Stuart Curran

MOTHERS OF THE NOVEL

Reprint fiction from Pandora Press

Pandora is reprinting, alongside this volume, eighteenth- and nineteenth-century novels written by women. Each novel is being reset into contemporary typography and reintroduced to readers today by contemporary women novelists. The **1986** paperback selection is as follows:

PANDORA

MOTHERS
OF THE
NOVEL

100 good women writers before Jane Austen

DALE SPENDER

London and New York

For my mother, Ivy Spender

First published in 1986
by Pandora Press
(Routledge & Kegan Paul plc)
11 New Fetter Lane, London EC4P 4EE

Published in the USA by Routledge & Kegan Paul Inc.
in association with Methuen Inc.
29 West 35th Street, New York, NY 10001

Reprinted 1986

Set in 10/11 Ehrhardt
by Columns of Reading
and printed in Great Britain
by TJ Press (Padstow) Ltd
Padstow, Cornwall

Library of Congress Cataloging in Publication Data

Spender, Dale.
Mothers of the novel.
Bibliography: p.
Includes index.
1. English fiction—Women authors—History and
criticism. 2. English fiction—18th century—History
and criticism. 3. English fiction—Early modern,
1500-1700—History and criticism. I. Title.
PR113.S63   1986   823'.009'9287   85-28377
ISBN 0–86358–081–5

British Library CIP data also available

Contents

Contents

Illustrations

Acknowledgments

Without the assistance of Candida Ann Lacey, this book would have had many more gaps. For the days that she has spent tracing references and finding books not deemed to exist, I am very very grateful; for the weeks she has spent reading novels and giving me the benefit of her insights and the luxury of good-humoured and inspirational support, I am most appreciative.

Helen Mott has also been a valuable colleague, and I am indebted to her for all the reading she has done, all the debates we have had, and for all the constructive comments that she has made.

My sister Lynne Spender has 'kept me in my place' (and I don't just mean sitting at my desk), and her wit and wisdom have been a constant source of strength – and enjoyment. Once more the postal services of England and Australia have played a most important part in conveying manuscripts and comments across oceans. Nothing has been lost and there have been no undue delays. For her constant feedback – and unfailing irony – I give her many thanks.

I want to thank Antonia Fraser who saved my sanity when I found that she too had read *Urania* and that I was no longer required to keep my thoughts on this early novel entirely to myself. Likewise, I want to acknowledge how rewarding it has been to receive a fund of information on early novels (and esoteric sources) from Cathy Davidson who is working on the development of fiction in the United States. And I am grateful to Debra Adelaide for her information on the Australian scene.

Susan Koppelman has provided me with some of the most illuminating insights into women writers and their lives and Joanna Russ – in her book *How to Suppress Women's Writing*, and in her private correspondence – has helped me to understand some of the dimensions of the problem – and to learn to live with the understanding.

To Cheris Kramarae I owe much for the steady stream of supportive letters; to Sally Cline I am grateful for her patience and consideration; to Margaret Bluman I owe many a delightful day – which could otherwise have been disastrous. To Anna Coote, I owe a great deal for

ix

her care – and her chauffeuring abilities – and to Renate Duelli Klein I have debts that I cannot hope to repay.

To Kate Jones for the correction of some of my prose, and to Ann Hall for the correction of some of my prejudices, I am grateful. And to the London Library where some of these old novels have been carefully preserved there should be a public expression of thanks.

I also want to thank Sue Butterworth and Jane Cholmeley of Silver Moon Bookshop for their willingness to try to find women's novels that are currently in print. And I want to thank Janet Todd for her superb *Dictionary of British and American Women Novelists 1600–1800*, which made my task of finding birth dates, death dates, and publication dates so much easier.

Without the assistance of David Doughan and Catherine Ireland at the Fawcett Library, I do not think that I would have been brave enough to have undertaken this task. And without the able typing skills of Glynis Wood, I would also have been daunted; not only has she done an excellent job in preparing this manuscript but the praise she has provided in her eagerness to collect each chapter and to get on with the story of the lost women novelists has been enormously encouraging.

From Ted Brown, who has taught me much about doing my 'homework', and who has ensured that it is not 'housework', I have received the greatest and most enduring support. And from my father, Harry Spender, who has good cause to complain of being a neglected male in my public records of acknowledgment, I have had (in my adult years) immense encouragement, assistance, and affection.

To Pippa Brewster, my editor, who has accepted a manuscript that bears no resemblance to my original proposal, I also want to acknowledge my thanks.

And to the more than 100 women novelists and their more than 600 novels which form the substance of this book, I have more than one debt. They have been for me one of the best things in life; for almost two years they have served as an excuse as I have been able to withdraw from the world . . . on the good grounds that I have had too many novels to read!

Introduction

This is not the book I started to write. Half-way through my research, I changed my mind. When I began my work on early women novelists – in the attempt to explore the relationship between women and fiction – I had assumed that women novelists had not really 'come into their own' until the entry of Jane Austen, and that the starting point for my work would be somewhere about the beginning of the nineteenth century. At that stage, I had no idea that for more than one hundred and fifty years before Jane Austen, women had been writing novels, and that to return to the early days of women's relationship to fiction meant to go back to the seventeenth, and not the nineteenth century.

But having embarked on my research, I soon 'discovered' more and more women writers, and more and more women's novels, in the eighteenth century, and the seventeenth century, and I began to realise that far from standing at the beginning of women's entry to fiction writing, Jane Austen was the inheritor of a long and well-established tradition of 'women's novels'. Yet this tradition, and the women who were part of it, had so faded from view as to be unknown. And it was at this point of recognition that I changed my mind. It was at this point that I decided to focus on the women before Jane Austen who had bequeathed to her such a rich legacy. So now this book concludes with women writers who started their careers before Jane Austen makes her appearance on the literary scene (*Sense and Sensibility* was published in 1811); it is a book I never could have envisaged at the outset.

One reason for my concentration on these early women writers is that this is where my questions about women's relationship to fiction led me. If I wanted to find out why women had begun to write novels I had to go back to 'the rise of the novel' and to women's role in the development of the new genre. But there is another – equally important – reason for my

1

concentration on these previously forgotten women writers. For the more women novelists I found, and the more women's novels I read, the more I was convinced of the desirability, and the necessity, of reclaiming this lost tradition, and of challenging the received wisdom of the literary establishment – that for women novelists it all started with Jane Austen.

When I realised that there was this great heritage of women novelists of whom most of us have never heard, whose existence we have not even suspected, I began to appreciate the significance of our loss and it became for me a priority, to 're-present' some of these women and their work to contemporary readers.

I cannot, however, begin to convey a sense of the joy I have experienced in finding these women writers. When I had thought that I had read most of the women novelists who had ever been published, the discovery of yet another one hundred 'new' old novelists was in itself a source of tremendous excitement. And the last two years of avid novel-reading has been, for me, one of the most moving and illuminating events of my life.

Always I have had mixed feelings about finding these women writers: on the one hand there has been the delight of discovering this treasure-chest; on the other hand, there has been the sadness, frustration, and anger, that such treasures ever should have been buried. And if it is difficult to separate the joy from the anger, so too has it been virtually impossible to separate the discovery from the burial. For there is no way of reclaiming these women novelists without wondering why they were lost.

These are not my only mixed feelings. While many of these novels have been enormously satisfying, they have also, frequently, been disconcerting. By the second half of the eighteenth century most of the women writers of serious fiction were concerned with ethical questions. They wanted to explore the human predicament and to understand human nature, and threaded through their novels are the issues of what is right and what is wrong, what can be improved and what cannot. They asked why human beings behaved in certain ways and whether they could behave differently. And they undertook all their explanations of character and judgment, of the relationship between the individual and the society, without knowing anything of Sigmund Freud and his psychology. It is strange to read these perceptive women writers who have no knowledge of the theories of Charles Darwin or Karl Marx. Yet far from casting aspersions on the limitations of their world view, I have found myself – repeatedly – asking awkward questions about the limitations and 'mind-set' of my own.

My present understandings have been considerably enriched by the very different perspective these women writers have provided. And while in some ways their eighteenth century world view stands in sharp contrast to my own, there are other ways in which the similarities between the old and the new are striking. For what is contained in these more than five hundred novels is a record of women's consciousness, a documentation of women's experiences as subordinates in a male-dominated society. In this context, the distance created by two centuries quickly collapses. Few contemporary readers will have any difficulty in identifying with this realm of women's experience as it is portrayed in these eighteenth century novels.

That the eighteenth century women should have written at all is in itself a contradiction. For women who had no rights, no individual existence or identity, the very act of writing – particularly for a public audience – was in essence an assertion of individuality and autonomy, and often an act of defiance. To write was to be; it was to create and to exist. It was to construct and control a world view without interference from the 'masters'. No woman writer was oblivious to this; all of them had qualms about the propriety of being a woman and a writer, and almost all felt obliged to defend themselves against attack. Which is why so many of them apologise for their audacity and presumption. I think it is also why so many of them 'reformed' the male characters in their novels.

However, that these women were asserting their identity in a society which did not grant them existence in their own right suggests that they were in this respect, at least, unrepresentative of their sex. But if by way of their writing they were atypical women, the fact that these one hundred women writers come from all walks of life also suggests that the early women novelists were not of one small and privileged class, and that in this respect, their experiences were more representative of their sex as a whole.

Women, of course, were not trained to write. While there are numerous accounts of the denial of literacy to slaves and the working classes, on the grounds that those who are literate are more difficult to control, there are few such accounts which relate to women's illiteracy. Yet one of the basic reasons for the systematic denial of education to women has been that those who are uneducated are more readily subordinated. The absence of formal and extensive education was the reality for *all* these women writers so it is understandable that the education of women is one of the most frequent themes in their writing.

When all women were denied education it borders on the ridiculous to try and make class distinctions between women on the basis of their education. Almost all the women novelists were, to some extent, self-taught. Clearly, women who grew up in families where books and leisure were available were likely to be better educated than milkmaids. But even so, there were more privileged women who were frightened of being thought 'bookish' and who avoided all literary pursuits, while milkmaids like Ann Yearsley found their way into print.

Which is why it is a nonsense to classify all these women novelists as middle class – unless, of course, literacy is taken as the mark of middle class.

Undeniably, a very few women did not rely on profits from their pens for their living. But the vast majority of women writers did. Most of the eighteenth (and seventeenth) century women novelists worked at writing to support themselves and their families. And if they couldn't get work as writers they had to find something else. With the range of occupations for women severely limited – and becoming more so, particularly as midwifery increasingly became the province of men – and with virtually every profession closed to them, these women did not have much choice about the work they could do. Although more than one hundred years apart. Aphra Behn and Agnes Maria Bennett had smilar work experiences; if they couldn't support themselves by writing they accepted positions as mistresses.

For the men of letters, with their monopoly on the literary scene, it was galling indeed to find these women who, despite their lack of education and in the face of the disapproval they encountered, continued to do so well in print. What I did not know a year ago and what I do know now is that during the eighteenth century, the majority of novels were written – by women! And the men were not amused by the women's prominence. They did much to 'discourage' the competition of women and there are signs that their backlash was successful. Whereas in the late eighteenth century when women were seen to be in the ascendancy, men writers had used female pseudonyms to try and find a favoured way into print, by the 1840s the practice had been reversed, and women writers were adopting male pseudonyms in order to find a publisher.

That it was women and not men who made the greater contribution to the development of the novel does not seem to me to be surprising upon reflection. It was a logical extension of women's role. When it is realised that women were not debarred from letter writing – and that most of the early novels took the form of letters – the relationship between women and the novel is more easily discerned. Denied education, disallowed in the public world, women had always been permitted the 'indulgence' of letter writing and were even permitted to excel at it. And letters are a good medium for exploring emotions and maintaining relationships. To me it seems quite obvious that it was a cunning move on the part of women to transform their private occupation into a public and professional activity.

They drew on the strengths they had been allowed and transformed their private literary indulgence into a public paid performance, and in the process they gained for themselves a voice and helped to create a new literary form. Women did not imitate the men; it was quite the reverse. And as the women writers produced this novel form, they forged for themselves an occupation which was intellectually stimulating, often lucrative, generally rewarding, and increasingly influential. They did all this before the men quite realised what was going on and began their policy of 'containment'. Today, when Tillie Olsen, Joanna Russ and Lynne Spender have all helped to establish that women do not constitute more than 20 per cent of the published writers, it is important to look back to the early stages of the novel and to recognise that it has not always been this way.

Of course, one of the reasons that the women novelists were so successful is that their books met the needs of the women readers. Excluded from so many social, political and economic activities, often isolated and not infrequently at a loss to know how to lead a meaningful life, many women seized upon women's novels as an entry to a new dimension of understanding – and living. To represent the woman reader of the late eighteenth century as a bored and listless woman who idled away her time with sentimental novels is to do great disservice to the readers – and the writers. (It is also to reveal how we can be taken in by myths constructed long after the event, and which discredit women.) For so many women, these novels meant access to the world of ideas, to self-analysis and social issues. These novels were women's intellectual foodstuffs. And women writers not only 'exploited' their role as letter writers, when they created the novel; they became the connecting medium for the experience of women.

Ideas, understandings, new realisations and questions spread among women as quickly as the publishers could print women's novels and the circulating libraries could get them into the hands of women (and men). These 'women's novels' to some extent constituted 'women's education' and were nothing short of subversive in their own context. And it is understandable that this new, exciting literature should have been so often and so churlishly condemned by many men. Once the 'women's novel' was so widely available, there is no doubt that women were more difficult to subordinate.

I think this also helps to explain in part why these women novelists have been suppressed.

It is precisely because these women writers are the bearers of women's traditions that they were vitally important to women in their own time, and that they are highly significant now. And I am not so credulous as to believe that it has been coincidence that has been responsible for the disappearance of more than one hundred good women novelists in favour of five men (Daniel Defoe, Henry Fielding, Samuel Richardson, Tobias Smollett and Lawrence Sterne). While I leave myself open to the charge of not having looked hard enough, I must confess that my researches have turned up more than one hundred women novelists before Jane Austen and no more than thirty men. But I am determined to be fair – if not positively magnanimous – so I am prepared to assume that there were only two good women novelists to each man.* Yet even with this generous allocation to men, it is still unreasonable if not outrageous to accept the premise of the literary establishment that five of the ostensible fifty men are to be preferred to one hundred good women.

Quite simply, and in the face of the verdict of the men of letters, it is my contention that women were the mothers of the novel and that any other version of its origin is but a myth of male creation.

With this in mind, I have divided the book into three parts. The first is concerned with a time which is difficult to envisage – when there were no novels as we know them now – and where the first seeds of fiction were sown by the women who began to write biographies, and epistolary novels. It concludes with Eliza Haywood – and her more than fifty novels, published in the first half of the eighteenth century.

The second part, 'Literary Standards', begins with an itemisation of the more than one hundred women writers (and their more than five hundred novels) who followed Eliza Haywood. Understandably, this section is concerned with finding an explanation for the disappearance of all these women from the literary scene. To have eliminated such a substantial body of work from the literary heritage was no mean feat but a rationale for this massive denial of women's writing is not difficult to find.

And the third part is devoted to some of these women writers – to an understanding of their lives and their work. It is an attempt to reclaim women's traditions and to make clear what it is we have been missing.

*Among the neglected men I have found Robert Bage, Henry Brooke, John Bunyan, Geoffrey Chaucer, Thomas Delaney, Emanuel Ford, William Godwin, Richard Graves, Robert Greene, Robert Henryson, Charles Johnstone, Charles Lever, M.G. Lewis, Thomas Lodge, Henry MacKenzie, Thomas Malory, Charles Maturin, Walter Scott, Philip Sidney, Horace Walpole . . . twenty, plus the recognised fathers of the novel . . . Daniel Defoe, Henry Fielding, Samuel Richardson, Tobias Smollett and Lawrence Sterne; generosity indeed to double the number!

Note: There is one deficiency which I want to draw attention to; try as I have it has been beyond me to ascertain what the print runs of various novels were. It has not been difficult to determine how many editions of a novel were published, but only on rare occasions is it revealed how many books were published in each edition. I have almost become an expert on the production of books and the costs of paper in my attempts to discover the quantities of books printed . . . but to no avail. So I have had to take the number of editions as my yardstick for popularity rather than the number of books. If anyone can enlighten me when it comes to print runs, I would be exceedingly grateful.

PART I

Literary Origins

CHAPTER 1

Fact and fiction

Lady Mary Wroath and Anne Weamys

In 1621 Lady Mary Wroath wrote *Urania* for publication. A member of the aristocracy, her purpose in writing was nonetheless financial: she hoped to make enough money to keep herself out of debtors' prison. And being a member of that half of humanity whose business it was to secure a living through relationships, Lady Mary Wroath wrote in part – about relationships.

It is tempting to state that she was the first in the long line of women writers of fiction: tempting it may be but a safe bet it most definitely is not, for until recently I would have sworn that Aphra Behn was the first, the founding mother of fiction, and yet Lady Mary Wroath's *Urania* was published nineteen years before Aphra Behn's birth. So all I am prepared to state is that, at this stage, it seems as though Lady Mary Wroath was the first woman to take up her pen for many of the same reasons that women today take up the pen – to earn money. And Lady Mary Wroath was the first (as far as I know) to find herself up against some of those constraints which worked against a woman writer then, and which continue to work against women writers in contemporary times.

Although the select club of 'the men of letters' had not come into existence at this time and begun its institutionalised practice of discriminating against the woman writer, the fact of being a woman in the seventeenth century was in itself a severe disadvantage for anyone who might wish to write. At the most elementary level a writer needs to be literate and to have time, and writing materials, yet even these bare essentials were out of the reach of almost all women in the seventeenth century. In her book, *The Weaker Vessel: Woman's Lot in Seventeenth Century England* (1984), Antonia Fraser documents the nature and extent of some of the disadvantages women experienced in relation to

11

men, and while there were vast differences between women, the activities of all women were restricted by legal and social custom. The denial of so many legal rights, of any form of independence, the lack of mobility, education and property, the insistence on the *weaker* nature of women along with the liabilities of child bearing and of being the 'disposable' property of men, was 'the lot of all women' in the seventeenth century and hardly conducive to literary aspirations let alone literary success. With so many obstacles – material and psychological – to be overcome, it was a considerable achievement for Lady Mary Wroath to write at all. But for her – as for so many women who followed her – writing was a necessity.

Privilege and a 'literary background' Lady Mary Wroath undoubtedly had, and given the possibilities for money making which she saw around her, it is understandable that she should have turned to writing as a way out of her financial difficulties. Born in 1586, the eldest daughter of the Earl of Leicester, she was not without literary antecedents (and not reluctant to make use of them) for her uncle was Sir Philip Sidney, the author of the highly successful pastoral romance *Arcadia*, and her aunt was the Countess of Pembroke, a renowned 'literary lady'. Married at eighteen to Robert Wroath, Lady Mary had every reason to believe that she had embarked on a successful path for life, as she was very much part of the court-world and in a position to act as a literary patron. Her support of literary men was substantial and she was frequently accorded their gratitude: Ben Jonson dedicated much of his work to her, including, in 1610, *The Alchemist*.

But success for a dependant is a precarious matter; it *depends* on someone else and takes little or no account of the efforts or achievements of the dependant. So although Lady Mary Wroath had chosen her occupation wisely and had worked responsibly and creditably, it all came to an end with the death of her husband in 1614: through no fault of her own she found her circumstances dramatically changed – virtually overnight – as she went from being able to provide support for others to being in desperate need of it herself. Her husband's financial position had not been sound, a fact unknown to his wife: she had not participated in the management of his estate but found on his death there was little but debts. As well, she had a young son to support. And the death of her son in 1614 was not only an enormous personal blow, it was also the end of valued work and she was left with no established means of making her way in the world. This was when she determined to 'write for her life' – a solution which was without social sanction but one which she saw as the only way open to her. (As it transpired, however, she did not make enough money from her daring venture to stave off her creditors and in 1623 she was obliged to petition the King for protection for one year.)

12

But could she write? What would she write? These are not just fascinating questions but were fundamental questions at the time when Lady Mary Wroath took up her pen, and it is difficult now for us to envisage the context in which she made her momentous decision. Today, when the prospect of success – however unrealistic – may tempt many to look favourably on writing, it is quite a feat to imagine the time when no woman would have written for fame! For women, fame was certainly not something that was sought as it was far more closely associated with *infamous* than *famous*. To acquire 'a reputation' these days may be for both sexes a plus in literary terms, but in the seventeenth and eighteenth centuries – and even into the nineteenth century according to Harriet Martineau in her *Autobiography* (1877) – for a woman to have any sort of reputation was for her to have a bad name and to be beyond the pale. To seek public attention – which was precisely what the *publi*cation of a book entailed – was for a woman to lay herself open to every charge of indecency.

Which is one reason that women, when they did write, often did so anonymously. It is also a reason that today, when we try to trace these women writers of the past, the task is made more difficult: when they did not write anonymously they frequently used pseudonyms. And even if they did use their 'own' names these would change upon marriage. So women's literary history is from the outset complicated in a way that men's is not. What is usually an elementary step in the literary tradition of men – the establishment of the identity of writers and the titles of their works – can constitute a major problem in the literary traditions of women.

It is not possible to examine women's literary heritage without reference to the social and political position of the female sex – because women's position has been so starkly different from men's. The one action could take on contrasting significance, according to whether it was performed by women or men. At the time when Lady Mary Wroath took up her pen – for the purpose of publication – her decision had implications and connotations which did not apply to men. For she was defying the social order by her action.

When women were unable to own property, when they themselves were considered property, for women to engage in property-making transactions was to flout the belief system and to break all conventions. Women who were in trade – who had something to sell* – were an offence because such activity was reserved for men. Of course women persistently defined the social order and often from necessity engaged in

---

*As Ruth Perry (1980) points out, it had not always been this way: she indicates that the economic position of women had been better during the Middle Ages – see pp. 27–62 of her book.

money-making activities, no doubt having decided that social ostracism was a smaller price to pay than starvation. Apart from waged women there were other women who persistently engaged in trade. It was not new for women to sell their bodies and to be denounced for supplying what the blameless purchasers were ready to buy. But it is interesting to note that the women in the seventeenth century who began to trade their creative resources, their minds, who started to sell their literary wares, were treated with much the same ribaldry and contempt as prostitutes. In fact, by the time of the Restoration when more and more women were earning their living by the pen, the distinction between the prostitute and the woman writer was so blurred as to be almost non-existent and it is possible that the opprobrium associated with both is more closely connected to the *selling* and the *money making* than it is to any particular commodity they were trying to sell.

Having elected to write for financial gain, however, the issue for Lady Mary was what to write: what would be profitable, what would readers want to buy? 'Market research' studies which sample consumer appetite might today provide a profile of the best seller for the benefit of the aspiring writer, but the absence of such assistance from market research surveys was not the only way in which Lady Mary's experience stands in marked contrast to the considerations of contemporary times. There was also the very basic question of who she was writing for.

England today is a literate society with a vast number of books printed annually and an extensive reading public waiting to receive them. But it hasn't always been this way and it comes as quite a shock to realise just how recent a development this is: writing in 1961, Raymond Williams declared that it was only in his generation that the reading of books had spread to a bare majority of the population (1975: p. 177).* The emergence of this mass reading public which has helped to shape literature could not have been envisaged in Lady Mary Wroath's time. In 1621 there were but the very elementary beginnings of the literary tradition with which we are familiar today and Lady Mary Wroath would have had none of the literary experiences of the modern world. For example, she would not have grown up with story books, or girls' own annuals, or a selection of novels about 'real' people which would make for satisfying Sunday afternoon reading in front of the fire. She would not have been able to read biographies or even to have looked at the newspaper, for both these forms had yet to appear. Any reading for leisure or pleasure would have consisted of versions of the classics with their heroes (and occasional heroines) of antiquity, or pastoral romances, based on conventions of courtly love, and which were unrealistic, highly extravagant and affected affairs, such as those written by Marie de

*For further discussion see chapter 8 of this book, 'Male romance'.

France in the twelfth century. 'Literature' was the pursuit and province of the upper class and the further it was removed from 'real life' the more prestige it enjoyed. The idea of reading fiction for the illuminating light it might shed on the world – or oneself – was not yet born.

Apart from the more imaginative offerings (some would say fantastical offerings) of the pastoral romance – where romantically named shepherds and shepherdesses gambolled in exotic surrounds and obeyed the ritualistic dictates of love, compounded by mistaken identities – there were also the more serious books directed towards the elevation of the spirit. There were sermons, tracts, and 'philosophies' which were associated with 'education'. This was hardly a literary diet which could foster the development of creative writing as we know it today.

Crucial to the growth of a mass reading public has been the growth of mass education, and just as there was in the seventeeth century a very small audience for literature, so too was there a very small group of educated people. While the model of education we now have was only beginning to emerge then it was, in one respect, significantly different: what little educational provision there was was intended for boys. This did not always mean that girls were entirely excluded: from the seventeenth right through to the nineteenth century a significant number of women from the upper classes who took to writing counted among their blessings the fact that they had brothers – brothers who had been provided with tutors. With a brother and a tutor in the house it was often possible for a sister to gain some learning although not infrequently she was obliged to resort to surreptitious means: sneaking into the school room or being tutored second-hand by a sympathetic brother himself were ways by which not a few women gained their education.

A surprising number of women educated themselves. 'Surprising' because in this day and age we are accustomed to think of even reading, for example, as something which must be *taught*, yet many are the women who seem to have acquired their skills with a minimum of tuition. And many are the women who taught themselves a foreign language – by means of a dictionary. (This was how Mary Wollstonecraft, in need of money from translations, taught herself French, Dutch and German.) Women frequently deplored the limited nature of their education – they 'grumbled about their inadequate instruction and the absence of a system, which they assumed was delivered only by institutional learning' (Janet Todd, 1984: p. 4) – and this was another reason they were prone to apologise for their printed efforts. But looking back over the obstacles that were placed in the way of women's learning one is far more struck by what women *did* achieve than what they did not.

For boys – of the upper class – things got better during the seventeenth century, as their education was placed on a more systematic footing and was oriented towards the study of Latin and Greek. But as girls were excluded from the formal education system, the increased emphasis on Latin and Greek served to widen the distance between the education of girls and boys. Latin and Greek did not lend themselves so readily to self-teaching methods and as the century wore on the education for privileged boys continued to get 'better', while for girls education continued to get 'worse' to the extent that Antonia Fraser (1984) writes that it was firmly believed by more than a few that there was a *decline* in girls' education in the seventeenth century (p. 139). As the education of girls had not been good to begin with, this was quite a serious matter. Even before the seventeenth century the education of girls had been undermined: 'The disappearance of the convents at the time of the Reformation had deprived English girls not only of convenient places of learning but also of a pool of women teachers in the shape of the nuns themselves' (Antonia Fraser, 1984: pp. 123-4).

The chances, then, of girls being literate – let alone educated – were not very good. Some upper class women were skilled at reading and writing and some could manage it at a pinch, though proficiency was by no means presumed. And some working women were literate: this was more likely if they worked in any of the great houses and even more likely if they found themselves employed by a benevolent (and literate) mistress, who was prepared to instruct them in order that they could read the Bible. But literacy was still rare among females: in London, in 1600, 90 per cent of the women were illiterate, although by 1640 this number had dropped significantly to 80 per cent: during the same period the illiteracy rate among women in East Anglia was calculated at 100 per cent (Antonia Fraser, 1984: p. 129).

Had it ever occurred to Lady Mary Wroath to write a book for women there would have been no need to consult the oracle to determine how her work would fare. Women did not constitute a substantial reading public: women were not an audience for women's books. So, in contrast to today, the questions of what to write and who to write for would have yielded very different answers for Lady Mary Wroath who worked without benefit of current literary traditions, and without the demands of an extensive audience of women readers.

The idea of writing a realistic story about people of her own time would probably not have crossed Lady Mary's mind because *fiction*, as it is commonly understood now, would have been an alien notion then. There are still problems associated with defining and accepting fiction – as any adult who has ever tried to teach the young the difference between telling stories (fiction) and telling lies (fiction?) will readily appreciate – but in Lady Mary's time, the present widespread

16

acceptance of fiction had not been developed. If anyone was going to tell a story it had to be crystal clear that it was indeed a story and not to be confused with the facts: so realistic stories, like those we are accustomed to today, would not have been acclaimed as literature, but would have been denounced as deception. If the story could have conceivably been true – and was not – if it was but an invention masquerading as truth, then it would have been viewed as a hoax, as a form of trickery. A 'proper story' – in the aristocratic tradition – was one which was as far removed from the real world as was possible. And there was a variety of conventions which helped to signal that the story was not true, and not to be taken *literally*: for example, there was the use of exotic settings, and the use of even more exotic names. Another sign was that of the poetic form, for among the literary persons of the time – Sir Philip Sidney being one of them – it was widely accepted, in the absence of the contemporary concept of fiction, that *all* creative and imaginary writing *was* poetry, and that it was therefore appropriate to couch stories in the poetic form. But if this was not enough to remind readers that they were in the realm of fantasy and not fact, then the unfolding of the most unlikely events in the lives of the most ethereal beings should surely have removed any last vestiges of confusion.

But if these pastoral romances existed they were not always sanctioned. That the mind could be quickly corrupted was a fundamental Protestant tenet – and it applied to books. In 1538 and 1543 censorship acts had been passed in England 'for the advancement of true religion and the abolition of the contrarie', and there had been 'a continuous campaign against plays and romances which were not serious reading' (Raymond Williams, 1975: p. 180). Although 'serious reading matter' was accorded more status and pronounced more desirable, this judgment did not prevent the publication of 'lighter' material. The romance (in the traditional sense) found its way into many an aristocratic home and the chapbook, the jest book, the ballad and the broadsheet – all made possible by the printing press and appearing in the sixteenth century – had by the seventeenth century attained 'wide' popular appeal.

Another common convention of the time which suggested 'serious purpose' but which in fact took a great deal of licence with this principle was the practice of relating a sober tale which was already known (and 'approved') and of embellishing it in the process so that it became lighter and more entertaining. (William Shakespeare made use of this device.) This custom had the advantage that the audience would not be led to believe that they were being party to any hoax or deception, for from the outset they were aware that they were being told an old story.

Today we would be inclined to look down on the new writer of stories who merely retells a tale that has been told before: in a literary world where creativity is everything, to be 'unoriginal' borders on committing a crime and the reputation of a fiction writer who is accused of being an imitator can be irretrievably ruined. But the same 'rules' did not apply in the seventeenth century and it would be a mistake to think that writers were any the less creative because their stories were not 'original'. Look at Shakespeare. He is not often rated as less than a genius on the grounds that his stories were not of his own making.

So when Lady Mary Wroath was looking round for something to write it would not have been an absence of creative ability or a lack of imagination or talent which led her to consider rewriting a story that was already known. Indeed, it's quite likely that Lady Mary Wroath, along with other budding writers of her time, might have thought solely in terms of finding an existing popular story which she could redo, in the interest of literary and financial credit. And she didn't have to look very far for the right story.

Wasn't her uncle Sir Philip Sidney, and hadn't he written *Arcadia* which had been published in 1590, and which had been an immense success? Here was a form that had already gained acclaim and which many reputable literary personages had tried their hand at, since publication: *The Ile of Guls*, written by John Day in 1606 had been – in his own words – 'a little string or rivulent drawn from the full stream of the Right Worthy gentleman, Sir Philip Sidney's well known *Archadea*'. Even William Shakespeare had borrowed from his pastoral fantasy of heroism and romance: the scenes between Gloucester and his son in *King Lear* are another version of the story of the dispossessed King of Paphlagonia in *Arcadia*. So, why not a new version of *Arcadia*, reasoned Lady Mary, for on many counts it seemed an eminently suitable choice? And she set about producing her variation on this elaborate pastoral tale.

To accuse her of plagiarism would be to misunderstand the conventions of the time: to suggest, however, that she revealed a ready measure of opportunism would be fair comment. She was after all writing expressly for money which meant that she was very interested in potential sales, so it made sound sense to establish as many links as possible between her own work and that of her famous and successful uncle. She hoped by association to share some of the literary esteem (and profits) that his writing enjoyed. And she was not averse to using the literary reputation of her aunt, to the same purpose, either. Hence the title page of *Urania*

The
Countesse
of Montgomeries
URANIA
Written by the right honourable the Lady
MARY WROATH

Daughter of the right Noble Robert
Earl of Leicester
And niece to the ever famous and renowned
Sr. Phillips Sydney, knight. And to
The Most exelent Lady Mary Countesse of
Pembroke late deceased

The inclusion of her aunt's name on the title page was also a public statement that women *could* write, and for Lady Mary Wroath, the very existence of such a close relation with such an established literary reputation probably helped to boost her confidence – if not her sales!

Urania is a complicated web of plot and subplots, written in the fantastical and flowery manner of the time as Lady Mary Wroath set about emulating the extravagances of her uncle. Urania, the heroine, is a shepherdess-cum-princess, who suffers and is saved, and whose noble origins are finally revealed. (There is a hero too, of course, Parselius, but it is interesting to note that it is the woman who is the focus, whose story is being told, and whose name is taken as the title for the book.) Of *Urania*, Brigid MacCarthy (1944), has written wryly that 'A jaundiced reader might be forgiven for thinking of the *Urania* as a succession of caves all full of royal personages, bemused and forewandered [*sic*], who sit about endlessly relating their misfortunes' (p. 57). But it all works out well in the end, and in accordance with the conventions of the heroic pastoral code: after many adventures, misunderstandings, and wanderings, the kings all regain their rightful positions and the lovers all gain their own true loves.

So, what is Lady Mary Wroath's achievement and why should the birth of women's novel writing be with her? The answer is not hard to find: apart from the fact that she is the first woman I have been able to locate who wanted to write for a public audience and for profit (as distinct from writing as an accomplishment for parade to one's private circle), Lady Mary Wroath made a most significant contribution in the history of women's writing. It comes not from her emulation of *Arcadia*, but in the variations, the additional subplots – and their style – which are very much her own invention, and which are very innovative, very *novel*. There is both the content of some of her subsidiary stories and the very realistic manner in which they are recounted, which not only have a bearing on the development of fiction, but which form some of the foundation stones of women's fiction writing.

First of all, the content: there is in *Urania*, for example, one 'digression' which is the story of Limena who is married to a jealous huband, Philargus. Although entirely innocent – of course – Limena's husband accuses her of loving Perissus and he gives her two days to either lure Perissus to his death, or else to die herself. Limena –

naturally – chooses her own death, and Philargus proceeds to beat her and torture her, which is not the usual fantastical turn that fate takes in a pastoral romance. What is fantastical, however, is the timely appearance of a knight in shining armour who slays the wife beater (my terminology, not that of Lady Mary Wroath), and whose presence on the scene is quickly followed by that of Perissus, who – predictably – just happens to be passing by. Limena and Perissus – obviously – live happily ever after.

Realism intrudes: and it is not just the realism of content. Lady Mary Wroath also introduces dialogue (there was no dialogue in *Arcadia*), and it is impressive and realistic dialogue. I am not the only one to have noticed this realistic element: it was also apparent to her contemporaries. One of the responses to *Urania* – and it was a response which could never have arisen in relation to *Arcadia* – was widespread discussion among writers and readers about *who* these realistic characters really were.

If Lady Mary had based some of her 'digressions' on the more titillating exploits of her real, live acquaintances, then she had indeed moved a long way from the fantastical conventions of the pastoral romance. She was heading in the direction of the novel. It is possible that the similarities between her characters and prominent social figures were quite deliberate: she had a few debts other than financial ones to repay, and she may have even been bitter about a society which had made much of her when she had possessed money to bestow as a patron, but which had quickly turned its back when she herself was in need. The temptation to expose certain individuals who had disappointed her, and to indulge in some scandalmongering, might have proved too great once the pen was in her hand and she was casting round for material for her subplots to add to *Arcadia*. If the use of real people and the seamy and secret details of their lives was intentional, then Lady Mary Wroath was the first woman writer to recognise – and exploit – the reading public's taste for thinly veiled gossip about the greats. Later this particular form of writing – the scandalous history with a 'key' to identify the real characters – would prove to be extremely popular with women writers. Both Delarivière Manley and Eliza Haywood excelled in the 'scandalous' histories or satires from which they earned the greater part of their living, but it was Lady Mary Wroath who many years before was first accused of this 'base' practice.

But, of course, it is equally possible that the scandal element of *Urania* was more accidental than intentional. What Lady Mary Wroath did in her departure from fantasy to realism was to break the rules which preserved a clear demarcation line between fact and fiction. Readers were confused because if the 'stories' in *Urania* were not fantasy (as clearly some of them were not), then it must follow that they were real, that they were true. There was no other category in which to place them at the time. And if they were real, what could be more logical than the search among the public figures to identify the jealous husband or the wife beater? It may well have been Lady Mary's failure to observe the rules of separating fantasy from realism, rather than any planned attack, which was at the core of the angry response of a number of prominent individuals to the publication of *Urania*. Not a few noblemen registered their objections and Lord Denny wrote some 'satirical' verse (which Lady Mary replied to) as his revenge on the author of *Urania* who, he believed, had maligned him: 'she doth palpably play upon him and his late daughter, the Lady Mary Hay, besides many others she makes bold with,' wrote a contemporary, 'and they say, takes great liberty, or rather license to traduce him she pleases' (quoted in Brigid MacCarthy, 1944: p. 62). But Lady Mary Wroath's characters may not necessarily have been based on anyone she knew. Then (as now), it was quite feasible that readers were reading something into the book which writers by no means intended. Writers can categorically declare that any resemblance between their characters and real people is purely coincidental (or the result of divine inspiration as Delarivière Manley was later to argue in her own defence): but readers who may have a penchant for glory can disregard such statements and persist in finding themselves reflected on the page. Lady Mary Wroath may equally well have been one of the first victims of the reading public's propensity for its own inventions, and it is feasible that she could even have been astonished that anyone should have thought they were the subject matter of her own literary imagination. And as for the scandal, she could have retorted – 'if the cap fits, wear it'!

Perhaps her stories, with their introduction of realism, were a bit of both. All imaginative writers may draw on what and whom they know without consciously seeking to portray particular individuals, and it can be a testimony to their talent as writers if the readers then find themselves represented in the work. But whether she simply failed to observe the conventions of keeping any hint of realism out of her writing, whether she deliberately aimed at an element of notoriety for the benefit it might bring to sales, or whether her stories were made into something which she had not foreseen, what cannot be disputed is that Lady Mary Wroath traced some of the first outlines in what would become the pattern of women's fiction writing.

Her narratives in which the experience of women filtered through, her understandings about the pressures placed on women, the emphasis on relationships and the unmasking of the idealised world to reveal some of the harsher realities beneath, were all to emerge as the hallmarks of women's writing. That Lady Mary Wroath did not earn much money from her writing, that she was abused for her efforts and that she and her work have no place in the literary traditions is also part of the predominant pattern of women's fiction writing.

But if she was the first woman to adapt *Arcadia* and to introduce more realistic considerations, she was by no means the last. Among the variations on the theme which regularly made their appearance was *A Continuation of Sir Philip Sidney's Arcadia*, by Anne Weamys, published in 1651. Although the formation of present literary traditions may have been in its very early stages, the publication of the *Continuation* suggests that some of the conventions of modern publicity were already in use: the bookseller, Thomas Heath, wrote a 'sales blurb' (in the form of an introductory letter) which glowingly stated that the lively ghost of Sir Philip Sidney was speaking through the pen of this 'inspired Minerva'. Given the language of the *Continuation* it is unlikely that Sir Philip Sidney would have endorsed the bookseller's claims, for while Anne Weamys adhered to the code of the pastoral romance when it came to subject matter – with lots of love and lots of adventure – she did not relate her stories in the elevated and artificial manner of Sir Philip Sidney. Never lapsing into the 'everyday language' of Lady Mary Wroath, Anne Weamys steered a straight and sensible course through the amorous adventures of her many heroes and heroines who showed not 'the slightest inclination to confide their troubles to lambs' (Brigid MacCarthy, 1944: p. 68). So she too made a contribution towards the evolution of realism in fiction, and towards the women's novel.

CHAPTER 2

•

Publish – and be damned . . . as a woman

Katherine Philips

During the earlier part of the seventeenth century, the literary offerings of Lady Mary Wroath and Anne Weamys were not the only ones penned by women, although these were the more public ones and the more significant contributions in relation to the birth of the novel. But while women were starting to set foot in the public arena (and were paying the price of going 'public'), there was a parallel private tradition among the literary ladies of the upper classes who were more inclined to follow the lead of the Countess of Pembroke, rather than that of her brother. Women who could write, who had the opportunity and materials to write, very often did write, for although a woman who wrote could be considered a little strange, it was not so much the writing itself but the *publi*cation of such writing which was considered a disgrace. So women who wrote, and who *also* wanted social acceptability, not surprisingly shrank from any publicity. Not only did this constrain women's writing (and set up many contradictions and problems for the woman writer), it also gave male authors a distinct advantage: the field was left to men who were not obliged to compete with women, and who therefore were much more visible as writers. Men were published in far greater numbers than women, then as now – though there was an aberration in the interim, in the eighteenth century – (with Tillie Olsen, 1978, Joanna Russ, 1984 and Lynne Spender, 1983 all setting the figures for women's publications overall at never more than 20 per cent of the total). But the greater publication rates of men cannot be taken as any accurate indication of the quantity or quality of women's writing: that only 20 per cent of the books published are authored by women is much more likely to be an indication of the efficiency of men's arrangements for keeping women out of this public and influential sphere.

The public world of letters was already by the seventeenth century a world of the 'men of letters', because so many women decided that the price of publicity was too high to pay, and made few or no attempts to encroach on this area of male territory. And this absence of women in print still has ramifications today, for, apart from the fact that it gave men a free hand to decree the literary conventions of the time (conventions which still make their presence felt), there is also the additional difficulty which is encountered when it comes to tracing the origins of women's literary traditions. Women published much less, and what they published was more likely to be anonymous, little favoured, and easily 'lost'. This is in contrast to the extensive, varied, *public* heritage of men which has been more readily preserved.

For example, the most renowned literary lady of the middle part of the seventeenth century was Katherine Philips (1631-1664), but there must have been many more women like her and of whom there is now no trace. One of the reasons we know about Katherine Philips is because *some* of her work was published (her collected poems, only after her death in 1667), but ironically it is the issue of publication itself which becomes the focus of the greater part of the little discussion that there is on her. Did she, or did she not seek publication? So the question becomes one of the personal attributes of a particular woman, and not the value of her work; likewise, the issue is generally phrased in terms of whether or not *she* was scheming, subversive, or sly, and not whether men were petty, punitive or pernicious in organising 'restrictive practices' designed to keep women from participating in the process of the printed word. This pattern of one rule for women and another for men, a pattern which is geared towards ensuring the predominance of men in print, has persisted since women found they could write – and proceeded to do so.

Katherine Philips was a member of a small literary circle in which everyone wrote, and read their work to the group. They all had romantic pastoral pseudonyms – her own being 'Orinda', and it became the 'Matchless Orinda' after her premature death from smallpox in 1664. Like the Countess of Pembroke, 'Orinda' wrote poems and worked on translations (in manuscript form), which she insisted were for the eyes of her literary friends only. Conforming to the edicts of her time, Katherine Philips kept the subject matter of her writing far removed from the real world and only once – as far as is known – did she pen a poem on a political issue of her day and that was when Charles I was executed, an event which she judged to be so extraordinary that she felt a comment was justified and that it could not detract from her position as a proper and private lady. She might have inwardly railed against the constraints which condemned her to writing for a small, select circle, while the male members of that same circle were free to have their work published if they so desired, but outwardly she dutifully observed all the

24

rules of decorum and disclaimed any desire to be a published writer – and an indecent woman.

Sometimes, however, it is a non-starter to try to measure women's popularity according to whether or not they were published. It was permissible for them to pass round their manuscripts among their friends and these were in turn copied and passed on to yet more friends. Such private circulation could even have resulted in the writer enjoying almost as many readers as a small print run would ensure. But in terms of posterity, printed matter has a better endurance record and so, again, the way that women's writing was made available has meant that it is more likely to have 'disappeared'.

But clearly Katherine Philips felt that there would be a bigger audience for her writing – if it was published. Her friends considered her translation of Corneille's Pompey so good that they prevailed upon her to publish it. After their praise and with their encouragement she consented to 'go public' only on condition, however, that the name of the translator did not appear. She stipulated that it should be anonymous.

Perhaps she was playing with fire but it is unfair to imply (as most critics who have ever referred to her do) that her protestations about acknowledgment and publicity were feigned. It is snide to suggest that she really sought the limelight and that there was some deficiency in her character simply because she wanted for herself what men writers took for granted – the right to a wide audience without automatically being damned as a human being. There was a real and painful conflict for women who could only be successful writers at the expense of their 'womanliness' and it should neither cause surprise nor warrant defence if women chose to try and resolve this conflict by being both – by being writers *and* women. It is the arrangement whereby women writers were outlawed which should be the focus of criticism and not Katherine Philips's ostensible attempts to get round it. And there can be no doubt that she was genuinely disturbed about the considerable risk she was taking with the publication of *Pompey*. In her correspondence to Sir Charles Coterel (whose pastoral pseudonym was 'Poliarchus') she wrote of *Pompey* that 'I would beg leave publicly to address it to the Duchess, but that then I must put my name to it, which I can never resolve to do; for I shall scarce ever pardon myself the confidence of having permitted it to see the light at all, tho' it was purely in my own defence that I did; for had I not furnished a true copy, it had been printed from one that was very false and imperfect. But should I once own it publickly, I think I should never be able to show my face again' (Katherine Philips, 1705: pp. 127-8).

This is no coy affectation: it would have been extremely difficult for Katherine Philips to have retained her place in society, and her womanly

25

reputation, had she publicly acknowledged her authorship (speculation was another matter entirely). Having to choose between being a woman and a writer represented an identity conflict for women – an identity conflict unknown to men for whom there was no incompatibility between being a man and a writer – and the toll that this conflict took should not be underestimated. For every woman who chose to write publicly, to defy convention and to risk the repudiation of her womanhood, there were sure to be women who settled for acceptability, and abandoned their aspirations as writers. And for the women who did choose to write and be damned, it is clear that the difficulties did not dissolve with the decision, but posed continuous problems which could well have undermined their writing. So although there were external constraints which reduced the number of women writers, there were also the internal constraints among the small band of women writers who had to first deal with the erosion to their confidence before they could ply their pens.

Katherine Philips was no daring rebel. She was a woman who wrote and presumably would have liked a wide audience for her work, and she was prepared to go to the limits of respectability in order to achieve this end. But she was not prepared to go *beyond* the limits of acceptable behaviour for a woman of her time, and far from being arrogant she was genuinely concerned about her ability, and even wondered whether or not she was being presumptuous in assuming that her writing was worthy of a wide audience. So it is understandable that she was distressed when – without her knowledge or permission – a London printer published a volume of her poems. She consistently and categorically denied that she had anything to do with the publication (and such 'pirate printings' were by no means uncommon and assuredly were facilitated when many manuscript 'copies' were in circulation), yet her word is doubted in the histories of literature and it is generally intimated that this was a wily scheme of Katherine Philips's – which backfired. (This is not to suggest that a woman might not use a few tricks to even the odds: Delarivière Manley was later to deliberately deny all knowledge of one of her publications and insist on its withdrawal, with the most beneficial result for sales.)

During the seventeenth century any woman who ventured outside the set limits and who obtained some learning, and took to writing, was sure to attract attention and to be under social surveillance, and Katherine Philips was aware that even as the unpublished 'Orinda' her womanliness was in jeopardy. With the publication of her poems she knew she would be a target for more than mere gossip and that the 'incident' would be seized upon as evidence of her unfitness for society. And there was little that she or any other woman could do in these circumstances, for it only made matters worse to engage in any public defence. The only course open to her was to 'retire' and to hope that the censure would cease and finally be forgotten.

To her acquaintance, Dorothy Osborne, she wrote:

> I must never show my face among reasonable people again, for some most dishonest person has got some collection of my poems as I hear and has delivered them to a printer – and this has so extremely disturbed me, both to have my private folly so unhandsomely exposed and . . . the most part of the world are apt enough to believe that I contrived at this ugly accident. I have been on the rack ever since I heard it, though I have written . . . to get the printer punished, the book called in, and me some way publicly vindicated. (See Julia Longe, 1911: pp. 38-42.)

To Poliarchus, she was even more emphatic as to what such publication would mean:

> The injury done me by that printer and publisher surpasses all the troubles that to my remembrance I ever had . . . who never writ a line in my life with the intention to have it printed. . . . I have rather endeavoured never to have those trifles seen at all, than that they should be exposed to all the world . . . sometimes I think that to make verses is so much above my reach, and a diversion so unfit for the sex to which I belong, that I am about to resolve against it forever; and could I have recovered those fugitive papers that have escaped my hands, I had long since I believe, made a sacrifice of them all to the flames. The truth is I have always had an incorrigible inclination to the vanity of rhyming, but intended the efforts of that humour only for my own amusement in a retired life, and therefore did not so much resist as a wise woman have done. (Katherine Philips, 1705: pp. 227-9.)

The printer *did* apologise and the book *was* withdrawn, and it is unlikely that any opportunistic and commercially minded printer would have consented to such arrangements had Katherine Philips indeed given permission for publication. Yet despite this vindication, Katherine Philips's reputation is now still much the same as it was three centuries ago, for the topic of 'Orinda' almost never gives rise to discussion of her writing – only to discussion of her motives for publication.

Katherine Philips did not regain her good name in her own lifetime, for six months after the publication of the pirated poems she died from smallpox. But the fact that three hundred years later her reputation rests on whether she tried to evade the restrictive practices rather than on the source of those practices, reveals a great deal about literary history and criticism. Within this body of knowledge, women are consistently censured *as women* and are judged not according to the value of their work, but according to whether they conform to the rules that men have set up for women, and which the 'men of letters' have shown great willingness to enforce.

Given the range of restrictions placed on women it is surprising that any woman should have got into print in the seventeenth century. Apart from the very real barriers that were designed to discourage women from taking up their pens (such as the denial of education to females), there were also the many intangibles which would have added to women's insecurities at the time, and made the task of writing doubly difficult. For women knew they were not educated and this must have prompted grave doubts about their ability to say anything worthwhile. They knew they were denied access to the public world and as they were led to believe this was the real world of human affairs, they would have been apprehensive about their ability to know, understand or comment on anything of significance. So if their writing was tentative, or even apologetic, if their dedications were self-deprecatory and were sometimes pleas for tolerance, this is not necessarily a sign of temerity on the part of the writers. On the contrary, it took great courage for a woman to write and any admission of the limitations of their knowledge could well have been a realistic assessment of their context rather than a personal confession of failure.

Yet even if they did overcome some of these difficulties, the problem of time in which to write still remained. The number of hours that were left in a day for writing for any woman who earned her living in service, in a rural occupation, cottage industry, or a trade, were precious few, and not sufficient to permit any sustained effort. It was really only women who were not in paid employment who in practice had the opportunity to write. But for these more privileged women, it was not all that easy either. A woman who went off on her own to read or write was viewed with distrust, partly because women were not supposed to have resources of their own, but instead were expected to make themselves available to men. This was the reality of dependence and the role of the weaker vessel. Women were required to 'be there' when their menfolk were present; they were required to be decorative and amusing. Any woman who had her own interests and gave them preference over her womanly duty of availability was, at the very best, considered selfish and regarded with suspicion. And if the men were not around, and if women were not engaged in domestic duties, they were continually distracted by the demands of society – for calling and visiting. Almost without exception, women who tried to write recorded the daily frustration of never being permitted a moment to themselves, and few of them had the audacity of Mary Astell (1668-1731) – who had no husband to please or placate – who insisted on her own writing coming first, and who would therefore defiantly announce from her Chelsea upstairs window that Mrs Astell was not at home, to the callers who came knocking at her door.

Despite all the difficulties, however, some women did manage to write, and during the second half of the seventeenth century, they started on another form of writing which helped to bridge the gap between fact and fiction. It was the beginning of the biography and autobiography (and the use of letters). That this should have been the next stage in breaking down the divisions between fantasy and reality is quite logical, for biographies and autobiographies – and letters – were supposed to be, as *truthful narratives*, an amalgam of the two.

CHAPTER 3

———————•———————

Biographical beginnings

Anne Clifford, Lucy Hutchinson, Anne Fanshawe, Margaret Cavendish

Obviously, biography was authentic, it was a 'true story' and it was difficult to dismiss it as but a form of trickery. It could also be very serious and written with a moral purpose. Yet because biography and autobiography incorporate some of the features of fiction – character, a story, the selection of detail and information, etc. – the category of real and true stories was being transformed as this new genre was introduced. For while a biography was true, there was no doubt that its veracity could be disputed; there was no doubt that the accuracy of an autobiography could be suspect, so even while this new form was taken as 'fact' there had now to be reservations among the readers about the factual nature of the facts, and the door was beginning to open on the possibility of the acceptance of fiction. The four women biographers of the seventeenth century – the Countess of Montgomery (Anne Clifford), Mrs Lucy Hutchinson, Lady Fanshawe and the Duchess of Newcastle (Margaret Cavendish) – all helped to launch new literary traditions when they blurred some of the distinctions between fact and fancy, but in such a way that it would have been difficult to charge them with the ruse of deliberate deception.

All these women biographers had different reasons for writing and they were by no means consciously and exclusively concerned with challenging the limitations of the prevailing literary conventions. For example, Anne Clifford, Countess of Montgomery, was for thirty-eight years involved in litigation over her claims to the Clifford estates, and she summarised the main events of her life as a record for her children – and their legal advisors – so that they would be familiar with all the detail. She did not publish her manuscript, which has, by circuitous means and after much copying, found a place in the British Museum, and it is worth noting that not only does the issue of its accuracy arise today, but that it was of interest from the beginning. For such a record is inextricably linked with questions about reliability and credibility when the very purpose for which it was written was to outline *one* side of the story in a legal dispute.

(i) Anne Clifford

Anne Clifford – who today deserves a biography – was a woman of courage and conviction whose life (and the comment is irresistible) reads stranger than fiction! She lived under six reigns, through the execution of Charles I, the Civil War, the Commonwealth and the Restoration, and she indicates that upper class women of the seventeenth century were not without political influence. When in the nineteenth century Barbara Bodichon was to make her case that votes for women was not something new but an ancient right which women had only relatively recently been denied, it was to Anne Clifford that she referred in her evidence (see Dale Spender, 1982a). Asked by an agent to support a candidate of Charles II in her pocket borough of Appleby, Anne Clifford wrote:

> I have been bullied by an usurper, I have been neglected by a court, but I will not be dictated to by a subject. Your man sha'nt stand. Ann Dorset, Pembroke and Montgomery.* (See Vita Sackville-West, 1923.)

Clearly, Anne Clifford had a considerable command of the language, and that she put it to novel purpose in her account of her husband's and her own claims to justice is not surprising. That she was, in the process, helping to form a new literary genre is, however, one of her more remarkable achievements.

(ii) Lucy Hutchinson

The seventeenth century was a most exciting time, with its shifts in political power, and with its rise and fall of kings there was, predictably enough, a rise and fall in the fortunes of many of the subjects. For this reason there was often a genuine need to present 'the facts' if estates were to be regained or reputations were to be vindicated, and Lucy Hutchinson was one woman who wanted to set the record straight about her husband – Colonel Hutchinson – and the part he played in the support of the Puritans during the Civil War. She also wrote some autobiographical sketches in which she took certain liberties with the age

---

*Anne Clifford's second husband was Philip Herbert, Earl of Pembroke and Montgomery; he was also a nephew of Sir Philip Sidney and first cousin to Lady Mary Wroath.

of her mother as well as herself with the result that it is difficult to determine the elementary facts of her birth and death: all that can be stated here was that she was born about 1620 and that she married Colonel Hutchinson in 1638.

She too was a very colourful woman who led a very eventful life, and Antonia Fraser (1984) describes Lucy Hutchinson as 'one of the most attractive of the gallery of seventeenth century women' (p. 135). For her to take up her pen to defend her husband's name was not such a dramatic move because she had the rare advantage of an education – she could read at the age of four, was soon bilingual in French and English, knew Hebrew and Greek, and was rather derisory about her tutor, the chaplain, who was 'a piteful dull fellow' – and all her life she showed literary leanings. She had read avidly and translated much, even after her marriage and the birth of her children, so although her purpose was somewhat different when she came to her husband's defence, the task of writing was not unfamiliar. She did, of course, select her material carefully: in the effort to establish the honourable reputation of her husband there would have been no point in including material which discredited him.

But Lucy Hutchinson made her own contribution to the battle between fact and fiction. First of all her material was usually well researched and helped to provide an additional and often contradictory version of major events – which suggests that historians, too, can suffer from the problem of trying to separate fact from fiction. Secondly, she wrote in the third person. Whether this was because she believed then, as so many academics do now, that the use of the third person automatically makes an account more truthful and magically removes the 'personal' and subjective, or whether she wanted to conceal her identity, one can only guess. But she certainly made use of the convention of removing her 'self' from the record and this practice persists in many forms to the present day, justified on the very spurious grounds that it permits disinterest and promotes authenticity.

Lucy Hutchinson did not publish her writing. Although offers of publication were made after her death they were refused for over one hundred years and her manuscripts were preserved by the family. They consisted of 'The Life of Colonel Hutchinson', plus an untitled book of research notes, a fragmentary account of her own life, and two books on religious matters. In 1806, under the title of *The Memoirs of Colonel Hutchinson*, his life and the sketches of her own were published, and in 1817 her religious writing was published as *Principles of the Christian Religion*. But as her writing was only widely available more than a century after her death, it was not influential on the writers of her time. What is significant about Lucy Hutchinson, however, is that she saw the potential of biography and autobiography and she proceeded to experiment. And what she could see, so too could other literary ladies of her time.

(iii) Anne Fanshawe

Anne, born in 1625, daughter of Sir John Harrison of Hertfordshire (and presumably of a woman too but this fact has been difficult to establish), and wife of Richard Fanshawe, wrote a memoir of her husband after his death for circulation among her family and for the express purpose of providing her sole surviving son with a testimony of the goodness of his father. Again, the motives for writing were highly partisan and her account of the life of the Fanshawes is more a tale of romance and adventure than many an imaginary invention could ever have been. But in setting down 'the facts', Lady Fanshawe took literature another step down the path to fiction.

Anne Fanshawe's fate was inextricably linked with the rise and fall of kings, at first by way of her father who supported Charles I, was imprisoned by Parliament and deprived of his property; upon his release in 1643 he joined the Court at Oxford. His family was poverty stricken and Lady Fanshawe wrote that:

> From as good a house as any gentleman of England had, we came to a baker's house in an obscure street, and from rooms well furnished, to lie in a very bad bed in a garret, to one dish of meat and that not the best ordered, no money, for we were as poor as Job, nor clothes more than a man or two brought in their cloak bags: we had the perpetual discourse of losing and gaining towns and men; at the windows the sad spectacle of war, sometimes plague, sometimes sickness of other kind, by reason of so many people being packed together, as, I believe, there never was before of that quality; always in want, yet I must needs say that most bore it with a martyr-like cheerfulness. For my own part I began to think we should all, like Abraham, live in tents all the days of our lives. (Lady Fanshawe, 1830: p. 57.)

All this was just the beginning. In 1644, aged nineteen, Anne married Richard Fanshawe (aged thirty-five), who had just been appointed Secretary of War to Prince Charles, then a boy of fourteen. For the next twenty years the fate of Richard Fanshawe and that of his wife is a chronicle of one adventurous episode after another. With the execution of Charles I they had to flee for their lives and narrowly escaped capture at Cork, only to find themselves in plague-ridden Galway. En route to Spain, Lady Fanshawe was in danger of being taken as a slave by a Turkish man-of-war, and she bribed the cabin boy for his clothes. 'I crept up softly and stood upon the deck by my husband's side as free from sickness and fear, as, I confess, from discretion,' she wrote, and only after the danger had passed did her husband realise the identity of the 'boy' at his side. 'And though he seemingly chid me, he would laugh at it as often as he remembered that voyage' (John Loftis, 1979: pp. 123, 128.)

With such tales of true life, with women in men's clothing, with flights and fights and Turkish pirates, where could the line be drawn between fact and fiction? And still there was more: in Lady Fanshawe's *Memoirs* there are stories of shipwreck and near starvation, of defending the house from robbers and of outwitting passport authorities, of childbirth in the most difficult circumstances, and of an enduring and exciting love between husband and wife. No wonder the conventions which would keep reality and fantasy apart were fast losing their force and efficiency.

Yet at the same time as she recounts a fantastic tale, Anne Fanshawe reveals her great talent for including the realistic detail which gives the flavour of everyday life. The diarist Samuel Pepys (1928) is persistently praised for his realism, his attention to detail, his unadulterated and uncontrived recording of daily life. But Samuel Pepys was not the only writer of the time to bequeath a document of immense social value as a picture of the period. Lady Fanshawe left an equally fascinating account although her contribution is not equally esteemed, nor her subject matter accorded the same significance.

Her description of clothing *other than her own* rivals that of Samuel Pepys, particularly when for example she is commenting on the customs of other countries, such as Spain. And the countryside produces a response in her which is missing from the pages of Pepys, as she observes and notes the natural beauty of her surroundings. She too has her own idiosyncratic and endearing habits, one of which is to put out of mind the perils of a place and to make much of any small delights that are available: while Pepys, too, enjoyed his food, he would have been far more likely to have shown great concern for his health than did Lady Fanshawe when fleeing from Bristol to Barnstaple to avoid the plague, for she notes that 'near Barnstaple there is a fruit called a masard, like a cherry, but different in taste, and makes the best pies with their sort of cream I ever eat' (Lady Anne Fanshawe, 1830: p. 212).

Yet once more there are further contentions about the authenticity of the *Memoirs* with claims that the original is in Lady Fanshawe's handwriting (S.E. Lee in the *Dictionary of National Biography*) and counter-claims that they were dictated (see preface to 1830 edition). But whoever wrote the first manuscript in 1676, there is no doubt about the second, which was copied one hundred years later by Charlotte Colman, a great granddaughter of Lady Fanshawe (and a scribe not known for her accuracy). In 1786 yet another copy was made and it was the version that was published in 1830, and of course there was ample opportunity for editing in the more than one hundred and fifty years between Lady

Fanshawe's original version, and the date of publication. Perhaps in this intervening period, when fiction developed and the novel came into its own, some of the touches were added which make Lady Fanshawe's *Memoirs* closer to fiction: but it is at least equally likely that those touches were there in the original and were pointers to the way literary conventions would move. What can be said with certainty is that she wrote with sensitivity and skill, that she wrote a good story which sustained the interest of the reader and which was most convincing and entertaining. In the end it doesn't matter just how true or objective her account was. What matters is that her *Memoirs* are one of the early models of good women's writing.

(iv) Margaret Cavendish

But if there is to be one woman singled out to represent the starting point of women's entry to the world of letters, it must be Margaret Cavendish, Duchess of Newcastle (1624–1674). She wrote and she wrote; she wrote poetry, prose, philosophy; she wrote about people and she wrote about science. For her, there were never sufficient hours in the day to find out all she wanted to know, and to set down all she felt compelled to write. And unlike any other woman before her (as far as I can determine) she not only looked on writing as her full-time employment, she unapologetically stated that her life was a quest for knowledge – and for fame. She was a strange woman – because she was avowedly ambitious. She wanted to be a writer, a serious writer, and a *recognised* writer, and because she did not shrink from public view, because she unashamedly sought publication and wasted not one whit of her time in trying to preserve or protect her reputation, she encountered the most savage and sneering response that society could devise. She was called 'Mad Madge' for her literary efforts and was publicly mocked and ridiculed. As Virginia Woolf (1928/1974) states, 'the crazy Duchess became a bogey to frighten clever girls with' (1974: p.63), and for her knowledge and writing – and her spirit – she was held up as a figure of fun. 'Her rare visits were one of the sights of the town', wrote Brigid MacCarthy (1944), 'and never failed to arouse the vociferous delights of the populace, the tittering amusement of the fashionable and the puzzled disgust of conventional citizens' (p. 80). Even the diarists Samuel Pepys and John Evelyn commented on her extraordinary discourse and her even more extraordinarily fanciful attire, with Samuel Pepys going out of his way to have a look at this irreputable woman, and then registering his embarrassment that she might make respectable institutions where she appeared and with which he was associated – such as the Royal Society – look ridiculous (Samuel Pepys (1928), April 26th and May 30th 1667; John Evelyn (1850), April 18th 1667).

But Margaret Cavendish defied such taunts and torments. Their viciousness strengthened her resolve and vindicated her stand; the woman who wrote 'women live like bats or owls, labour like beasts and die like worms' (quoted in Virginia Woolf, 1928/1974: p. 63) was not to be cowed by jeers and gibes. The more she was condemned for her quest for knowledge and fame, the more she was calumniated for being a woman with intellectual resources, then the more confirmed she was in her beliefs that women and their intellectual resources were held in contempt. Her reaction to the sneers was to write more, not less; to know more, not to abandon the search. This independence, courage and persistence of the Duchess of Newcastle stands out starkly. Whereas Katherine Philips had tried (understandably) to squeeze into the bounds of decency by insisting that she did not seek publication and could not contemplate fame, and whereas Anne Clifford, Lucy Hutchinson and Lady Fanshawe retained their respectability by refraining from publication and insisting on the propriety of their writing – for it was in a good cause – the Duchess of Newcastle not only broke, but decried all the rules which pertained to her sex, and claimed women's right to write on the same terms and for the same reasons as men.

Behind her claim was much thought and analysis. She did not just rail against convention as some of her contemporaries were prone to do, nor did she simply object to her treatment on the basis of justice or fair play: instead she used her not inconsiderable powers of reasoning to come to an understanding of *why* the world was as it was and why women were treated the way they were. Margaret Cavendish was a feminist who reflected at length on the position of women and the power of men.

Around her was ample evidence of the 'inferiority' of women and Margaret Cavendish was never the sort of feminist who condoned or excused the behaviour of her sex on the grounds that they were victims of a society which abused them. Having herself found the courage to defy convention, it was beyond her comprehension that other women could not consider themselves capable of resistance and rebellion, and do the same. If she could pursue knowledge, persist with her writing, procure publication and pay the price – and survive – then such a course of action *was* possible, and she had no patience with women who would protest – feebly – and yet continue to *endure* the restrictions placed upon them. For although these women could also perceive the injustice of their lot, they did not support Margaret Cavendish. They did not see that where she went the way might be made easier for them to follow: rather some women were among the first to condemn her for venturing where they themselves feared to tread.

Dorothy Osborne, for example, could so easily have benefited from Margaret Cavendish's pioneering efforts. Dorothy Osborne could have been a writer – if it had been considered suitable for women to engage in writing. But Dorothy Osborne was not one to challenge convention, she was one who conformed, and although she wrote, it was not 'proper' writing which encroached on the domain of men: Dorothy Osborne wrote letters, and as Virginia Woolf (1928/1974) says, 'Letters did not count. A woman might write letters while she was sitting by her father's sick bed. She could write them by the fire whilst the men talked without disturbing them' (1974: p. 63); so letter writing posed no threat, and Dorothy Osborne wrote many letters. And on the publication of one of the Duchess's books, Dorothy Osborne wrote in a letter, 'Sure the poor woman is a little distracted, she could never be so ridiculous else as to venture at writing books and in verse too, if I should not sleep this fortnight I should not come to that' (quoted in Virginia Woolf, 1928/1974: p. 63; modernised spelling). If Dorothy Osborne saw nothing to unite her with the Duchess in her effort to be a woman writer, it is not surprising that the Duchess should have seen nothing to unite her with Dorothy Osborne and the many other women who were free with their censure and supercilious sneers. In fact, far from seeing women as victims of a system, Margaret Cavendish was of the opinion that women had a great deal of influence – with men, and that it was primarily women who were at the source of her dismissal from society. In her 'Preface to the Reader' in *The World's Olio* (1655), Margaret Cavendish wrote, 'I believe all of my own sex will be against me out of partiality to themselves, and all men will seem to be against me, out of compliment to women', for, she continues in her appraisal of her own sex, 'women's tongues are like stings of bees' (quoted in Joan Goulianos, 1974: p. 55).

It is fair to say that Margaret Cavendish did not have a very good opinion of women, but then, she didn't have all that good opinion of humanity in general, which given her circumstances is not at all surprising. She did, however, go to great lengths to *dissociate* herself from the deficiencies of her sex which she thought to be by no means inevitable, and she caustically castigated those women who 'lived down to' the lowest expectations which men held for them as silly, flighty, dependent ornaments. She was fierce in her fulminations against the folly of female flirtatiousness and devastatingly denounced 'romance' as a sentiment which could guide or structure one's life. While she showed the greatest warmth and loyalty, affection and companionship for her own husband (who supported her writing), she could categorically claim that 'amorous love, I never was infected therewith, it is a disease; or a passion, or both, I only know by relation, not by experience' (*The True Relation of My Birth, Breeding and Life*, 1656/1973, p. 195). Critical of the 'romantic', there was little likelihood that Margaret Cavendish would use her pen to follow in the tradition of Sir Philip Sidney or to cater for the foolish interest in courtly love and chivalrous intrigues.

Women *could* aspire to serious concerns, of that she was quite sure, for after all, she was a woman and she was intensely serious; she was almost consumed by a passionate need to know and understand. Of the doubts which plagued so many women of the time who would have liked to indulge their intellectual curiosity – and their pen – the Duchess of Newcastle had little experience. When it was believed that it was not possible for a woman to be a true woman *and* an intellectual being, Margaret Cavendish derided and denied the belief, rather than fencing herself in with a contradiction that demanded she choose one or the other.

Of course women were intellectual beings, she insisted, and if this was not obvious, there was only one reason for it; their lack of education. And she was certainly not going to blame women for this – although she was puzzled as to why so few of them were prepared to do something about it. As Mary Wollstonecraft was to do almost one hundred and fifty years later (and it was still a radical stand to take in 1792), Margaret Cavendish argued that if women and men were to have the same educational opportunities they would very soon demonstrate the same intellectual capabilities. 'Whereas in nature we have as clear an understanding as men', it was women's lack of education that gave them the appearance of inferiority, and all would be well, 'if we were bred in schools to mature our brains and to manure our understandings, that we might bring forth the fruits of knowledge' (from *The World's Olio*, 1655, quoted in Joan Goulianos, 1974: p. 56).

She did not deny the limitations of her own learning but nor did she take the approved path of apologising for any of her deficiencies. That she would not be undermined or intimidated by the handicaps that were imposed on women but instead claimed her achievement in not being held back by them, was typical of Margaret Cavendish: 'As for Learning, that I am not versed in it, no body, I hope, will blame me for it, since it is sufficiently known, that our Sex is not brought up to it, as being not suffered to be instructed in Schools and Universities', she wrote in the 'Reader' Preface' to *Observations on Experimental Philosophy* (1666), and she went on to add audaciously, 'I will not say but many of our Sex may have as much Wit, and be capable of learning as well as Men; but since they want instructions, it is not possible they should attain to it; for Learning is Artificial, but Wit is natural.' Conceded she may have her lack of education – through no fault of her own – but accept that her work was inferior, she would not: what she lacked in training was more than compensated for by natural ability in her view.

It is not a view shared by her critics, past or present, who have been quick to point to the enormous errors of her ways. Because the Duchess of Newcastle wrote so much and on such a wide range of topics – from scientific experiments to morality and manners, from whether optic perception was confined to the eye or was a function of the brain, from the nature of knowledge of the world to the nature of self-knowledge – she is a ready target for accusations of an absence of discipline and an abundance of errors. But Virginia Woolf, like the Duchess herself, lays the blame where it deserves to be placed, on the social arrangements which were so harsh to women. 'What could bind, tame, or civilize for human use that wild, generous, untutored intelligence?' asks Virginia Woolf (1928/1974), 'It poured itself out, higgeldy-piggeldy, in torrents of rhyme and prose, poetry and philosophy which stand congealed in quartos and folios that nobody ever reads. She should have had a microscope put in her hand. She should have been taught to look at the stars and reason scientifically. Her wits were turned with solitude and freedom. No one checked her. No one taught her. At Court they jeered her' (1974: p. 62). The wonder of it is that she wrote what she did and that she continued to write in the face of so much opposition and derision: to carp on the mistakes instead of marvelling at the achievement is to ignore the prejudice, the penalties – and the pain – that Margaret Cavendish contended with.

Perhaps she was able to survive the censure and persevere with the publications because she had found a means of explaining the reaction to her and her work. She was able to distance herself from the abuse, to not take it personally, because she understood that much of it was directed towards her sex, and not her *self*. Where other women then, and now, may flinch at a full recognition of the relationship between the sexes and resort to a veneer of romance to gloss over the reality, Margaret Cavendish had no use for such sentiment and focused on the relationship between women and men with a steady gaze. She stated plainly that 'men from their first creation usurped a supremacy to themselves, although we were made equal by nature', and this 'tyrannical government they have kept ever since' and showed no signs of relinquishing. The consequences for women have been dreadful, she writes, for 'we could never come to be free, but rather more and more enslaved' as men have insisted on 'using us either like children, fools or subjects, that is, to flatter or threaten us, to allure us or force us to obey'. She knew that what men had – including their domain of the literary world – they would not willingly give away, for they 'will not let us divide the world equally with them, as to govern and command, to direct and dispose as they do.' And all this, she added, has taken its toll on women, for our 'slavery has so dejected our spirits, as we are become as stupid as beasts are but a degree below us, and men use us as but a degree above beasts' (*The World's Olio*, 'Preface to the Reader', 1655, quoted in Joan Goulianos, 1974: p. 56). Such chilling analysis suggests that Margaret Cavendish knew full well the threat of her public, independent and intellectual actions. She understood the significance of her solitary and serious quest as a woman, for knowledge and fame, and she was able to explain not only society's response to her, but her own response – and rebellion – to the social restrictions which circumscribed women's lives.

In an age where it was not uncommon for women to have ten or more children, she could see sound reasons for women's involvement in the family and men's involvement with the business of provision. But although she subscribed to some separation of the interest-areas of the sexes, she endorsed neither marriage nor motherhood as ends in themselves and she certainly would not romanticise either of these aspects of women's lives. 'A bad husband is far worse than no husband', she declared; and she warned, for every good husband there are one thousand bad ones. Her message was plain: women beware (*Sociable Letters*, XVIII, 1664, quoted in Joan Goulianos, 1974: pp. 65–6).

Likewise, Margaret Cavendish was puzzled as to why women should be distressed by the absence of children, for again, 'where one child proves good, as dutiful and wise, a thousand prove disobedient and fools, as to do actions both to the dishonour and ruin of their families.' Without children herself, the Duchess of Newcastle was critical of motherhood to the point of being unable to see why women should want it, which is usually taken by commentators as a sign of sour grapes on her part. She is generally referred to as 'barren'. Yet when she sets out the disadvantages of maternity she shows good cause for women to be disenchanted with motherhood.

Margaret Cavendish accepted that a woman might want a child 'to keep alive the memory of . . . husband's name and family by posterity' but women, she warned, should be quite clear that it was for the father's sake, and not their own, that they were having children.

A woman does not even have an identity to pass on to her children, wrote Margaret Cavendish, for 'her name is lost as to her particular in marrying for she quits her own and is named as her husband.' Nor, as someone not allowed to possess property, can a woman make any claim on her child, for as a woman 'neither name nor estate goes to the family according to the customs and the laws of the country.' And while a woman has little to gain she has much to lose in having children, for 'she hazards her life by bringing them into the world, and has the greatest share of trouble in bringing them up.' Through Margaret Cavendish's realistic and unsentimental eyes it seemed as though a woman should express gratitude, not grief, if she found herself without children. That was her own stand, and while it may well have been a rationalisation, making the best of what she could not change, if there was anything outrageous in her position it resided not in her reasoning but in her challenge to the sanctioned and idealised vision of motherhood.

The comments of the Duchess of Newcastle on maternity are

brusque but by no means embittered, yet when she turns her attention to daughters it is possible to detect a more personal and more accusing note. For women there might be little comfort in sons, but there is even less in daughters, she declares, for

> daughters are but branches which by marriage are broken off from the root whence they sprang and grafted onto the stock of another family, so that daughters are to be accounted but as moveable goods or furnitures . . . (*Sociable Letters*, XCIII, 1664, quoted in Joan Goulianos, 1974: p. 65).

It was as maid of honour to the Queen (a service Margaret Lucas volunteered for but one which brought her much misery) that she went to Paris, and met the Duke of Newcastle. He was a widower of fifty-three and they were married in 1645 when Margaret was twenty years of age. Fortunately, the two of them shared – in Brigid MacCarthy's (1944) words – 'a magnificent indifference to worldly possessions' (p. 88), and in her autobiography, *The True Relation of My Birth, Breeding and Life* (1656), the Duchess of Newcastle recounts with remarkable equanimity a life in exile where the predominant activities were the flights from creditors and the frequent and flurried attempts to find a place to live. In part the financial difficulties and the exile abroad were the result of her husband's championship of the Royalist cause and the consequent confiscation and destruction of his property during the Civil War. After their many years in exile, the Duke and Duchess of Newcastle returned to England after the Restoration, when they 'retired to their ruined estate and devoted the rest of their lives to each other and to their particular pursuits' (Brigid MacCarthy, 1944: p. 91). There is no need to state which pursuit held the interest of the Duchess.

After her autobiography came, in 1667, the biography of her husband – *The Life of the Thrice Noble high and puissant Prince, William Cavendish, Duke . . . of Newcastle* – which ran to three editions during his own lifetime. Again, as did all the biographies written by women during this period, the autobiographical and biographical writing of the Duchess of Newcastle marked a transformation in literary conventions. Ironically, although she could not have been further removed from the romantic tradition (and indeed, she even borders on cynicism on occasion), her story of a Duke and Duchess with its subject matter of exile and ruin, of the court, the execution and the restoration of a King, and even of her devotion to her husband, was the very stuff from which romance is wrought. Her witty, lively, realistic and provocative style of writing – along with her sensitivity – was guaranteed to get the reader in, and her own eccentricity – or notoriety – including the name under which she wrote ('The Thrice Noble, Illustrious and Excellent Princess', in *Letters*,

1664) all helped to spice her true narrative and to end the distinctions between reality and romance. It would have been a remarkable fiction which could have competed with Margaret Cavendish's facts. Some of her 'adventures' may have been located in far-off places but there could be no doubt about their authenticity – particularly the avoidance of debt collectors – and the reading public was beginning to find something worthwhile, even pleasurable, in life-like characters in a life-like world, and not just in the fantastical figures of nobly born shepherds and shepherdesses who inhabited a dream world compounded of a mixture of classical antiquity and medieval chivalry.

In the social ferment in which a king was executed, a Civil War conducted, great men pulled down and other men put up, when a commonwealth was tried and the monarchy reinstated, a change in social values is to be expected and understandably will manifest itself in the reading and writing interests of the time. For those who lived through this period of upheaval, the recognition that individuals could be changed by the fluctuation of events was a new one which contrasted sharply with the outlook of the Elizabethans who had accepted as set and static the nature of human beings and the world order. An appreciation of history began to emerge so that the presentation of an amorphous and fanciful Arcadian past – or of an eighth century Denmark or a Renaissance Italy which were indistinguishable from sixteenth century England, as Shakespeare would have it – was simply not sufficient to satisfy an increasingly sophisticated society which was becoming fascinated by the relationship of individuals to their *particular* circumstances.

In her writing Margaret Cavendish was a product of her own place and time but as she was read she also helped to clarify and extend the interests of her time and place. Her introduction of real characters who confronted real crises, who sought self-knowledge, who met with the problems of everyday life, and who tried to make decisions and learn from experience, who suffered and survived, was the substance from which the novel was to grow. After Margaret Cavendish set down the details of her life, fiction as an accepted genre was not far away. Not that she is given such credit or accorded this place in the history of letters.

Biographical writing was not, however, the only contribution that she made to the development of the novel. Her interest in science also led her to construct an imaginary world which contains the kernels of later science fiction and utopian writing. But again, instead of being given credit for her literary innovation she has been discredited for her scientific inaccuracy in *The Description of a New Blazing World* (1666). Her setting may have been bizarre, but no more so, I suspect, than 'star-wars' settings which are also unlikely to stand the test of time and could prove to be as 'scientifically inaccurate' three hundred years hence as the 'science fiction' of the Duchess of Newcastle appears today. But if the authenticity of the setting of the *New Blazing World* leaves something to be desired, the reality of the characters in it cannot be disputed. The heroine, Margaret the First, is a down-to-earth character who holds discourses with wise men on the nature of atoms, 'spirits, snails, air, lice, nettles, the sun, sight and innumerable other problems' (Brigid MacCarthy, 1944: p. 126), and bears a striking resemblance to the Duchess herself!

Margaret Cavendish's autobiography appeared as part of *Nature's Pictures Drawn by Fancie's Pencil to the Life* (1656), which also contains much else of interest – it is a collection of tales, fables and dialogues and the autobiography is but one section. All of the sections, with their many innovations, help to push the boundaries just a little further to make way for the fictional form, and all of the stories persistently portray women in a positive role. It is salutary to see women in this seventeenth century context being anything but victims as they use their wits, and display their capacity for being very far from defenceless. What they say still has an authentic ring today and how they say it represents a new development for the time: like Lady Mary Wroath, Margaret Cavendish introduced realistic dialogue.

There was a grave Matron, who came to visit a young Virgin, whom she asked why she did not marry, since she was of marriageable years. 'Truly', said she, 'I am best pleased with a single life.' 'What!' answered the Matron, 'will you lead Apes in Hell?' The young lady said, it was better to lead Apes in Hell, than to live like Devils on Earth, for, said she, 'I have heard that a married couple seldom or never agree, the Husband roars in his drink, and the wife scolds in her Choler, the Servants quarrel, the Children cry, and all is disorder, than 'tis thought Hell is, and a more confused noise.' Said the Matron, 'Such are only the poor, meaner sort of people that live so; but the noble and rich men and their wives live otherwise; for the better sort as the noble and rich, when they are drunk are carried straight to bed and laid to sleep, and their wives dance until their husbands are sober.' Said the Lady, 'If they dance until their husbands are sober, they will dance until they are weary'; 'So they do,' replied the Matron (*Nature's Pictures*, Book II, 'The Discreet Virgin', quoted in Brigid MacCarthy, 1944: 1944: pp. 129-30).

You can't get much more matter-of-fact than this, and the 'discreet virgin' goes on to air many of the Duchess's own down-to-earth views on the nature of men and their domineering manners. 'This is only one example of Margaret Newcastle's habit of using her characters as mouthpieces for her own opinions,' writes Brigid MacCarthy (1944), and

'She herself is her favourite heroine, and she stalks through all her plays and most of her stories, talking commonsense about life . . . challenging all comers to argument, fencing according to a wild and whirling fashion of her own' (p. 130). Although the distance between herself and her characters may not have been great in terms of the fiction to which we are accustomed today, that she created such lively and likeable – and female – characters, at all, is a testimony to her achievement. 'The discreet virgin' is much more a creature of fiction than John Bunyan's abstractions in *The Pilgrim's Progress* (1675), which Walter Allen (1954/1980) holds up as the prototype of fiction.

One of the most appealing stories of Margaret Cavendish (from my point of view) is *The Matrimonial Agreement*. This action-packed story is of a woman who distrusts the permanency of married love and who therefore only agrees to marriage on condition that her husband make over to her part of his estate, so that if he does not remain faithful she will be in a position to leave him. He agrees, finding it at first no liability to remain true to his wife. But with the passing of time, fidelity becomes more onerous to him and although he temporarily resists temptation (for the simple reason that he knows the consequences of being caught – the loss of a substantial part of his estate), eventually he succumbs, and is, of course, found out by his wife. She shows little compunction about claiming her share, but she does *not* – romantically – withdraw from the world or retire from society. Instead she uses her financial independence as maintenance, while she embarks on the same course as her husband and conducts her own affairs. To my mind a more realistic if not a less moral or less conventional ending.

The Tale of the Traveller is more moral although no less innovative than many of Margaret Cavendish's other stories. It is about a man who sets out to try just about everything the world has to offer, only to discover that what he is seeking is in essence to be found at home. Apart from the quest for self-knowledge that this journey represents, there is the descriptive detail of the travel writer – yet another innovation which would be drawn upon by future writers of fiction and travelogues – and such accounts of foreign scenes are not without their realistic elements, partly because of Margaret Cavendish's direct experience of living abroad.

A survey of the writings of the Duchess of Newcastle reveals that despite the many limitations of her circumstances, she opened up for literature a vast range of opportunities which had not previously been perceived. So many of the genres and conventions which are today taken for granted began to take shape and substance in her creative writing. And it would be remiss to make no mention of her letter writing, for in this form as well she tried to portray real life, to present real problems and possible resolutions and to unify her epistles with a semblance of narrative. But as Virginia Woolf has so caustically pointed out, the letter writing of women has never been taken seriously; it has never posed a threat to the male-dominated literary establishment because men have never counted women's letters as 'real' writing. (Needless to add, the same rule does not apply to the letter writing of men which can come under the heading of 'literature'.) Historically and currently women have been predominantly the 'private' letter writers (and diary keepers) with the results that this is one area at least where women do have an extensive heritage, see Dale Spender (ed.; in press). Yet because women's letters – and diaries – have never been systematically included among the works of literature, this rich heritage has never received the attention it deserves. But like biography, letter writing too stands at the starting point of fiction and it is no coincidence that those literary works which are held up as the first novels – and which are written by men – are either ostensible accounts of a 'true life' (Daniel Defoe's *Robinson Crusoe*) or else are volumes of letters (Samuel Richardson's *Pamela*). They are presented, however, without female precedent.

In his history of the English novel, Walter Allen (1954/1980) makes no reference to any woman I have so far discussed as a contributor to the formative stages of the novel. Instead, Walter Allen goes back to Chaucer's fourteenth century prologue to *The Canterbury Tales* and to *The Wife of Bath's Tale* in the effort to trace the origin of the novel. He shows the influence of Shakespeare in the presentation of a 'fiction' and he refers to the contribution of Sir Philip Sidney and the comparable writings of Robert Greene, Thomas Lodge and Emanuel Ford; but there is no hint of the existence of Lady Mary Wroath or Anne Weamys. He lists lofty male poets but omits Katherine Philips and, for all his intents and purposes, Anne Clifford, Lucy Hutchinson, Lady Fanshawe and the Duchess of Newcastle do not exist. Yet the Duchess of Newcastle – at least – was as well if not better known as a writer in her own time than many of the men who have a place in his pages.

The exclusion of women from the literary heritage has not been confined to efforts to keep them out of print but has extended to keep them out of consideration even when they are in print. That the history of English letters is primarily the history of the writing of men is more in the nature of a revelation of the importance men attach to their own deeds than it is an assessment of women's writing. 'The comparatively sudden appearance at the turn of the seventeenth century of the novel as we know it was a manifestation of a marked change in men's interests,' writes Walter Allen (1954/1980: p. 21) and his statement is not only significant for the primacy it accords men and their interests, but for the blind spot that such partiality portrays: perhaps if he had taken a closer look at the literature of women, the appearance of the novel would not have seemed quite so sudden. For in the biographical, narrative, and letter writing of the Duchess of Newcastle, we can identify the shape of fiction in embryonic form.

'Men of letters' have excluded women and women's writing from both participation and consideration within the literary circle, and they have compounded their errors of judgment with their failure to mention that there are different rules for the women, whom they have not included. Only individuals who are determinedly partisan could have for centuries practised a double standard which judged the woman writer as a true woman and the man writer as a true writer; only individuals who are in control and who wish to stay that way could have consistently refused to admit the part they were playing in keeping women out of the world of letters. Why is it that half the human population who are deemed to be more than proficient at writing when it is undertaken in school or seen as an accomplishment are held to be 'not up to standard' when they are measured against men – and by men? And why is this not a central topic of discussion in literary circles, for it is not a new understanding: it is something women have known for centuries and it is why so many of them have tried to conceal their sex in their attempts to obtain a fair hearing.

There can be no more illuminating case study of men's exclusion of women from full participation in the production of culture than that afforded by the men of letters. And not until women are equal partners in the world of letters and not until the historic exclusion of women is a central topic in literary discussion will we have a history of letters, an assessment of our literary heritage, that is more fact than fiction. Until that time, we are obliged to take as valid the partisan versions of the men of letters who would have us believe, for example, that the prototype of the modern novel is John Bunyan's (1678) *Pilgrim's Progress*. I do not take exception to this acknowledgment of paternity but I cannot accept yet another story of creation in which it is the father who gives birth and where it is held that there were no mothers of the novel.

CHAPTER 4

---•---

'The fair triumvirate of wits'

Aphra Behn, Delarivière Manley, Eliza Haywood

(i) Aphra Behn

The seventeenth century, with its upheaval of the Civil War and the goings and comings of the monarchs, was an age of increasing uncertainty. When one year the king rules by divine right and the next the common man is judged to be better-fitted to the task, considerable mental adjustment has to be made. In such a context where old values lose the hold they once had, literature can play a part as a clarifying force, both drawing on and feeding into the changes of the time. This is one reason that the literature of the Restoration period is significantly and substantively different from the literature which preceded it: it was responding to, reflecting and shaping some of the new values. It was written in a very different spirit and for a different and growing audience.

The grim reality of executions and the Civil War, and the narrow concerns of the Puritan reign in which life had been but a preparation for death with literature moulded accordingly, had hardly been fertile ground for the growth of a mood of gay abandon. But with the return of a pleasure-seeking king, society was in a frame of mind to put aside the bitter past, and to turn to more joyous pursuits. A new spirit of enjoyment entered the age, and there emerged – in the words of today – a very 'permissive' society.

Nowhere was this more obvious than in the theatre. Condemned and closed during the Puritan ascendancy, the re-opening of the playhouses in the reign of Charles II was met with great enthusiasm: and royal patronage was assured, for the king himself was inclined towards many of the pleasures the theatre had to offer. The popularity of the stage and the revitalisation of the drama – and 'immoral' and bawdy drama at that – reflected the shift in interest and taste, and suggested new realms of literary possibility. It was probably because all was in a state of flux,

47

because the old guidelines had gone and the new ones had not been fully established, that women were able to make their entry to the theatrical world at this point. This was the era when women found their way on to the stage and when they established their credentials as dramatists.

It has been said that the novel was the 'late developer' in literary terms because for so long it was the drama that attracted all the attention and drew the talented writers towards it. Certainly Christopher Marlowe, William Shakespeare and Ben Jonson made magnificent contributions to literature during the Elizabethan period, and it does seem plausible to suggest that while these writers and the dramatic form flourished, there was no great pressure to meet the need for story telling through the development of fictional forms.

The drama also flourished during the Restoration period, and if the first *real* novel is taken to be Daniel Defoe's *Robinson Crusoe* (1720) – and it usually is – then there seem to be some grounds for the theory that the novel stagnated while the drama thrived. But there is just one problem. One of the great dramatists of the Restoration *also* wrote thirteen novels – more than thirty years before *Robinson Crusoe*. Only if this contribution is *excluded* is there any validity in the (well-established) theory that it took a fall in drama to lead to the rise of the novel.

Of course, the author of these thirteen novels which have been excised from the history of letters was a woman: Aphra Behn (1640-1689). She was one of the leading literary lights of the Restoration period who began by writing highly successful plays, but who seems to have turned to novel writing after wearing thin her theatrical welcome – probably by giving offence to some prominent Whigs whom she consistently attacked in her plays. In her case, however, the need to write a story in prose form was no mere matter of finding a creative outlet: it was financial necessity. If she did not write and publish, she did not eat. So when she was 'warned off' the stage it seemed logical and most desirable to publish her dramatic stories in prose form. While it may seem that this was a very radical departure, this switch from one genre to another is not so startling as it first appears. With only two playhouses in London, it had become common practice to publish plays in order that they should reach a wider audience than those who could get to see them. This meant that Aphra Behn was quite used to thinking of the presentation of her dramatic stories in printed form. It also meant that the reading public had been prepared for prose stories in print through their familiarity with published plays.

But first a little more about Aphra Behn. She is not an easy subject to embark upon because there has been (this century) considerable controversy about whether she did what she was supposed to have done,

1   Aphra Behn

or indeed, whether she did or did not exist. Ernest Bernbaum (1913) was of the opinion that the accepted biography of Aphra Behn was a fiction – he seemed to find it preferable to disprove Aphra Behn and her achievement rather than to admit that a woman could write so well. And if her writing is going to be – euphemistically – 'overlooked', disputes about her existence can be quite useful as a means of discrediting her work.

Although it is established practice for men of letters to devalue the achievement of women writers, Mr Purvis and Mr Bernbaum (and a few others) seem to have gone to extremes to make their points: the weaknesses in their theories were obvious and they have now been dismissed (see Angeline Goreau, 1980: p. 10). Yet, ironically, although they have been discredited, the denial of Aphra Behn, as it is represented in the work of these men, still contributes to the devaluation – and neglect – of the *writing* of Aphra Behn, for it moves the focus of discussion from her writing to the details of her life.

It is partly the old division between fact and fiction which is responsible for some of the interest in the *real* story of Aphra Behn, for whether her own writing is a *true* account of her experiences or an *imaginary* tale, makes – or is supposed to make in the framework of literary judgments – a difference to her status as a *narrator*. If, for example, she really did go to the West Indies and meet a slave prince, then her story *Oroonoko* is (supposed to be) a very different sort of writing from that of 'making it all up'.

From this distance it seems to me ludicrous that any evaluations of the writing of Aphra Behn should hinge on whether the details of her life are true or false. From my point of view, the only real certainty *is* her writing, and it is this which should be the basis of any assessment of her achievement. And any survey of her plays and novels (and poems and translations) reveals that her work *is* a great literary achievement, and that the efforts which have been made to exclude it from the history of letters are unpardonable.

Although during my own formal literary education I never once heard reference made to Aphra Behn, earlier this century she did enjoy favour among literary women: Vita Sackville-West wrote a biography of her in 1927, and she was something of a model for Virginia Woolf, who wrote, 'All women together ought to let flowers fall upon the tomb of Aphra Behn, which is, most scandalously but rather appropriately in Westminster Abbey, for it was she who earned them the right to speak their minds. It is she – shady and amorous as she was – who makes it not quite fantastic for me to say to you tonight: Earn five hundred a year by your wits' (Virginia Woolf: 1928/1974: p. 66). It is generally agreed that Aphra Behn was the first woman to earn her living by the pen. And as she had not the 'benefit' of a classical education, and was neither a member of the aristocracy nor of the male literary establishment, her writing was *popular*. She drew on her experience of the world – including women's place in that world – for her writing.

Writing, however, was not her only claim to fame, and because I think it cannot be bettered, I quote Angeline Goreau's (1980) summary of the life of Aphra Behn:

> The life she led would have been extraordinary in any age, but for a woman of the seventeenth century not born to fortune or position it was nearly unheard of. Aphra Behn was an adventuress who undertook the long and dangerous voyage to the West Indies, became involved in a slave rebellion there, and visited a tribe of Indians who had never before seen Europeans. She was a spy for Charles II against the Dutch. She was a debtor imprisoned for expenses incurred in the service of the King. She was a feminist who vociferously defended the right of women to an education, and the right to marry whom they pleased, or not at all. She was a sexual pioneer who contended that men and women should love freely and as equals. She was a political activist who urged the Royalist point of view at Will's Coffee House and from the stage at Drury Lane theater. She was an early abolitionist whose novel *Oroonoko* contained the first popular portrayal of the horrors of slavery. Finally, she was a writer who not only insisted on being heard, but successfully forced the men who dominated the jealous literary world of Restoration England to recognize her as an equal. In a London that boasted only two theaters she had seventeen plays produced in seventeen years. She wrote thirteen 'novels' (thirty years before Daniel Defoe wrote *Robinson Crusoe*, generally termed the first novel) and published several collections of poems and translations (Angeline Goreau, 1980: pp. 3-4).

No wonder this magnificent woman who fought such an open battle for women's rights – including the right to write for money – served as a model for Virginia Woolf, although even Virginia Woolf could not refrain from reference to Aphra Behn's shady and amorous lifestyle. And in the deprecation of Aphra Behn's moral standards there hangs another tale which helps to explain how and why the mothers of the novel have had their contribution denied.

From the vantage point of the present 'permissive' age, Aphra Behn's writing in a 'permissive' age of the past does not appear as shocking as it has seemed to commentators in the intervening years: almost without exception they feel obliged to apologise for her lewd and lurid ways and her scandalous style. But the fact that so many of the critics have been outraged by the circumstances of her life and the shamelessness of her

51

writing is not just an interesting observation: their incensed response has had its uses. In trying to explain why it is that Aphra Behn's novels have been 'ignored' and that pride of place has been accorded to Daniel Defoe, it emerges that there have been clear links between Aphra Behn's 'immorality' and her expulsion from the literary mainstream. Her work has not been fit for study.

(Needless to say no such criterion applies to her male colleagues who, although they did not write novels, wrote plays which, less successful at the time, have not since been outlawed on the basis of their 'immorality' or 'poor taste'.)

In 1862, an anonymous writer in the *Saturday Review* made the explicit connection between Aphra Behn's indecency and her place in English letters. Five hundred copies of a selection of her works had been reprinted and even if she had had the capacity to deprave, it is unlikely that such a small circulation could ever have led to the widespread corruption of the morals of English society. Yet the reviewer is adamant that the writer is dangerous, and that in the reprinting of Aphra Behn's work there had been five hundred copies too many published. 'It is a pity her books did not rot with her bones,' he wittily pronounced. 'That they should now be disinterred from the obscurity into which they have happily fallen is surely inexcusable.' He was convinced that if anyone did read Aphra Behn's work it could not be for 'literary appreciation' but could 'only be for a love of impurity for its own sake, for rank indecency', and he was for banishing Aphra Behn 'from all decent society' (vol. 33, 27 January 1862, p. 109).

By such means are women writers removed from the literary mainstream. What with the attempts to prove that she didn't exist, didn't do what she said, and even if she did wasn't fit to be read, the wonder of it is that her work has survived these scurrilous attacks, and that it is now possible to restore her to her proper place – as one of the mothers of the novel.

Aphra Behn broke with all the literary traditions of her time for women. She was no literary lady who took to writing for the pleasure of the task. She was a professional writer who wanted to know about payment, and she made shrewd guesses about the market place: if it was bawdiness the public wanted – and would pay for – then it was bawdiness she would provide. And if this cost her her reputation as a lady, it had the compensation of providing her bread.

With Aphra Behn we turn a very important corner in the history of women's writing, said Virginia Woolf, in 1928: 'We leave behind, shut up in their parks among their folios, those solitary great ladies who wrote without audience or criticism, for their own delight alone. We come to town and rub shoulders with the ordinary people in the streets' (1928/1974: p. 64). And if Aphra Behn provided what the public wanted, she did so on her own terms and in her own distinctive style. It is the life of London, in all its realistic and 'immoral' detail, that she is familiar with, and which is present in most of her stories. Even where 'romance' enters in the form of noble souls with pastoral names, it is their realistic behaviour and speech as rather indecent if not debauched 'locals' which is part of the humour and the attraction of the work.

Of course, the fact that Aphra Behn did not know Latin and Greek, could not write according to the laws of the classics, and with her 'low' characters mocked the lofty literary traditions which were much prized, brought her into conflict with the writing men of the time. To the charge of 'inferiority' she defiantly retorted that she suffered from the same limitations as Shakespeare (who knew no Latin and Greek) and she then proceeded to add insult to injury by becoming more popular than her male colleagues, by generally earning more, and by confronting them with a version of reality which they preferred not to see.

This was brought home to me – dramatically – when recently one of Aphra Behn's plays (*The Lucky Chance*) was restaged (first appearance on the London stage for two hundred and fifty years, the advertisements at the Royal Court announced!). Apart from the fact that I found it immensely amusing (which no doubt says something about my own 'moral' standards), I was intrigued by the shift in style. The play was very much in the manner of Restoration comedy with infidelity and mistaken identities constituting the greater part of the drama: but there was a significant difference, because the women were not presented as fools – and the men were not flattered. The women were not spiteful, vindictive or sexually insatiable, and the men did not get the best of every situation. The women were astute judges of the options available to them and were prepared to settle for a steady income in lieu of a more stimulating occupation, but just as for centuries men have thought it not unreasonable to want both, so too the women would have preferred wealthy husbands who were also stimulating and attractive.

Throughout this play – and throughout all the writings of Aphra Behn – it was men who were being measured by women's standards, and this provides a welcome and refreshing change. When women are the reference point, men do not have it all their own way. Which is one of the reasons Aphra Behn did not find favour with all her male colleagues then; and, no doubt, one of the reasons she has not found favour with the literary critics since. Yet this is not *sufficient* reason to exclude from literature half the representations of humanity: or at least I don't think it's sufficient reason to judge women's writing as 'below standard'. It might not be the standard men like or to which they are accustomed, but it is a standard which I find illuminating and valuable. But while ever the history of letters is primarily the history of men's writing, it will be a standard we will not have recourse to. We are being disallowed women's portrayal of women – and men – and the world, and we are being offered instead a partial and distorted literature which has a limited capacity to clarify and resonate the human condition.

This is why it is important to reclaim the writing of the mothers of the novel: not just because it is unjust to exclude them – although this in itself is reason enough – but more importantly, because without them we are without the symbolic meanings and understandings of half of humanity. Without the women writers, literature is reduced to the level of propaganda, the medium for the unchallenged view of the dominant sex.

With her representation of the world which is distinctly *not* that of the dominant sex, Aphra Behn symbolises the nature and extent of the omissions, while women are excluded from the literary canon. In her choice of subject matter, her commentary, and her style, she illustrates some of the differences in outlook between women and men; even her sense of humour – which frequently makes men the butt of the joke – contrasts markedly to the forms to which we are accustomed, and in which it is the humour of men that prevails.

For example, during the Restoration period there were many men who were prepared to enumerate all the advantages of a 'permissive' age, and much of the literature of men at this time suggests that all members of society were more than satisfied with their new sexual freedoms. Yet this is *not* the view that we get from the writing of Aphra Behn. Write, she would, on sexual permissiveness, because that was what was popularly demanded, but she had little praise for these new freedoms. She thought they went against women's interest. It was all very well, she stated again and again in her writing, for men to be pleased that social convention now permitted so many more women to be available to them, and it was even the case that the reputation of a man was enhanced by his capacity for amorous conquests. But what did this mean for women? They could hardly be delighted by the prospect of being required to be available to more men, and they certainly didn't gain in stature by repeatedly being 'conquered'.

In her criticism of the permissive age, Aphra Behn makes the significant point that women see society as arranged for the convenience of men (right down to the education they provided for themselves), and with little regard to the consequences for women. Perhaps, if for the last three hundred years these understandings of Aphra Behn's had been retained in the history of letters it would not now be necessary to go over the same ground again in today's permissive society, for we would have come to understand the issues – centuries ago. But because her woman's perspective has been kept out of the literary heritage, it has only been recently – and with great effort – that the writing of Aphra Behn has been recovered and that we are able to enjoy some of the benefits of hearing her side of the story.

Not that she was completely free to write what she wanted. All writers who want to earn a living must to some extent cater for the interests of their time, and this necessarily reduces the number of options available. But for women writers there has always been an additional problem: most, if not all the judges of their writing, are men. As just about every woman writer who has ever got into print has commented, in order to even get an audience a woman writer must first please men (who are the publishers, advisers, critics), in a way that no man writer has ever been required to please women. In Aphra Behn's age – and right up to the present day – it is men who have made the decisions about what gets into print (see Tillie Olsen, 1978; Joanna Russ, 1984; Lynne Spender, 1983); it is men who decide whether the manuscript is worthwhile, valuable, likeable – saleable! And not surprisingly men make their decisions in accordance with their own value system. On this point, Virginia Woolf is just one among the multitudes of women who have had something to say:

> When a woman comes to write a novel, she will find that she is perpetually wishing to alter the established values – to make serious what appears insignificant to a man, and trivial what is to him important. And, for that, of course, she will be criticized; for the critic of the opposite sex will be genuinely puzzled and surprised by an attempt to alter the current scale of values, and will see in it not merely a difference of view, but a view that is weak or trivial, or sentimental, because it differs from his own. (Woolf, 1972, vol. 2: p. 146; written in 1929)

And when Aphra Behn became the first woman to seek systematic commercial publication, she plunged right into the problem that has plagued women writers ever since. The problem of having to obtain the approval of men. If this situation were reversed, if in order to get published men had to submit their writing to a panel of women (to one of the relatively recently established women's presses, for instance, for which there is a demonstrable need), if men had to obtain the stamp of approval from women literary critics – there would be an outcry. Such an arrangement would be called unjust, unfair: there would be accusations that this constituted censorship, that it constrained what men were permitted to write – even that it inhibited them, undermined their confidence, and caused writer's block – and that it allowed for the publication of a distorted and 'politically correct' view. But for hundreds of years, since Aphra Behn, this is the predicament that women have faced. And men have said never a word. They have even on occasion treated with disdain, if not contempt, the 'ridiculous' woman writer who has raised the issue. This fundamentally significant topic has not featured on the agenda of the men of letters: their silence is a testimony to just how far women's view has been excluded from the realms of literary debate.

Aphra Behn, and Delarivière Manley who followed her, never failed to remember that they were dependent on men, that they were being judged as women and by men, and that their livelihoods rested on their ability to please. But neither of them could resist the temptation to lay their own charges, and Aphra Behn's writing is replete with references to women being able to write as well as men and that any judgments to the contrary were a better gauge of men's prejudice than of women's talent.

Aphra Behn believed that justice called for a single moral standard for both sexes and she skilfully satirised the many conventions which decreed that what was good for the goose was not good for the gander. Yet even though she demanded the same code of morality for both sexes, she did not think that women and men could lead the same sort of lives. She may not have conformed herself but she was still aware that the predominant 'occupation' for women differed radically from the predominant 'occupation' of most men, and the occupation of women interested her and was often the substance of her writing.

If it were a fair and just world no doubt we could have novels about women's work and men's work; no doubt they could complement one another and, standing side by side, they could together provide a comprehensive account of the diversity of human existence. But it is far from a fair and just world that we inhabit, with the result that before the novels are even read, they are assigned very different values: those which explore women's occupation (decreed to be obtaining a living by obtaining a man) are from the outset accorded a lower status than those which are concerned with men's occupation (obtaining a paid place in the world). And with the first step of the first professional woman writer into the world of women, we encounter the dilemma that has confronted women writers ever since. If they choose to explore their own experience of the world, if they elect to concentrate on the world as it is viewed by women, they are, usually, willingly placing themselves in the category of 'minor writer'. They are by definition producing substandard work. This has nothing to do with the quality of their writing – or the quality of the world they choose to depict – but is a value judgment, pure and simple, about their limited, inferior, and insignificant subject matter.

Because, as so many women have written, the sanctioned business of woman's life has for so long been to ensure a livelihood by obtaining a man, women have had 'career' aspirations and strategies which have relied heavily on the management of human relationships. Of course, this is by no means the only reason that women have been concerned with exploring, understanding and utilising relationships. That women are so often held responsible for domestic relationships, for the rearing of children and the psychological well-being of the family, has also contributed to this dimension of women's lives. But let a woman writer concern herself with 'relationships', particularly relationships between the sexes, and she brands herself as the writer of that inferior class of novels – *romantic fiction*. Immediately her work is classified as *outside* the bounds of literary consideration.*

The term 'romantic fiction' is used in much the same way to designate the printed word of women as 'gossip' is used to designate the spoken word of women. It is an all-encompassing (and derogatory) term which places women's words beyond serious consideration. Neither 'romantic fiction' nor 'gossip' warrant analysis. Their inferior status is based not on an analysis but quite the reverse: such labels *preclude* analysis. And by lumping together the diverse writing of so many women (from Aphra Behn to Barbara Cartland) and labelling it romantic fiction, the contributions of many, many magnificent women writers are automatically placed outside the literary mainstream.

There is no equivalent 'catch-all' category for men's writing, no male equivalent to romantic fiction (or gossip) which automatically renders certain concerns of men as beneath consideration. If Barbara Cartland portrays a caricature of the feminine, there are plenty of caricatures of the masculine to be found – but they are not dismissed out of hand. Indeed, they are not even all lumped together in one indiscriminatory category but have been evaluated, refined, divided into subgenres of spy story, thriller, western, detective story, etc. And such classification does not necessarily bar them from serious literary appraisal. Too readily can I recall my own postgraduate courses in literature where not only was there not one single woman author, but where I was required to spend an entire semester engaged in the serious business of studying the artistic skill of Raymond Chandler! Aphra Behn I knew nothing of, but Margaret Drabble was then an 'emerging' novelist. When I asked to be allowed to study her I was informed that as she wrote 'romantic fiction' she was ineligible for inclusion in a literary course. So, Raymond Chandler it was. And the recognition that it is not that men do not gossip – or portray their sex in postures of gender-excess – but that when they do it, they call it by a different name: they call it

*For further discussion see chapter 8, 'Male romance'.

something grander and more prestigious.

This double standard is not new. From the advent of the first woman novelist we have a value system which automatically places women's concerns, and the literature which reflects them, in a subordinate position and generally beneath notice. Women's lives and experiences are held to be less important and less significant than men's, and women's literature which gives them expression can be excluded from the literary tradition by virtue of its association with women, and without regard to its literary merit. This practice persists to the present day where the genre 'romantic fiction' is held in considerable contempt, and as this genre has never been the subject of serious or systematic analysis within the literary tradition,* the evaluation is not based on the writing. The result has been that there is a vast body of women's writing which the men of letters have never seen fit to examine or include in the literary canon. This is how the writing of the mothers of the novel has been deemed not to exist in the history of letters.

The 'romantic fiction' of Aphra Behn bears little resemblance to the 'romantic fiction' associated with the current Barbara Cartland industry, which is another reason that the overall label is inappropriate, and why there is a need to distinguish and refine some of the many different strands of this imprecise and deprecatory categorisation. But the inaccuracy of the term would be small consolation to Aphra Behn whose 'romantic' stories have enjoyed much the same fate as if they had been of the Barbara Cartland variety. In essence, Aphra Behn wrote no novels of the 'woman-gets-man' variety. Her characters – of both sexes – were prone to pursue perilous paths in the name of love, but there was little of the courtly love tradition in their adventures. Bigamy, incest, and murder, all making their presence felt in her plots, were not part of the chivalric code, and were indications of the distance she had moved from the pastoral romance of Lady Mary Wroath.

Held against me though it may be (given her 'indecency'), I must admit to laughing out loud when reading some of Aphra Behn's novels. I suspect that the charges of 'immorality' are linked with her complete carelessness of convention, her habit of turning the value system upside down, and her irreverence for all things sacred. For example, three of her novels are about nuns (*The Fair Jilt of Tarquin and Miranda*, *The Nun or The Perjured Beauty*, *The Nun or The Fair Vow-breaker* – it is not possible to date them accurately), but the nuns who are the heroines are scarcely recognisable as women with religious vocations. As Brigid MacCarthy (1944) has written wryly, 'Generally the nun is an incredibly immoral woman, and the convent a kind of elegant brothel with the

*See Margaret Ann Jensen (1984), and chapter 8, 'Male romance', for further discussion.

added piquancy of a grille' (p. 159). Exhausted by the demands of their love life, some of the women retreat to the nunnery for respite, to get their second wind, before once more venturing into the tumultuous territory of requited – or unrequited – love.

Yet, despite these departures from convention, Aphra Behn was not uninfluenced by the literary traditions which flourished until the Restoration period. She makes use of some of the devices of pastoral romance with, for example, her choice of characters of ostensibly high birth and with distinctly high-sounding names. To this she adds another – almost contradictory – practice of adamantly insisting that the story she is relating is a true narrative. So we have in her novels another move towards fiction as we know it, in her unusual combination of fantasy and reality. Her means of cultivating the sense of realism and authenticity are interesting. She is forever vouching for the truth of her tale: the story comes from first-hand experience, she was there at the time, the characters were personally known to her, she saw them with her own eyes and heard their utterances with her own ears so all she is doing is simply relating an account of real life no matter how unlikely the events may appear. By this technique, Aphra Behn attempted to reassure her readers that they were not being party to any deceit but were privileged to be able to learn of these remarkable affairs.

The realistic detail in her writing, however, is such that it conveys a greater sense of authenticity than all her explicit assurances of truthfulness could ever do. She has the talent for minute observation, astute assessment, the portrayal of fine realistic detail. So many of her descriptions 'ring true'; one which struck me particularly was that of Isabella (in *The Nun or The Fair Vow-breaker*), preparing her two lovers for death.

Having renounced her lover, Villenoys, to become a nun, Isabella is later prevailed upon by Henault to abandon the veil and to marry him – whereby he is promptly disinherited by his father, who will only forgive him if he redeems himself by going off to war. So to battle goes Henault, only to fall, and to entrust to his fellow warrior – who is, of course, Villenoys – his dying message to Isabella. Villenoys takes back the message and takes up his love affair with Isabella, and they are soon married.

But – and it is not difficult to guess what is coming – Henault did *not* die in battle, and one day he returns. Such a plot borders on the melodramatic but Aphra Behn far exceeds this particular limitation when she presents in her characters and evokes for her readers a drama of great force. It is the very real agony of Isabella when she confronts Henault and realises she has committed bigamy which Aphra Behn is able to express, and there is no lessening of the tension and no descent from the powerful dramatic style, when the author shows Isabella facing

59

the consequences, and making her decisions about what to do.

Isabella contemplates suicide, but dismisses it as an unsatisfactory solution. She thinks of taking Henault back and of banishing Villenoys, but she has reached the stage where she knows it is Villenoys, and not Henault, that she wants. She can't send Henault away – but she can get rid of him and resume the life she and Villenoys happily shared. It is this option that she chooses.

She smothers Henault and informs Villenoys that he died of shock on hearing that she had 'remarried'. Villenoys accepts her story but is uneasy because he recognises that no matter how 'innocent' they are, the death of Henault is so convenient, they will both be suspected of foul play. So he decides to remove the evidence and to throw Henault's body in the river. But Isabella has observed Villenoy's reaction and his fear: she knows that *she* can live with her crime but she realises that Villenoys will not be able to live with even public suspicion of it. There can be no return to their days of unperturbed happiness: Henault has separated them, in his death.

Going along with Villenoy's scheme to dispose of the body, Isabella methodically stitches up the sack in which Henault has been deposited. Then, on the pretence that all is not concealed, she begins to readjust the sack which Villenoys has hoisted on to his back. And with deftness and deliberation she calmly stitches the sack to Villenoys, and urges him to throw with all his force when he hurls the sack into the river. When he follows her instructions, of course, he throws himself in as well; the stitches do not break but keep him joined to Henault's body and the weight drags him down to drown.

This crime, Isabella cannot live with: she gives herself away, and is executed.

The *stitching*: the ordinariness and extraordinariness of Isabella's scheme. There is no question of the realism, the authenticity; the crude dimensions of the bigamy plot fade in the face of this most convincing episode. In the combination of old and new conventions, in the blend of the romantic and the tragic, in the unique mixture of fantasy and reality which is the hallmark of Aphra Behn, an entirely new form emerges, and it is the basis of the novel. She creatively fuses so many of the elements which were supposed to be kept separate, and in so doing, she reveals the extent of her genius: there is no better example of her 'craft' than in *Oroonoko*, the novel which enjoys the greatest reputation of all her work. It is even referred to (and it constitutes the first reference to an English woman writer) by Walter Allen (1980) in his history of the novel: if we were to accept his judgment, however, we would be in no great haste to read it.

On the basis of *Oroonoko*, Walter Allen grants Aphra Behn originality in two respects: the first is that she writes about 'the noble savage' seventy years before Rousseau, and that her work is 'the forerunner of all anti-imperialist or anti-colonial literature'. The second aspect of her originality is that she claims to have been to Surinam in the West Indies, where the story is set: 'It now appears unlikely that she ever was in Surinam, and the source of background material was probably George Warren's *Impartial Description of Surinam* published in 1667', he states in supercilious tone (pp. 34-5). And this acknowledgment of Aphra Behn's 'originality' is what is generally termed a 'back-handed' compliment which denies all the achievement of 'the forerunner of all anti-imperialist or anti-colonial literature', for by ironically praising Aphra Behn for the invention of her biographical details, Walter Allen places her in the ranks of those who are not to be trusted.

This is *very* interesting. Leaving aside for the moment the question of whether or not Aphra Behn really *did* go to Surinam (all the evidence being that she *did*), why should Walter Allen resort to the outdated distinction between fact and fiction to undermine the value of the contribution of the first woman he mentions in the history of the English novel? Such a standard is not applied to any other author he includes in his pages. It is not even applied to other women writers: indeed, he would probably be scoffed at, if it were.

This treatment of Aphra Behn is as remarkable as it is inconsistent; an imaginative writer is being dismissed because her writing is so imaginative. The absurdity of such an evaluation is not wasted on Brigid MacCarthy (1944): 'Would Jane Austen be a better kind of novelist', she asks 'if it could be proved that she knew Elizabeth Bennet, Darcy, and Mr Collins in real life, and that she had actually lived at Longbourne and visiting Rosings?' For Brigid MacCarthy assumes that credit is to be given for creativity – across the board. Yet the rules are being applied selectively – even randomly – when on the one hand Ann Radcliffe 'is praised by literary critics for her ingenuity in creating convincing backgrounds of travel and letting her imagination play round them' (p. 179), while those who suspect that Aphra Behn is engaged in a comparable activity condemn her on the grounds that it is her imagination that she is making use of.

Not even Daniel Defoe is now condemned for his lie that *Robinson Crusoe* is a true account; rather he is commended for his realistic detail and his construction of authenticity. But when it suits, a woman is dismissed for employing these same skills with good effect: Aphra Behn, who wrote more than thirty years before the appearance of *Robinson Crusoe*, and more than one hundred years before Ann Radcliffe, and without benefit of models, is systematically and snidely devalued because in the minds of some men it cannot be admitted that she led the life she did. Her imaginative powers are taken out of their literary context, are given the connotation of 'lies and deceit', and are then used as a justification for not taking her work seriously.

This is marvellously convenient. It is also a fabrication of 'reasons' long after the facts. If there are those who deserve not to be taken seriously, they are the critics who have devised this particular form of dismissal. Apart from the fact that the case against her visit to Surinam is not nearly as substantial as the case for her visit (see Angeline Goreau, 1980, for a summary of all the evidence), we are asked to accept that while for two centuries after her death her visit was not questioned, *on the basis of no new material*, the critics of this century have seen fit to advance the theory that Aphra Behn was a liar and that this debases her work. Is it just a striking coincidence that, as it becomes more difficult to deny her contribution on the grounds of indecency, there developed a growing tendency among the men of letters to dismiss her on the grounds of dishonesty?

These absurd standards of decency and honesty have never figured crucially in assessments of the quality of the literature of men, yet not only have they been brought out to deny the value of the writing of the first woman to make her mark upon the novel, but in the case of the accusation of dishonesty, what is being used against Aphra Behn is nothing other than a trumped-up charge. The last person who would have been surprised by this deviousness would have been Aphra Behn herself, although she might have been surprised to find that in the space of three hundred years men had not mended their ways and were still jealously guarding their literary domain as their right, and were 'protecting' it from female intruders. In her own day, Aphra Behn was more than familiar with the range of tricks which were used to deny her achievement and she was continually obliged to defend herself against the charges that her work could not be good because she knew no Latin or Greek, or if it were good it could not have been her own, but must have been written for her – by a man.

Such determined efforts to devalue Aphra Behn should not, however, deflect us from a proper consideration of her writing, which defies the shabby slurs and stands as a remarkable achievement with its synthesis of the old and the new. *Oroonoko*, published in 1688, abounds with detailed descriptions of Surinam – its flora, fauna, scenery, housing – and it must be acknowledged that for English society at the time, this exotic reality would have been extremely romantic. So too is the 'romance' balanced by realism, for in her own journey to Surinam, Aphra Behn meets an outstanding man who happens to be a slave, but who like the shepherds of the pastoral romance is obviously of noble blood as is evidenced by his lofty bearing. He has been a prince in his own country, and lured into slavery because of his love for Imoinda whom the King (his grandfather) wants for his harem but whom Oroonoko takes as his wife. Imoinda is also sold into slavery and the two noble lovers meet in Surinam where they are happy – but in search of their freedom. To subdue the influential and princely Oroonoko, his masters promise him his freedom at a future date, but Oroonoko soon realises he is being deceived and attempts escape. He is captured and tortured, but agonises more over the dreadful fate he knows awaits his wife than over his own injuries. He gains a little time and kills Imoinda before being himself recaptured – and hacked to pieces in the most vicious and brutal manner.

So much is turned upside-down in this novel: the romance of the real scenery, the reality of the romance, the factual nature of the fiction and the imaginative nature of some of the facts, these all help to make a black prince a slave and a hero, and his white masters but debased men.

Oroonoko is not presented as an average human being who is awfully wronged: there were few precedents for such a leading character and few premises about human rights at the time. It is the fact that he is a prince which in the terms of the day helped to make his slavery an outrage, and as a prince, Oroonoko has little compunction about trading other more humble slaves in return for his own freedom. But that he can retain his aura of nobility in degrading circumstances is intrinsic to Aphra Behn's presentation of him as a hero, even if such an account is rather fanciful. As Vita Sackville-West has suggested, 'Oroonoko resembles those seventeenth century paintings of negroes in plumes and satins, rather than an actual slave on a practical plantation.' Aphra Behn 'dresses him, it is true, in a suit of brown hollands; but nonetheless the plumes continue to wave in the breeze and the satins to glisten in the sun' (1927: p. 74). And nonetheless we are presented with a black nobleman who acts and dies honourably in contrast to his white masters, and nonetheless we are provided with a horrific portrayal of slavery. There is no doubt we are intended to deplore its practices.

Aphra Behn's journey from popularity to obscurity is not related to the quality of her writing. I think she is one of the most gifted writers our culture has produced. And I want her back on the literary scene – centre-stage – where her work can be read, evaluated, debated, and can become part of our well-known literary heritage.

To reclaim her, I do not think it is necessary to systematically disparage the efforts of men so that women's writing will appear in a positive light.* This would be but a reversal of the treatment which men have accorded women. I do not think we have to detract from men's achievement: Daniel Defoe too made his own unique and valuable contribution to the development of the novel. I want this achievement to stand – but I want it to stand *alongside* the achievement of Aphra Behn. I

---

*This by no means precludes me from comparing (unfavourably) the writing of some men with that of women.

want the mothers of the novel acknowledged equally with the fathers. This will provide us with a radically different literary tradition.

Table I: Aphra Behn (1640-1689)

1	1671	*The Forced Marriage, or The Jealous Bridegroom*, a tragi-comedy
2		'That Beauty I adored before,' a song in *The Westminster Drollery*
3		*The Amorous Prince, or The Curious Husband*, a comedy
4	1672	(*Covent Garden Drollery*, edited by AB, and conjecturally attributed to Aphra Behn, by Mr G. Thorn Drury)
5	1673	*The Dutch Lover*, a comedy
6	1676	*Abdelazer, or The Moor's Revenge*, a tragedy
7		*The Town Fop, or Sir Timothy Tawdrey*, a comedy (1677, 1699)
8	1677	*The Rover, or The Banished Cavalier*, a comedy. (1709, 1735, 1757)
9		(*The Debauchee, or The Credulous Cuckold.* This is credited to Aphra Behn in the British Museum catalogue, but is not included in any collection of her plays)
10		(*The Counterfeit Bridegroom, or The Defeated Widow.* Sometimes attributed to Aphra Behn but not given as hers in the usual authorities)
11	1678	*Sir Patient Fancy*, a comedy
12	1679	*The Feigned Courtesans, or A Night's Intrigue*, a comedy
13	1680	'Œnones epistle to Paris,' paraphrase included in *Ovid's Heroical Epistles*, translated by various hands (1683, 1701, 1712, 1725)
14	1681	*The Rover, Part II*, a comedy
15	1682	*The City Heiress, or Sir Timothy Treatall*, a comedy
16		*The Roundheads, or The Good Old Cause*, a comedy
17		*The False Count, or A New Way to Play an Old Game*, a comedy
18		Prologue and Epilogue to *Romulus and Hersilia*
19		Epilogue to Randolph's *The Jealous Lovers*
20	1683	*The Young King*
21		*Young Jemmy, or The Princely Shepherd*, a song
22		(*Love Letters between a Nobleman and His Sister*, attributed to Aphra Behn, but not included in her 'Works.' It was entered at Stationers Hall, Oct. 28, 1683)
23	1684	*The Adventures of the Black Lady*, a novel
24		*Poems Upon Several Occasions, with A Voyage to the Island of Love* (1697)
25		Prologue to Fletcher's *Valentinian*
26	1685	*A Pindaric on the Death of Charles II*
27		*A Miscellany*, poems by AB and other writers
28	1686	*La Montre, or The Lover's Watch*, translated from the French
29		*Æsop's Fables*, rendered into English verse (1687, 1703)
30	1687	*The Lucky Chance, or An Alderman's Bargain*, a comedy
31		*The Emperor of the Moon*, a farce

32   *To the most Illustrious Christopher Duke of Albermarle*, verses on his
         departure for Jamaica

33   *To Henry Higden, Esq., on his Translation of the Tenth Satire of Juvenal*,
         verses prefixed to that work

34   *The History of Oracles*, translated from the French (1699, and see no.
         57)

35 1688 *A Discovery of New Worlds*, translated from the French (1700, 1718)

36   *On the Death of E. Waller, Esq.*, verses contributed to a memorial
         volume

37   *A Pindaric Poem to the Rev. Dr Burnet, on the Honour he did me of
         Enquiring after me and my Muse*

38   *A Congratulatory Poem to Her Most Sacred Majesty on the Universal Hopes
         of all Loyal Persons for a Prince of Wales*

39   *A Congratulatory Poem to Their Majesties on the Happy Birth of a Prince*

40   *Oroonoko, or The Royal Slave, a True History* (1759, 1777, 1800, 1886,
         1890; dramatised, and translated into French and German)

41   *Lycidus, or The Lover in Fashion*, in prose and verse

42   *Agnes de Castro, or The Force of Generous Love*, a novel; translated from
         the French

43   *The Fair Jilt, or The History of Prince Tarquin and Miranda*, a novel
         (1886)

44   *The Unfortunate Bride, or The Blind Lady a Beauty*, a novel

45   *Two Congratulatory Poems to Their Majesties on the Hope and the Happy
         Birth of a Prince*(1689, see also nos. 38 and 39)

46 1689 *The Lucky Mistake, a New Novel*

47   *A Congratulatory Poem to Her Sacred Majesty Queen Mary Upon Her
         Arrival in England*

48 1690 *The Widow Ranter*, a tragi-comedy

49 1693 *Of Trees*, a translation of Book 6 of Abraham Cowley's *Of Plants* (This
         is the earliest known edition, but the work was entered at Stationers
         Hall, April 5, 1688)

50 1696 *The Histories and Novels of the Late Ingenious Mrs Behn . . . Together with
         the Life and Memoirs of Mrs Behn, written by One of the Fair Sex* (1698,
         1705, 1718, 1735 8th edn)

51   *The Younger Brother*, a comedy

52 1697 *Poems, Second Edition, Also the Lover in Fashion, to Which is Added a
         Miscellany of New Poems*

53   *The Nun, or The Fair Vow Breaker*, a history was entered at Stationers
         Hall, Feb. 3 (*The Nun, or The Perjured Beauty*, 1886)

54 1698 *Poetical Remains*, edited by Charles Gildon

55 1702 *Plays*, in two vols (1718)

56 1711 *Works*, in three vols (1712)

57 1718 *The Theory and System of Several New Inhabited Worlds; The History of
         Oracles; The Unfortunate Bride, etc.* (See nos. 34, 35, 44)

58 1724 *Plays*, in four vols
59 1755 *Poems*, included in *A Select Collection . . . of Love Letters, etc.*, edited by
          G. Gaylove
60   *Poems* included in *Poems by Eminent Ladies, etc.*, edited by M. Barber
61 1771 *Novels*, included in a *Collection of Novels*, edited by Elizabeth Griffith
62 1871 *Plays, Histories and Novels*, in six vols
63 1886 *The Fair Jilt, or The Amours of Prince Tarquin and Miranda* (see no. 43)
64   *The Nun, or The Perjured Beauty* (see no. 53)
65   *Oroonoko* (1890; see no. 40)
66 1905 *The Novels of Aphra Behn*, edited by E. A. Baker; comprising *Oroonoko*;
          The Fair Jilt; *The Nun*; *Agnes de Castro*; *The Lover's Watch*; *The Case
          for the Watch*; *The Lady's Looking-Glass to Dress Herself By*; *The Lucky
          Mistake*; *The Court of the King of Bantam*; and *The Adventure of the
          Black Lady*
67 1908 *Selected Poetry of Aphra Behn*, edited by J. R. Tutin
68 1915 *Complete Works of Aphra Behn*, in six vols, edited by Montague
          Summers
69 1927 *Aphra Behn, the Incomparable Astrea*, by V. Sackville-West

---

(ii) Delarivière Manley

There was a further development in fiction in 1714 with the publication
of *The Adventures of Rivella*. It purported to be the biography of
Delarivière Manley by one Sir Charles Lovemore: the title page states:

The Adventures of Rivella
or
The History of the Author of the Atlantis
with Secret Memoirs and
Characters of Several
Considerable Persons, her
Contemporaries

Delivered in a Conversation to the Young
Chevalier D'Aumont in Somerset House Garden,
by Sir Charles Lovemore.

Done into English from the French.

In fact, Delarivière Manley (1663-1724) – the author of the *Atlantis* –
was herself the author of this 'biography', which she had written at great
speed. A publisher – Edmund Curll by name – had commissioned from
Charles Gildon a biography on the famous (or more acurately, the
infamous) writer of 'scandals', Delarivière Manley. On seeing the
advertisements for this forthcoming publication, Delarivière Manley

offered to provide Edmund Curll with her own account on the condition that Charles Gildon's work did not appear. She knew full well that with her record of exposing the follies and weaknesses of prominent figures, it would be no flattering portrayal that Charles Gildon would provide of her, and so with characteristic flair and daring she promised the publisher that she would produce 'better' copy. He accepted, and later said that she had delivered the bulk of the manuscript – of her biography supposedly written by Sir Charles Lovemore – in about a week, although the publication date indicates that she may have taken a little longer (see Patricia Koster, 1971: p. xx). But it was typical of Delarivière Manley that she should have organised such an 'outrageous' publication: to write her 'biography' – where she could control her own image – and to 'pass it off' as the considered judgment of an independent observer. She was particularly adept at 'managing the media' and by providing this 'faction' she was not only able to promote a positive image of herself but to confound more disinterested reporters of her life for years to come. And arranging for Sir Charles Lovemore's version of the life of the remarkable author had not been without its complications for she was at the time living with her regular publisher, Alderman Barber, who, presumably, would have had more than one objection to her secret meetings with his rival. No doubt a less spirited woman would have seen no alternative to the 'publish – and be damned' philosophy at the prospect of the Charles Gildon biography, but to Delarivière Manley, resignation was a quality with which she was not familiar.

No one could become acquainted with the life and writing of Delarivière Manley and remain unimpressed – or unamused. Not that it is all that easy to separate her life from her writing, because *Rivella* was not the only publication in which she presented her own portrayal of her life – and there is some inconsistency when one account is compared with another. Commentators on Delarivière Manley have had more than their share of problems in trying to disentangle the details of her life from the embellishments of her writing and it is interesting to note that while Margarette Smith (1984) says of *Rivella* that it appears to be an 'honest' biography for the author 'does not make light of her faults, nor does she make extravagant claims for her obvious generosity and loyalty to her friends' (p. 211), Patricia Koster (1971) classifies *Rivella* as a novel. Which just goes to show what difficulties abound whenever any attempt is made to wholly divide fact and fiction. Certainly, in Delarivière Manley's case it is a complex business trying to separate the real romance from the romanticised reality but one fact which emerges and which remains incontrovertible is that she was a woman who wrote for her living (poems, plays, novels, satires, political journalism) and who was ranked in her own time, if not now, as one of the most renowned writers of the day. (This is not to suggest that she was the most liked writer: she offended a great many people.)

Her novels 'irritated Pope, Swift, Fielding and Lady Mary Wortley Montagu into acid comments' but this was not the only effect she had, for they also 'elicited irritations from Defoe and lesser writers' (Patricia Koster, 1971: p. v). Ignored she may have been ever since, but there was no ignoring Delarivière Manley in her own time.

Her date of birth is a matter of some conjecture, as Delarivière Manley provides a number of variations on this theme (and this is coyly commented on by some critics, who have proceeded to 'generalise' about the disinclination of all women to reveal their age). What we do know, however, is that her father, Sir Roger Manley, supported the Royalist cause, was obliged to leave England in 1646 for fourteen years abroad, and returned on the Restoration of Charles II when he was rewarded for his loyalty and made the Lieutenant Governor of Jersey. He held this post until 1674 when he became Governor of Landguard Fort in Suffolk. He was a well-educated man, the author of *History of Late Wars in Denmark*, and *De Rebellione* in Latin, and a *History of the Rebellion* in English, which was published in 1691, the year after his death. 'Dela' as she signed herself was probably born in 1672 in Jersey.

All we know of her mother is that by 1674 when Sir Roger arrived with his family of five children in England, she was dead.

John Manley, Dela's cousin, was made her guardian on the death of her father in 1690, and here begins an episode in her life which was to appear in many forms throughout her 'fiction'. For John Manley, who had been married, declared that his wife had died, and he persuaded the young Dela (who is barely fourteen in some versions) to marry him. But the protective and persuasive man becomes a tyrant upon marriage, and Delarivière Manley gives an account of their life together in her novel *Atlantis*, where she refers to herself as 'Delia' and to John Manley as 'Don Marcus'.

He took her to Angela (which is the code word for London in *Atlantis*), she writes, where he confined her to remote quarters and allowed her no visitors. 'Delia', who, as she states, had certainly not married 'Don Marcus' for his company alone, was greatly distressed by this imposed isolation:

> I thought this a very rough proceeding, and grieved the more
> excessively at it, since I had married him only because I thought he
> loved me; those that know his person will easily believe that I was not
> in love with him. He was about twenty-three years older than I was
> . . . as to his person, his face and shape had never been handsome.
> You know him vain, talkative, opinionated, mixing a thousand
> absurdities with every grain of sense; then so perfect a libertine, that

he never denied himself the gratification of his passions; every way a debauchee. (*Atlantis*, vol. II, p. 185)

Such 'pen-portraits' flowed freely in Delarivière Manley's writing (and they help to explain why she provoked heated responses), but her isolation, and the fact that her husband was unattractive, soon became the least of her worries.

I was uneasy at being kept a prisoner but my husband's fondness and jealousy was the pretence. . . . Soon after I proved with child, and so perpetually ill that I implored Don Marcus to let me have the company of my sister and my friends. . . . Having first tried all the arguments he could invent, then the authority of a husband, but in vain, for I was fixed to my point and would have my sister's company; he fell upon his knees before me with so much confusion, distress and anguish, that I was at a loss to know what could work him up to such a pitch. At length, with a thousand interrupting tears and sobs he stabbed me with the wounding relation of his wife's being still alive! (*Atlantis*, vol. II, pp. 186-7)

It may be tempting to mock Delarivière Manley's melodramatic account of this tragic event in her life, but there can be no denying that for a woman of her time – and in her position – the disclosure that she had entered upon a bigamous marriage must have been deeply shocking. The realisation was not only traumatising – it meant ruin. Without means, money, or the likelihood of further marriage, the prospect for a woman looked bleak indeed. She had to leave John Manley (who never contested her story despite ample opportunity) for she could not pardonably live with him once she knew the relationship was bigamous: but where could she go? She was pregnant and obliged to support herself and if she was fourteen – or even eighteen – it would be no exaggeration to suggest that she must have felt that there was no hope for the future.

She gave birth to a son: this much we know because the one comment that she makes about him is that she was filled with dread when she looked upon him, the product of an 'illicit union'. But any generalisations about 'maternal instinct' would have to make an exception of Delarivière Manley: she never refers to her son again and we have no idea what happened to him. On one other occasion she appears to have been pregnant but again, she does not refer to children in *Rivella*. Although she was a writer who freely revealed her personal feelings and who was most interested in exploring emotions she makes little or no comment about relationships between mother and children and there are no expressions of regret at their absence in her own life.

After the revelation of John Manley and her separation from him, Delarivière Manley seems to have survived by being 'adopted' by Barbara Villiers, Duchess of Cleveland, and one-time mistress of Charles II (by no means an exclusive position). For six months she lived with the Duchess, acting as companion and secretary, and was invited to mix with some of the most influential political figures of the day. Her entry to this circle (whose members appear to have had somewhat shady dealings and intrigues) was later to prove a valuable resource when she took to writing. But just as readily as she was adopted, so too her services were dispensed with (and there was the implication that Delarivière Manley had her own amorous intrigues with the Duchess's son). So within six months, Delarivière Manley was back to square one: where should she go, what should she do?

Her own account of this period of her life portrays a world-weary young woman who wants to withdraw to the country, where she is unknown. In June 1694, she set out for the West of England and she also took up her pen. She wrote *A Stage Coach Journey to Exeter* which consists of a series of letters about her travels. The letters contain light-hearted and entertaining stories about her adventures, her travelling companions and herself. As a writer she can be attractively and amusingly self-mocking, and while the first letter is the young woman who wants to get away from it all and enjoy the beauty of the country, the second is the record of how quickly the delights of the country (and travel) can diminish. And these letters, slender volume though they may comprise, represent an early contribution to the development of the tradition of 'letters' in literature.

For two years from 1694, Delarivière Manley was 'out of town' and there is some speculation as to how she supported herself at this time with one favoured explanation being that she returned to John Manley, in Truro, Cornwall (see Walter and Clare Jerrold, 1929: p. 98). But wherever she was or however she supported herself she nevertheless persisted with her writing. During these two years she wrote two plays and whether it was good luck or good management – or the use of the 'casting couch' which is often implied – she succeeded in arranging to have them both staged in 1696, one at each of the two playhouses.

She returned to London for the events in 1696, and naturally enough she was concerned that her plays should be extremely popular and provide her with a living. She knew she was an 'unknown' and that publicity was called for. So she collected her letters in *A Stage Coach Journey to Exeter* and had them published: the book included 'announcements' about the forthcoming plays. But Delarivière Manley's promotion efforts did not stop here: just before the plays were due to be staged she announced that *A Stage Coach Journey to Exeter* had been published without her permission, and she had it withdrawn. Understandably, the law of supply and demand came into operation and not only was there a demand for the withdrawn book, there was also a great deal of publicity about the author, and her forthcoming plays. Delarivière Manley laid some of the foundation stones of literature: she also laid some of the foundation stones of the practice of the publishers' 'hype' – the fabricated publicity designed to increase sales. Others were not slow to follow where she had gone: Alexander Pope later deigned to use a similar method to put his own letters before the public.

Despite all the promotion, however, the plays were not the success that Delarivière Manley had hoped they would be. *The Lost Lover or The Jealous Husband* was performed at the Theatre Royal in 1696 (produced by Sir Thomas Shipworth who was supposed to be having an affair with Mrs Manley), and it was damned on the first night. When it was later published, Delarivière Manley wrote a foreword to it in which she makes it very clear that women and men writers are treated very differently by public and publishers alike: 'I am satisfied the bare name of being a woman's play damned it beyond its own want of merit,' she wrote.

Not long after *The Lost Lover or The Jealous Husband*, Delarivière Manley's tragedy *The Royal Mischief* was produced at Lincoln's Inn Field's Theatre and it enjoyed a somewhat better fate, although, again, it would not have accorded her any financial independence for any length of time.

After the performance of her plays, however, literature does not seem to have been the main concern of Delarivière Manley's life: love makes an entry. John Tilly, the Warden of Fleet Prison, was the man concerned, and the existence of his wife and children seems not to have been an obstacle for Delarivière Manley. On the contrary, she seems to have preferred a part-time relationship, for when John Tilly's wife died, and he was in financial difficulties, although he wanted to marry Dela she persuaded him to be sensible and to marry a rich widow instead. His second marriage, however, was not as 'convenient' as his first, either for himself or Dela – who had great difficulty meeting him. After 'four years of uneasiness' his mind gave way, and in three more years her handsome lover was dead.

Again, what should she do? How should she earn a living? She was by now in her thirties and her needs were pressing.

In 1705 the 'scandals' started. Delarivière Manley published *The Secret History of Queen Zarah and the Zarazians; being a looking glass. . . . Faithfully translated from the Italian copy now lodged in the Vatican at Rome and never before printed in any language.* While the book was ostensibly about other people in other places and other times, the characters and events it related were in fact much closer to home: *The Secret History of Queen Zarah* was an exposé of people and practices in the political life of the day. The book was a huge and instant success.

Whether Delarivière Manley was the originator of this particular form of fiction does not seem to me to be a matter of great moment today. It has been stated – meanly I think – that of course she did not create this form, but was merely imitating some earlier publications which had appeared in France. But I suspect that it is far more likely that given her shrewd understandings and her economic needs she was quite capable herself of devising this money-making venture without recourse to copying anything at all. She was certainly blatant about what she was doing, and why; and in marked contrast to Lady Mary Wroath who, almost one hundred years before, had denied any connection between her characters and real people, Delarivière Manley exploited such connections to the full. Published separately – and involving, not coincidentally, a second sale – was the *key*, which made explicit the links, and listed the code words and corresponding names of real people and places. So Zarah was the Duchess of Marlborough, and Angela was London.

Delarivière Manley was by no means an apolitical person. She wrote political journalism, worked with Jonathan Swift on the *Examiner* and succeeded him as editor in 1711. And part of the reason for the huge success of the 'scandals' was that she was acutely aware of the political implications of many of her disclosures. With the emerging appearance of a middle class and the consequent test of the balance of power, Delarivière Manley 'dramatized the conflict between the aristocracy and the middle classes' and added the appeal of the personal (and the romantic) to the public issue by exploiting 'the popular mythology of innocent maiden seduced by aristocratic libertine' (Margarette Smith, 1984: p. 210). Yet further reason for her success was that her accounts could not be summarily dismissed: as Patricia Koster (1971) says, Delarivière Manley 'did not mention a scandal without foundation' (p. vii). She had found an excellent blend of fact and fancy which enjoyed favour with the reading public.

She provided them with something very different, and which they were more than eager to read. Her audience waited with impatience for her next volume and endured extremes of frustration if they were unable to purchase the book and the 'key' simultaneously. Unfortunately, however, the very elements which were responsible for such high levels of interest in her writing in her own time make her books less than meaningful today. Their immediacy and relevance no longer apply and many of her episodes have lost their fascination because we are not always aware of the significance of her references.

But Delarivière Manley's inventions take 'fiction' one step further. Whereas Aphra Behn had provided realistic accounts of fantastical exploits – convincing stories of noble slaves and wayward nuns – it was precisely the reverse blend of fact and fiction which was utilised by Delarivière Manley: she introduced a fantastical rendition of real-life happenings.

In 1709 appeared the two volumes of *Secret Memoirs and Manners of Several Persons of Quality of Both Sexes from the New Atlantis, an Island in the Mediterranean, written originally in Italian.* That the book was supposedly translated from the Italian was not merely a device for adding romance: a far more practical consideration was that it afforded protection against libel suits – an issue of priority for Delarivière Manley. For while the New Atlantis is presented as an allegory, with Astrea, the goddess of justice, being shown round the wicked world by Intelligence, the events outlined are by no means allegorical, but are accounts of scandalous happenings among the great and famous in the thirty years prior to publication.

'The sensational aspects of Mrs Manley's writing, with accounts of drunkenness, orgies both hetero- and homosexual, seduction, rape and incest, are the main reasons why her works have so long remained in obscurity,' states Patricia Koster (1971), although she does not indicate whether it is because she is a woman writer that such censure has been applied to Delarivière Manley. 'Under the aspect of Victorian morality, volume 2 of the *New Atlantis* is the most objectionable of the novels, beginning with a section on incest and carrying on with some anecdotes about the *New Cabal*, a group of rich lesbians' (p. xiv). Volume II also contains some of the strongest women characters – and some of the most entertaining – and Mrs Nightwork, the gossiping midwife, regales the reader with secrets and becomes one of the first comic characters in fiction.

Delarivière Manley is a superb story teller (in every sense of the word) and there are many 'detachable' episodes woven into her scandals which are virtually 'novellas' in themselves. She 'has a good ear for tricks of speech and a keen eye for details of dress, furnishings, and behaviour' (Patricia Koster, 1971: p. xiv) and this, along with her presentation of the goddesses as fashionable society ladies, ensures that her readers are aware that they are 'home-truths' which they are learning. If Aphra Behn could carry English manners away to exotic Surinam, Delarivière Manley could bring exotic Atlantis straight back to the English front door.

That she extended the possibilities for fiction is abundantly clear. Other writers were to profit from her contribution, and even to emulate her directly. One of them was, of course, Daniel Defoe who in 1711 'complimented Mrs Manley by issuing a small book entitled *"Atlantis Major.* Printed in Olreeky, the chief city of the north part of Atlantis Major."' This was a "spoof" historical narrative of remarkable happenings in the great island "lying in the Ducaledonian Ocean"'

(Walter and Clare Jerrold, 1929: pp. 126-7). From Atlantis, the distance to other imaginary islands was not so great with Daniel Defoe again revealing his links with Delarivière Manley in *Robinson Crusoe* (1720). And Jonathan Swift, who knew Delarivière Manley well (and who had few words of praise for her – although in his case it is significant that he accorded her any praise at all), also follows in a tradition she helped to establish when he makes use of an imaginary island setting to stage his own political satire in *Gulliver's Travels* (1726). Despite her development of fiction, Delarivière Manley has been marginalised almost to the point of invisibility in the history of letters: she does not even rate a mention in Walter Allen's *The English Novel* (1954/1980), and this bears no relation to the significance of her writing.

Her significance in her own time, however, was not determined by literary judgment. Although she kept up a running battle with Richard Steele (who evidently refused her financial aid when she was in need), who had started the *Tatler* on April 12, 1709, this exchange promoted rather than minimised her writing in the eyes of the reading public. And it wasn't the reading public who, scandalised by her disclosures, wanted to see an end to this new and highly entertaining fictional form. It was the individual members of the government whom she had so roundly criticised and attacked, who took the first steps in the attempt to silence Delarivière Manley.

A warrant was issued against the printer, publisher and author of the *New Atlantis* and according to 'Dela' (in *Rivella*), because she was concerned about the fate of the printer and publisher, she would not flee – even though she knew in all probability she would end up in jail. She was examined by John Hopkins, Under Secretary of State, who was primarily concerned with her sources of information.

But Delarivière Manley would not reveal her sources – if indeed she had any other than her own shrewd ability to put two and two together. When it was insisted that she must have obtained inside information – that there must have been 'leaks' – she took the stand that if she knew anything she was not supposed to, it must have come by way of *divine inspiration*. This was perfectly consistent with her much reiterated and 'innocent' defence that she didn't want to write about such indecent happenings and only did so out of conscience and a sense of public duty. In *Memoirs of Europe* (1710) she was later to write, 'I think it's hard, and I have often wondered at it, why one should be thought uncharitable, a satirist or libeller, who repeats with the pen what everybody fearlessly reports with their tongue' (vol. I, p. 254).

But despite her protestations of 'innocence', on October 29th, 1709, Delarivière Manley was sent to prison where she was allowed neither book nor pencil, and where, she claims, she was barbarously insulted. For one week she remained in prison and was then released on bail. In

February 1710, the prosecution was dropped.

By 1711, Delarivière Manley was working regularly with Jonathan Swift on the Tory periodical (or more precisely, the anti-Whig periodical), the *Examiner* (she took over the editorship in June) and was writing other political pamphlets. Again it is interesting to note the double standard which is used to evaluate the writing of women and men – particularly in regard to politics. For while Jonathan Swift is seen first and foremost as a political satirist, Delarivière Manley, who was interested in the same issues, who was equally politically minded, who worked with Jonathan Swift and wrote on the same topics – often interchangeably – has been consigned to the category of *scandalmonger*. The only difference is the sex of the writer. This helps to explain why it is that few if any women writers are ever considered satirists: it is not that they don't write satire but that when they do, it is called something else – gossip, scandal, or irony (if they are fortunate). So satire remains primarily the preserve of men.

Nowhere can I find a reference to Delarivière Manley as a serious political being. Whenever the political dimensions of her writing are referred to they are 'glossed over' in but a few words. Yet here is a woman who gives ample evidence of her political interest, who makes significant political interventions through her writing, and who stands as the first woman political journalist (who would not reveal her sources). If Jonathan Swift is to be granted the stature of a political commentator, why not Delarivière Manley? And if Jonathan Swift is still considered worthy of retention in the literary canon, and worthy of continued study, why not Delarivière Manley?

And why no recognition of the fact that this achievement on her part was even greater than his? Not for her had there been the security of a 'living', the benefit of a university education, the patronage of influential men – or even the servants who could leave her free to write. That she should have been such a successful writer, that she should have been so fictionally innovative and so politically influential, is a remarkable achievement for a woman of her day. And yet this aspect of *women's* writing, this acknowledgment of the disadvantages and the difficulties – not to mention the double standard – is missing from any discussion of writers and their work.

Whether it was the difficulty of being a woman writer which led Delarivière Manley to 'seek security' with her publisher Alderman Barber, it is difficult to tell. She gives no indication that her decision was motivated by any great passion and it is more than likely that despite the success of her books she was once more 'financially embarrassed'. 'It was not the authors who made much money out of their books in those days,' write Walter and Clare Jerrold (1929) – and one is tempted to add that this is still the case – and 'Barber's biographer says that he certainly made a good bargain in the matter for he acquired large sums from "her writings, the *Atlantis* (in this case he mentions thousands of pounds), her novels, the play of *Lucius*, with many political pamphlets." He adds that she brought Barber acquainted with Lord Bolingbroke, Dr Swift, Mr Prior, and others, who made him their printer' (p. 132).

'Popular' books were a new phenomenon and their appearance marked a transfer in influence from the aristocracy to the growing middle class. With the spread of literature to a wider audience comes the distinction between 'literature' and 'blotterature' which is with us still. It is a distinction which is based on fear, according to Raymond Williams (1975): 'There is the fear that as the circle of readers extends, standards will decline and literature be threatened by "blotterature",' he writes. And there is also the 'essentially political fear that, if the common man [sic] reads, both quality and order . . . will be threatened'. This is why, he continues, 'different authorities have at certain periods openly exerted their power to prevent or limit the growth of reading or to prevent or limit the education from which it naturally follows' (p. 179). Raymond Williams refers only to men, but does not his argument apply to women?

Is this why education – and reading and writing – were denied for so long to women? Is this why there are so many obstacles to women's entry to the literary world? Because by extending the circle of readers – and writers – to include women, the standards will be lowered? Because once women can freely read and write they pose a threat to order? This is certainly part of the rationale behind the exclusion of women from the literary tradition. This is why even today women are still frequently omitted from consideration as writers and readers because to acknowledge their existence in the literary heritage is ostensibly to dilute the quality of that heritage. (I am not going to argue against the assertion that reading and writing women pose a threat to established order: judging from the number of times women have claimed, 'This *book* changed my life', it could well be the case that literacy in women has led to a challenge to male power. But it is interesting to note that Raymond Williams acknowledges that groups in power have gone to considerable lengths to protect it by trying to keep illiterate those without power: he does not extend this argument to include women, however.)

But women were in at the beginning when popular literature was seen as a threat to standards and order. The writing profession opened its ranks and the trading started, with both writers and booksellers playing their part. And the custodians of the privileged aristocratic tradition registered their protest. Among them was Alexander Pope, who deplored the development of this upstart literary industry and who tried to preserve literary standards by retaining the pursuit of literature as the occupation of the upper class. These new books, which masqueraded as true accounts of real happenings, or which were fanciful versions of 'gossip', which required no classical or formal education to write and which made no pretension to being part of a lofty literary tradition, incensed Alexander Pope. Yet the very reasons he had for dismissing such books were the same reasons that women were able to enter the field of writing.

It would be a mistake, however, to think that women were well paid in their new profession. Many worked 'long cramped hours for miserable pay on Grub Street. For the most part writers sold their work outright to booksellers and had to turn out new material in order to keep eating' (Ruth Perry, 1980: p. 67).

Delarivière Manley may have sold her manuscripts outright to Alderman Barber and for not a very great sum but it must be remembered that the sales of 'popular' books in the eighteenth century were nothing like sales today. 'The audience for whom these early novels were written were generally Londoners with enough education and leisure to read, and enough money to buy the books,' writes Ruth Perry (1980), and since the books 'cost six pence to six shillings at that time (one or two shillings being the common price) they were out of range of all but the well-to-do' (p. 12).* And this new breed of writers, Delarivière Manley among them, encountered the obstacle which persists to this day: they had to convince the booksellers that their work would sell well and not simply find favour among a few of refined judgment. Perhaps Mary Delarivière Manley found she could be more persuasive from inside Alderman Barber's house. By 1711 she was living with him although, again, she does not appear to have been very happy. Like John Manley, Alderman Barber seems to have become something of a tyrant – and a debauchee – on cohabitation, although it was his coarseness and rudeness which distressed her far more than his 'mistresses'. But her sister Cordelia joined her and they both remained with Alderman Barber until their deaths. In Cordelia's case it was clear that she had no other choice: she had nowhere else to go.

Clearly, Delarivière Manley did not make a lot of money from her writing, which is somewhat surprising given her self-promotion, and her success. For she capitalised splendidly on the public taste of the time and was always ready to co-operate with the booksellers who were willing to declare that every epistolary item that came their way was the genuine article. Much of the commentary that surrounded Delarivière Manley's works was concerned with establishing that these were indeed real letters from real people and that only by some strange quirk of fate had the bookseller managed to obtain them. The customary format was to establish that the letters had never been intended for publication, that

*For further discussion, see Part II of this book, particularly chapters 6 and 8.

they had been inadvertently mislaid – or lost, stolen, broke open – and always published at great risk to the bookseller.

That Delarivière Manley 'co-operated' in such sales promotion reveals that she was quite familiar with some of the conventions of literary hoaxes, and not averse to presenting fanciful versions of her own making as facts. So to have written her own biography and to have presented it as the work of Charles Lovemore – and translated from the French – was no sudden departure from some of her established practices. And my reading of *Rivella* suggests that she understandably relished the liberty of constructing a flattering account of her life and circumstances. While in *Rivella* there is abundant evidence that she wants to get the reader 'on side' there is also clear evidence about her personality which has not been manipulated.

Introducing *Rivella*, Sir Charles Lovemore (alias Delarivière Manley) declares that 'Her virtues are her own, her vices are occasioned by her misfortunes, and yet as I have often heard her say, IF SHE HAD BEEN A MAN, SHE HAD BEEN WITHOUT FAULT.' This is not the only indication of Rivella's that she objects to the double standard. The charter of the female sex being so much more confined than that of males, continues Sir Charles Lovemore, that 'what is not a crime in men is scandalous and unpardonable in women as she herself has very well observed in diverse places, throughout her own writings' (Manley, 1714: pp. 7–8).

Delarivière Manley objected to women being required to trade their bodies for male support and she resented the way women's bodies had to be shaped to meet male approval. But this genuine protest has been dismissed by some of her critics who have designated her stand as one of 'sour grapes' and to give credence to their case have pointed to the flattering (and supposedly inaccurate) portrayal she provides of herself in *Rivella*:

Her person is neither tall nor short: from her youth she was inclined to fat: when I have often heard her flatterers liken her to a Grecian Venus. It is certain, considering that disadvantage, she has the most easy air that one can have; her hair is of a pale ash-colour, fine and in large quantity. . . . But to do Rivella justice, till she grew fat, there was not I believe any defect to be found in her body; her lips admirably coloured; her teeth small and even, her breath always sweet. Her complexion fair and fresh; yet with all this you must be used to her before she can be thought thoroughly agreeable. Her hands and arms have been publicly celebrated; it is certain I never saw any so well turned . . . her feet small and pretty (Manley, 1714: p. 8).

In later life, Delarivière Manley had dropsy. Her feet were swollen.

That she should make mention of her small feet is mocked by many commentators. Yet I find there is little that is pathetic in this self-description. She declares she is fat – but why not like a Grecian Venus? That her teeth are small and even and her breath sweet, seems to me to be a practical consideration and worthy of comment. And I have no doubt that once plagued by dropsy she would dwell on the time when she had small feet. I am more interested in the statement that you had to know her well before you found her agreeable, but it is not this admission that has attracted the attention of her critics. Instead, she has consistently been presented as a fat and deluded scandalmonger well able to make a nuisance of herself because of her absence of ethical and decent standards. If referred to at all in the literary tradition she is presented in terms of her morals and appearance and the assertion is that in both respects she left a lot to be desired.

The entry I would like to see for Delarivière Manley in the history of letters would be as follows: A prolific and innovative writer who helped to develop the genre of fiction by her use of the epistolary form and her introduction of political satire. A woman of independent mind who resisted many of the limitations placed on women and who, despite her success, could not acquire the independent financial means to give her thoughts full reign. The first woman political journalist, who ranked with Jonathan Swift and who shared the editorship of the *Examiner* with him. A founding contributor to the precept that journalists should not disclose their sources and should attempt to outwit any government which tried to silence them. An audacious woman who established new literary conventions and who showed a particular capacity for devising book promotions schemes. A playwright who understood the politics of the theatre, who anticipated the reaction of men who wished to protect their own preserves, and who well understood the reasons behind the anonymous *The Female Wits* which was a scandalmongering attempt to discredit herself, Mary Pix, and Catherine Trotter who were enjoying some success in the theatre (see Fidelis Morgan, 1981 for further discussion). Jonathan Swift and Daniel Defoe are but two writers who are indebted to this talented woman who was one of the mothers of the novel.

This would be a far more accurate entry than some of those which currently exist. Like Aphra Behn, Delarivière Manley has been deprecated and dismissed. Delarivière Manley has not even sparked off any controversy about whether or not she did what she was supposed to do: nor was she honoured by burial in Westminster Abbey. In 1717 her play *Lucius* was performed and in 1720 it had a second run: during these years she wrote many political pamphlets, some poems, and began a volume of novels which were published in 1720 as *The Power of Love: in Seven Novels*. This was her last work. She died on July 11, 1724 and was buried in the middle aisle of the church of St Bennet, Paul's Wharf. The inscription on her grave stone reads

Here lies the body of
Mrs De la Rivière Manley
Daughter of Sir Roger Manley, Kt.
Who, suitable to her birth and education, was
acquainted with several parts of knowledge; and
was the most polite writer both in the French and
English tongues. This accomplishment, together with
a greater natural stock of wit, made her conversation
agreeable to all who knew her, and her writings be
universally read with pleasure.

This is Mary Delarivière Manley at her impudent best. I believe her.

Table 2: Delarivière Manley (1663–1724)

1	1696	*Letters written by Mrs Manley* (see also no. 22)
2		*The Lost Lover or The Jealous Husband*, a comedy
3		*The Royal Mischief*, a tragedy
4	1705	*Secret History of Queen Zarah and the Zarazians* (1711, 1745, 1749; French translation 1708) (see also no. 14)
5	1707	*Almyna, or The Arabian Jew*, a tragedy
6	1709	*Secret Memoirs and Manners of Several Persons of Quality of Both Sexes. From the New Atlantis*, vols 1 and 2 (1720, 1736, French translation 1713-1716 (see also no. 7)
7	1710	*Memoirs of Europe towards the Close of the Eighth Century. Written by Eginardus*, in 2 vols (afterwards printed as vols 3 and 4 of *New Atlantis* (see also no. 6)
8	1710-1712	*The Examiner: or Remarks on Papers and Occurrences*
9	1711	*A True Narrative of What Passed at the Examination of the Marquis of Guiscard* (reprinted in the *Somers Tracts*, vol. 13, 1809)
10	1711	*Court Intrigues in a Collection of Original Letters from the Island of the New Atlantis*
11		*A Comment on Dr Hare's Sermon*
12		*The Duke of Marlborough's Vindication*
13		(*A Relation of the Several Facts and Circumstances of the Intended Riot and Tumult on Queen Elizabeth's Birthday*)
14		*Secret History of Queen Zarah*, with the addition of a second part (French translation with key, 1712)
15	1713	*The Honour and Prerogative of the Queen's Majesty Vindicated and Defended against the Unexampled Insolence of the author of 'The Guardian'.*

(iii) Eliza Haywood

'The female Defoe' and 'the forerunner of Richardson' are comments which have been used to describe Eliza Haywood (1693–1756) by the very few critics who have allowed her a place in the literary tradition. Whether it is preferable to be seen only in relation to men, or not at all, it is difficult to decide, but both such views do an immense disservice to Eliza Haywood who was one of, if not *the* most versatile, prolific and popular writers of her day. Only more extraordinary than her achievement is its removal from the records of literary innovation and accomplishment, for this outstanding writer, who was responsible for some of the most significant developments in fiction, is not mentioned in the two standard evaluations of the novel (Walter Allen, 1980, *The English Novel* and Ian Watt, 1957, *The Rise of the Novel*).

Yet Eliza Haywood's writing life spanned a period of almost forty years from 1719 and it was during this time that the novel assumed the basic form with which we are familiar today. And Eliza Haywood was among the first with every experiment, and among the few who could claim success. She wrote novels of every kind – epistolary novels, sentimental novels, 'thrillers', moralising novels and realistic novels. She wrote scandals, and histories, and conduct books. She set up as a publisher, started newspapers for women, wrote 'agony columns', translated, and wrote plays – and acted in them. Her output was astonishing, with George Whicher (1915) listing 67 works by her – and more 'possibles' – and Walter and Clare Jerrold (1929), attributing 93 publications to her (see page 108). And yet in the history of letters it is almost as if she had never existed.

Where her name does arise in literary history, when it is not her

2 Eliza Haywood

morals that are at issue, she is generally referred to pejoratively as an imitator with the distinct implication that she was without creative ability. It is partly because of this devaluation of her to the level of opportunistic copier that I have been tempted at times to engage in the quibbling task of establishing that certain of her works – which are supposed to be emulations of her 'superiors' – did, in fact, precede the so-called originals. But in the end it is not all that important whether *The Unfortunate Princess* first published in 1736 and reprinted in 1741 predates the achievement of Samuel Richardson (or even whether it was appropriated or exploited by Samuel Richardson); what is important is that for almost forty years (with a significant gap of more than four years) Eliza Haywood was among the foremost writers of her time, not just in terms of her talent but also in terms of her sales. (During this 'gap' in literary production, George Whicher (1915) suggests that she could well have been writing anonymously – which would mean an even longer list of publications!) Beginning with *Love in Excess or The Fatal Enquiry* published in 1719, through to *The History of Betsy Thoughtless* in 1751, we witness in the work of Eliza Haywood, the rise of the novel.

The growth and development of the novel can be illustrated with reference to the writing of this one woman, who reveals an extraordinary creative ability, who freely experiments with form and style, and who produces an unprecedented and perhaps unparalleled range of novels. Every enduring and exemplary feature of the new genre is to be found in her writing, and yet she has never been given the credit for her contribution. And with the denial of her achievement it has been possible to locate the origins of the novel in the writing of men. So to Daniel Defoe, Henry Fielding, and Samuel Richardson go the laurels; not because they were necessarily first, foremost or fundamental, but because with the removal of Eliza Haywood, there is no female challenge to their pre-eminence.

As with so many other women writers of the eighteenth century, Eliza Haywood has been so effectively buried and denied it is not easy to recover some of the definitive details of her existence. And Eliza Haywood herself is of little assistance in the task. Like Delarivière Manley who dealt with departures from decency in the lives of others, Eliza Haywood too had good reason for protecting her own life from public view, particularly since it contained some 'irregularities'. Yet even had the behaviour of Aphra Behn, Delarivière Manley and Eliza Haywood been above reproach, it is still more than likely that their reputation as writers would soon have procured for them a reputation as loose women. Indeed, it is more as immoral women than as writers that all three have been 'included' in the history of letters; and of course, to be included on these grounds is in effect to be dismissed. As Walter and Clare Jerrold (1929) write,

. . . it is their lack of niceness in social behaviour rather than their literary achievement which is most frequently made matter for comment. They are not only blamed for being what they were, but it is even made a matter of reproach that they were not something else; that they wrote when coarseness of thought and expression was characteristic of the age is not to be blamed against them – it would have been yet more remarkable had they proved pioneers for their sex into the first of the professions in which it was to win a footing (p. 202).

The 'reputation' as loose women which these writers are accorded today was acquired in part in their own time and helps to explain why they were concerned to provide for their enemies no more evidence than they could help, for they knew that it would assuredly be used againt them not just as women, but as writers. So some mystery surrounds the details of their lives: an anonymous 'friend' wrote Aphra Behn's biography* and Delarivière Manley took some liberties with her own; Eliza Haywood, however, went further and ensured that there was no biography and not much material for anyone who thought of attempting such a work.

She covered her tracks so well it is now virtually impossible to find out anything she did not want known. But even the defensive measures Eliza Haywood took in her own lifetime did not afford her any protection then, or now; what was not known could always be invented. And many of the details and much of the 'disgrace' of Eliza Haywood is nothing other than invention. Even Alexander Pope made a contribution: unconstrained by considerations of truth or justice he unleashed a vituperative attack on Eliza Haywood in *The Dunciad* (1728) and yet claimed as justification for his scurrilous efforts the high moral purpose of exposing the low moral calibre of the scribblers of the literary industry. That it can be established that many of the 'sins' which he attributes to Eliza Haywood were more the manufacturings of *his* own mind than the products of *her* pen, has done little to restore her literary reputation. Nor has it done much to detract from his, even though his spurning attack did her much harm and explains the gap in her writing career. That Alexander Pope made Eliza Haywood the 'heroine' of *The Dunciad* is more the source of any of her current 'fame' than is her own writing, and it is a sad comment on the history of literature that it is Alexander Pope's spiteful account of Eliza Haywood which is considered worthy of commemoration and not her remarkable writing.

It must have been dreadfully demoralising and distressing for these

*'History of the Life and Memoirs of Mrs Behn, by One of the Fair Sex', in *All the Histories and Novels Written by the late Ingenious Mrs Behn*, 1696, reprinted 1705.

women writers to encounter so much deprecation, scorn and harassment. For while James Sterling wrote a complimentary poem *To Mrs Eliza Haywood on Her Writing* (and considered that Eliza Haywood, Delarivière Manley and Aphra Behn formed 'the fair Triumvirate of Wit'; see Jane Spencer, 1984a: p. 160), he was among the very few at this stage of literary appraisals to give credit where it was due. More common was the classification of women writers – and actors – as low and loose creatures who were selling their wares, and who were to be allowed no place among the decent and respectable literati.

Women writers have experienced enormous difficulties, simply because they were women, yet no serious attempt has been made in the literary establishment to examine the conditions under which women have been required to work, or to assess the influence of these conditions on their writing. As Marion Glastonbury (1978) has pointed out, however, in one of the rare discussions on the different working contexts of the sexes, most writers who are extolled as 'great' have generally had the benefit of 'a wife'. Not only do women writers not have wives, they are often in the position of *being* wives, and this in itself can introduce a conflict not experienced by 'great men'. For the wife who wants to write not only forgoes many of the services customarily provided for men, she also has to come to terms with her own inability or reluctance to provide such services. 'The Woolfs lived austerely,' writes Marion Glastonbury, indicating what happens when the wife wants to write. 'Virginia struggled to suppress domestic guilt. She called it killing the angel in the house' (p. 35).

Women writers have consistently dwelt upon this issue; from Lady Mary Wortley Montagu and Mrs Thrale in the eighteenth century (see Marion Glastonbury, 1978), to Adrienne Rich (1980) and Tillie Olsen (1978) in the twentieth. One writer who well summed up the problem was Katherine Mansfield, writing to her lover, John Middleton Murry:

> . . . the house seems to take up so much time if it isn't looked after with some sort of method. I mean . . . when I have to clear up twice over or wash up extra unnecessary things I get frightfully impatient and want to be working. So often this week, I've heard you and Gordon talking while I washed dishes. Well, someone's got to wash dishes and get food, otherwise – 'There's nothing in the house but eggs to eat'. Yes, I hate hate *hate* doing these things that you accept just as all men accept of their women. I can only play the servant with a very bad grace indeed. It's all very well for females who have nothing else to do . . . and then you say I am a tyrant, and wonder because I get tired at night! The trouble with women like me is – they can't keep their nerves out of the job in hand – and Monday after you and Gordon and Lesley have gone I walk about with a mind full of

ghosts of saucepans and primus stoves and 'Will there be enough to go round?' . . . and you calling (whatever I am doing) '*Tig*, isn't there going to be tea? It's five o'clock' as though I were a dilatory housemaid.

I loathe myself today. I detest this woman who 'superintends' you and rushes about, slamming doors and slopping water – all untidy with her blouse out and her nails grimed. I am disgusted and repelled by the creature who shouts at you. 'You might at least empty the pail and wash out the tea leaves!' Yes, no wonder you 'come over silent'. (Katherine Mansfield, 1913 in C.K. Stead, 1981, pp. 43-4)

Clearly John Middleton Murry was free to write (and entertain) while Katherine Mansfield washed his dishes as well as her own. But Katherine Mansfield, a writer, living in the same house, was a woman and did not have a man's opportunities or privileges.

Nor is this the only area where women's working conditions are different – and detrimental – when compared to those of men. That it is men who sit in judgment on the writing of women as well as men, is a factor which has played a crucial role in women's literary work. 'No male writer has written primarily or even largely for women or with the sense of women's criticism as a consideration when he chooses his materials, his themes, his language,' writes Adrienne Rich (1980). 'But to a lesser or greater extent, every woman writer has written for men, even when, like Virginia Woolf, she was supposed to be addressing women' (pp. 37-8). And if the men are not pleased with the women's work they appear to have little compunction about showing it.

They do not feel obliged to confine themselves to the merits of the writing but almost without exception slide effortlessly into an evaluation of the merits of the woman. Women critics, in contrast, seem not to have descended to the same insulting level when commenting on the writing of men. Search though I have through some of the most rigorous feminist 'literary criticism' I cannot find attacks on the masculinity of male authors which begins to approach the virtually standard attacks on the femininity of women writers. From a woman I can find no pronouncement on a man which comes close to that made on Eliza Haywood:

Swift considered her a 'stupid, infamous scribbling woman'. Walpole contemptuously refers to her as the counterpart of Mrs Behn, Pope lashes her with scorpions in the *Dunciad*. In a note he describes her as one of those 'shameless scribblers who, in libellous memoirs and novels reveal the faults and misfortunes of both sexes, to the ruin of public fame or disturbance of private happiness' (Brigid MacCarthy, 1944: p. 233).

Apart from the fact that the goddess only knows what Alexander Pope thought *he* was doing, there is the question of how far such abuse affected the writer. Surely it would not have been easy to continue writing, to persist in making oneself so vulnerable, in the face of such hostility?

But we can certainly appreciate why Eliza Haywood went to such lengths to conceal the intimate details of her life: they would have been but more grist to the mill. One of the very few personal comments she ever made in writing was in a private letter to the publisher Edmund Curll (who printed it – which is why we know of it), to whom she mentioned 'the little inadvertencies of my own life'. Through the pen of Alexander Pope this statement is translated into 'two love babes' which were born after she had been deserted by her husband.

According to the scandal of the time Eliza Haywood was supposed to have had two children (paternity unknown) and to have been abandoned by her husband. Alexander Pope could have been reporting these rumours: he could also have been starting them. But Eliza Haywood did not bite. There was little to gain and a lot to lose if she became involved in any drawn-out dispute about her own morals. To simply have one's morality made a matter of discussion was for a woman to be damned: better to ignore the implications than to draw attention by defence.

If it suited society to believe ill of her and to give credence to the gossip that she had been deserted by her husband, it wasn't likely that she would go up in estimation by announcing that it wasn't he who left her, but she who left him. So quiet was she on this subject that it was not until 1915 that the scandal was repudiated and the more accurate picture provided by George Whicher, who had undertaken extensive research for his book *The Life and Romances of Mrs Eliza Haywood*. Although, however, he was able to put together some of the 'missing pieces' it must be noted that there is still very little known about the life of Eliza Haywood, and that his reference to 'romances' is in relation to her writing, and not to any personal involvements on her part.

It is generally accepted that Eliza Fowler was born about 1693 and the only information available on her early life comes from her own acknowledgment that she was proud to have received an education which was unusually liberal for a girl. She was married in either 1710 or 1711, and according to the *Dictionary of National Biography*, after a brief married life, her husband left her with two children to support. However, the investigations of George Whicher (1915) revealed that it was the Reverend Valentine Haywood that she married, that he was a serious gentleman fifteen years her senior, and that Eliza Haywood embarked on her writing career while she was still living with him. In 1719, when she was almost thirty years of age (give or take a bit), she published *Love in Excess* and it was so enormously successful that she followed it up with a second volume almost immediately, and then in 1720 with a third, thereby becoming a pioneer of the three-volume novel. With the publication of *Love in Excess*, however, came the taste not only for the literary life, but for independence as well. On January 7th, 1721, the following declaration appeared in the newspaper, *The Post Boy*:

> Whereas Elizabeth Haywood, wife of the Reverend Mr Valentine Haywood, eloped from him her husband on Saturday 26th November last past, and went away without his knowledge or consent: This is to give notice to all persons in general, that if anyone shall trust her either with money or goods, or if she shall contract debts of any kind whatsoever, the said Mr Haywood will not pay the same.

'Elope' meant much the same then as it does now, so it is clear that the Reverend Haywood, at least, was prepared to claim that his wife had gone off with another man – though it is of course possible that this was a claim made to protect his pride, it being more acceptable that she should go off with a man than that she should leave him for no one at all. But we will never be able to tell: from Eliza Haywood there is not one word on this subject. We can only speculate on why she left him. From her writing it is clear that she had many objections to women's position as subjugated wives and she often registers her protest against women's vow of mindless obedience to their husbands; she also recommends the life of independence for married women who are burdened with more than they can endure. Not a few of her heroines leave their husbands, and escape a dreadful fate.

There have been suggestions that Eliza Haywood's views originated from her personal experience of marriage. The Reverend Haywood appears to have been disposed towards obedience in a wife. But perhaps this was not the only bone of contention between the couple: the Reverend Haywood was also a writer.

In 1719 he too published a book – *An Examination of Dr Clarke's Scripture Doctrine, with a confutation of it.* This volume was hardly compatible with his wife's *Love in Excess*, nor was the husband's success comparable to the wife's. While *Dr Clarke's Scripture Doctrine* seems to have sunk without trace, *Love in Excess* not only extended to a three-volume novel, it ran to six editions in the following four years.

The strains on the relationship of the Reverend Haywood and his wife can be the subject only of speculation, but given the mores of the time, it is not difficult to determine what some of them would have been. It was most unfitting for the Reverend's wife to be enjoying such literary prominence and he could well have wanted her to refrain from future forays into the world of print. He could even have insisted on submission and obedience in his wife and have demanded the customary services 'the lord' was entitled to expect – and this would have been particularly galling for a woman of Eliza Haywood's spirit. If she was intent on writing (and it seems that she was), it is not unlikely that she realised it was going to be well nigh impossible while she remained under her husband's roof. No doubt she too experienced something of the same conflict as that described by Katherine Mansfield – the conflict between being a writer and being a wife – and in the case of Eliza Haywood the difficulties were overcome when she removed the demands of being a wife.

But the significant issue is not *why* Eliza Haywood 'eloped': that she left at all is extraordinary, and it says much more about her than some of the snippets of information that have been assembled. For a woman to leave the protection of her husband was a daring move indeed in the early part of the eighteenth century. And if she did have children to support, and she did propose to earn her living with her pen, she must have had enormous courage – and confidence. She could look to no other women for guidance. There were no thriving women who had established themselves as respected writers who were enjoying an independent income. There were no inspirational 'models', and no signs that the way would be anything other than hard. And yet Eliza Haywood was by no means an idealistic or naive young woman when she made her decision to lead her own literary life. When it was not uncommon for women to be married at thirteen and dead at thirty, Eliza Haywood was already old in the terms of her time when she embarked on her life of independence. Because she was astutely aware that women 'declined into disfavour' with the passage of time, it is irrational – and snide – to suggest that she sought to support herself by selling sexual favours rather than the products of her pen. There is no evidence which would contradict the reasonable premise that Eliza Haywood, having attained a considerable measure of success with the publication of *Love in Excess*, elected to continue her writing career and left her husband to do so. This is nothing other than the move of an independent woman; but she has been labelled an adventuress for her efforts.

But her chances of success, of being able to support herself by her writing, were somewhat better than they had been for Aphra Behn and Delarivière Manley. In the forty years since Aphra Behn had written her novels, many of the social changes which had occurred were conducive to the emergence of a popular woman writer. An increasing middle class which was increasingly literate, while still far removed from the mass reading public of today, was nonetheless making its presence felt as a growing and demanding audience. And for the first time an appreciable part of that expanding reading public was women. While the emerging middle class was in general looking more to reading as a source of information, enlightenment and entertainment, middle class women in particular were looking for confirmation and clarification of their own new lifestyles. Here, Eliza Haywood came into her own. She was able to provide such representations for women and to take advantage of the developments in the publishing industry. She tried her hand at every type of fiction but was always sensitive to the social context in which her work was received.

She started her writing career with the licentious *Love in Excess*, and the pinnacle of her achievement, published towards the end of her writing life, was *The History of Betsy Thoughtless* (1751). In between is an astonishing number of publications which testify to her considerable creative powers and her extraordinary versatility. But if women writers can be condemned for the narrowness of their vision and the limited conformism of their style, this does not necessarily mean they will be praised when they reveal their ability to do precisely the reverse. For this is what Eliza Haywood did: she leapt from one form to another and from one style to another and yet far from gaining kudos for her diversity she is more often derided for her inconsistency. Because her achievement in fiction virtually extends from one end of the literary spectrum of the time to the other, where her work has been assessed it is often labelled as 'shallow'. She is seen not as a skilful writer but as a 'hack' who shifts and starts, simply to give the public what it wants.

To suggest, however, that Eliza Haywood prostituted her talents merely to give the fickle reading public what it wanted to read, is not only to do disservice to her talent but to portray her in a purely passive role. She was part of the society she was writing about and writing for, and she helped to *shape* as well as to reflect the social values of her period. It is absurd to think solely in terms of her reaction to public demand, and to omit any consideration of the role she played in stimulating, extending and developing the tastes of her audience. While she was – understandably – concerned with sales, it is nothing short of a denial of her literary ability to cast her in the role of a hack, a writing machine who wrote to formula!

To have been capable of writing in so many styles and so many forms, to have been able to adapt, shift, progress, to have modified and experimented, to have consolidated and innovated as Eliza Haywood did, was in itself a literary achievement of great merit. One cannot help but think that if these had been the characteristics of a male author, the novels would have been hailed as those of a genius. But it was a woman whose writing showed such remarkable versatility and the work has faded and been forgotten.

Despite her retreat after the attack of Alexander Pope (and whether her disappearance was voluntary or enforced – or whether she continued to write under pseudonyms – we cannot know), Eliza Haywood did not fade or get forgotten during her own time. One reason for her sustained popularity was that she represented the middle classes who were becoming the backbone of the publishing industry, so that many of the views and values which found expression in her fiction chimed with those of her reading public. Growing steadily stronger, this new middle class audience was beginning to flex its muscles, to exert its influence and to demand the presentation of its own lifestyle in literature, and it found in Eliza Haywood a spokeswoman for its concerns.

There was some jostling for positions going on between the upper and middle classes and whereas adulatory accounts of the distanced aristocracy had once been accepted as the only fitting subject of literature, the emerging middle class was no longer content with the practice of drawing all heroes and heroines from the aristocratic ranks. The new reading public wanted its own existence validated, it wanted its own kind centre-stage, at least some of the time; and it was by no means averse to the inclusion of some satirical criticism of its traditional 'betters'. So a change begins to take place. Far from supplying the heroes for fiction, the aristocracy becomes the recruiting ground for 'villains'. And I suspect that this version of class politics could only have originated in a woman's view of the world.

Aphra Behn had started to move away from the aristocratic frame of reference: her characters may have retained their high-sounding names but their behaviour more closely resembled that of low-born Londoners on occasion. Delarivière Manley had gone further with her class-based political satires which exposed the aristocratic leaders as less than perfect – even less than honourable or deserving of respect. But although she proceeded in the same self-consciously middle class direction, Eliza Haywood gave a different twist to developments: she introduced a new type of villain (from the aristocracy) but she introduced a new heroine as well – from the middle class. And the stage was set for the dual drama of the conflict of class interest worked out through the battle of the sexes.

It is not with Samuel Richardson and *Pamela* (1740) that the poor but honest heroine – harassed by the upper class rake – makes her appearance, but with Eliza Haywood. Quite intentionally she moved towards the middle class as the source of her material and in 1728 she defended the practice of finding in ordinary people a fit subject for literary treatment in *The Disguised Prince, or The Beautiful Parisian*:

> Those who undertake to write Romances, are always careful to give a high Extraction to their *Heroes* and *Heroines*; because it is certain we are apt to take a greater Interest in the Destiny of a *Prince* than a *private Person*. We frequently find, however, among those of a middle State, some, who have Souls as elevated, and Sentiments equally

91

noble with those of the most illustrous Birth: Nor do I see any reason
to the Contrary; *Nature* confines her blessings not to the *Great* alone.
. . . As the following Sheets, therefore, contain only real Matters of
Fact, and have, indeed, something so very surprising in themselves,
that they stand not in need of any Embellishments from Fiction: I
shall take my *Heroine* such as I find her, and believe the Reader will
easily pass by the Meanness of her Birth, in favour of a thousand
other good Qualities she was possessed of. (p. 1–2)

A middle class heroine – and a moral purpose! This was a recipe for
instant appeal for a significant segment of the novel-reading public, who
were middle class women intent on a moral purpose.

Of course not all middle class women had easy access to novels.
There was a matter of money: the circulating libraries did not appear
until the 1740s and although Eliza Haywood's novels ranged in price
from one shilling to three shillings (see Jane Spencer, 1984a: p. 158),
there were few women of sufficiently independent means who could
afford such purchases.* And if lack of funds was not an obstacle, lack of
'availability' certainly was because it was out of the question for
respectable women to venture into bookshops which were very much the
preserve of men. Even as late as the end of the eighteenth century it was
still impossible for decent women to walk into a bookshop as Mary
Somerville found when she wanted a copy of Euclid's *Elements of Geometry*:
there was simply no way she could get it (Dale Spender, 1982a): p. 169).

But for middle class women the pressure to read novels outstripped
the difficulties in obtaining them, and this was partly because these
women were beginning to find themselves in the position where there
was very little else for them to do. They were becoming a class of people
who were prohibited from *working* and more and more they turned to
reading, as a constructive pursuit.

Because they were not engaged in paid work and were no longer
required to directly produce many of the goods which had traditionally
been made in the home, it is not uncommon to find this entire group of
diverse middle class women pejoratively labelled as idle and frivolous,
and their novel-reading propensities condemned as a form of
dissipation. Yet such a broad and belittling generalisation reveals more
about the historical bias against women than it does about the women
themselves. For while no doubt many of them found fiction an
entertaining diversion and a means of filling in time, it is also clear that
many of these women looked to this evolving genre for a more edifying
diet. They wanted substance, they wanted something serious, they

*For further discussion of circulating libraries and the cost of novels see
chapter 8, 'Male romance'.

wanted something which explained the world and caused them to think. This helps to account for the transition from the more sensational to the more moral and reflective novels, a transition which is reflected in Eliza Haywood's own writing career. Under the influence of women readers and women writers, the novel began to assume the dimensions of a commentary on the human condition.

Eliza Haywood was at the forefront of these developments. She was among the first to assert the validity of middle class experience, among the first to insist on the significance and the humanity of 'ordinary people' and among the first to explore the conflict of interest between the classes and sexes. And in so doing she helped to modify the very essence of a story and its meaning.

Until this time, the conventional basis of a traditional story had been the test of a *man's* honour. But suddenly, with the entry of Eliza Haywood, there is a dramatic switch, and we find that it is the *woman's* honour that is being tested. The whole perspective has changed. Men are no longer the reference point. Women are no longer seen only in relation to men, cast in the role of seductress, intent on luring men away from their high moral purposes. Instead, with the poor but honest heroine, it is women's view which becomes central, and in this context men are seen in relation to women. And it is not a particularly flattering portrayal of men which begins to emerge: for every honourable man we are confronted with we also encounter a number of debauched, debased and deceptive rakes – who try to lure women to their ruin.

This represents quite a change. Such a switch supports Virginia Woolf's statement, in an essay written in 1929, that the values of a woman are not the same as those of a man and that the woman writer reveals this with her perpetual alteration of the values established by men (1972: p. 146). Eliza Haywood (and to some extent, Aphra Behn as well as Delarivière Manley) is an excellent example of this thesis as she presents the world through women's eyes and sees in men what they do not ordinarily see in themselves. That since her time the test of a woman's honour has become a conventional plot for novels – with men from Samuel Richardson onwards making use of this form* – does not detract from her achievement of introducing the reality of a middle class woman as the reference point. What has happened with this – as with so many other innovations that have originated with women – is that her contribution has gone unacknowledged and then has been taken up by a man, who is not only presumed to be better, but with the passing of time is taken to be the real innovator.**

*I do not include Daniel Defoe's *Moll Flanders* (1722) in this category for it does not qualify as a test of a woman's honour.
**For further discussion see chapter 6, 'Power and propaganda'.

This shift in emphasis which can be traced in the writing of Eliza Haywood seemed to me sufficiently marked and significant to warrant the attention of literary historians, so I spent a considerable amount of time trying to find references to it in the accounts that deal with the rise of the novel. I even thought that some protest might have been made by men of letters who saw their own sex not only being displaced in her writing (and in that of other women novelists as well) but who would have been displeased to find that male characters were being distorted and discredited. But search as I have through all the 'authorities' I cannot find any discussion of the important change from the test of a man's honour to the test of a woman's honour. And certainly there is no reference to Eliza Haywood's contribution in this regard: when she rates not a mention it is easy to deny her achievement.

What I have found, however, is that this conceptualisation introduced by women is turned around so that it is viewed through the eyes of men. Far from identifying with the harassment that is experienced by women, Walter Allen (1980), for example, filters this new subject matter through the reference point of men and labels this development – as represented in the writing of Samuel Richardson – as one based on 'the principle of procrastinated rape' (p. 40).

There are two people involved in rape and two perspectives on rape: there is the one who is raped and the one who does the raping, and their experiences are realms apart. And while Eliza Haywood was concerned with the world as it impinged on those who were raped, this dimension of human experience is 'mocked' where it is not 'overlooked' by most male critics.

Identifying with women's view as I do, I see in these novels of 'heroine testing' by women writers one instance of sexual harassment after another, one instance of male brutality after another, one instance of injustice after another. But this is not what male readers see, judging from their comments. J.B. Priestley, and his evaluation of Eliza Haywood is a case in point:

> The ensnaring of innocent maidens . . . appears almost to have been the chief pastime of the eighteenth century gentleman, the one to which he devoted most of his time, energy, skill and patience. This fact is not really a tribute to the beauty and initial virtue of the eighteenth century maidens. It is explained, I fancy, by the lack of resources for the idle man of that century. With no golf, no bridge, no cars, these gentleman had to pass the day somehow, and if they did not care for hunting, drinking, politics or literature, they had to go seducing out of sheer boredom. And I suspect that they were careful, like good sportsmen, to choose the most difficult subjects, so that the

end would not come too quickly. Mrs Heywood [sic] offers us some good specimens of the seducer, but of course she does not understand them. She thinks it is a question of unbridled desire, and does not see that these long pursuits and elaborate stratagems argue an intellectual interest. (J.B. Priestley, 1929, p. xii)

Such is the *literary* standard by which Eliza Haywood is judged – and found wanting. It is a *literary* standard which denies women's humanity and reduces them to 'prey', which is patronising in the extreme, which scorns women's view and values, and which reveals more about J.B. Priestley's sense of male centrality and significance than it does about Eliza Haywood's writing. Yet it is the judgment of J.B. Priestley – and his peers – which prevails, and which pushes Eliza Haywood from any place in our literary heritage. Eliza Haywood is one of the mothers of the novel but the male critics have called her unfit and allowed her no part in the novel's growth and development.

Her input to the novel in its early stages, however, was not confined to matters of content (the middle class heroine put through a moral test), but extended to structure as well, and Eliza Haywood was one of the writers who helped to establish the epistolary novel. *Letters* – partly because of their seeming veracity and their obvious flexibility – were probably the most popular writing form of their day, and were making their appearance in a variety of places. They were a perfect vehicle for travel reports, and for tales of adventure from far-away places. They were an excellent means of conveying on-the-spot news reports, and indeed, newspapers were really little more than a collection of letters on a range of topics, and all published together. ('Edward Ward, for example, was a hack writer who liked to masquerade his sensational exposés as on-the-scene reports back home in the form of letters' [Ruth Perry, 1980: p. 7] and was probably the first supposedly 'foreign correspondent' to send his 'letter' home.)

John Dunton started the practice of printing the editor's reply along with the anonymous letters which were purportedly from readers, and so popular did this item prove to be that it was not only taken up then by the *Spectator*, the *Tatler* and the *Guardian*, but it is a practice which persists to the present day.

There were Letters which were designed to guide one through life, to explain the finer points of etiquette, and to serve as 'manuals' in all manner of situations. 'Defoe, always willing to supply the needs of the reading public,' writes Ruth Perry (1980), 'contributed *The Family Instructor* (1715), a collection of sample dialogues for sticky situations which might occur between a father and son, or a mother and daughter – a "how-to-do-it" manual for family life – and *Conjugal Lewdness* (1727) which warns married couples at great length against too heavy an emphasis on the sexual side of their union' (pp. 8-9).

The popularity of letters as a published form had many implications for women. Because they had been permitted letter writing, because it was familiar to them – and because it was a form of writing in which they were even held to excel – women did not feel they were debarred from participation in this new field of professional writing. Instead of being disqualified by their education and experience – as they had been when writing was associated with aristocratic tastes and classical education – women now found that they were peculiarly fitted to be published writers – in letter form. And the letter form was peculiarly suited to the expression of women's experience. Letters were the perfect place for poignant and painful outpourings. The suffering heroine, who had so little opportunity to act in the world or to influence the course of events, could nonetheless retire and unburden herself in letters or journals.

So too could letter writing serve as a means for self-inspection. This was becoming a valued activity of middle class society, and fiction which could deal with self-examination meshed with the growing social awareness that human beings were capable of reflection, change – and improvement. Psychological fiction and stream of consciousness novels might have been a long way off, but the epistolary novel was an excellent vehicle for allowing characters to be introspective, to examine their circumstances, and weigh their motives and decisions. Human beings seem to have a constant need to know what is happening in the lives of other people and to make sense of it in relation to their own (which explains the popularity of many forms besides fiction – scandal sheets, many newspaper exposés, soap operas – and even 'gossip'), and one of the most direct means of access to private lives is through personal letters and diaries. So fiction appropriated the letter – and the diary – and developed in leaps and bounds. And women writers were at the very centre of this development.

For the woman reader, what could have been more convincing, more authentic – and more appealing – than the personal revelations of another woman? And for the woman writer, what could have been simpler to provide?

By the middle of the eighteenth century women were a growing reading public but they were not the major reading public: financial constraints and 'unobtainability' continued to play their part. But if women could not enter bookshops and browse, looking for books, they were able to peruse catalogues – and to subscribe.

Publishers then were as wary of risk taking as they are now and rather than lay out their own money for publication, readers were solicited to pay in advance: when sufficient subscriptions had been collected the book was published to the benefit of all concerned, for the author was published, the readers received their copies (often with their names as subscribers printed in the book), and the publisher was not in danger of losing a fortune. Sometimes publishers would only publish books if the author organised the subscriptions and came not just with manuscript in hand but with finance (or pledged finance) as well. Sometimes, too, prominent people were sought after for subscriptions on the grounds that where they went others would follow, and what they considered to be a good investment they would hold up to their friends. So women who had money of their own could exercise some influence over the selection of publications through the process of subscription. But still at this stage women were not the majority of the subscribers. Eliza Haywood seems to have published only one book by subscription – *Letters from a Lady of Quality to a Chevalier* (1721) – and of the three hundred and nine people who subscribed (at a cost of three to five shillings, depending on the binding) one hundred and twenty-three were women.

But if the publishers could cover their risks there were few assurances for writers. Often they were paid only once for their manuscript: they sold it outright and frequently for a very small sum. If their book proved to be a success then it was the publishers'/booksellers' good fortune, and the only advantage for the writer was the possibility of raising the price of the *next* manuscript to be delivered. But the next manuscript also had to be written, and many writers produced at great speed – in order to survive. By 1724 'she . . . rushed into print no less than ten original romances, besides translating half a lengthy French work, "La Belle Assemblée" . . .' (George Whicher, 1915: p. 15). Between 1724 and 1727 Eliza Haywood wrote seventeen epistolary novels – as well as other novels, a play, poems and translations – which not only gives some idea of the rapidity with which she worked (about thirty-eight publications in all) but also reveals her popularity as a writer – of the epistolary form, particularly. At this rate of writing it is quite possible that she could have made a living but she must have been under enormous pressure to keep her pen flowing. It is unlikely that she had much time to revise.

She tried to supplement her income in other ways. Wealthy people often paid to have kind words written about them. (Letitia Pilkington (1712-1750), for example, tried without much success to support herself by penning panegyric poems for the powerful which they then circulated.) 'Dedications' were often paid for by the person to whom they were dedicated – which helps to explain the fulsome and flattering praise that is sometimes to be found in these offerings to the great (the majority of whom were women). Eliza Haywood has some most effusive dedications to some very wealthy people and while there must have been times when the 'trick' didn't work, she clearly received grateful payment on occasions.

The theatre, however, was where there was money to be made. A long run meant a lot of money for a writer and this was one reason Eliza Haywood tried her hand at play writing. Another reason was that she was passionately interested in the theatre, and not just in writing, but in acting as well. On August 12th, 1973, her play *A Wife To Be Let* was staged at the Drury Lane Theatre and one of its attractions was that the author was appearing in it. This was explained in terms of the sickness of the actress who had been engaged to play the part, but judging from the text this could well have been a ruse for it appears that Eliza Haywood had every intention of performing. The following speech was contained in the prologue:

> Critics! be dumb tonight – no skill display;
> A dangerous woman-poet wrote the play;
> One, who not fears your fury, though prevailing,
> More than your match, in everything but railing.
> Give her fair quarter, and whenever she tries you
> Safe in superior spirit, she defies you;
> Measure her force by her known novels, writ
> With manly vigour, and with woman's wit.
> Then tremble, and depend, if you beset her,
> She, who can talk so well, may act yet better.

Despite the writer's challenge – and performance – the play was not a success. But this did not discourage her from writing or appearing in further dramatic productions. During the 1720s most of her energies went into writing but during the 1730s she was to be found more frequently as an actress: this was after the denunciation of Alexander Pope and it has been suggested that she was forced on to the stage because she was forced out of the literary world. However, even if acting were the only field open to her it was evidently no hardship, although this is not to suggest that she made a handsome living from it.

There is some debate about the start of Eliza Haywood's acting career, with Jane Spencer (1984a) among those who date it from 1715 in Dublin, where Eliza Haywood is supposed to have played the part of Chlöe in *Timon of Athens, or the Man Hater*. But there are some inconsistencies in the evidence, not the least of which is what would the Reverend Haywood have thought of his wife going on the stage – and in Dublin? Other claims, however, can be made with more certainty. Among her associations with the theatre were the production of her play, *Frederick, Duke of Brunswick-Lunenburgh* (1729) and her performance in William Hatchett's *Rival Father* at the Haymarket in 1730. In 1732 she acted in *The Blazing Comet*, and in 1737 in *A Rehearsal of Rings*. She co-operated with William Hatchett on *The Opera of Operas or Tom Thumb*, and in 1736 played Mrs Arden in *Arden of Faversham* which as Jane Spencer comments was 'an adaptation she may have written herself'. But her 'stage career ended when the Haymarket closed down after the Licensing Act' (p. 158).

But if she made her mark in the theatre, it was in fiction and in journalism that Eliza Haywood excelled and which was her main source of financial support.

Walter and Clare Jerrold (1929) have said of Eliza Haywood that, 'Between the first triumphant success scored with *Love in Excess* and the serious check to her popularity caused by the indecent attack on her by Alexander Pope, there was something like a constant stream of romantic fiction, of translations and of excursions into that field first staked out by Mrs Manley, which must have made the name of Eliza Haywood that of one of the most familiar writers of the time' (p. 223). Five years after the popular *Love in Excess* her writing was so much in demand that the booksellers issued her *Works* in four volumes, and 'by 1724 it would seem that she had attained a position equal to that of the "best sellers" of our day' (p. 225). Eliza Haywood is not referred to in Walter Allen's (1980) *The English Novel*.

In other contexts, Eliza Haywood's name and achievement is linked with that of Daniel Defoe, although the reference is, of course, to her as 'the female Defoe' and not to him as 'the male Haywood' despite the fact that there was little to distinguish between them at the time – except that she was the more prolific of the two. But similarity in achievement – and style – is not the only factor which is responsible for the connections between these two writers.

It may have been 'a token of esteem' or it may have been a clever marketing strategy, but Delarivière Manley was not the only woman author to have her titles appropriated by Daniel Defoe. In 1723 Eliza Haywood's *Indalia, or the Unfortunate Mistress* was published and not long afterwards Daniel Defoe brought out *The Fortunate Mistress* which was certainly a play on Eliza Haywood's title. But there seems to have been no ill-feeling between these two writers – no battle of words like that conducted by Delarivière Manley and Richard Steele – but rather there is evidence of 'overlap' and even the suggestion of collaboration. When in 1720 Daniel Defoe's *History of the Life and Adventures of Mr Duncan Campbell* (the deaf and dumb fortune teller) was published, it contained an 'announcement' that it would soon be followed by 'a little pocket volume' of the letters of Duncan Campbell and his correspondents. This 'little pocket volume' finally appeared in 1724, with the grand title *A Spy Upon the Conjurer, or A Collection of Surprising Stories, with Names, Places and Particular Circumstances relating to Mr Duncan Campbell commonly known by the Name of the Deaf and Dumb man; and the astonishing Penetration and Event of his Predictions. Written to my Lord by a Lady, who for more than twenty years past has made it her Business to Observe all Transactions in the Life and Conversation of Mr Campbell.*

This work was issued with four separate title pages in 1724 and three of them declare the 'author' to be Eliza Haywood. This has not prevented many critics from ascribing the work to Daniel Defoe, although the writing style is recognisably that of Eliza Haywood. Of course, it is quite possible that Eliza Haywood read Daniel Defoe's 'announcement' in the *History*, and took the initiative, although she does not seem to have felt the need to 'borrow' the ideas of other writers. Alternatively, and more likely, is the possibility that her writing was done with the co-operation of Daniel Defoe: in 1730 Duncan Campbell died and he had been such a popular character in the public mind that it made good sense to publish his 'memoirs' – no matter whether or not he had actually left any – and it seems as though Daniel Defoe began this project but became too ill to continue, and that Eliza Haywood completed it (see Walter and Clare Jerrold, 1929: p. 228). So perhaps there was some form of collaboration between these two best-selling writers. But even if Eliza Haywood were to be included in the history of letters, and to be given her place alongside Daniel Defoe, such is the bias of literary men that we would be bound to hear of Eliza Haywood in terms of her indebtedness to Daniel Defoe. There is little likelihood that the question of her influence on Daniel Defoe would arise: not even the question of her influence on the novel has been raised although clearly she helped to shape its form and substance, in its early stages.

The public wanted epistolary novels and epistolary novels it got – in abundance – from Eliza Haywood, but even as she produced this new form she also wrote in the 'tried and true' form of Delarivière Manley, with the regular publication of 'satires' and 'scandals'. The most daring of these was *The Secret History of the Present Intrigues of the Court of Caramania* (1727) which was an exposé of the affair between the Prince of Wales (who became George II just after the book was published) and Henrietta Howard (later the Countess of Suffolk). There was no doubt who the principal characters were in 'real life', and showing a little more prudence than Delarivière Manley, Eliza Haywood ensured that her name did *not* appear on the title page. Nor did the names of the printer or bookseller appear, so even though there had been some tightening of the libel laws since the days when the author of the *New Atlantis* had created havoc in high places, Eliza Haywood seems to have evaded the long arm of the law.

She did not, however, avoid being an object of attack among some of the literary men of her day. Apart from Alexander Pope, there was also Richard Savage who unleashed the full force of his furious pen against her. According to the 'wisdom' of the day, Eliza Haywood and Richard Savage were at one stage more than just good friends – although whether this is accurate or not, it is difficult to say, for there is not one word of confirmation – or refutation – from Eliza Haywood on the subject. But whatever their relationship and however it began, it obviously ended on a bitter note with Richard Savage seeking printed revenge: he even parodied her play, *A Wife To Be Let* (1724) with a production of his own in 1732 – *An Author To Be Let.*

'The degree of intimacy between Eliza and Richard Savage can only be guessed at today,' write Walter and Clare Jerrold (1929), and 'that she was prepared to forgive and forget we may gather, but he seems to have pursued her after the break with something like malice', and they go on to add that it could well have been Richard Savage who 'was in some way responsible for the unenviable position of publicity into which she was thrust by Pope's *Dunciad*' (p. 241). For *The Dunciad* also had a 'key' – not that it ever classified as a scandal of course: *it* is a serious literary satire (still much studied in educational institutions today). In the 'key' to *The Dunciad* it was intimated that it was Richard Savage who was the father of the 'two babes of love' with which contemporary scandal credited Eliza Haywood.

Although Eliza Haywood was more than capable of hitting back – and had ample opportunity to do so – she kept silent when the men attacked her in this way. (She was not silent when her work was criticised, and often came back with an impudent defence.) But to have responded to the denunciations of Richard Savage or Alexander Pope would only have made matters worse.

It is tantalising to know so much and so little about Eliza Haywood. To know so much about the writing, and so little about the writer. To know that she was so unusual, so adventurous and independent, obviously so talented and so determined, and yet to know so little about the feelings of this woman who made her living from exploring and disclosing the feelings of others. How did she live? How did she see herself as a woman writer? How did she respond to some of the attacks upon her? Answers to all these questions can only be speculative.

That she had a cheeky sense of humour with a satirical bent – and that it contained a liberal dash of irreverence – is indisputable, and was probably an asset when it came to surviving some of the difficulties she encountered. Her stage appearance – and the prologue – in *A Wife To Be Let* reveal her defiant and semi-protective humour, and *Anti-Pamela, or Feigned Innocence Detected* (1741), her response to Samuel Richardson's *Pamela* (1740), displays all her satirical skills, and is arguably the best of all the many *Pamela* derivatives (although, of course, it rarely rates a mention in this context in literary evaluations). When *Betsy Thoughtless* was published in 1751 – to considerable public acclaim – a carping critic

Literary Origins

unfavourably compared Eliza Haywood with Henry Fielding and Tobias Smollett, and in her next novel, *Jemmy and Jenny Jessamy* (1753), the author to some extent got her own back with the comment that it 'contains none of those beautiful digressions, those remarks or reflections which a certain would-be critic pretends, are so distinguished in the writings of his two favourite authors; yet it is to be hoped, will afford sufficient to please all those who are willing to be pleased' (vol. 9, ch. 8). Eliza Haywood was never cowed and if we knew more about her life we would be able to make more of many of the satirical and humorous comments in her writing.

But it was also as a journalist that Eliza Haywood best used some of her satirical and comic talents. A mother of the novel she undeniably is, but she is also *the* mother of women's magazines. Her first venture was an essay-paper, similar to the *Tatler*, which was called *Tea Table* and which was published every Monday and Friday from 21st February to 21st June 1724 (thirty-six numbers in all). Then in 1728 another periodical appeared – the *Parrot* – and the pseudonym of the editor/writer was Mrs Penelope Prattle. (A later *Parrot* was issued in 1746 and Eliza Haywood acknowledged authorship in this instance and as Alison Adburgham (1972) states, the similarities in style between the old *Parrot* and the new – and their close resemblance to the *Female Spectator* – 'leaves little room for doubt as to the true identity of Mrs Penelope Prattle' (p. 78).)

It must be understood that newspapers and periodicals represented much the same problems for women as books. They were the property of men. They were concerned with men's affairs and were not considered suitable reading matter for women. Newspapers and periodicals were not brought into the home but were read by men in coffee houses – where women were not allowed to go. So any woman who wished to be informed about the affairs of the day (business affairs, current affairs, or amorous affairs) encountered real obstacles. She could neither purchase nor read newspapers and was therefore entirely dependent on men for information at a time when men were becoming increasingly sure that women should not worry their heads with politics or business. So there was a great need for a women's newspaper which would be accepted as 'appropriate for the ladies', which could provide some coverage of current affairs and some material of substance but which would be distinguished by its high moral tone and its treatment of topics considered suitable for the well-bred gentlewoman.

Ever adaptable, and ever ready to meet the needs of a growing and changing reading public, the author of *Love in Excess* showed her skill for moving with the times by taking up her pen for a more moralising and crusading purpose in the *Female Spectator*. A monthly essay-paper – this time modelled on the *Spectator* – it made its appearance in 1744. In the

102

first issue Eliza Haywood introduces herself to her readers and makes an explicit statement about the transformation of her own life – which may have been an accurate account but which could have equally been 'good journalism' for there is no doubt that her acknowledgment suits her new and more respectable purpose:

I have run through as many scenes of variety and folly as the greatest coquet of them all – dress, equipage and flattery were the idols of my heart. My life for some years was a continual round of what I then called pleasure: and my whole time engrossed by a hurry of promiscuous diversions. . . . The company I kept was not, indeed, always so well chosen as it might have been, for the sake of my own reputation; but then it was general, and by consequence furnished me, not only with the knowledge of many occurrences, which otherwise I had been ignorant of, but also enabled me, when the too great vivacity of my nature became tempered with reflection, to see into the secret springs which give rise to the actions I had either heard or been witness of . . . to judge of the various passions of the human mind, and distinguish those imperceptible degrees by which they become masters of the heart, and attain dominion over reason. With this experience, added to a genius tolerably extensive, and an education more liberal than is ordinarily allowed to persons of my sex, I flattered myself that it might be in my power to be in some measure both useful and entertaining to the public.

What better than a reformed coquet to warn women against the pitfalls of lack of sensible judgment? Eliza Haywood was in an unchallengeable position to caution women against loss of reputation. She was, she stated, going to help them guard against the dangers of the world and to do this she intended to expose vice and its dreadful consequences, and folly and its resulting misfortunes. Her 'spies' would send reports not just from the resorts of Bath and Tunbridge, but from foreign parts as well, although the *Female Spectator* was definitely not to be confused with a scandal sheet, for it would be the *actions* and not the *persons* which would stand condemned:

The sole aim of the following pages is to reform the faulty and give an innocent amusement to those who are not so; all possible care will be taken to avoid anything that might serve as food for the venom of malice and ill-nature. Whoever, therefore, shall pretend to fix on any particular person the blame of actions they may happen to find recorded here, or make what they call a key to these lubrications, must expect to see themselves treated in the next publication with all the severity so unfair a proceeding merits.

103

As Alison Adburgham writes, 'Thus did Mrs Haywood whet the appetite for libel and scandal, while at the same time declaring a crusade against the sins of Society' (1972: p. 97). Certainly the morals of many of the essays are that wantonness does not pay and that virtue is rewarded, but in the terms of the times this was reasonably self-evident and although Eliza Haywood professes to be the bearer of wise counsel, it should not be surmised that she was writing reforming or elevating tracts. Her essays are still very lively– a little of the licentiousness lingers – but the difference is that these narratives are placed in a context which cautions women against being caught by censure to the cost of their own welfare and happiness. It could be that the author was speaking with the voice of experience, but if so it was not an embittered or cynical voice and there is the sneaking suspicion that Eliza Haywood favoured the subversive belief that it was better to have loved and lost, than not to have loved at all.

In many respects the essays in the *Female Spectator* – like those in the *Spectator* – are attempts to provide more information so that better decisions can be made. The essays are moral in that they assume the value of reason and judgment and urge readers to acquire these habits in preference to the dictates of perfidious fashion. As with Joseph Addison's and Richard Steele's 'advice to the gentlemen', Eliza Haywood's 'advice to the ladies' is based on similar motives and provides much the same sound sense: but the status of such advice is startlingly different – depending on the sex to whom it is addressed. For whereas Joseph Addison and Richard Steele are held up in literary history as fine examples of serious moralists with their advice to young men, Eliza Haywood is scorned and deprecated for her silliness, with her advice to young women. The men's words become the substance of literature (both Joseph Addison and Richard Steele were required reading in *my* schooldays) while those of the woman are superciliously dismissed under the label of 'gossip' or 'rules of etiquette': the men are concerned with morals but because Eliza Haywood addresses women, she is judged to be concerned with manners. Sex makes a significant difference in literary criticism.

The *Female Spectator*, the first women's periodical of some duration run by a woman, ran for two years and afterwards appeared in four volumes which ran into seven editions (the last appearing in 1771). Many of its features still find a place in the women's magazines of the present day and one of them was the forerunner of 'the agony column'. Letters, not surprisingly, played a prominent part in the *Female Spectator* and some of the letters from readers (and the editor's response), whether they were authentic or not, continue to have their entertainment value. One mother writes to lament the foolishness of her daughter of fourteen who thinks nothing of dashing off for public breakfasts and pleasure places – and what shall she wear? What does Mrs Haywood advise, asks the mother? Should the daughter be isolated and sent to a relation in Cornwall who is twelve miles from the nearest neighbour?

The editor expresses her sympathy for the mother yet tells a sad tale of the young woman who was overly confined by her parents and who – to escape – eloped with the first young man who came her way. And Eliza Haywood's advice about divorce (and remember – it's 1744) sounds curiously familiar today:

> When both parties are equally determined to maintain their different opinions, though at the expense of all that love and tenderness each has a right to expect of the other, and instead of living together in any manner comformable to their vows at the altar, it is the judgment of every member of our Club [the non-existent 'staff' of the *Female Spectator*] that it is less violation of the sacred ceremony which joined their hands, to separate entirely, than it is to continue in a state where to persons mutually dissatisfied, the most trifling words or action will be looked on as fresh matter of provocation.

No-fault divorce? With or without alimony? How much Eliza Haywood's advice reflected her own personal circumstances we can only guess, but in her living and her writing she held firmly to the principle that wives should not be expected to submit to unreasonable demands. The case is stated quite unequivocally in her two last novels, *The Wife* (1756) and *The Husband in Answer to the Wife* (1756) where the suggestion is that she is alluding to her own domestic life and difficulties by way of illustration.

There is one account of a quarrel between wife and husband where the husband wants the bedchamber to be reorganised and the wife maintains that it would be impossibly awkward, and she would rather it stay as it is. To this her husband replies that 'the best quality a wife can be possessed of is her obedience to the commands of her husband; and you ought to have known that after marriage it would not be your province to dispute, but to submit to whatever I should think fit to enjoin'. Eliza Haywood thinks this a preposterous demand and unhesitatingly points to the consequences of such tyrannical behaviour. 'Their life together was an almost continual scene of dissension till tired with the tyranny of a husband, she flew to the embraces of a lover, with whom she went to Paris and still resides there' (quoted in Walter and Clare Jerrold, 1929: p. 213).

Note: the wife does not seem to be dreadfully punished for her actions. This was not the customary approved outcome for the times.

Of all Eliza Haywood's works, it is *The History of Betsy Thoughtless*

(1751) which is accorded the greatest claim to (limited) fame. This was the novel that Fanny Burney credited with being the inspirational source for *Evelina* more than twenty-five years later, and this in itself indicates how popular and enduring *Betsy Thoughtless* proved to be. It is a much more carefully crafted novel than some of Eliza Haywood's earlier efforts and although it follows the 'picaresque' style, with one episode after another, it has a decisive unity. (This was brought home to me when I undertook the practical task of trying to cut the novel for reprinting: unlike many other picaresque novels – such as those of Daniel Defoe or Henry Fielding – I found it impossible to remove any one episode without being obliged to add information on what had been omitted, so tightly woven together and interdependent are all the many events.)

It is also a novel of rivetting interest where plot, character and dialogue all work to ensure a lively and demanding read. Alison Adburgham (1972) has said of it that it is 'crammed with excellently depicted characters, each chapter packed with incident and ending at a point in the plot that compels you to start reading the next' (p. 104). And the dialogue has not lost its power to amuse even today: 'Madam, perhaps we may never more meet between the sheets,' declares Mr Goodman to his wife on discovering her deception.

Although Evelina and Elizabeth Bennet would later emerge as young women who had learnt from the error of their impressionable ways and who had acquired sound moral judgment in the process, it was Betsy Thoughtless who first appeared in this role. Brigid MacCarthy (1944) has described her as 'a skittish young lady with a genius for involving herself in incriminating situations' (p. 245), and although appearances may be against her, Betsy Thoughtless *is* innocent and stays innocent throughout, despite the treacherous currents of the world in which she moves. Her crime is that she doesn't think, but by the end of the novel her impetuosity has given way to a more reflective and responsible frame of mind.

The heroine's honour is tested in a variety of ways. She is faced with two suitors, the sober Saving and the profligate Gaylord, and while she is being swayed by superficial values, the admirable Mr Trueworth is obliged to witness her thoughtless escapades. (Note the similarity with Jane Austen's *Emma*.) Finally, out of patience with Betsy, Mr Trueworth marries Harriet Lovitt, and Betsy makes the mistake of taking the heartless Munden for her huband.

Interestingly, Eliza Haywood does not find it necessary to get her characters out of trouble *before* they are married, although admittedly, this places a strain on the plot, when the spouses of both Mr Trueworth and Betsy are obliged to die in order that the hero and the heroine can get together. But both have learnt from marriage and one thing that

Betsy has learnt is what a tyrant a husband can be. Eliza Haywood provides a painful portrayal of the plight of wives and makes no bones about what she thinks of such arrangements.

Yet neither this remarkable novel, nor its remarkable and prolific author, has any place in the history of literature. If it were desirable to choose but one author to represent the growth and development of the English novel, sex bias aside, the lot would undoubtedly fall to Eliza Haywood, whose writing encompasses all the significant innovations and enduring and exemplary achievements of the early novel. Through a study of her work the entire range of shifts and changes in style and content can be readily traced. From her use of 'romantic' names in her earlier novels to her move to 'personality' names in her later novels (Trueworth, Lady Trusty, Miss Forward) we witness the shift in values that occurred in fiction during her lifetime. Yet she is virtually never quoted as a pioneer in the history of the novel.

In her work we can document the emergence of the novel, for the distance between *Love in Excess* (1719) and *Betsy Thoughtless* (1751) is much greater than the distance between *Betsy Thoughtless* and *Evelina* (1778) or *Pride and Prejudice* (1813). And it is nothing other than falsification to excuse her exclusion from literary history on the grounds that she was only reflecting or mimicking the changes which the men around her were implementing. This might be an explanation which is consistent with the image of men as culture makers, but it is one that is inconsistent with Eliza Haywood's work.

She was as much an active force (and arguably a greater force) in shaping the novel as were Daniel Defoe and Henry Fielding, and she was as good and as great a social commentator as were Richard Steele and Joseph Addison. She helped to 'create' the reading public while she responded to the needs of that same public, and any evaluation of her which does not grant her a prominent place in the birth of the novel – or which excludes her completely from consideration – can only be based on her sex.

Eliza Haywood died as she lived – very privately. No record of her death, burial, or of a memorial has been found in any of the normal sources of information. Even the writer of *Biographica Dramatica*, writing not so long after her death in 1782, confessed himself defeated. 'All I have been able to learn,' he states in the only record that exists, 'is that her father was in the mercantile way, that she was born at London, and at the time of her death, which was on the 25th January, 1756, she was about sixty-three years of age.'

While much about Eliza Haywood must remain a mystery, there is no mystery about why she has been omitted from the world of letters and who is responsible for the omission.

Table 3: Eliza Haywood

1	1719	*Love in Excess, or The Fatal Inquiry*, a novel. Parts 1 and 2
2	1720	*Love in Excess*, Part 3
3		*Love in Excess* (3rd edn 1721, 1722, 1724, 6th edn, 1725)
4	1721	*The Fair Captive*, a tragedy (1724)
5		*Letters from a Lady of Quality to a Chevalier*, translated from the French (1724)
6	1722	*The British Recluse, or The Secret History of Cleomira* (2nd edn 1722, 1724, 1725, 1732; see no. 14)
7	1723	*The Injured Husband, or The Mistaken Resentment* (2nd edn 1723, 1724, 1725)
8		*Idalia, or The Unfortunate Mistress* (2nd edn 1723, 1725)
9		*Lasselia, or The Self-Abandoned* (1724, 1725)
10	1724	*A Wife to Be Let*, a comedy (1729, 1735)
11		*The Rash Resolve, or The Untimely Discovery* (2nd edn 1724)
12		*Poems on Several Occasions* (1725)
13		*Works*, in 4 vols. I. *Love in Excess* II. *The British Recluse; The Injured Husband; The Fair Captive* III. *Idalia; Letters from a Lady of Quality* IV. *Lasselia; The Rash Resolve; A Wife to be Let; Poems on Several Occasions*
14		*The British Recluse . . . and The Injured Husband*, two novels (see nos. 5 and 6)
15		*The Surprise, or Constancy Rewarded* (1725)
16		*A Spy Upon the Conjurer, or A Collection of Surprising Stories . . . relating to Mr Duncan Campbell, etc.* (two other edns 1724, 1725)
17		*The Fatal Secret, or Constancy in Distress* (2nd edn 1724)
18		*The Masqueraders, or Fatal Curiosity, Part 1* (3rd edn 1724; see no 23)
19		*The Arragonian Queen, a secret history* (2nd edn 1724, 1727)
20		*La Belle Assemblée, or The Adventures of Six Days* Parts 1, 2 and 3 (forming vol. 1) translated from the French (see nos. 39 and 66)
21		*The Force of Nature, or The Lucky Disappointment*, a novel
22		*Fantomina, or Love in a Maze*
23	1725	*The Masqueraders*, Part 2 (see no. 18)
24		*Memoirs of a Certain Island Adjacent to the Kingdom of Utopia*, vol. I (see no. 42)
25		*Bath-Intrigues in Four Letters to a Friend in London* (3rd edn 1725)
26		*The Lady's Philosopher's Stone, or The Caprices of Love and Destiny*, a historical novel, translated from the French
27		*The Unequal Conflict, or Nature Triumphant*, a novel (1726; see no. 31)
28		*The Tea-Table, or A Conversation between Some Polite of both Sexes, at a Lady's Visiting Day*, Part 1 (4th edn 1725; see no. 36)

Intrigues; The Masqueraders, Part 2; The Perplexed Duchess

53 1728   *The Mercenary Lover . . .* to which is added *The Padlock, or No Guard Without Virtue* (see no. 35)

54   *The Agreeable Caledonian, or Memoirs of Signora di Morella, a Roman Lady, etc.* (see nos. 60 and 89)

55   *Irish Artifice,* included in *The Female Dunciad*

56   *Persecuted Virtue, or The Cruel Lover*

57   *The Disguised Prince, or The Beautiful Parisian,* Part 1, translated from the French (17633; see no. 59)

58 1729   *Frederick, Duke of Brunswick-Lunenburgh,* a tragedy (2nd edn 1729)

59   *The Disguised Prince,* Part 2 (1733; see no. 57)

60   *The Agreeable Caledonian,* Part 2 (see nos. 54 and 89)

61   *The Fair Hebrew, or A True but Secret History of Two Jewish Ladies Who Lately Resided in London* (2nd edn 1729)

62   *Mrs Haywood's Select Collection of Novels and Histories, Written by the Most Celebrated Authors, in several languages. All newly translated from the originals, by several hands,* in 6 vols

63 1730   *Love Letters on All Occasions lately passed between Persons of Distinction*

64 1732   (*Secret Memoirs of the Late Mr Duncan Campbell*)

65 1733   *The Opera of Operas, or Tom Thumb the Great,* with songs by E.H. and William Hatchett

66 1734   *L'Entretien des Beaux Esprits. Being the Sequel to La Belle Assemblée* (see nos. 20 and 39)

67 1736   *Adventures of Eovaii, Princess of Ijaveo. A Pre-Adamitical History* (see no. 68)

68 1741   *The Unfortunate Princess, etc.* This was a reprint of no. 67, with a new title

69   (*Anti-Pamela, or Feigned Innocence Detected in a series of Syrena's Adventures* (1742))

70   (*The Busy Body, or Successful Spy,* translated from the French)

71 1742   *The Virtuous Villager, or The Virgin's Victory,* translated from the French

72 1743   *A Present for a Servant Maid, or The Sure Means of Gaining Love and Esteem* (1743, 1744, 1745; see no. 90)

73 1744   *The Fortunate Foundlings, etc.* (3rd edn 1748)

74 1745   (*Leonora, or Characters Drawn from Real Life*)

75 1745-6 *The Female Spectator,* in monthly numbers, and then in 4 vols (1747, 1748, 1750, 1755, 7th edn 1771. Translated into French, 1751)

76 1746   *The Parrot.* With a Compendium of the Times. In nine weekly numbers

77 1748   *Life's Progress Through the Passions, or The Adventures of Natura*

78 1749   (*Dalinda, or The Double Marriage*)

79   *Epistles for the Ladies* (1753, 1776)

80 1750   (*A Letter from H G Esq.* (Translated into French, 1757))

81		*(The History of Cornelia)*
82	1751	*The History of Miss Betsy Thoughtless*, in 4 vols (1751, 1765, 4th edn 1768, 1783)
83	1753	*The History of Jemmy and Jenny Jessamy, in 3 vols (1753, 1785)*
84	1755	*The Invisible Spy (1759, 1766, 1773, 1778)*
85		*(Matrimony*, a novel in 2 vols)
86	1756	*The Wife* (1756, 1762)
87		*The Husband, in Answer to the Wife*
88		*The Young Lady*, in twopenny numbers, only three of which were published
89	1768	*Clementina*, a re-issue of *The Agreeable Caledonian* under a new title (see nos. 54 and 60)
90	1772	*A New Present for a Servant Maid* (see no. 72)
91	1778	*The History of Leonora Meadowson*
92	?1770	*Love in a Madhouse, or The History of Eliza Hartley, the Distressed Orphan* (see no. 37)
93	1771	Several Novels of EH included in Elizabeth Griffith's *Collection of Novels*
94	1915	*The Life and Romances of Mrs Eliza Haywood*, by George Frisbie Whicher, PhD

PART II

---•---

Literary Standards

CHAPTER 5

———————•———————

Gross deception

100 women novelists

I have no reason to suspect that my own university education was peculiarly biased or limited. On the contrary, it appears to have been fairly representative. Yet in the guise of presenting me with an overview of the literary heritage of the English-speaking world, my education provided me with a grossly inaccurate and distorted view of the history of letters. For my introduction to the 'greats' was (with the exception of the famous five women novelists) an introduction to the great men. Even in the study of the novel where women were conceded to have a place, I was led to believe that all the initial formative writing had been the province of men. So along with other graduates of 'Eng. Lit.' departments I left university with the well-cultivated impression that men had created the novel and that there were no women novelists (or none of note) before Jane Austen.*

There was no reason for me to be suspicious about what I was being taught. I was a student in a reputable university being tutored by experts who referred me to the literary scholars who, without qualification, asserted the ascendancy of men. For example, the authoritative treatise on the early novel was by Ian Watt and was entitled *The Rise of the Novel: Studies in Defoe, Richardson and Fielding* (1957) and it opened with the

*I have since checked the current course offerings of the English Department of Sydney University; in 1985, of twenty-five courses, only *one* is devoted to a woman writer, and *only three include women writers*! What is more, the course entitled 'The place of women' gives pride of place to men, with three out of the four texts used being by male authors. I am indebted to Debra Adelaide for her assistance in gaining these figures and I deplore the fact that in twenty-five years and with the pressure of the contemporary women's movement, no progress has been made to give women recognition in this reputable university establishment.

bald statement that the novel was begun by Defoe, Richardson and Fielding, and that it was the genius of these three men that had created the new form (p. 9). Had it even occurred to me to be dubious about the frequency with which I was asked to accept men's good opinion of men, by what right could I have questioned the scholarship and authority of such established and sanctioned critics?

Besides, what contrary evidence was available? No matter where I looked around me, I encountered almost exclusively the publications of men. Like Virginia Woolf in the British Museum (*A Room of One's Own*, 1928) I too found that the library catalogue and shelves were filled with books predominantly authored by men. And in the bookshops a steady stream of new and attractively packaged editions of early male novelists helped to reinforce the belief that it was only men who had participated in the initial production of this genre. I neither stumbled across fascinating 'old' editions of women's novels on the library shelves nor found interesting republications when browsing through bookshops. As far as I knew both the old and the new were representative of the books that had been published, and as there were virtually no women among them, it had to be because women had not written books.

So I had no difficulty accepting the statements of Ian Watt: men were to be congratulated for the birth of the novel. Women – or more precisely, one woman – entered only *after* men had ushered the novel into the world: Jane Austen, writes Ian Watt in 'A Note' at the end of *The Rise of the Novel*, provided a steady and guiding influence for this new form but neither she, nor any other woman, had helped to bring it into existence. In his book in which Fanny Burney is mentioned on only three occasions (and in less than three lines) he does say that 'Jane Austen was the heir of Fanny Burney' (p. 296), but as this is the only cursory reference, the impression remains that when it comes to women novelists there was no one to speak of, before Jane Austen.

It does not, of course, strain the limits of credibility to believe that for women, Jane Austen started it all. Her novels reveal such a great talent that it is possible to accept that she was capable of bringing forth – in fully fledged form and without benefit of female 'models' – those superb novels which to my mind still stand as one of the high points of achievement in English fiction. But if it is possible to accept this version of women's literary history, I have discovered since that it is exceedingly unwise. For to see Jane Austen as a starting point is to be dreadfully deceived. Any portrayal of her which represents her as an *originator* and not as an *inheritor* of women's literary traditions is one which has strayed far from the facts of women's fiction writing. And when Jane Austen is seen to *inherit* a literary tradition this has ramifications not just for the history of women novelists but for the history of novelists in general.

For more than a century before Jane Austen surreptitiously took up

116

her pen, women, in ever increasing numbers and with spectacular success, had been trying their hand at fiction. And not just the few women already referred to either, although obviously the Duchess of Newcastle, Aphra Behn and Delarivière Manley had played an important part, and Eliza Haywood, 'a woman of genius', had helped to conceive the possibilities and realities of fiction. And not just the 'refreshing' Fanny Burney or the 'worthy' Maria Edgeworth who are sometimes briefly acknowledged in passing for their 'historic interest'. (Maria Edgeworth is not mentioned in Ian Watt's *The Rise of the Novel*.) But a whole gallery of women: women from different backgrounds, different regions, and with different concerns, who all published well-acclaimed novels by the end of the 1700s.

That such women and their writing exist raises numerous questions about the traditions of women: this also raises questions about the traditions of men!

Without doubt the novel came into its own during the eighteenth century; the publication figures in themselves tell a story of sure and steady growth: 'The annual production of works of fiction, which had averaged only about seven in the years between 1700 to 1740, rose to an average of about twenty in the three decades following 1740 and this output was doubled in the period from 1770 to 1800', writes Ian Watt (1957: p. 290). About two thousand novels in all, by the end of the century. And the distinct impression that they were written mainly by men.

Now, it's not possible to make definitive statements about how many of these two thousand novels were written by women, and how many by men. In quite a few cases, the sex of the author remains unknown – particularly because of the penchant for anonymous publications, a practice, it must be noted which was more likely to tempt (particularly modest) women rather than men. But even if the 'sex unknown' authors are subtracted from the list of novelists of the 1700s, the number of women novelists and their works which remain is little short of astonishing, given that we have been led to believe that women played no part in these productions. As a result of a little detective work and a great deal of perseverance, I have been able to find one hundred good women novelists of the eighteenth century and together they were responsible for almost six hundred novels.

This means that even by the most conservative standards women would have to be granted a half-share in the production of fiction in the 1700s. And yet they have *all* 'disappeared'. It must be noted that this is not a reference to the occasional obscure woman writer who has slipped through the net of literary standards, not the 'one-off' achievement that has unfortunately been lost, not the eclipsing of one woman of genius like Eliza Haywood. This is at least half the literary output in fiction over a century; it is six hundred novels which in their own time were accorded merit.

And if since the eighteenth century it has become a well-established fact that women did not write novels during the 1700s, or that women did not write good novels, this was a fact which was *not* known at the time. For it was then widely appreciated that women wrote novels, and wrote them well. So firmly entrenched was this belief that it affords a most unusual and interesting chapter in the history of letters. While ever since it has been men who have been seen as the more significant and better novelists – to the extent that on occasion women have tried to increase their chances of publication by pretending to be men – it was not unknown during the eighteenth century for men to masquerade as female authors in the attempt to obtain some of the higher status (and greater chances of publication) which went with being a woman writer.

So frequent had this practice become that as early as June 1770 the *Gentleman's Magazine* thought it proper to conduct its own investigations as to the sex of authors, in the interest of being able to provide its readers with information on whether the latest production from a supposedly female pen was indeed genuine. For as the reviewer commented, 'among other literary frauds it has long been common for authors to affect the stile and character of ladies' (page 273). Which means that eighteenth century readers knew something that twentieth century ones do not; namely that in the beginning, and for quite a long time thereafter, the novel was seen as the female forté.

In 1773 the *Monthly Review* stated that when it came to fiction the field was filled by ladies, and well into the nineteenth century it was conceded that not only were women novelists plentiful, but that they were good.

Yet by the twentieth century when Ian Watt comes to outline the rise of the novel, women are no longer held in high esteem. He does – in passing – acknowledge that *the majority of eighteenth century novels were written by women*, but how very damning is this faint and only praise.

How is it that we have come to lose this knowledge about many good women novelists? How have we come to lose it so completely that its one-time existence does not even register, so we are blissfully unaware of what has been lost? So that we do not even appreciate the significance of the single sentence that once women wrote (and published) reams? For so thoroughly have early women novelists been edited out of the literary records and removed from consciousness, their absence does not even ordinarily prompt comment, let alone concern. When early women novelists are simply not presented as part of the literary heritage it takes a peculiar degree of paranoia to suspect that the records have been tampered with and the evidence of their existence eliminated. Far more likely is it that those who are being initiated into the literary traditions will innocently presume that all is open and above board in the practices of the men of letters. So if no women are to be found among the early 'greats' it would undoubtedly be because women have not written anything 'great'. In such a context, any question about what the men have done with the women writers would not generally arise.

Not all that is written could be preserved; not all that is written is worth preserving. This is why we have literary experts and critics. They are entrusted with the task of judging what is worthy of inclusion in the literary heritage and what is not. Of the approximately two thousand novels that were written during the eighteenth century, only a very few have been preserved and passed on in the literary canon. This in itself is no cause for complaint. But when to this is added the information that about half these novels were written by women and *all* of them have since failed the test of greatness, then explanations are required. Either the laws of probability are in need of revision or there are good grounds for hypothesising that some other law is operating in the selection process.

Quantity alone does not satisfy the criteria for excellence. But quantity alone suggests that the criteria in relation to the early novels are not being made explicit. When during the 1700s so many novels were written by women and *not one* of them qualifies now for a prominent place in the literary heritage, it seems reasonable to claim that what is meant by the standards of excellence is that in order to be great, one must be a man.

Because *quantity* is an issue when it comes to women's writing, because women wrote so many novels which, without exception and regardless of the acclaim they enjoyed at the time, now fall short of greatness – and because these women and their writing have been so completely lost that they are now genuinely unknown – it seems appropriate to include here a list of eighteenth century women novelists and their work. It is by no means a definitive list. It is, however, one measure of the degree to which women writers have been eliminated from the literary traditions.

Table 4: 106 women novelists before Jane Austen: 568 novels

Note: The list excludes the women discussed so far, e.g. Eliza Haywood (and her many novels).

1 Penelope AUBIN 1679-1731	1721	*The Strange Adventures of the Count de Vinevil and His Family*	
novelist, translator,	1721	*The Life of Madame de Beaumont*	
playwright	1722	*The Nobel Slaves, or The Lives and Adventures of Two Lords and Two Ladies Upon a Desolate Island*	

	1722	*The Life and Amorous Adventures of Lucinda*
	1723	*The Life of Carlotta du Pont*
	1726	*The Life and Adventures of Lady Lucy*
	1728	*The Life and Adventures of the Young Count Albertus, the son of Count Lewis Augustus, by the Lady Lucy*

2 Jane BARKER

novelist and poet

	1715	*Exilius, or The Banished Roman*
	1723	*A Patchwork Screen for the Ladies, or Love and Virtue Recommended*
	1726	*The Lining of the Patchwork Screen*

3 Agnes Maria
BENNETT
died 1808
novelist

	1785	*Anna, or The Memoirs of a Welch Heiress*
	1788	*Juvenile Indiscretions*
	1789	*Agnes de Courci*
	1794	*Ellen, Countess of Castle Howel*
	1797	*The Beggar Girl and her Benefactors*
	1800	*De Valcourt*
	1806	*Vicissitudes Abroad, or The Ghost of My Father*

4 Elizabeth BONHÔTE
1744-1818
novelist and essayist

	1772	*Rambles of Mr Frankley and His Sister*
	1773	*The Fashionable Friend*
	1787	*Olivia, or The Deserted Bride*
	1789	*Darnley Vale, or Emilia Fitzroy*
	1790	*Ellen Woodley*
	1797	*Bungay Castle*

5 Elizabeth BOYD

poet and novelist

	1732	*The Unhappy Unfortunate, or The Female Page*

6 Sophie BRISCOE

novelist

	1771	*Miss Melmoth, or The New Clarissa*

7 Eliza BROMLEY

novelist

	1784	*Laura and Augustus, an authentic story; in a series of letters*
	1803	*The Cave of Cosenza: A Romance of the Eighteenth Century, altered from the Italian*

8 Frances BROOKE

	1763	*The History of Lady Julia Mandeville*

1724-1789 novelist, dramatist, essayist, translator	1766	*The History of Emily Montague* (first Canadian novel)
	1774	*All's Right at Last, or The History of Miss West*
	1779	*The Excursion*
	1790	*The History of Charles Mandeville*
9 Indiana BROOKS novelist	1789	*Eliza Beaumont and Harriet Osborne*
10 Mary BRUNTON 1778-1818 novelist	1810-11	*Self Control*
	1814	*Discipline*
	1818	*Emmeline* (posthumous)
11 Mrs BURKE novelist	1787	*Ela, or Delusions of the Heart: A Tale Founded on Fact*
	1788	*Emilia de St Aubigne*
	1796	*Adela Northington*
	1796	*The Sorrows of Edith, or The Hermitage of the Cliffs: A Descriptive Tale, Founded on Facts* (attributed)
	1800	*Elliott or Vicissitudes of Early Life* (possible author)
12 Fanny BURNEY 1752-1840 novelist and diarist	1778	*Evelina*
	1782	*Cecelia*
	1796	*Camilla*
	1814	*The Wanderer*
13 Sarah Harriet BURNEY 1770-1844 novelist	1796	*Clarentine*
	1806	*Geraldine Fauconberg*
	1812	*Traits of Nature*
	1816-20	*Tales of Fancy* (3 vols)
	1839	*Romance of Private Life* (3 vols)
14 Lady Charlotte BURY 1775-1861 novelist, diarist, editor, biographer	1812	*Self Indulgence*
	1822	*Conduct is Fate*
	1826	*Alla Giornata, or The Day*
	1828	*Flirtation*
	1830	*The Separation*
	1830	*The Exclusives*
	1834	*The Disinherited/The Ensnared* (two novels published together)

	1836	*The Devoted*
	1837	*The Divorced*
	1837	*Love*
	1840	*A History of a Flirt*
	1841	*Family Records, or the Two Sisters*
	1842	*The Manoeuvering Mother*
	1844	*The Wilfulness of Woman*
	1853	*The Roses*
	1856	*The Lady of Fashion*
	1864	*The Two Baronets, a novel of Fashionable Life* (posthumous publication)
15 Mary BUTT/Mrs SHERWOOD 1775-1851 novelist, writer for children	1795	*The Traditions: A Legendary Tale. Written by a Young Lady*
	1802	*Susan Grey*
	1818	*The Fairchild Family*
	1891	*The Juvenile Library* (posthumous publication of children's tales)
16 Lady Mary CHAMPION de CRESPIGNY 1748(?)-1812 novelist, poet, educational writer	1796	*The Pavillion*
17 Charlotte CLARKE 1713-1760 novelist, playwright, autobiographer	1755	*The Mercer, or Fatal Extravagance*
	1756	*The History of Henry Dumont, Esq and Miss Charlotte Evelyn*
	1758	*The Lover's Treat, or Unnatural Hatred* (40pp)
	n.d.	*The History of Charles and Patty* (attributed tale)
18 Mary CHARLTON novelist, poet and translator	1794	*The Parisian*
	1797	*Andronica*
	1798	*Phedora*
	1798	*Ammorvin and Zallida*
	1799	*Rosella*
	1801	*The Pirate of Naples*
	1802	*The Wife and the Mistress*
	1802	*The Reprobate* (transl.)
	1803	*The Philosophic Kidnapper* (transl.)
	1804	*The Rake and the Misanthrope* (transl.)
	1813	*The Homicide*

1820	*Grandeur and Meanness*
1830	*Past Events*

19 Harriet CHILCOT

poet and novelist

| 1790 | *Moreton Abbey* |

20 Emily CLARK

novelist

1798	*Ianthe, or The Flower of Caenarvon*
1800	*Ermina Montrose, or The Cottage of the Vale*
1805	*The Banks of the Duora, or The Maid of Portugal*
1817	*Tales at the Fireside, or A Father and Mother's Stories*
1819	*Esquimaux, or Fidelity*

21 Jane COLLIER
1709(?)-1754
satirist and novelist

| 1753 | *An Essay on the Art of Ingeniously Tormenting* |
| 1754 | (with Sarah Fielding) *The Cry: a new dramatic fable* |

22 Mary COLLYER
(?)-1763
novelist and translator

1742	*The Virtuous Orphan, or The Life of Marianne* (transl.)
1746	(same novel as above, different title) *The Life and Adventures of Indiana*
1744	*Felicia to Charlotte: Being Letters from a Young Lady in the Country to her Friend in Town*

23 Anne Seymour DAMER
1748-1828
novelist

| 1801 | *Belmour* (3 vols) |

24 Mary DAVIS
1674-1732
novelist and playwright

1700	*The Ladies' Tale*
1704	*The Amours of Alcippus and Lucippe*
1705	*The Fugitive*
1724	*The Reformed Coquet*
1725	*Works* (including earlier pieces)
1727	*The Accomplish'd Rake*
1732	*The False Friend*
n.d.	*The Merry Wanderer*
n.d.	*The Cousins: Familiar Letters Betwixt a Gentleman and a Lady*

123

25 Anne DAWE novelist	1770	*The Young Sister, or History of* *Miss Somerset*
26 Anne EDEN novelist	1790	*Confidential Letter of Albert; from his first* *attachment to Charlotte to her death. From* *the Sorrows of Werter*

27 Maria EDGEWORTH
    1768-1849
    novelist and
    educational writer
	1795
	1800
	1801
	1804
	1805
	1806
	1809-12
	
	1814
	1817
	1834
		Letters for Literary Ladies
		Castle Rackrent
		Belinda (3 vols)
		Popular Tales (3 vols)
		The Modern Griselda
		Leonora (2 vols)
		Tales of Fashionable Life (1809 *Ennui and*
		Manoeuvering, 1812 *Emilie de Coulanges*
		and *The Absentee*)
		Patronage (4 vols)
		Ormond and Harrington
		Helen (3 vols)

28 Elisa FENWICK
    (?)-1840
    novelist and children's
    writer
	1795	*Secresy, or The Ruin of the Rock*

29 Sarah FIELDING
    1710-1768
    novelist and scholar
	1744
	1747
	
	1749
	
	1753
	
	1754
	
	1757
	1759
	1760
		The Adventures of David Simple
		Familiar Letters between the Principal
		Characters in David Simple
		The Governess, or The Little Female
		Academy
		The Adventures of David Simple, Volume
		the Last
		The Cry: a new dramatic fable (with
		Jane Collier)
		The Lives of Cleopatra and Octavia
		The History of the Countess of Dellwyn
		The History of Ophelia

30 E.M. FOSTER novelist	1795 1800 1803 n.d. n.d. n.d.	*The Duke of Clarence* *Frederic and Caroline* *Light and Shade* *Federetta* *Rebecca* *Miriam*

31 Anne FULLER	1786	*Alan Fitz-Osborne*
(?)-1790	1789	*The Son of Ethelwolf*
novelist	1786	*The Convent* (attributed)

32 Phoebe GIBBES	1764	*The Life and Adventures of Mr Francis Clive*
novelist	1767	*The Woman of Fashion*
	1784	*The American Fugitive, or Friendship in a Nunnery*
	1788	*The Niece*

31 Mrs A. GOMERSALL	1789	*Eleanora*
	1790	*The Citizen*
novelist and poet	1796	*The Disappointed Heir*

34 Sarah GREEN	Author of twelve novels
novelist	

35 Elizabeth GRIFFITH	1757	*A Series of Genuine Letters Between Henry and Frances*
1720(?) 1727(?)-1793		
playwright and novelist,	1769	*The Delicate Distress*
translator	1771	*The History of Lady Barton*
	1776	*The Story of Lady Juliana Harley*
	1777	*A Collection of Novels* (edited)
	1780	*Novellettes* (including thirteen stories she published in *Westminster Magazine*)

36 Susannah Minifie GUNNING	1763	*The Histories of Lady Frances S___ and Lady Caroline S___* (plus three other novels)
1740-1800		
novelist	1764	*Family Pictures*
	1766	*The Picture* (with sister Margaret Minifie)
	1768	*Barford Abbey*
	1769	*The Cottage*
	1770	*The Hermit*
	1783	*Coombe Wood*
	1792	*Anecdotes of the Delborough Family*
	1793	*Memoirs of Mary*
	1796	*Delves*
	1797	*Love at First Sight*
	1800	*Fashionable Involvements*
	1802	*The Heir Apparent* (posthumous)

125

37 Elizabeth HAMILTON 1796 *Letters of a Hindoo Rajah*
   1758-1816   1800 *Memoirs of Modern Philosophers*
   Essayist, poet, satirist, 1808 *The Cottagers of Glenburnie*
   novelist

38 Lady Mary 1776 *Letters from the Duchess de Crui*
   HAMILTON 1777 *Memoirs of the Marchioness de Louvoi*
   1739-1816 1778 *Munster Village*
   novelist 1782 *The Life of Mrs Justman*
                        1801 *Duc de Popoli*

39 Mary Ann HANWAY 1798 *Elinor, or The World As It Is*
                        1800 *Andrew Stuart, or the Northern Wanderer*
   novelist and journal 1808 *Falconbridge Abbey: A Devonshire Story*
   writer 1815 *Christabelle, The Maid of Rouen*

40 Laetitia Matilda 1811 *The Countess and Gertrude, or Modes of*
   HAWKINS   *Discipline* (4 vols)
   1759-1835 1814 *Rosanne, or Father's Labour Lost* (3 vols)
   novelist, memorist 1821 *Heraline, or Opposite Proceedings* (4 vols)
   miscellaneous writer 1824 *Annaline, or Motive Hunting* (3 vols)

41 Mary HAYS 1796 *Memoirs of Emma Courtney*
   1760-1843 1799 *The Victim of Prejudice*
   novelist and polemical 1804 *Harry Clinton, or A Tale of Youth*
   writer 1815 *The Brothers, or Consequences. A Story of*
                          What Happens Every Day
                        1817 *Family Annals, or The Sisters*

42 Mary HEARNE 1718 *The Lover's Week* (dedicated to
                           Delarivière Manley)
   novelist 1719 *The Female Deserters*
                        1720 *Honour the Victory and Love the Prize,*
                           Illustrated in Ten Novels by Mrs Hearne
                           (including two above)

43 Elizabeth HELME 1787 *Louisa, or The Cottage on the moor*
                        1788 *Clara and Emmeline*
   novelist 1794 *Duncan and Peggy*
                        1796 *The Farmer of Inglewood Forest*
                        1799 *Albert, or The wilds of Strathnavern*
                        1801 *St Margaret's Cave, or The Nun's Story*
                        1803 *St Clair of the Isles*

	1805	*Pilgrim of the Cross, or The Chronicles of Christabelle de Mowbray*
	1812	*Magdalen, or The Penitent of Godstow*
	1814	*Modern Times, or The Age We Live In* (posthumous)

44 Elizabeth HERVEY
1748-1820(?)
novelist

1790	*Louisa* (2 vols)
1796	*The History of Ned Evans*
1797	*The Church of St Siffrid*
1800	*The Mourtray Family*

45 Mrs HOWELL

novelist (Minerva Press)

46 Anne HUGHES

poet, novelist,
dramatist

1787	*Caroline, or The Diversities of Fortune*
1788	*Henry and Isabella*
1787(?)	*Zoraida*

47 M. (Harley) HUGILL

novelist

1786	*St Bernard's Priory*
1788	*The Castle of Mowbray*
1793	*Juliana Ormeston*
1794	*The Prince of Leon*
1797-8	*Isidora of Gallicia*
1798	*The Countess of Hennebon* (now lost)

48 Maria HUNTER

novelist, actress

| 1792 | *Fitzroy, or Impulse of the Moment* |
| 1798 | *Ella, or He's Always in the Way* |

49 Elizabeth INCHBALD
1753-1821
playwright, novelist
and critic

| 1791 | *A Simple Story* |
| 1794 | *Nature and Art* |

50 Susanna KEIR
1747-1802
novelist

| 1785 | *Interesting Memoirs by A Lady* |
| 1787 | *The History of Miss Greville by the author of Interesting Memoirs* |

51 Isabella KELLY

novelist, poet,
educational writer

1794	*Madeleine, or The Castle of Montgomery*
1795	*The Abbey of St Asaph*
1796	*The Ruins of Avondale Priory*
1797	*Jocelina, or The Rewards of Benevolence*

127

	1795	*Eva*
	1801	*Ruthinglenne, or The Critical Moment*
	1802	*The Baron's Daughter*
	1803	*A Modern Incident in Domestic Life*
	1805	*The Secret*
	1813	*Jane de Dunstanville, or Characters as They Are*

52 Anne KERR

novelist

1799	*The Heiress de Montalde, or The Castle of Bezarto*
1800	*Adeline St Julian, or The Midnight Hour*
n.d.	*Ederic the Forester*
n.d.	*Emmeline, or The Happy Discovery*
n.d.	*Modern Faults*

53 Sophia KING
1781(?)-(?)
novelist and poet

1798	*Waldorf, or The Dangers of Philosophy*
1799	*Cordelia, or A Romance of Real Life*
1801	*The Fatal Secret, or Unknown Warrior*
1801	*The Victim of Friendship: A German Romance*

**54 Ellis Cornelius
KNIGHT**
1758-1837
scholar, historian
novelist, translator,
poet

1790	*Dinarbus*
1792	*Marcus Flaminius, or A View of the Military, Political and Social Life of the Romans in a series of Letters from a young patrician to his friend*
1833	*Sir Guy de Lusignam*

55 Sarah LANSDELL

novelist

1796	*Manfredi, Baron St Osmond*
1798	*The Tower, or The Romance of Ruthyne*

56 Mary LATTER
1725-1777
miscellaneous writer

1759	*The Miscellaneous Works in Prose and Verse* (short epistolary novel, essays, letters and verses)

57 Harriet LEE
1757-1851
novelist and playwright

1786	*The Errors of Innocence*
1797	*Clara Lennox*
1797-99; 1801; 1805	*Canterbury Tales* (with sister Sophia)

58 Sophia LEE
1750-1824
novelist and playwright

1783-85	*The Recess*
1786	*Warbeck*
1797-99;	*Canterbury Tales*

128

	1801; 1805	(with sister Harriet)
	1804	*The Life of a Lover*

| 59 | Charlotte LENNOX
1720, 1727, 1729,
1730(?)-1804

novelist, translator
magazine editor, poet
and playwright | 1750
1752
1758
1760

1766
1790 | *The Life of Harriot Stuart*
The Female Quixote
Henrietta
The History of Harriot and Sophia
serialised in *The Lady's Museum* (later
published as *Sophia* in 1762)
The History of Eliza (attributed)
Euphemia |

| 60 | Charlotte MacCARTHY

novelist and religious
writer | 1745
1767 | *The Fair Moralist*
Justice and Reason |

| 61 | Anna Marie
MACKENZIE

novelist | 1783
1789
1790

1791
1792
1793
1795
1796
1798
1800
1809 | *Burton Wood*
Calista
Monmouth: A Tale Founded on Historical
Facts
The Danish Massacre: An Historical Fact
Orlando and Lavinia
Slavery, or The Times
Mysteries Elucidated
The Neapolitan
Dusseldorf, or The Fratricide
Feudal Events of Days of Yore
The Irish Guardian: Errors of Eccentricity |

| 62 | Jean MARSHALL

novelist | 1766

1767
1789 | *The History of Miss Clarinda Cathcart*
and Miss Fanny Renton
The History of Alicia Montague
A Series of Letters |

| 63 | Eliza MATHEWS
(?)-1802
poet, novelist,
miscellaneous prose
writer | 1785
1789
1790
1793
1801

1802 | *Constance: a novel*
Argus, the Housedog of Easlip
Arnold Zulig: a Swiss Story
The Count de Hoensdern: a German Tale
Morning's amusements, or Tales of
Animals etc.
Anecdotes of the Clairville Family to which
is added the History of Emily Wilmont |

	1807	*Griffith Abbey, or Memoirs of Eugenia* (posthumous)
	1809	*Elina, or The Young Governess* (posthumous)
	1809	*Afternoon Amusements, or Tales of Birds* (posthumous)

64 Anna MEADES
1734(?)-(?)
novelist

1757	*The History of Cleanthes an Englishman of the Highest Quality and Celemene the Illustrious Amazonian Princess*
1771	*The History of Sir William Harrington*

65 Mary MEEKE
(?)-1816(?)
novelist and translator:
24 books under her own
name; many as
'Gabrielli'

1795	*Count de Blanchard*
1795	*The Abbey of Clugny*
1797	*Palmira and Ermance*
1801	*Which is the Man*
1802	*Midnight Weddings* (plus 11 more novels)

'Gabrielli'

1797	*The Mysterious Wife*
1799	*Harcourt*
1801	*The Mysterious Husband*
1802	*Independence*
1804	*Something Odd*
1806	*Something Strange*

66 Margaret MINIFIE

novelist (sister of
Susannah Minifie
Gunning)

1763	*The Histories of Lady Frances S___ and Lady Caroline S___* (with sister)
1766	*The Picture* (with sister)
1780	*Le Count de Poland*

67 Hannah MORE
1745-1833
poet-playwright,
religious writer

1809	*Coelebs in Search of a Wife*

68 Lady MORGAN
(Sydney OWENSON)
1778-1859
novelist, essayist,
poet, travel writer

1803	*St Clair, or The Heiress of Desmond*
1804	*The Novice of St Dominick*
1805	*The Wild Irish Girl*
1807	*Patriotic Sketches*
1809	*Woman, or Ida of Athens*
1811	*The Missionary*
1814	*O'Donnel*
1818	*Florence Macarthy*

	1827	*The O'Briens and the O'Flahertys*
	1833	*Dramatic Scenes from Real Life*
	1835	*The Princess or the Beguine*
	1859	*Luxima* (rewrite of *The Missionary*)

69 Elizabeth NORMAN   1789   *The Child of Woe*

novelist

70 Amelia OPIE

70 Amelia OPIE	1790	*The Dangers of Coquetry*
1769-1853	1801	*Father and Daughter*
novelist, didactic	1804	*Adeline Mowbray*
writer	1806	*Simple Tales*
	1812	*Temper*
	1813	*Tales of Real Life*
	1816	*Valentine's Eve*
	1822	*Madeline*

71 Charlotte PALMER	1780	*Female Stability, or the History of Miss Belville* (5 vols)
novelist and children's	1792	*It is, or It is not* (2 vols: attributed)
author	1792	*Integrity and Content: an allegory*

72 Mary Elizabeth
PARKER   1795   *Orwell Manor*

73 Catherine PARRY   1784   *Eden Valley*
(?)-1788
novelist

74 Eliza Phelp PARSONS	1790	*The History of Miss Meredith* (2 vols)
1748(?)-1811	1792	*The Errors of Education* (2 vols)
novelist	1793	*Woman as she should Be, or The Memoirs of Mrs Melville*
(60 novels)	1793	*The Castle of Wolfenbach: a German story* (2 vols)
	1793	*Ellen and Julia* (2 vols)
	1794	*Lucy* (3 vols)
	1795	*The Voluntary Exile* (5 vols)
	1796	*The Mysterious Warning* (4 vols)
	1796	*Women as They Are* (4 vols)
	1797	*The Girl of the Mountains* (4 vols)
	1798	*Anecdotes of Two Well-Known Families* (2 vols)

131

	1799	*The Valley of St Gothard* (3 vols)
	1800	*The Miser and His Family* (2 vols)
	1801	*The Peasant of Ardenne Forest* (4 vols)
	1802	*The Mysterious Visit* (4 vols)
	1804	*Murray House* (3 vols: occasionally misattributed to Mary Meeke)
	1807	*The Convict, or Navy Lieutenant* (4 vols)
	n.d.	*The Wise Ones Bubbled, or Lovers Triumphant* (attributed)
	n.d.	*Rosetta* (attributed)
75 Susanna PEARSON	1794	*The Medallion*
poet and novelist		
76 M. PEDDLE	1785	*The Life of Jacob in Ten Books* (historical novel)
miscellaneous writer	1789	*The Rudiments of Taste; in a series of letters from a mother to her daughter*
77 Mary PILKINGTON	1797	*Edward Barnard*
1766-1839	1798	*The Mirror for the Female Sex*
novelist, translator,	1798	*Tales of the Hermitage*
short story writer,	1799	*Biography for Girls*
children's author	1799	*Biography for Boys*
	1802	*Memorial Tales*
	1813	*The Sorrows of Caesar, or Adventures of a Foundling Dog*
78 Mary PIX	1696	*The Inhuman Cardinal*
1666-1709	1704	*Violenta*
playwright and novelist		
79 Arabella PLANTIN	1727	*Love Led Astray, or The Mutual Constancy*
1700(?)-(?)	1727	*The Ingrateful, or The Just Revenge*
novelist	1727	*Letters to the Lady Wharton and Severall Other Persons of Distinction* (including both of above)
	1727	*Whartonia, or Miscellanies in Verse and Prose by the Wharton Family* (including reprint of all above)
80 Elizabeth PLUNKETT	1794	*The Packet*
1769-1823	1794	*Lord Fitzhenry*

novelist and translator	1795	*Memoirs of Mme de Barneveldt* (trans.)
(daughter of Susannah	1799	*The Gypsy Countess*
Minifie Gunning:	1803	*Plurality of Worlds* (trans.)
numerous publications)	1808	*Exile of Erin*

81 Ann RADCLIFFE
1764-1823
novelist

1789	*The Castles of Athlyn and Dunbane*
1790	*The Sicilian Romance*
1791	*The Romance of the Forest*
1794	*The Mysteries of Udolpho*
1797	*The Italian*
1826	*Gaston de Blondeville* (posthumous)

82 Mary Anne RADCLIFFE
(?)-1809
novelist

1790	*The Fate of Velina de Guidova* (attributed)
1790	*Radzivil* (attributed)
1809	*Manfrone, or The One Handed Monk*
1802	*Radcliffe's New Novelist's Pocket Magazine*

83 Clara REEVE
1729-1807
novelist and critic

1777	*The Champion of Virtue* (later *The Old English Baron*)
1783	*The Two Mentors*
1788	*The Exiles*
1791	*The School for Widows*
1792	*Plans of Education*
1793	*Memoirs of Sir Roger de Clarendon*
1799	*Destination*

84 Mary Darby ROBINSON
1758-1800
poet, novelist, actress ('Perdita')

1792	*Vancenza, or The Dangers of Credulity*
1794	*The Widow, or A Picture of Modern Times*
1796	*Angelina*
1796	*Hubert de Severac*
1796	*The Wanderings of the Imagination*
1797	*Walsingham: The Pupil of Nature*
1799	*The False Friend*
1799	*The Natural Daughter*

85 Regina Maria Dalton ROCHE
1764-1845
novelist

1789	*The Vicar of Landsdowne*
1793	*The Maid of the Hamlet*
1796	*The Children of the Abbey*
1798	*Clermont*
1800	*The Nocturnal Visit*
1806	*The Discarded Son*
1807	*Alvondown Vicarage*
1810	*The House of Osma and Almerida*

	1812	*The Monastery of St Colombe*
	1813	*Trecothic Bower*
	1814	*Anna of Edinburgh*
	1814	*London Tales* (short stories)
	1819	*The Munster Cottage Boy*
	1823	*Bridal of Dunamora, and Lost and Won*
	1825	*The Castle Chapel*
	1828	*Contrast*
	1834	*The Nun's Picture*
	1834	*The Tradition of the Castle*

86 Elizabeth Singer ROWE 1728 *Friendship in Death: in Twenty Letters*
1674-1737 *from the Dead to the Living*
novelist, poet, religious 1728, *Letters Moral and Entertaining*
writer 1731,
1733

87 Susanna ROWSON 1786 *Victoria*
1762-1824 1788 *The Inquisitor*
British/American 1790 *Charlotte Temple: A Tale of Truth*
novelist, actress, 1791 *Mentoria*
playwright 1792 *Rebecca, or Fille de Chambre*
1795 *Trials of the Human Heart*
1813 *Sarah*

88 Elizabeth RYVES/ 1789 *The Hermit of Snowdon*
REEVES
1750-1797
novelist and playwright

89 Charlotte SANDERS/ 1787 *Embarrassed Attachment*
SAUNDERS
novelist, poet,
children's writer

90 Sarah Robinson 1750 *History of Cornelia*
SCOTT 1754 *Agreeable Ugliness*
1723-1795 1754 *A Journal Through Every Stage of Life*
novelist, historian 1762 *A Description of Millenium Hall*
1766 *A History of Sir George Ellison*
1772 *A Test of Filial Duty*
(histories)
1761 *The History of Gustavus Erikson, King of Sweden*

	1762	*The History of Mecklenburgh*
	1772	*The Life of Theodora Agrippa D'Aubigne*

91 Frances SHERIDAN 1724-1766 novelist and playwright

1761	*Memoirs of Miss Sidney Biddulph* (3 vols)
1767	*The History of Nourjahad*
1791	*Eugenia and Adelaide* (posthumous)

92 Ann Emelinda SKINN 1746(?)-1789 novelist

| 1771 | *The Old Maid* |

93 Eleanor SLEATH novelist

1798	*The Orphan of the Rhine*
1802	*Who's the Murderer?, or The Mysteries of the Forest*
1808	*The Bristol Heiress*
1809	*The Nocturnal Minstrel, or The Spirit of the Wood*

94 Charlotte SMITH 1749-1806 poet and novelist

1788	*Emmeline, or The Orphan of the Castle*
1789	*Ethelinda, or The Recluse of the Lake*
1791	*Celestina*
1792	*Desmond*
1793	*The Old Manor House*
1794	*The Wanderings of Warwick*
1794	*The Emigrants*
1794	*The Banished Man*
1795	*Montalbert*
1796	*Marchmont*
1798	*The Young Philosopher*

95 Sarah Emma SPENCER novelist

| 1788 | *Memoirs of the Miss Holmsbys* |

96 Miss TAYLOR novelist

| 1799 | *Josephine* |

97 Jane TIMBURY novelist and poet

1770	*The Male-Coquette, or The History of the Hon. Edward Astell*
1790	*The Philanthropic Rambler*
n.d.	*The Story of Le Fevre*
n.d.	*The History of Tobit*

98 Elizabeth TOMLINS 1763(?)-1828 poet, novelist, translator	1787	*Conquest of the Heart: a Victim of Fancy*
	1792	*Memoirs of a Baroness*
	1799	*Rosalind de Tracey*
99 Jane WARTON 1723-1809 poet, novelist, essayist	1782	*Letters Addressed to Two Young Married Ladies on the Most Interesting Subjects* (2 vols)
	1783	*Peggy and Patty, or The Sisters of Ashdale* (4 vols)
100 Jane WEST 1758-1852 novelist, poet and playwright	1793	*The Advantages of Education*
	1797	*A Gossip's Story* (similar theme to *Sense and Sensibility*)
	1799	*A Tale of the Times*
	1827	*Ringrove* plus five more novels
101 Helena WELLS 1760(?)-(?) novelist (born in America)	n.d.	*The Step-Mother*
	n.d.	*Constantia Neville*
102 Helena Maria WILLIAMS 1762-1827 chronicler and novelist	1790	*Julia, a novel*
	1801	*Perourou, the Bellow Mender* (satire, later adapted for stage)
103 Mary WOLLSTONECRAFT 1759-1797 polemical writer and novelist	1788	*Mary, a Fiction*
	1798	*Memoirs and Posthumous Works, including The Wrongs of Women*
104 Mrs A. WOODFIN novelist	1756	*Northern Memoirs, or History of a Scotch Family*
	1762	*The History of Miss Harriet Wilson*
	1763	*The Auction*
	1764	*The Discovery of the History of Miss Marian Middleton*
	1765	*History of Sally Sable*

105	Ann YEARSLEY 1752-1806 poet and novelist ('Lactilla' and 'The Poetic Milkwoman')	1795	*The Royal Captives*
106	Mary Julia YOUNG (?)-1821 novelist and poet	1799	*The East Indian*
		1799	*Ragamount Castle*
		1803	*Lindorf and Caroline*
		1803	*Moss Cliff Abbey*
		1803	*Right and Wrong*
		1804	*The Mother and Daughter*
		1805	*Donatan*
		1807	*A Summer at Brighton*
		1808	*A Summer at Weymouth*
		1810	*The Heir of Drumoindra*
		n.d.	*Lenora*

If the laws of literary criticism were to be made explicit they would require as their first entry that the sex of the author is the single most important factor in any test of greatness and in any preservation for posterity. And perhaps if such acknowledgment was duly made – perhaps if Ian Watt, for example, prefaced his discussion on the rise of the novel with the blatant declaration that in his terms as only men can be considered great he had confined his analysis to only men – then at least the sense of deception might be removed, even if the sense of injustice were to remain. At least there would need to be open debate on the whys and wherefores of such sexual inequality. But because the process of literary evaluation which has been conducted almost exclusively by men has been masked with a façade of disinterestedness, gross deception not only takes place but is removed from the realm of challenge. So questions such as – what have the men done with all the women, and why? – are considered out of order, and the deception proceeds unchecked. Or, this is how it has been, anyway.

CHAPTER 6

●

Power and Propaganda

All these unknown women novelists! More precisely – all these *buried* women novelists. This was not an easy list to compile: women novelists have been securely hidden and there have been no readily accessible inventories which would even hint at the wealth of women's writing that existed in the eighteenth century.* But the presentation of such a list helps to make clear one dimension of the problem we are facing. It provides incontestable proof that women were there in their numbers at the beginning of the novel and that it is only since then that they have been put *out*.

And it is not because they were all no good that these hundred women novelists and their six hundred novels have been consigned to oblivion. For when the pronouncements of the literary establishment are perused for the case against the worth of these women writers, a curious omission comes to light. *There is no case against them.* If these many novels have been evaluated, the findings are not contained in the official literary records. And when the worth of women writers is not being based on any consideration of their writing, the only conslusion which can be drawn is that their worth is being determined by their sex.

That the writing of women does not count because it is written by women is the distinct impression given by Ian Watt. While his assertions about the quality of male novelists are based on a detailed examination of their writing it is clear that he thinks the stand he takes on the absence of quality in women's writing does not even call for substantiation. He devotes three hundred pages to his assessment of

---

*Now that Janet Todd's *Dictionary of British and American Women Writers 1660-1880* (1984) is available, this task has been made much easier.

male novelists and restricts his assessment of females to a single sentence: 'The majority of eighteenth century novels were actually written by women' (p. 298). With no further discussion of the women, no entry to them in the index, and no explanation for his failure to discuss 'the majority' of novels of the eighteenth century, Ian Watt indicates that it is not necessary to examine the writing of women to know it is of no account.

Perhaps Ian Watt offers no evidence for the simple reason that it does not support his beliefs.

In the eighteenth century it was not known that women writers did not count. Quite the reverse. Charlotte Lennox, Mary Wollstonecraft, Fanny Burney, Elizabeth Inchbald, Mary Hays, Amelia Opie and Maria Edgeworth were not just 'actually' the majority, they were the *esteemed* majority. They were highly praised by readers and reviewers alike. They were valued by some of the best educated and most distinguished persons – of both sexes. And if today they do not count among the scholars and critics this was not how it was in their own day, when their writing was read and studied, when their efforts were consistently applauded, when they enjoyed extensive and positive reviews, when they were congratulated on their contribution to literature. (One way of rediscovering these women novelists is to go through the review sections of the literary periodicals of the day.)

Strange that those who read the novels then should have found them so good when today the verdict is that they are so bad they do not warrant examination. This is a most interesting additional insight. Now when we are presented with an exclusively male literary tradition – and this is how the early novel *is* presented – we must bear in mind that this is not because women did not write, could not get published, or went unacclaimed. Women qualified on all these counts. It was only later that they were disqualified.

How do we explain this transition from prominence to negation? What does it mean when women who were esteemed in their own lifetime are later denied and dismissed? It could be the rationale of an 'individual case' when earlier this century attempts were made to prove that Aphra Behn did not even exist but such an explanation will not suffice when we are confronted with one hundred women whose work appears to have been systematically denied. Could it be that there is pattern and purpose in this treatment of women?

Germaine Greer (1974) certainly thinks so. She has referred to the 'phenomenon of the transience of female literary fame' and not just in relation to the novel. It is her contention that there have always been good women writers, in every area and every era, and that they always disappear. Since the days of Aphra Behn, she states, there have been 'women who have enjoyed dazzling literary prestige during their own

139

lifetimes, only to vanish without trace from the records of posterity'
(p. 784).

Once acclaimed, but now denied. This is the problem of women
writers and it is one which almost every woman critic of the past few
decades has addressed. Although in some circles it may be in order to
'accept' the disappearance of women writers as just a strange and
random quirk of literary history, such an explanation has no place
among women critics who have noted that the same fate does not await
men. Of course many male writers have fallen by the wayside with the
passage of time – but not *all* of them, not one hundred of them over a
century. And not those who were widely acclaimed in their own day.
Enough men are retained to allow for an uninterrupted tradition of men
writers. The same is not true for women.

In the eighteenth century women wrote in much the same (if not
greater) numbers than men, with much the same (if not more) success
than men, and attained much the same (if not more) status than men.
Yet not only has this achievement of women been edited out of literary
history, but a false version has been substituted in its place. A distorted
version which makes no mention of women's former greatness, but
which presents the birth of the novel solely in terms of men. So Daniel
Defoe's *Robinson Crusoe* (1720) is transformed into the first novel;
Samuel Richardson's *Pamela* (1740) becomes a turning point in the
development of the novel and is celebrated; Henry Fielding, Lawrence
Sterne and Tobias Smollett are accorded the status of proud parents of
this new form. And all this with little or no regard for 'the facts of life'.

How is such a falsified version of events to be explained? And is it a
practice of the past or one that persists in the present? For if the denial
of women's literary achievement continues to this day, what fate awaits
some of the current women writers who enjoy considerable literary
acclaim? They too could be consigned to oblivion so that future
generations would neither know nor suspect that there has been an
'explosion' in women's writing over the last few years. To those who are
yet to come could be bequeathed the legacy of Norman Mailer, Anthony
Burgess, Graham Greene and it could be as though Fay Weldon, Alison
Lurie, Edna O'Brien, Erica Jong, Marilyn French, Anita Brookner,
Mary Gordon, Margaret Drabble and so many more – never existed.

A range of explanations has been offered for the transience of female
literary fame. At one end of the spectrum are rationalisations that as
literature became increasingly institutionalised during the eighteenth
and nineteenth centuries, the decision making powers were concentrated
in the hands of men who not surprisingly found the good and the great
among their fellow men. While the novel was in a state of flux – as it was
in the earlier part of the eighteenth century -- while there was much new
activity and little form to follow, women had been able to find a place in

literature – as had Aphra Behn in the ferment which accompanied an earlier literary upheaval during the Restoration; but once things settled down, once patterns and experts and credentials were established, the traditional relationship of the sex reasserted itself, and the dominance of men as critics and writers soon became the reality of the literary world.

Such an account is plausible. It posits a male-dominated society and presumes a male-dominated literary tradition as a result. It is based on the premise that when women and men are equal, they will have literary traditions in which women and men are equally represented.

But there are women critics, past and present, who have gone further than this explanation of men finding in favour of their own sex; further even than arguing that men find fault with women. They have introduced the argument that in a male-dominated society, women are denied the right to their own creative resources and that these resources are *taken* by men to augment their own. And such a conceptualisation provides a very different framework for interpretations of the treatment of women writers.

It suggests that the men of letters are not blind to the achievements of women but instead of according them validity in their own right, men take from women what they want and leave the rest – which they determine to be of no value – to fade from view. So men writers and critics can deny women's creativity and appropriate women's efforts, claiming women's achievement as their own. So Eliza Haywood can be reduced in stature to a mere copier, her contributions appropriated by her male colleagues and in the eyes of the critics her achievement is denied and becomes the property of the men.

This explanation is plausible when applied not just to Eliza Haywood, but to all the women novelists of the eighteenth century. It is not just that Walter Allen or Ian Watt neglect to include the women writers, but that they deny the way the men profited from the women's work. The end result is that the reputation of men is built at the expense of women and, in the words of Matilda Joslyn Gage (1873/1980), this is nothing other than the *theft* of women's creativity.

Men 'steal the fruits of women's creative labour,' declared Matilda Joslyn Gage, and according to some contemporary women critics men continue to engage in such illicit literary practice. Hilary Simpson (1979) has pointed to the extent to which D.H. Lawrence, for example, appropriated the creative resources of women and passed them off as his own: and she has also noted that within the literary establishment there has been no accusation of foul play.

Without acknowledgment of his sources, D.H. Lawrence 'solicited notes and reminiscences from Jessie (Burrows), from his wife Frieda, from Mabel Dodge Luhan and others ... he also took over women's manuscripts and rewrote them, as in the cases of Helen Corke and

141

Mollie Skinner . . .' (p. 155). If one such distinguished man of letters could feel that it was in order to take these creative contributions to enhance his own achievement, then the possibility can be admitted that a collective of men of letters could act in the same way, and take the contributions of the early women novelists to enhance their own claims.

If F. Scott Fitzgerald could take the creative resources of Zelda Fitzgerald's diaries as his own property and build his novels upon them, if he could see *her* creativity as the raw material for *his* work – and if the law upheld his right to do this and prevented Zelda from publishing her own work (which it did) – then the practice of men stealing women's creativity is hardly outrageous or unknown (see Nancy Milford, 1975). It is accepted practice and as such its widespread presence should be expected.*

Were these but isolated examples, the evidence in support of Matilda Joslyn Gage's thesis of theft would not be so strong: but Samuel Richardson, Thomas Hardy and William Wordsworth are among other great writers known to have similar propensities for taking the writing of women and using it for their own ends. Further investigations in this area might even yield more examples of men at this work. Perhaps behind the dedications or ritual brief acknowledgments to 'the skills of the wife' there lie more examples of women's intellectual and creative resources being appropriated by men to lend substance to their own claims to fame. Marion Glastonbury (1978) certainly thinks so. With these examples in mind – and more to follow – it seems reasonable to suggest that it could have become routine for literary men to perceive women's work as available for their own use. And unless challenged why should they not continue with this arrangement?

However, whether the men of letters have overlooked women's writing, or whether they have exploited it, what can be stated unequivocally is that they have in effect suppressed the traditions of writing women. And the question that arises is – does this matter? Does it really matter to past, present, future generations of women – and men – that the early women writers have been removed from the literary heritage so it is as if they never existed? Is it not a little short of fanatical to dig up all these lost women and to confront the seemingly benign men of letters with an accusation which borders on being a charge of malign conspiracy? What possible difference can it make to writers, readers, or the world in general to know that contrary to what we've been led to believe, women as well as men (and even more significantly than men) participated in the conception and development of the new genre, the novel?

The answer depends on the role and importance that is attached to

*See also chapter 16 and the discussion on Maria Edgeworth

tradition. On the one hand it won't make an immediate and tangible difference to insist on the acknowledgment of women's literary contributions – or to challenge the massive censoring exercise that has been undertaken by men. It won't lead to direct improvements in women's poverty or bring a dramatic end to world wars. But on the other hand, the reinstatement of women's meanings and achievements within the culture could make a very big difference: Virginia Woolf thought that in the long run it would even make a difference to women's poverty and to the prospects of war.

No one can quantify but few would want to totally repudiate the influence that the cultural heritage of the past has on the attitudes and values of the present. And when that heritage of the past blatantly mistreats and devalues half of humanity why should it not be assumed that this predisposes the society which possesses such a heritage to mistreat and devalue human beings?

When, for example, the literary traditions represent the views and values of one small select group of men who agree that those who are not in their own image are not worthy of recognition – or that they are available for exploitation – then the divisions of good and bad, rich and poor, dominant and subordinate, are readily constructed. And the implications of such divisions extend far beyond the confines of the woman writer; they affect women, men, the whole society. This was the stand taken by Virginia Woolf in *A Room of One's Own* (1928) where she made the connections between women's cultural poverty and women's material poverty; it was the stand she took in *Three Guineas* (1938) where she linked the male domination of the cultural heritage with exploitation, violence and war.

She associated the injustice of the suppression of women's meanings with social injustice on a grand scale and she insisted that it was imperative – for the sake of society and the survival of the species – that women's *different* meanings should be reinstated in literary (and other cultural) traditions. Part of Virginia Woolf's argument was based on the premise that *one* world view – the view of men who exercised power – was simply not enough to provide full understanding about the way the world worked. It was too limited: too much was left out. It was the very perspective of those who did *not* exercise power, over whom power was exercised, and who were defined as alien, other, and unworthy of recognition, that was needed for a full view of the world, she insisted. It was her fundamentally simple assertion that women could see much that men – because of their position – could not; that women could see in men precisely what men could not see in themselves; it was this that led her to argue that the meanings forged by women, and represented in their writing, should be included in the cultural heritage. Only then would it provide a fair and reliable basis for

143

making sense of the world.

This is the argument of many women: that in the broadest possible sense, the knowledge of women's contribution could make a significant difference to the judgments and practices of the whole society. Women, whose philosophies are as far apart as Dora Russell's (1984), Elizabeth Robins's (1924), Kate Millett's (1970) and Adrienne Rich's (1980) have nonetheless agreed on the central point that male dominance means women's silence and that society can no longer afford to neither hear nor heed the voice of half of humanity. These women – and many others as well – have insisted that while ever women are kept out of the cultural traditions we have a heritage which is comprised of nothing other than political propaganda, in which the powerful decree their world view as the *only* world view, and in which those who differ from the powerful are censored, suppressed, outlawed. To reclaim and revalue the women writers men have removed is, in this framework, to do more than challenge a biased version of literary history: it is to take a political stand and to challenge the propaganda of a dictatorship.

Whether or not one subscribes to the theory that women should seize and control their own creative resources, or concedes the sweeping claim that the reinstatement of women in the literary traditions will lead to a better society, it seems safe to assert that the establishment of the existence and extent of the cultural heritage of women could make a big difference to women. A big difference to the image of women and to the reality of female achievements. While the catalogues, the library shelves, the bookshops, the reviews, the courses of study, all help to suggest that women are without a literary tradition, the belief in female inferiority is surely sustained. And it erodes women's confidence; it undermines the woman writer; it produces doubts. If women were indeed without a great literary tradition, much could be said for the advisability of inventing one, for the positive influence it could provide for women and women's literary endeavours. Such is the power of a tradition.

CHAPTER 7

———————•———————

*The myth of the isolated achievement**

But it is not necessary to *invent* a literary tradition for women, only to rewrite the records and to put in what men have left out. For we do have a splendid but suppressed tradition of women writers (by no means confined to novelists) which when reclaimed is not only a source of comfort, confidence and inspiration for contemporary women writers, or even a lesson in limitations for men; the uncovering of such a tradition also affords a fascinating and illuminating area of study which, for two centuries or more, has been denied.

It is a refreshing and rewarding experience to return to those many early women novelists and to trace among them the connections which form the fabric of a tradition. But these connections reveal more than the relationships among women writers; they also expose the means whereby the great number of female novelists who perceived themselves as part of a collective of women writers were later separated, severed from their sources, and reduced to a chosen, isolated few. So the pattern of isolated achievement which is the product of this imposed selection process is exposed as a myth when the women novelists are returned to their interconnected and collective context. This means that as we come to know more about Jane Austen and her relationship to other women writers, for example, the more we are obliged to question and qualify the judgments of men which have placed her in a category of her own.

While Jane Austen is presented as a solitary figure and a starting point of women's literary achievement – and then is followed by the rare and equally isolated examples of Charlotte Brontë, George Eliot, Virginia Woolf and (sometimes) Doris Lessing – we are being asked to accept a

———————

*With thanks to Joanna Russ.

most extraordinary premise. That only five women novelists are worthy of acclaim. Five women against tens of men.* Even more, that these five women are not just the sum total of women's literary achievement but that in their very isolation they are representative of women writers as a whole.

So absurd is this premise that one could be forgiven for expecting to find it a matter of discussion and debate among those authorities who explore and explain the literary traditions. But it isn't; the question – of why only five women?, or in the case of Jim Hunter's *The Modern Novel in English* (1966), why *no women at all?* – almost never arises. Literary criticism cannot be said to be characterised by an interest in the issue of why or how it has come to receive so few women in its ranks of the great. Rather it assumes the normalcy of this slight token representation, and then proceeds to build meanings and explanations on the *fact* that when it comes to women writers they are very, very few.

This is another form of falsification. It is not a *fact* that there were few women writers of fiction; the fact is that this is the impression which men have constructed. From the broad stream of women writers, the literary critics have plucked but a few and have *imposed* the pattern of isolation on the women by removing them from their milieu. And then they have gone on to develop theories about the absence of connections among women and to present the myth of the isolated achievement. Rarely is there any revelation that this isolation is man-made, created by the very men of letters who refer to it.

Women critics however have been known to have a different view and frequently determine to discuss these practices which men appear reluctant to disclose. For example, in *A Literature of Their Own* (1977), Elaine Showalter points out that while there have been novelists there have always been women among them, but that the extraordinary range and diversity of these writers has been reduced to a tiny band of the 'great' who are then made the subject of literary theories. 'Criticism of women novelists,' she writes, 'while focusing on these happy few has ignored those who are not "great"** and left them out of anthologies, histories, textbooks and theories. Having lost sight of the minor novelists** who were the links in the chain that bound one generation to

---

*According to Ian Watt, men began the novel in the eighteenth century: according to Jim Hunter (1966) there are *only* men in the traditions of the modern novel. His publication, *The Modern Novel in English*, includes not one woman; instead there are D.H. Lawrence, James Joyce, Ernest Hemingway, John Dos Passos, Graham Greene, Joyce Carey, Samuel Beckett, William Golding, James Baldwin, Angus Wilson, David Storey and John Updike.

**I would make it clear that 'great' and 'minor' are terms of which we should be highly suspicious. They are political terms.

the next we have not had a very clear understanding of the continuities in women's writing' (p. 9).

Overall, women have been removed from the mainstream literary tradition to the point where – in England* in poetry and drama, they have virtually no presence at all. And in the novel, only five: an elite of five who are the focus for theories on women's writing. Bad enough if there had been only five; outrageous when there have been hundreds (thousands?) whose writing has been denied. Yet if we are to have any appreciation of women's literary heritage we must reclaim and study these writers who have been lost. For only if we can free ourselves from the bias and limitations of familiarity with the favoured few, only if we can escape from the myth of the isolated achievement, will we be able to look at women writers collectively and see among them the 'imaginary continuum, the recurrence of certain patterns, themes, problems and images' that have linked women writers in their own time and bound one generation to the next (Elaine Showalter, 1977: p. 11).

This is not the only reason that it is important to unearth our literary foremothers. 'When the memory of one's predecessors is buried,' writes Joanna Russ out of her own personal experience as a writer, 'the assumption persists that there were none and each generation of women believes itself to be faced with the burden of doing everything for the first time. And if no one ever did it before, if no woman was ever that socially sacred creature, "a great writer," why do we think we can succeed now?' (1984: p. 93).

As far as Joanna Russ is concerned it is not just more women writers we need to reclaim; it's more writing by women with whom we are already familiar. For the myth of the isolated achievement suggests not just solitary women – but a solitary work of art. How many people think Charlotte Brontë only wrote one novel – or one good novel – *Jane Eyre*, asks Joanna Russ? With one exception her students thought this was the case. And, writes Joanna Russ, 'I must add, embarrassingly, that I shared my student's reaction, that I assumed *Jane Eyre* to be Brontë's best book (and the others vaguely dull) until a description Kate Millett gave of *Villette* (in *Sexual Politics*) sent me on a hunt for *Villette* which eventually broadened to include *Shirley*, *The Professor*, Charlotte Brontë's juvenilia, Jane Austen's juvenilia ... Fanny Ratchford's books on the Brontës, and Emily Brontë's Gondal poems' (1984: p. 64). A whole literary heritage.

But the discovery of another woman writer, or of another book by a known woman writer, does not mean that these works can easily be

*This may not be the case in the United States where Emily Dickinson can be included in the literary traditions.

introduced into the literary heritage. Joanna Russ wanted to acquaint her students with *Villette* but soon encountered the problem of women's absence from the world of print. For it was almost impossible to get *Villette* into the classroom as 'there was not one edition of *Villette* in print in the United States, whether in paperback or hard-cover, and,' she writes, 'I finally had to order the book (in hard-cover, too expensive for class use) from England. (The only university library edition of *Villette* or *Shirley* I could find at the time were the old Tauchnitz editions; tiny type and no leading)' (1984: p. 63).

Despite the difficulties, however, it is imperative that these writings of women be reclaimed. For when we go back to the many books written by the many women writers we come to realise – partly because the authors tell us themselves – that far from feeling cut off from one another, it was much more common for them to see the bonds between them which brought them together. In the absence of formal education, university training or unchaperoned access to the wide world, it was to other women novelists that women writers turned for guidance. 'The personal give-and-take of the literary life was closed to them,' writes Ellen Moers (1977). 'Without it, they studied with a special closeness the work written by their own sex, and developed a sense of easy, almost rude familiarity with the women who wrote them' (p. 64). It is 'borrowings', influences and commonalities that characterise women novelists, not isolation at all.

Because women's literary traditions have for so long been suppressed, it comes as something of a shock to find that women have always had 'a literature of their own'. As Elaine Showalter has said, the idea is so much at variance with the received wisdom, it takes some getting used to. Yet once it is accepted that women have written so much for so long, the beliefs about women and writing – and about the practices of literary critics – are altered dramatically. For whenever women writers have been 'considered in relation to each other, the lost continent of the female tradition has arisen like Atlantis from the sea of English literature' (Elaine Showalter, 1977: p. 10). Not only does the study of the relationship among women writers challenge to the core the theories about literature and women – and the criteria of the critics – but it is through such a study that the female literary tradition emerges. Which is why we cannot accept Jane Austen as an example of isolated achievement, why we are victims of a man-made-myth if we continue to see her as a writer who came from nowhere – and started it all.

Jane Austen may have been excluded from the literary milieu of men, declares Ellen Moers (1977), but she was perfectly at home in the world of writing women and well aware of their work. Even her own correspondence makes this clear: women writers are regularly reflected upon and their influence on her writing referred to. If today Mary

Brunton and her novel *Self Control* (1811) has failed and faded, it should be noted that it exerted great influence on Jane Austen at the time she was revising *Sense and Sensibility*, and starting *Mansfield Park*. So good did Jane Austen find Mary Brunton's writing she was nervous about the effect it would have on her own work. Mary Brunton was 'clever' and Jane Austen hoped she wasn't 'too clever', that she wouldn't intimidate, for in the face of such achievement, Jane Austen was frightened of finding that her own story and characters had been forestalled.

'She did however read and reread the Brunton book and said (jokingly), "I will redeem my credit . . . by writing a close imitation of 'Self Control' . . . I will improve upon it",' writes Ellen Moers (1977: p. 67).

Ellen Moers goes on to say that it could be argued that Jane Austen achieved the perfection she did precisely 'because there was a mass of women's novels, excellent, fair and wretched, for her to study and improve upon. Mary Brunton and the rest of the ladies were her own kind; she was at ease with them.' The literary tradition in which Jane Austen placed herself contained women, not men, and the 'fact is that Austen studied Maria Edgeworth more attentively than Scott, and Fanny Burney more than Richardson; and she came closer to meeting Mme. de Staël than she did to meeting any of the literary men of her age' (p. 67).

The uncovering of all the connections between Jane Austen and the other women writers who preceded her is not then just an interesting inventory exercise. It is the uncovering of a literary tradition from which she has been summarily removed. Placing her back in the context of women writers helps to dismantle the artificial structure of the favoured few: it calls into question the practices of the literary establishment and helps to map the contours and commonalities of women's writing.

Great satisfaction can be found in seeing the links between Catherine Morland – Jane Austen's heroine of *Northanger Abbey* (1818) – and her predecessors in the novels of earlier women writers. A 'victim of romantic fiction', Catherine Morland follows in the footsteps of Charlotte Lennox's Arabella (*The Female Quixote*, 1752) and bears a striking resemblance to Agnes Maria Bennett's Rosa, of *The Beggar Girl and her Benefactors* (1797). And the similarities between Jane Austen and Agnes Maria Bennett do not end with their heroines Catherine and Rosa; before the traditions of the early women novelists were suppressed it was not unusual to find men of letters comparing the achievements of these two writers, with Samuel Coleridge, for example, according them the same highly commendable status (see Dorothy Blakey, 1939: p. 54).

Northanger Abbey reveals in detail some of the connections between Jane Austen and her fiction-writing foremothers – so much so, that in 1927 Michael Sadleir wrote an article entitled *The Northanger Novels*.

And did we not know that 'Miss J. Austen, Steventon' was on the subscribers' list prefixed to Fanny Burney's *Camilla* (1796), we would find from the pages of *Northanger Abbey* that this novel, along with Fanny Burney's *Cecelia* (1782) and Maria Edgeworth's *Belinda* (1801), were familiar to the author, and were held in high esteem.

Catherine Morland (of *Northanger Abbey*) frequently discusses the novels of Ann Radcliffe, especially *The Mysteries of Udolpho* (1794) and *The Italian* (1797) – and the influence of the gothic novel plays a not inconsiderable part in the plot, and the plight of the heroine. Eliza Phelp Parsons, who wrote about sixty novels, has two of them mentioned in *Northanger Abbey* (*The Castle of Wolfenbach: a German story* (1793) and *The Mysterious Warning* (1796) and Regina Maria Dalton Roche, another 'best seller' of the 1790s, is included in the discussion of women's novels when reference is made to her book *Clermont* (1798). And these are by no means all the women novelists quoted by Jane Austen.

Not all of them, of course, are held up by Jane Austen as great novelists whose work is worthy of emulation. But then it is not necessary to praise or to imitate one's predecessors in order to be the inheritor of a tradition they have forged. One can just as easily criticise as commend the work that has gone before. It is not mandatory that Jane Austen or any other woman writer should like or approve of her literary links: what is mandatory if she is to be part of that tradition is that she should know of them. And clearly Jane Austen was aware of her surrounds, even if we are not.

So when Ian Watt (1957) takes Jane Austen out of context and presents her without peer or precedent, it must be remembered that Jane Austen did not see herself in this way. And if we are to get away from the myth of the isolated achievement, if we are to escape the belief that women writers of significance are few and far between, if we are to understand and appreciate the breadth and depth of women's literary endeavours then it is the word of Jane Austen and not that of Ian Watt which must serve as our guide.

Not that Jane Austen is alone in evaluating the writing of women and their influence on her work. Many are the eighteenth century women novelists who acknowledge their dues and debts to their female literary peers. For Fanny Burney, Eliza Haywood's *The History of Betsy Thoughtless* (1751) was an inspirational model for *Evelina* (1778). Charlotte Smith, Elizabeth Inchbald, Amelia Opie and Mary Brunton all praised Frances Chamberlain Sheridan and declared that her *Memoirs of Miss Sidney Biddulph* (1761, 1767) was a favourite and a source of great influence on their work.*

To see the precursor of Jane Eyre in Elizabeth Inchbald's *A Simple*

---

*Which is more than her son did. Many of the scenes from *Memoirs of Miss Sidney Biddulph* are to be found – unacknowledged – in his work.

Story (1791 and to trace the effects of Sarah Fielding's *The Governess* (1749) on the writing of Maria Edgeworth is to begin to appreciate some of the rich and varied interweavings that are the substance of women's literary traditions. And still this is only a beginning, only a superficial survey of a few of the more obvious connections in some of the (comparatively) better known early women novelists. Imagine how much more complex, comprehensive and considerable women's literary heritage would be if women had been accorded the same opportunities as men to establish the size and shape of 'a literature of their own'. The same amount of time and space devoted to a similar number of female literary personages; the same number of women authors as men on the literary shelves, in the bookshops, as subjects for study in literary courses; the same number of great women writers as men have claimed for their own sex.

As early as 1792, and by no means the first woman to give voice to such an opinion, Mary Wollstonecraft claimed that women possessed the same human creative potential as men. Which means that there is nothing inherent in the nature of women which would lead to the sexually differentiated pattern of isolated achievement. There is no good reason that women should not be equally represented in the galleries of the literary great. No good reason, that is, in relation to women; only good reasons that relate to men, and dominance.

CHAPTER 8

———————•———————

Male romance

'Romance: picturesque falsehood' *O.E.D.*

Jane Austen read 'women's novels'. So too did the reverend gentleman, her father. What is frequently 'forgotten' is that he also made his regular visits to the circulating library for the latest novel by a woman, who explored the implications of many a moral question of his time. And Mr Austen's reading habits were by no means unusual for a man in his position.

'Women's novels' are also plentiful today, but few if any are accorded the same superior significance they enjoyed in Mr Austen's lifetime. Rather the term 'women's novel' (which can be variously used to mean written by women or written for women, but with *women* always as the key word) has come to be one of relative abuse. It is used to disparage a diverse field of writing and to classify it as undeserving of critical attention.

Little distinction is made among women's novels and this is often illustrated not just in the more esoteric literary publications but in reputable periodicals and newspapers where all the fiction written by women can be grouped together under one heading (see Dale Spender, forthcoming). Little differentiation is made in relation to form, style or purpose. Whether the novels are written with a mass audience or a small, specialised audience in mind, the entire range of women's novels can be swept into a single category, defined by the prefix woman.

Needless to say, there is no such broad category of *men's novels*. Even the subcategory of mass market novels addressed primarily to men is broken down yet further into westerns, thrillers, spy stories, detective stories, etc. But for women's novels, there is virtually only *one* category, and it is referred to derisorily as romance.

Thus all women's fiction can be reduced to a stigmatised 'single

152

issue'. And this is not a feature of the writing which – *if examined* – would reveal that it was as various and as worthy of the same number of subdivisions as the writing of men. It is a feature of male dominance which lumps together all that is 'other' and assigns it an undifferentiated and inferior status. And it is this male dominance which has determined the fate of women writers, past and present, and which, regardless of the content, has cemented the links between women's fiction and the 'dastardly romance'.

Given the current mass publications of companies such as Mills & Boon and Harlequin* there are probably more 'romances' among women's writing than there is any other 'specialised' category. But even so, this does not justify the reduction of women's writing to one theme, nor does that theme warrant the vilification it has incurred (see Margaret Jensen, 1984). Yet because now women's novels are held in such low repute, many women's novels of the past have retrospectively been tarred with the same brush and have been deprived of the merit that was once bestowed. It is assumed that no person of refinement or taste would descend to the vulgar level of reading romances – in the twentieth century or the eighteenth century. And so while it is unlikely that the reverend gentleman of the twentieth century eagerly awaits the latest *mass* publication of Mills & Boon, so it is presumed that the reverend gentleman of the eighteenth century did not seek the 'mass' publication of the circulating libraries. But to project present values on to the past is to make a grave error.

It is partly because *mass* audience and vulgar *romance* are so closely interwoven in the received wisdom that such a mistake can arise. The eighteenth century is held to be the age in which this new entity, 'the reading public', emerged and erroneous assumptions about 'the masses' and their reading tastes of the time are frequently made. For the novel was not the only innovative form in print to make its appearance during this period. This is the era of the rise of the newspaper as well. The thrice weekly *Tatler* commenced publication in 1709 and the daily *Spectator* started in 1711. A whole host of periodicals, journals and magazines followed, including the successful experiment of the *Gentleman's Magazine* in 1735. And these were just the 'newspapers' of men: those of women had an equally expansive and

---

*The number of romances sold, is often not appreciated: Harlequin, one of many publishers in this field has a 28 per cent share of *all* paperbacks sold in Canada and a 10 to 12 per cent share of *all* paperbacks sold in the USA. *Publishers' Weekly* (USA) estimates that there are over 20 million readers in America who annually buy half a billion dollars' worth of romances (Margaret Jensen, 1984: p. 15).

colourful beginning (see Alison Adburgham, 1972, for an account of the growth of women's newspapers and magazines). All these journalistic endeavours began to feed into and to respond to the recently created, growing, and highly influential fee-paying audience – the reading public.

The introduction of these new media and the establishment of a popular reading audience helps to suggest that during the eighteenth century there developed a mass audience, the counterpart of today. With their statements that they had watched England become a nation of readers (and that the readers were too partial to pulp) Dr Johnson and other commentators on the social scene help to reinforce this impression of a mass audience with vulgar tastes. No doubt it did seem to them that 'everyone' had become a reader and that literary standards had been broadened – or lowered: when contrasted with the aristocratic influence on literature and the extensive illiteracy of the early 1700s the growth of the reading public would have assumed spectacular proportions and the expansion in the books and newspapers that were available would have appeared quite disturbing. But literacy and novel reading was nowhere near as widespread (and vulgar) as these commentators might lead us to think.

Such reading activities were still very much the province of an elite. In 1790 Edmund Burke estimated that of a population of six million only about eighty thousand were literate. And not all who were literate would buy or read novels or newspapers. This is a far cry from today. And to impose on the eighteenth century the contemporary links between mass audience and substandard women's novels/romance, is a fanciful rewrite of history – a picturesque falsehood.

Alexander Pope could deplore the 'degradation of letters' that he believed went with the shift from aristocratic patronage to the vulgarities of the bookseller and the market place, but the percentage of the population to whom he referred as 'lowering the tone' was probably not much different from the percentage who attend opera and ballet today. Newspaper and novel reading was not the entertainment sought by 'the masses' but the leisure and pleasure pursuits of a small and privileged group.

Like Dr Johnson, Alexander Pope was comparing the new developments to what had once been and his references to the masses and their philistine tastes are more of a protest against the movement of literature from the control of the aristocratic few than they are an accurate description of the reading public of the time.

Alexander Pope thought it outrageous that those who had not had the benefit of a classical education should suddenly become influential in the world of letters. The very emergence of 'an audience' had introduced new considerations on the literary scene: those with literary pretensions were being asked to take the audience into account, to address themselves to the issues of what the reading public would like to read, and want to buy. Such gross commercial concerns were an anathema to Alexander Pope. He resented the rise and power of the bookseller; he condemned the new breed of upstart critics who needed only to be able to read to feel competent to comment and criticise – without regard to the old established rules for literary criticism. Even women, for so long completely excluded from the educated literary world, were finding their way into print and were an appreciable part of this audience. No wonder literature was being debased.

But Alexander Pope's protest must be taken in context. It reveals more about his values than those of the reading public. For by today's standards this new audience was small and select indeed. Despite Alexander Pope's accusations to the contrary, the 'reading public' was comprised predominantly of educated people who saw themselves – and wished to be seen by others – as persons of refinement and taste. These were the people who were reading – and praising – some of the novels of women, and they were particularly proud and protective of their distinguished status. It is through their eyes, as well as our own, that we should try to see and appreciate the contribution that the women writers made.

That the reading of novels was an activity enjoyed only by a few is not surprising, given the social and political conditions of the day. First of all there were the barriers to literacy which ensured the exclusion of the majority of the population. Although literacy could be acquired at home (and even a high percentage of the women writers state that 'they taught themselves to read') this demanded certain prerequisites – like books, for example. Alternatively, reading and writing could be learnt at school, but this too required a prerequisite in the form of a school. And schools for the majority of the population were not in abundant supply. In 1788, one quarter of the parishes in England had no school at all and where there were schools for working class children they were provided on a haphazard basis which was matched by haphazard attendance. When in 1792 Mary Wollstonecraft wrote *A Vindication of the Rights of Woman*, one of her main grievances was the absence of educational provision.

School fees of even a few pence a week were sufficient to be prohibitive for many when the average labourer's wage amounted to about £1 per week. Besides, children did not ordinarily have money spent *on* them. Rather, they were required to earn it, to assist with family expenses. Sometimes they were wage earners from as early as five years of age. And even the children who did attend school usually did so for only a short period and generally on a very irregular basis.

Anyway, school attendance of itself was no guarantee of literacy. Quite intentionally many students were not taught to read or write.

Literacy can mean more than the mechanics of reading and writing. It can mean access to ideas. Which is why the extension of literacy has often been blocked (see Raymond Williams, 1975). When from certain groups in society submission has been expected, dire warnings have been delivered on the dangers of allowing them to become literate. The argument has been that such people would only be unsettled if they were able to read and write. They would no longer be content to cheerfully perform the menial tasks required of them. So – for their own good – it would be better if they were kept illiterate. Ignorance being bliss.

Such arguments have been used against women; they were used against slaves in the United States and against the working classes in England.

'Reading, writing and arithmetic are very pernicious to the Poor,' wrote Bernard Mandeville in 1723 in his *Essay on Charity and Charity Schools*. Such expertise was to be discouraged and, instead, the poor were to be put to work as early as possible. 'Men who are to remain and end their days in a laborious, tiresome and painful situation of life, the sooner they are put upon it at first, the more patiently they'll submit to it ever after.' The same rationalisation was applied to women. When there was a widespread belief that a wife who could read and write could well prove to be troublesome, literacy was not at the top of the list of desirable skills in women.

However, the lack of educational opportunity to learn to read and write was not the only factor which worked to keep the novel reading public very small. The cost of books – and novels – must also be taken into account. Novels averaged about three shillings bound and one shilling unbound, and this put them out of the reach of most of the population. According to Daniel Defoe, more than half the population were without the bare necessities of life and in such circumstances a novel – even at one shilling – would not have been an item of purchase.

Besides, assuming that most people even wanted to read novels (a hypothetical assumption indeed), when would they be able to do so? When would they have the time, the privacy – or the light to read by? Working people were employed during the daylight hours, six days a week, virtually every week of the year. They lived in crowded and dark conditions (there was a window tax) which made lighting for reading a necessity. Yet candles too came into the luxury category. And when Sunday came round and for many, relaxation and enjoyment were the order of the day (I suspect that this applied primarily to men!), how favourably would private reading rate (granted that it were possible) in comparison to the more gregarious social attractions, such as gin sipping?

The theatre was different. Because of the social opportunities they provided, plays sometimes attracted bigger audiences in the sixteenth and seventeenth centuries than novels did in the eighteenth. And literacy was not necessary in order to enjoy a play by William Shakespeare or Aphra Behn. Nor was great wealth a requirement. Less than one pence a performance was needed for entry to the pit. So, ironically, plays could provide more 'mass' entertainment than the novel.

Ironically, because unlike the *women* novelists, the *male* playwrights (and with the exclusion of women playwrights, like Aphra Behn, only the men are left), have not been charged with lowering the standards of literature and dismissed for their inferior contribution. The reputation of William Shakespeare has not suffered because he had *mass* appeal. On the contrary, his popularity is generally cited as one of his strengths.

And the male novelists have not been outlawed because of their mass appeal, or on the grounds that because they were popular, they wrote romance. *Moll Flanders* is praised and *Pamela* is celebrated and both are preserved at the forefront of the literary heritage, despite the fact that they were both popular and about heroines and 'love'.

It is only the women novelists who have been brought into disrepute for their supposed popular appeal, their penchant for petty romance, and their consequent debasement of literature.

The link between women writers of the eighteenth century and vulgarising romance seems spurious indeed. It seems as though when men are popular or write of romance it is called by another name which does not disqualify it from preservation in the canon.

For it simply is not the case that the one hundred women writers of the eighteenth century were all sensational and sentimental and were read only by frivolous women who had nothing better to do than spend their time on 'escapist' literature. Novel reading was confined to a small segment of the population and it was often the most 'respectable' segment who would not have been pleased with titillating romances. Because novel reading could be seen as far more refined and decent than play going it was often favoured in the most decorous households: at the upper end of the social scale where puritanical fathers and husbands could take exception to their women folk attending the public and rowdy entertainment of the playhouse, no such objections could be raised against the private and reflective practice of reading. In places where play going could be considered coarse and condemned, novel reading could be considered uplifting and condoned. It could even be positively encouraged where the novels were judged to have an edifying purpose.

And throughout the eighteenth century, many women novelists had been steadily moving towards a more serious moral justification for their work. This shift is reflected in the writing of Eliza Haywood: when in the work of one woman we see the titillating *Love in Excess* (1719) giving way to a consideration of responsibility and ethics in *The History of Betsy Thoughtless* (1751) we become aware of the extent to which the rationale for novel writing had changed.

It is trite to dismiss this development as an example of chameleon writers who turned their pens to churning out whatever their fickle audience required. The 'reading public' is not an isolated entity; it is as much influenced by writers as it influences them. While women novelists did reflect the values of their age – and of the reading public of which they were part – they also helped to foster and shape some of those values. They made a contribution towards the demand for *serious* literature.

There was more than one reason for their move in this direction. It was an area that interested their audience. It was also an area that had advantages for the woman writer: any criticism which might be levelled at the dubious character of the independent female author could be more easily deflected by reference to the educational and uplifting nature of their writing. Furthermore, writing about serious matters was more likely to lead to the writers being taken seriously. Although most of the women novelists wrote for money, this does not mean that they all thought themselves without merit. Many of them sought to be accepted as good writers.

Elizabeth Singer Rowe was one woman whose work represents some of the initial shifts of the time. *Letters Moral and Entertaining* (1729-33) marks a transitional phase from religious literature to polite fiction: while undoubtedly an early epistolary novel it is also a series of 'sermons' for young ladies, and for almost a century it was recommended for the education of young women.* It is the precursor of Samuel Richardson's *Pamela*, not only in content and epistolary style, but in its moralising as well.

But many of the women novelists did not confine morality to the necessity for female chastity. They had a much broader vision and explored a range of political issues through the medium of fiction. Elizabeth Inchbald used *A Simple Story* (1791) to develop understandings about Catholicism in an often hostile Protestant England. Charlotte Smith raised questions about authority and democracy. Lady Morgan unapologetically justified her fiction writing with the purpose of

*See Clara Reeve (1785/1970) for example.

exposing the plight of Ireland. And far from endorsing the Richardsonian principle that a lecherous man and a virtuous woman can be happily united in the end, Mary Brunton wrote of *Self Control* that her intentions had been 'to show the power of the religious principle in bestowing self-command and to bear testimony against the maxim, as immoral as indelicate, that a reformed rake makes the best husband' (Alexander Brunton, 1842: p. 22).

Such writers were not frivolous; they were not sensational, they were not titillating and they were not without merit. They were accorded stature in the literary world of their time. To read them could confer an aura of distinction and breeding on the reader – Jane Austen's father included. To remove these women from the literary records on the grounds that they were mass market and vulgar is just as false as removing them on the grounds that they *only* wrote romance or novels of manners. Not simply because of the double standard which allows manners to women and morals to men (see Eliza Haywood and *The Female Spectator*, page 104) but because the often highly formalised concern with manners meant something quite different then. Novels of manners for those who defined themselves and their position in society by their manners (as many of the novel-reading public did) were not to be treated lightly or scorned.

To imply however that all the women writers of the eighteenth century were motivated by high concerns which were executed with admirable artistic integrity is just as limiting as any assertion that they were all base and wrote bad prose. It is the *diversity* of women's writing – then and now – which has been denied. There were good, bad, and indifferent women writers in the eighteenth century as there are in the twentieth century and although it is simplistic and silly to equate good with a small audience and bad with a mass audience, the expansion of the novel-reading public which came with the advent of the circulating library – and the pressures this introduced – opened up the field for women writers. For it was not just that the circulating libraries which were opened by booksellers in search of new markets extended the novel-reading public; it was that more manuscripts were suddenly required. More manuscripts which had to be written very quickly if new books were to keep pace with the new demand. And many women rose to this challenge: the pens flowed at great speed.

Started in 1742 by entrepreneurial booksellers, the circulating libraries became increasingly popular, and one of the most successful publishers in this area was William Lane, of the Minerva Press. He began his venture in about 1770 (although the name 'Minerva' did not appear until 1790) and was the first to establish circulating libraries outside London. He published hundreds of novels (the majority by women) and although according to a number of critics few of them were of permanent value (an assertion I do not automatically accept), many of the most popular women writers of the day were on the Minerva list. For example, Agnes Maria Bennett's *The Beggar Girl and her Benefactors* was a 'best seller' of 1798 and other novels of hers were also published by Minerva. Regina Maria Roche, Eliza Parsons and Mary Meeke were 'best selling' Minerva writers and Mrs Howell, Isabella Kelly, Elizabeth Bonhôte, Anna Maria Mackenzie, Agnes Musgrave and Mary Charlton all featured in the Minerva catalogue.

In 1790, writes Dorothy Blakey (1939), '"Lane's General and Encreasing Circulating Library" contained over ten thousand items, a figure which gives some weight to the claim of the proprietor in 1794 that

> from the number of Books in this selection, and the manner in which it is conducted, it can now boast being the first in London' (p. 13).

However, while it was the biggest circulating library, ten thousand volumes is not a lot – particularly not by today's standards;* and the fees of the circulating libraries were still beyond the reach of most of the population.

'The price of a subscription at the Minerva,' writes Dorothy Blakey (1939), 'like the price of the novels themselves, rose steadily during the period. In 1798, subscribers who paid a guinea a year were entitled to all the new publications. ... The highest class of subscription in 1798 – three guineas – entitled the holder to eighteen volumes in town or twenty four in the country. ... Yearly subscribers in the country had to pay for "Boxes with locks and keys" which were provided by the proprietor, and for "carriage and porterage" to and from the library. They were also requested to pay the postage on their letters' (p. 116). This was far too expensive for most of the population. And while there were lower rates, they were not likely to lead to a mass influx to the circulating libraries.

'Readers who could not afford a yearly subscription could still be accommodated at the Minerva,' continues Dorothy Blakey. 'They were required to deposit the value of the books they took away and to pay fees which were fixed in various ways ... in 1798, plays cost twopence a day. ... Other books were rented by the week. In 1798, folios, new quartos, and books valued at over a guinea, cost a shilling; duodecimos, threepence' (p. 118). And new books were only allowed out for four

---

*The London Library has currently more than one million volumes, which serves as a basis for comparison.

days!

Circulating libraries did contribute to the growth of the reading public and certainly provided an opening for a cross-section of women writers. But like all new ventures, the circulating library was welcomed by some and condemned by others. Leigh Hunt was among those who gave it his stamp of approval and while still at school was a subscriber to the Minerva, 'the famous circulating library in Leadenhall Street', and ever afterwards 'a glutton of novels' (Dorothy Blakey, 1939: p. 113). Not everyone however was like the Austen family – 'great novel readers and not ashamed of being so' (Jane Austen to Cassandra, December 18th, 1798).

The power of novel reading to corrupt or to enervate was a belief held by more than a few and novel selling and novel reading were often undertaken in secrecy. But such resistance to this new form does not for a minute mean that all the novelists were of a uniformly low calibre. There are many in more recent times who have attributed to television the power to corrupt and to enervate, but this does not make all television programmes uniformly bad.

If we want to explain the dismissal of early women novelists from the literary heritage is is necessary to go much further than the misleading accounts about mass audiences and sensation, sentimental 'blotterature'. For in the eighteenth century, many of the women novelists who were writing for a small, refined and morally conscious audience, were held in very high repute. It is only *since* their time that the pervasive notion of silly novels by silly women novelists has held such sway.

The systematic devaluation of women writers and their concerns is more a product of the nineteenth century. By this time women's position as novel writers was so well established that there were more than mutterings among the men about the dangers of women's pre-eminence in the genre. That novel writing had become a debased profession because of the influence and presence of so many women was a frequent assertion and could well be explained in terms of a male backlash to female success. There is no shortage of examples of men's hostility towards the woman writer (see Elizabeth Helsinger *et al.*, 1983, *The Woman Question: Literary Issues 1837–1883*), and there is no doubt they were doing their best to deter her from venturing on to the literary scene. The wife and mother, apart from being labelled as limited by her experience, was branded as irresponsible, selfish and unwomanly if she were sufficiently assertive to take up her pen – and to profit. But women who were unmarried were also warned against literary indulgence. Again, there are numerous examples of this determination to dissuade women from competing with men: from Robert Southey's rebuke to Charlotte Brontë to J.M. Ludlow's pronouncements in the *North British*

Review:

> . . . what is to become of the women who remain unmarried, and yet
> have gifts such as fully qualify them to do good service in literature?
> Gently, and with all reverence must we tell them – Endeavour to find
> for your gifts other employments. Precisely because your lot is a
> solitary one, do not make it more so by literary labours. . . . Because
> you have leisure, which the wife and mother has not, spend that
> leisure upon others. . . . To you belongs the daily working, the
> drudgery of all charitable institutions. . . . Who does not know some
> one old maid who is the blessing of a whole circle? (*North British
> Review*, 1853, 19, pp. 169–71)

But although the men might decry, the women would not desist.
Because women continued to write, and even went so far as to
'deceive' when they adopted male pseudonyms around 1840, the
strategy of *containing* women's writing came into play. It is here
that the categorisation of women's novels as romance makes its
appearance.

Women who persisted with their literary endeavours were enjoined –
implored – to confine themselves to what they knew. They were advised
that their strengths lay in their exploration of women's world, in
romance, the domestic scene. And once this categorisation of women's
writing ability was pronounced, it was soon achieved. If not in the
writing of women, certainly in the minds of men. And so we have in the
containment of women, a male romance, a 'picturesque falsehood'
constructed in male interest.

For once the rule could be established that women's novels were *by
definition* doomed to the domestic scene it was no longer necessary to
regard them as an exploration of human nature. Women's efforts could
be reduced to the scale of a little love story, and therefore were of no
account.

So the division and differential status between women's and men's
writing was imposed. It is not a distinction which arises from an analysis
of the writing – for more often than not the writing of women is not
analysed. It is a distinction which is based on sex and power. Once the
distinction was made there would be no more *Pamela*, where a romance
was invested with universal significance. Henceforward, women writers
could be appreciated for their drawing room observations, their
emphasis on manners, their attention to fine detail; they could be
motivated by concerns of the heart. In contrast, men writers could be
appreciated for their largesse and vigour, their emphasis on morals, their
broad canvas of the wide world; they could be motivated by concerns of
the mind.

With the imposition of such a division the stage is set for the devaluation of women's writing. Looking forward, Virginia Woolf becomes 'limited and ladylike ("tragedy at the tea party" . . .)' (Joanna Russ, 1984: p. 90). Looking backward the women writers of the eighteenth century are denied their serious concerns: they are lumped together under the deprecating rubric of *romantic fiction* writers. It seems that it is not – as is frequently asserted – that they wrote romances for a mass audience that is at the source of their dismissal, but that they were women.

That Jane Austen, Maria Edgeworth, Fanny Burney and many more good women novelists wrote 'love stories' is not in dispute. What is at issue is the way in which the love stories of women have been devalued. For it is not that male novelists from Samuel Richardson to D.H. Lawrence have not written love stories, but that when they have done so they are called by a different name – and are accorded a more deferential status. D.H. Lawrence is not labelled as a writer of romantic fiction: his reputation would be eroded if he were.

That women writers have had their mobility constrained and their access to certain areas of life reduced, is not at issue. But so too have men. And what is at issue is that the partial experience of half the population – that of women – is judged to be narrow, second rate, specialised, while the partial experience of the other half – that of men – is held to be supremely significant and universal. Such a value judgment which is associated with the status of the sex and not the quality of the experience leads to the absurd situation where Jane Austen is patronised as a prisoner of the country parsonage while the parameters of T.S. Eliot's office pass without critical comment.

Even if it were the case that women writers were unable to directly participate in the more turbulent and treacherous ebb and flow of life (and to assume that male experience is more turbulent, treacherous and 'alive' than that of women is questionable indeed) there is no evidence that direct participation in the entire gamut of human involvements and emotions is necessary in order to portray them convincingly in writing.

It would be difficult to defend James Joyce against the charge that his solitary walks around a few streets of Dublin did not provide a broad and balanced view of life: yet such limitation did not prevent him from perceptively portraying part of the human predicament. Nor should women be outlawed for the limitations imposed on them. Not just because limitations in themselves can provide the fabric for cutting the cloth of humanity, but because women writers have so frequently transcended those limitations.

Much praise was accorded to the author of *Evelina* who knew so intimately the 'top' and the 'bottom' of life, and when it was revealed

163

that Fanny Burney was the writer there was astonishment that such a young woman who had led such a supposedly secluded life could have been so familiar with the wide world and so shrewd about the human condition:

> 'But *where*, Miss Burney, *where* can, or could you pick up such
> characters? *Where* find such variety of incidents, yet all so natural?'
>   'O Ma'am, *any*body might find who thought them worth looking
> for!'
>
> (Fanny Burney, Diary, MSS, Berg, pp. 843-4).

The male world does not have a monopoly on human experience, even though men have a monopoly on determining the significance of experience.

Women novelists are not consigned to the low status category of romantic fiction because of either the quality of their experience or the quality of their writing. Far more important as the deciding factor is their sex. Numerous studies have been undertaken on everything from essay writing to publisher's rejection slips and academic editors' partiality (see Gene Maeroff, 1979) which suggests that the sex determines the status of the writer, and as Philip Goldberg (1974) found, many years ago, the same piece of writing is judged to be *mediocre* when thought to flow from the pen of Joan Smith, and *impressive* when thought to be the work of John Smith. Not that it is always necessary to set up 'experiments' to detect this practice in operation. From the 1840s onwards, when females began to adopt male pseudonyms, women writers have been aware that, in principle, male authors get a fairer hearing and a better reception. Which is why women have taken various steps to avoid the inferior connotations of their sex.

When it was believed that *Mary Barton* was written by a man, the *Athenaeum* (1848) was full of praise for the author's grasp of politics and the fair and forcible portrayal of the working classes (p. 1050). But when known to be written by a woman, the whole tenor of the criticism changed. It is not the political acumen of Elizabeth Gaskell but her ability to promote sympathy which becomes the focal point. Her emotionalism, her lack of objectivity are soon 'discovered' and the broad canvas of class politics is reduced – by the critics – to a 'sweet and fragrant' love story. The literary records are tampered with and rewritten to the extent that Elizabeth Gaskell's 'mental palate fed always as it was on the fruit and frothing milk of her nursery days, kept a nursery simplicity and gusto. And in consequence her whole picture of life is touched with a peculiar dewy freshness, shimmers with a unifying, softening light' (see Anna Walters, 1977:

p. 38).

This is the woman writer who not only provided a fair and forcible account of class politics but who, in Victorian times, dared to write about prostitution, unmarried mothers and dominated wives – from a woman's point of view. But it is her sex – and in complete defiance of her writing – which ultimately determines her (minor) place in the history of letters. Elizabeth Gaskell may have been consigned to the derided category of 'romantic fiction' but it is not her writing which places her there.

The rule is that women and romantic fiction go together and it is not coincidence that both are devalued. Which is why it is understandable that even today women who want to be taken seriously as writers on the *human* condition will go to considerable lengths to try and avoid the connotations of woman, and romance, with their writing.

Elaine Showalter (1984) has drawn attention to this denial of sex among many contemporary women writers. It is a defence against the pejorative labelling of *woman* writer and her classification with the contemptible and circumscribed 'romance'. Not only do these women writers want to be free of the links of woman and writer, states Elaine Showalter, they want to be free of the contaminating links with the woman reader as well. For to be seen to write about women or for women is to be damned. It is to be placed in a ghetto. Hence the insistence by many established women writers that they are not women writers; hence the denial of their sex.

There is Doris Lessing, writes Elaine Showalter, who 'has been outspoken for years about her wish to dissociate herself from her devoted female reading public', and she is by no means alone. Many other distinguished women writers 'have been protesting that they are not "women writers" or "women's writers" (apparently worse) but *writers only*, less concerned with "female subjects" or "women's lot" than with the human predicament...' (p. 1). As if to write about half the population is to write *not* about the human predicament. Some of these protesting writers – who simply happen to be women – inadvertently reveal that they share the values of a male-dominated society when they assume that women are not fully human subjects.

What so few fail to confront is that it is the value attached to the sex, and not to the writing, which is primarily responsible for women's exclusion from the literary heritage. The U.K. Book Marketing Council can provide statistics to show that fewer men buy novels and fewer men read novels, and if numbers alone were the rationale for a 'ghetto' it would be comprised of 'men's novels', novels by or about men – which would be classified as the minority view. But of course to use *men* as a *qualifying* term is a nonsense: male is the norm, it is female which is the qualifier. No wonder Iris Murdoch has chosen a male persona for six of her first person novels. A simple strategy for enhancing status and ensuring *human* significance.

It is not at all difficult to see why women writers who are consigned to the subhuman 'women's world' want to repudiate the limitations of their sex. And when the choices consist of denying their 'womanliness' or changing the values of a male-dominated society, it is not surprising that some should select the former although – as Elaine Showalter suggests and I fully agree – it would be preferable if they were to try the latter: if they were to direct their attention to those who define the categories and do the consigning. For the devaluation of women, women's world, women's lives, is a manifestation of male dominance; it is a devaluation that applies to all that is female and from which not even writers are exempt.

To be seen as a woman writer is to be seen in a subcategory and to be concerned with subsidiary issues. It is to be 'minor' by definition – and all this can take place without any examination of the writing. For the bulk of women's writing which is dismissed has not even 'benefited' from the light of literary criticism.

The terms 'women's novels' and 'romance' are often used interchangeably and to signify deprecation. Whether this is the result of the low status of women being transferred to 'romance', or the low status of 'romance' being transferred to women, is not possible to determine. But as there is little justification for the wholesale devaluation of women, so too is there little justification for the wholesale devaluation of 'romance'. As Margaret Jensen (1984) has pointed out, such dismissal generally occurs *before* and not after an examination of the facts. The deprecation of women's writing is not based on a close study of the writing; rather the term 'romance' is used to indicate that such writing does not warrant close study. Once classified as 'romance', women's writing can be disqualified from analysis.

Which put very simply means that you don't have to read 'women's novels' to know they are awful: you just call them 'romance' and then all persons of proper taste and judgment will know such novels are not worth bothering about. By such unfair and unthinking means the bulk of women's writing can be consigned to the 'does not count' category. And this has happened to women's writing of the past while it still happens to women's writing in the present.

There can be no clearer example of this than that provided by John Cawelti (1976) in his study of popular literary culture, entitled *Adventure, Mystery and Romance*. A professor of English and humanities and presumably aware of the scholarly precepts that demand unbiased evaluations before judgment is pronounced, John Cawelti purports to analyse the elements of popular novels. Yet he feels no necessity to discuss or assess the 'largest single selling category in the paperback market' (Margaret Jensen, 1984: p. 23) – that of romance. His dismissal of this genre is total: he 'deals with romances in one and a half pages, the same amount of space that he devotes to the discussion of alien beings' (Margaret Jensen, 1984: p. 22). John Cawelti assumes that the only reference which needs to be made to this enormous body of writing is that it exists. No reasonable person would expect it to be evaluated.

To completely exclude such writing from consideration is not, however, the only reaction to the bulk of women's writing. 'When romances are not ignored,' writes Margaret Jensen, 'they are vilified as is no other category of popular fiction' (p. 23). Women's writing is maligned in a manner that has no counterpart when it comes to the writing of men. But when it is realised that this disparagement of women's writing is not based on an examination of the writing, the only conclusion that can be drawn is that it is based on sex; that it is the woman and not the unanalysed writing which is at the source of 'the vilification of romance'.

Now anyone who has defied convention and actually studied women's writing would not want to contend that all women writers are excellent and all romances works of art. But most would want to suggest that it is nonsense to lump together all women's novels and to call them 'romance': most would want to suggest that it is ridiculous to reduce women's writing to one undifferentiated category, and then to brand it with the pejorative label – romance. Not only is this practice unjustified in terms of the diversity of the writing: it is unjustified in terms of the bad name it gives to romance.

For there is nothing inherently inferior or deficient about romance. When it is the substance of men's writing it can become an exploration of human relationships and provide an insight into the human condition. And to think that the status of the *woman writer* could be improved by the repudiation of romance is just as misguided as thinking it could be improved by the repudiation of sex. The derisory connotations of *woman* and *romance* are equally undeserved and there are good grounds for seeking to reclaim both woman and romance, instead of subscribing to the inferiority of either.

Admittedly, romance is such a maligned category it's an uphill battle trying to invest it with *positive* meaning. But to continue to dismiss romance while it is inextricably interwoven with the status of women is to do an immense disservice to women's writing which may, or may not, fall into the category of romance. It is to continue to make it possible for women writers to be dismissed out of hand whether they are writing now or have written in the past.

For one of the most successful strategies for burying female writers of the past has been to label them as the authors of romance. And the issue cannot be that they were *not* women writers or that they did *not* write romance. The issue must be that this is nothing other than name calling. That the literary establishment has outlawed women writers by giving them and their writing a bad name and by establishing the reality that there is no need to read women's writing, for it can be taken for granted that it's no good.

If any consistent romancing has been going on, any sustained attempt at 'picturesque falsehoods', it would appear to be more in men's minds than women's writing, more a product of the fanciful imagination of the men of letters than of women's pens. For women's writing is every bit as diverse, as wide-ranging, as perceptive, profound, insightful, valid and as good, as that of men's; any verdict to the contrary is but a romance.

In this chapter I have examined the many indictments of women's writing that have been used to substantiate the conviction that would have one hundred women writers of the eighteenth century being inferior to five good men. And I have found that not only is there insufficient evidence for this judgment, but that women have been 'framed'. Most of the charges and much of the evidence that has been brought against women by the men of letters has been false.

That it is right and proper to exclude one hundred women writers because they were of popular, 'mass' appeal and therefore debased literature, is a judgment based on an accusation without foundation; they were not 'mass' in today's terms and no more 'mass' than some of the men of the time who were not condemned for their popular appeal – and besides, to appeal to a broad spectrum of readers is not by definition to be a bad writer who does not warrant attention. The whole issue of vulgar women writers who produced mass, meretricious, and mundane romances – and lowered the tone of literature – is an irrational and inconsistent case, constructed after the event, and without recourse to the facts of the writing.

The removal of these women writers from the literary heritage cannot be explained by the subsidiary nature of their concerns, the silly nature of their content, or the sensational nature of their style. And it cannot be explained by comparison with their male colleagues, for the men who wrote in similar vein have been retained within the tradition. The only explanation that suffices to account for women's crime – is their sex.

One hundred women writers have been outlawed not because of their writing, but because they were women. And there could be no more blunt statement of this double standard as it operates in literary evaluations than that provided by Norman Mailer: to be a great writer, one must have balls.

Once more we confront the traditions of the men of letters. In order to write well, about the human condition, and to be numbered among the great, it is almost always necessary to be male.

This is a picturesque falsehood; it is one which the elaborated code of literary criticism has helped 'to come true'.

PART III

Literary Achievements

CHAPTER 9

---•---

Women's view: women critics

To go back and assess the achievement of those one hundred women novelists in their more than six hundred novels is out of the question in this particular context. Such an exercise could take a lifetime – for a community of scholars – and be the substance of a series of books. Yet it is important to provide an indication of the worth of the writing of these badly treated women. Some small glimpse of what has been dismissed, some small appreciation of what has been lost, is necessary if we are going to insist that the novel was created by mothers. But where to start? How to choose? How even to begin to find all these novels (many of which appear to have been lost for ever), how to read them and to assess the achievement of the writers?

Initially I thought it would not be possible to formulate a sensible basis for selection. But that was before it occurred to me to look to the women critics for guidance. And of course one reason I was so slow to turn to the 'women of letters' was because I didn't know they were there.

But there have been women critics: there have been women critics for almost as long as there have been women novelists. And they have linked themselves with the women writers not simply by their efforts to assess the quality of women's work – but by coming to share much the same fate as the women they wrote about: oblivion.

Yet there they are, and found some of them can be, and a detailed study of their comments is not necessary for it to become patently clear that this is another area where the values of a woman stand in stark contrast to those of a man. Women commentators have had an entirely different perspective on writers and writing from their male counterparts.

In the first place I can find no mandatory separation of the writer and the writing in the approach of the women critics. On the contrary, they reveal a radical departure from 'literary convention' by placing almost as much emphasis on the *life* of the writer as on the text, and it is refreshing and rewarding to see a woman's circumstances and the conditions in which the writing was undertaken accorded almost as much attention as the writing itself.

Far from seeing this as a sign that women have not met the 'standards' of male critics, I find this framework of the female critics part of the evidence that women have formulated different 'standards' from men. And the standards women have set up are predictably different. It is understandable that women critics should have concerned themselves with the *personal* details of the existence of women writers – whether they were educated, married, had children – because these personal factors could play such a crucial role in the writing life of a woman in a way that is not matched in the writing life of a man. Whether a man is married or has children has no systematic correlation with his literary productivity, but marriage and children can be determining forces in the literary productivity of women.

When snide comments are made about a writing woman's reluctance to marry it is not necessarily the sometimes suggested 'frigidity' which is at the source: it can be the very real consideration of whether marriage and motherhood will mean the end of a literary career. No fantastical fear this, as the life and death of Charlotte Brontë reveals.

When Sydney Owenson procrastinated about her marriage it was not coyness or coquetry but critical concern which caused her to delay: she had established for herself a literary career and against great odds had won an independent life, and she was aware that marriage and motherhood could mean an end to all she had set out to do. She was not to know that she would not have children. She could not know how far Charles Morgan's support for her writing would extend after marriage: while assuring her that she would be free to write *he* would not have been blamed if after marriage he had insisted that she was free to write *after* his comforts had been attended to. So when she was considering his offer of marriage it had to be in the context of whether she was prepared to abandon her work – for love. Few men are placed in such a painful predicament. The fact that the personal dimensions of love, marriage, parenthood, are absent from critical evaluations of great male writers is primarily because they do not affect the writing; not because it is a 'superior' sort of discussion when such considerations are omitted.

Who Henry Fielding was married to seems to have mattered little to his writing, but if his sister, Sarah Fielding, had married – and had seventeen children – chances are that she would not have written at all. Had Elizabeth Inchbald's husband lived longer – and had she had children – she might not have given us the volume of writing that she did; and once widowed she was adamant that she wanted to write, to be independent, and that she would not marry again despite the many offers that she received. Why should anyone be surprised by this decision and how could anyone divorce the wife and mother from the writing?

When Mary Wollstonecraft and Mary Brunton died in childbirth after each having written only two novels, we have the stark facts about the way women's literary careers can come to a sudden end. When the Duchess of Newcastle, Aphra Behn, Sarah Fielding, Elizabeth Inchbald, Maria Edgeworth, Amelia Opie, Lady Morgan – and Jane Austen herself – are seen to be writing women who had no children, it simply is not possible to exclude the issue of children from a discussion of women's writing.*

When women needed the support (or non-interference) of a husband to be able to write (as did Anne Finch, the Duchess of Newcastle, Ann Radcliffe, Lady Morgan) or needed to leave their husbands in order to write (as did Eliza Haywood, Charlotte Lennox, Charlotte Smith) then the choice of a husband can make a much more significant difference to the writing than the choice of a wife. Male critics may have been able to ignore the choice of a spouse or the presence of offspring in the lives of male writers but for female critics these factors are of fundamental concern in their discussion of women writers.

Because women critics were women and writers they invariably experienced some of the complications and contradictions of female authorship and it is to be expected that they should comment on the common concerns of women writers. It is to be expected that their criteria for assessment should be different from those employed by men.

But attention to the conditions under which women writers work is not the only element which distinguishes the female critic from the male. In studying the women critics who have traced the development of the novel, what emerges – and what for me has been the source of some amusement – is the widespread reluctance among them to endorse men's good opinion of the achievement of the male sex. Again and again 'subversion' sets in as the great male tradition is called into question by

*See also Tillie Olsen's indictment of the world of letters and her list of women without children who have been writers: 'Willa Cather, Ellen Glasgow, Gertrude Stein, Edith Wharton, Virginia Woolf, Elizabeth Bowen, Katherine Mansfield, Isak Dinesen, Katherine Anne Porter, Dorothy Richardson, Henry Handel Richardson, Susan Glaspell, Dorothy Parker, Lillian Hellman, Eudora Welty, Djuna Barnes, Anais Nin, Ivy Compton-Burnett, Zora Neale Hurston, Elizabeth Madox Roberts, Christina Stead, Carson McCullers, Flannery O'Connor, Jean Stafford, May Sarton, Josephine Herbst, Jessamyn West, Janet Frame, Lilian Smith, Iris Murdoch, Joyce Carol Oates, Hannah Green, Lorraine Hansberry' (1978: p. 31).

the women. After reading so many accounts which have emanated from men on the glories and greatness of the early male novelists – and the shortcomings of the females – I found Clara Whitmore's (1910) 'reversal' not simply satisfying in terms of justice, but entertaining as well.

She simply cannot see why so much has been made of the men whom she finds limited – and boring – and she cannot understand why their writing has been so lavishly praised as realistic, when from her perspective it is full of fanciful illusion. Commenting on the contributions of Henry Fielding, Samuel Richardson, Tobias Smollett and Lawrence Sterne in the period 1740-1771, she challenges the claims that have been made for them with her statement that 'The plot of most of their fifteen realistic novels is practically the same' (p. 24), and she finds this all rather tedious:

> The hero falls in love with a beautiful young lady, not over seventeen, and there is a conflict between lust and chastity. The hero, balked of his prey, travels up and down the world where he meets with a series of adventures, all very much alike, and all bearing very little on the main plot. At last fate leads the dashing hero to the church door, where he confers a ring on the fair heroine, a paltry piece of gold, the only reward for her fidelity, with the hero thrown in, much the worse for wear, and the curtain falls with the sound of wedding bells in the distance (Clara Whitmore, 1910: pp. 24-5).

Clara Whitmore is not at all impressed. It's what men *would* find exciting and a cause for celebration, isn't it, you can almost hear her sigh? And with this dramatically different view from the 'other side' we have a much altered context in which to assess the justification for the fulsome flattery that critics like Ian Watt have accorded the men.

To me it is clear that the male critic finds that the women writers all seem very much the same – and are unconvincing; the female critic, however, finds the men are all very much the same – and are unconvincing. And if the world of letters had been the province of female critics as well as male we would be the possessors of differing views on the achievements of women and men writers. But of course, the critical establishment has been dominated by men with the result that the judgment of men has prevailed. So we possess a literary heritage which is based on the view of men that women writers are undifferentiated, are all 'much the same', are unconvincing, and are not worth preserving. Men tell only half the story but they have been in a position to have it accepted as the real story; and we have been left with the literature of men.

I do not want to insist that the view of Clara Whitmore is 'right' and that of Ian Watt 'wrong': I do not want to simply reverse the value judgments (although, admittedly it is tempting and I have no objections to reparations). Rather I want to make a case for women being equally represented in the critical establishment and for their views being accorded equal weight, so that both sides of the story can be heard, and so that the writing of both sexes can find a place in the literary heritage. Encountering the consistent praise for women writers among women critics (and conversely, encountering the consistent undermining of the achievement of men) has convinced me of the need for women and men critics, of women's and men's writing, for women and men readers. Only if and when women critics have equal status with men can we expect to have a literary heritage that is comprehensive, representative, and based on a consideration of the human condition. Such an eventuality is a long way hence.

Part of the reclamation of women writers consists of the reclamation of women critics who have worked within a very different tradition and constructed a very different literary heritage. Like Clara Whitmore they have not only challenged the pre-eminence of the men, they have also asserted the greatness of women. And it is these women critics (who did read the novels and who made their own selections) who can provide some guidance on the one hundred women novelists of the eighteenth century. There is among them a consensus about which women writers were great and worth preserving, and while there are problems in accepting the untested value judgments of critics, I offer as my rationale the fact that I am working within a female critical tradition, when I select a few from the many early women novelists.

The first 'woman of letters' I can find who concerns herself with an assessment of fiction is Clara Reeve who in 1785 wrote *The Progress of Romance*. She was herself a novelist (the author of the highly praised Gothic novel, *The Old English Baron*, 1777, among others) and in her book of literary criticism she was interested in tracing the origin and development of 'romance', and women's contribution to the genre. 'Romance' then did not enjoy the despised status it does today but was used as a more general term to designate fiction, and Clara Reeve returned to the 'romances' of the antiquities, and to the earlier French romances of glorious happenings among the good and the great, as she presented a history of 'the story'. And as she brought the history more up to date, male fiction writers like Henry Fielding and Samuel Richardson were included in her progress of romance. To Clara Reeve, 'romance' was an honourable form even if some writers fell short of its standards, and if its increasing popularity during the eighteenth century aroused some resistance.

Her commentary takes the form of a discussion with three characters – who are themselves blessed with romantic names: Hortensius,

Sophronia and Euphrasia. These three assess the many different romances and their relative merits and among the women writers accorded praise are Sarah Fielding, Charlotte Lennox, Frances Sheridan, Frances Brooke and Elizabeth Rowe. Some women writers who are mentioned are not ranked among the great: Elizabeth Griffith, for example, 'though moral and sentimental does not rise to the first class of excellence', though her novels 'may fairly be ranked in the second' and while 'very unexceptionable' they are 'entertaining books' (p. 45).

Poor Susannah Minifie Gunning however fares not nearly so well. All her novels 'are in the class of mediocrity', according to Euphrasia, who adds, 'if I were to mention such it would make our talk too long and tedious' (p. 45).

In the very early stages of the novel Clara Reeve was differentiating among women writers, putting to one side Elizabeth Griffith and Susannah Minifie Gunning and reserving a place in the literary tradition for Sarah Fielding, Charlotte Lennox, Frances Sheridan, Frances Brooke and Elizabeth Rowe, and as some of these names keep recurring in the work of later women critics we see the beginning of a female tradition of novel writing in the process of construction. Not all later women critics were to share Clara Reeve's opinion, of course. Frances Sheridan falls by the wayside, which is regrettable and not entirely explicable for the *Memoirs of Miss Sidney Biddulph* (1761) is to my mind a classic which ranks with *Evelina*, and reveals that Frances Sheridan bequeathed more than her talent to her son who made considerable use of her novel as a source for his own writing. But I must acknowledge few regrets for the fading of Elizabeth Rowe although I would want to insist that no discussion of *Pamela* would be complete without reference to Mrs Rowe's *Letters Moral and Entertaining* (1729–33): if it is in order to comment on the imitations of *Pamela*, why is it not in order to address the issue of the imitations IN *Pamela*?

By 1843 when Anne Elwood (another writer of works that were not literary criticism – *An Overland Journey to India*) gave her view in *Literary Ladies of England,* we find that additional names have been incorporated in the female novel-writing tradition. Anne Elwood singles out Charlotte Smith, Elizabeth Inchbald, Fanny Burney, Mary Wollstonecraft, Ann Radcliffe and Mary Brunton – and of course Jane Austen – as the writers who are worthy of a place. Julia Kavanagh (1863) (author of *Nathalie, Adele,* etc. and *French Women of Letters*) holds up some of the same women again as deserving of study and praise in her book *English Women of Letters.* Her work indicates that at least in 1863 there was an awareness of the extent and diversity of the female tradition and the women she includes in her evaluation are much the same as those who have been discussed (or will be discussed) here. She brings back Aphra Behn, retains Sarah

Fielding, and gives prominence to Fanny Burney, Charlotte Smith, Ann Radcliffe, Elizabeth Inchbald, Maria Edgeworth, Amelia Opie, Lady Morgan – and Jane Austen.

With *Women's Work in English Fiction* (1910) – Clara Whitmore's contribution to an assessment of the female literary tradition – we find that the one hundred women novelists before Jane Austen have settled into a pattern; we have a selection, with some variations, but in which familiar names can be found. Eliza Haywood returns to take her place along with Sarah Fielding and Frances Sheridan; Fanny Burney, Charlotte Lennox, Charlotte Smith and Elizabeth Inchbald are all duly acknowledged and praised; Clara Reeve stands alongside Ann Radcliffe and Harriet and Sophia Lee in the discussion of the Gothic novel; Maria Edgeworth, Lady Morgan, Amelia Opie and Mary Brunton all find acclaim in Clara Whitmore's frame of reference.

These are by no means the only women critics, of course, but reference to even these few is sufficient to serve as guidance for the selection of women who warrant further discussion. And the existence of these women critics also helps to show that even while the men have been 'mainstream' and have been putting forward the achievements of men, there has been 'alternative', equivalent (but obscured) activity among women critics, who have continued to put forward the literary achievements of women.

CHAPTER 10

Sarah Fielding and misrepresentation

'*Little is known* of the life of Sarah, the third sister of Henry Fielding, the novelist' (1969: p. ix: my italics), begins Malcolm Kelsall in what has become the ritual introduction to early women writers. Despite her own very considerable achievements as a novelist – sufficient to challenge the supremacy of her brother during his lifetime – Sarah Fielding (1710-1768) is, nevertheless, defined in relation to *the* novelist, Henry. But one should be grateful for small mercies: without such a relationship to a famous man we would undoubtedly know much less about Sarah Fielding than we do. However, it is still galling to consult the 1969 Oxford University Press edition of her novel *The Adventures of David Simple* and to find that the chronological table of *her* life begins three years before her entry into the world, with the date of birth of her brother Henry.

Nowhere can I find a chronological table on Henry which even includes the birth of Sarah, although this could have been an 'event' in his life in contrast to the fact that his birth had no relevance in hers. But while the birth of a man may be granted precedence in the life of a woman, it seems that the reverse does not apply. In my search through numerous chronological tables on the lives of men, I can find no such table that begins with the birthdate of a woman before his time, no matter what his relationship, or her fame.

Still, as efforts have been made to document the life of Henry, they can be drawn upon, on occasion, to provide some of the details of the life of Sarah. Whenever the two shared a common existence – as they did when young and when Sarah dwelt with Henry to care for his motherless children – the picture of Sarah's life is more complete than it is for most of the other women writers in the eighteenth century. Yet it is significant that when Sarah Fielding's presence is no longer required in Henry's establishment, and she leaves (as she did upon his remarriage), she fades almost entirely from view. There is something rather eerie in finding that because of the sex bias in values and scholarship, Sarah Fielding virtually does not exist except in Henry's presence.

In many respects, Sarah Fielding's 'elusiveness' is characteristic of women's treatment in historical records and is a product of women's marginality. That even the information on her memorial tablet in Bath is inaccurate, is symptomatic of the 'mistakes' in the documentation of women's lives:

> In this City died Sarah, second daughter
> of General Henry Fielding,
> By his first wife, daughter of Judge Gould,
> Whose writings will be known
> As incentives to virtue and
> honour to her sex
> She was born in 1714 and died April 1768.
>
> Her unaffected manners, candid Mind,
> Her Heart benevolent and Soul Resigned
> Were more her praise than all she
> knew or thought
> Though Athens' Wisdom to her Sex She Taught.

She was born 1710: she was the third and not the second daughter; her father was General Edmund Fielding, not Henry.

That she warranted a memorial stone at all, however, is indicative of the esteem she enjoyed in her own lifetime. Sister of Henry Fielding, second cousin of Lady Mary Wortley Montagu, friend of Samuel Richardson, and much admired among the leading literary figures of her day (including Elizabeth Carter, Elizabeth Montagu and Catherine Talbot), if Sarah Fielding has been eclipsed it is not because she was a crass writer producing books for the discredited circulating libraries. 'Her novels were discussed by the blue-stockings and subscribed for by the aristocracy' (Malcolm Kelsall, 1969: p. ix). So this is another case of women being damned if they do, and damned if they don't: damned to obscurity if 'popular', and equally damned if 'refined'.

While Sarah Fielding came from a semi-privileged background which places her more within the traditions of the literary lady, it was by no means a secure background either materially or emotionally. There was much psychological drama in her early life and it has echoes in her later writing. In 1718, when she was seven years of age, her mother died, and for a short period her great aunt was in charge of Sarah and the other five children. But there was family friction when her father remarried (a Roman Catholic) and the new stepmother (then called a 'mother-in-law') and new siblings were introduced to the household. Evidently the family quarrels were all too much for Colonel Fielding, who soon decided to disperse the family: the three older girls were sent to boarding school, Henry was sent to Eton, and the two youngest were despatched to their maternal grandmother, Lady Gould.

But Lady Gould was convinced that her grandchildren were not being provided for in accordance with her late husband's will and there were many recriminating scenes when she accused the Colonel of improperly using the children's money for his own use. Lady Gould decided on a law suit to gain custody of the children and to control their finances (I doubt whether a woman would have been able to act in this way in the nineteenth century) and Henry, who sided with his siblings and his grandmother, ran away from Eton to join the family faction against his father.

Lady Gould was obviously right in her judgment. On 28th May, 1722, the Lord High Chancellor ruled against Colonel Fielding and awarded the control of the children (and their inheritance) to the grandmother. Which given women's position under the law seems remarkable indeed.

Obviously it was no secure and happy childhood that Sarah enjoyed. While details of the court case are interesting today – particularly in the controversial matter of what the children were given to eat under their father's roof, for it was Lady Gould's contention they were not even properly fed – the examinations, and cross-examinations, must have been traumatising for the children. And in the days when it was considered almost sinful to go against one's father, it would have been extremely difficult for the children who were confronted with the necessity of having to do so.

There is however a positive element to emerge from this unfortunate situation. Because the facts of Sarah Fielding's life were presented in Chancery, we do have information about her which might otherwise have been unknown. For example, we know that after the law suit the three older girls were sent to a boarding school run by Mrs Mary Rookes. And it must have been quite a good school given Sarah's later scholarly achievements.

She became renowned for her learning. As Malcolm Kelsall has said, 'She was something of a bluestocking. She read English poetry and French criticism, and knew enough of the classics to write a psychological study of Octavia and Cleopatra. It is recorded that she could repeat "a thousand lines at a Time" of classical poetry and she had enough Greek to translate Xenophon's Socratic *Memorabilia* and *Apology* (the latter work at one time reprinted in Everyman's Library)'

(1969: pp. ix-x).

No benefit of Eton for Sarah Fielding but a great deal of self-education and some assistance with Latin from the father of her friend, Jane Collier. Arthur Collier not only taught Sarah Fielding, he thought she was an excellent pupil and Henry was also aware of her talents. Hester Salusbury Thrale was another of Dr Collier's students and he told her that 'Henry Fielding, who encouraged his sister when she read and wrote in English, became jealous when she was able to read Virgil' (see Katharine Rogers, 1982: p. 29).

But despite her learned background, Sarah Fielding simply could not afford to live the life of a refined literary lady and the reason she took her immodest step into the commercial world was the same reason as women from Aphra Behn onwards have taken to writing novels – to earn her living. Not that we know much about the circumstances that brought her to this decision.

After the court records state that Sarah Fielding is to be sent to boarding school, and she and her brother go their separate ways, there is very little information on Sarah Fielding until 1744, when her first novel (and but the first part of it) *The Adventures of David Simple* appeared in print. This, however, was not the first time she had been published: again, in relation to Henry a little more can be gleaned about Sarah's literary life.

Joseph Andrews was published in 1742 and chapter 4 of Book II contains a series of letters, one of which is entitled 'Leonora to Horatio'. Of this letter, Henry Fielding said that it 'was written by a young lady' on reading the preceding letter. According to Jill Grey (1968), 'it is generally presumed that the young lady in question was Sarah. Sarah is also presumed to have been the author of a story in *A Journey from this World to the Next* which first appeared in Henry's *Miscellanies* on 12 April 1743, as told by Anne Boleyn' (p. 13).

The combination of pressing economic need and the opportunity for writing and publishing were no doubt sufficient to set Sarah Fielding on her novel-writing path, although it does seem very superficial to describe the more than twenty years of her life from 1722 to 1744 as the period in which she made up her mind to write novels.

What we do know of Sarah Fielding during this period is that from 1722 she lived with her grandmother in Salisbury; that during the 1730s her brother was increasingly successful in the literary world with four of his plays being produced in six months in 1730; that in 1733 her grandmother died and she and her sisters continued to live on in the house chaperoned by an aunt. We know that she had a close friendship with Jane Collier – who also turned to writing and with whom Sarah Fielding later collaborated on the novel, *The Cry* (1754). And we know that in 1737, when her younger brother came of age, her grandmother's estate was sold and the money divided up among the grandchildren. But it was not enough for Sarah Fielding to support herself for when *The Adventures of David Simple* was first published, it contained the following 'Advertisement to the Reader':

> Perhaps the best excuse that can be made for a woman to write at all, is that which really produced this book – distress in her circumstances, which she could not so well remove by any other means in her power. If it should meet with success, it will be the only good fortune she has ever known.

It sounds as though thereby hangs a sorry tale. It is clear that Sarah had not led a life of happy revelry.

However, she did enjoy the only good fortune she had ever known: *The Adventures of David Simple* met with substantial success. There was only one cloud on the horizon: because it did so well numerous readers concluded that it was the work of Henry – of course!

Henry Fielding had been 'out of town' while Sarah had written her novel, although no doubt he knew that the work was in progress and almost certainly he recommended it to his publisher, Andrew Millar. But on his return, and the advent of publication, Henry decided, for many reasons, to add his name to Sarah's work. In order of decreasing generosity the reasons were – to help with her sales, to testify that she was indeed the author, to defend himself against the charge that he had written a slanderous publication attacking the legal profession, and to add the characteristic Fielding stamp of quality to a work which bore the family name, by correcting and polishing Sarah Fielding's style (see Malcolm Kelsall, 1969: p. x).

So in the second edition of *The Adventures of David Simple* (which was required but a few months after the first) the 'Advertisement to the Reader' was replaced with a preface by Henry Fielding. He vouched for the fact that Sarah Fielding was the author and had received but a few hints and a little advice from him. But the second edition was not quite so much Sarah's work as the first had been and Henry graciously acknowledged his contribution:

> There were some grammatical and other errors in stile in the first impression, which my absence from town prevented me from correcting, as I have endeavoured, though in great haste, in this edition . . ., small errors, which want of habit in writing chiefly occasioned and which no man of learning would think worth his censure in a romance; nor any gentleman in the writings of a young woman (*David Simple*, 1782 edn: pp. iv-vi).

In the preface to a successful novel by a woman, few more blatant statements could be found on the superiority of men and their literary authority. And more than one critic has declared that Henry's interference in 'polishing' Sarah's style (and in 'advising' her on her future writing) was less than beneficial for Sarah. 'The influence of her brother drove her to dissipate her interest,' states Malcolm Kelsall (1969: p. xii) who has made a comparison of the first and second edition, and who has attempted to analyse the extent of Henry's 'interventions'.

But Henry's influence aside, *The Adventures of David Simple* brought Sarah Fielding considerable acclaim. Arthur Murphy, an established literary critic of the day, held Sarah Fielding to have a lively and penetrating genius and, writes Malcolm Kelsall, 'There can be few novelists of the time whose style was to win the approval of Lady Mary Wortley Montagu, whose psychological penetration was praised by Samuel Richardson' and who, when *The Lives of Cleopatra and Octavia* was later published, prompted the comment from the critic in *The Monthly Review* (July 1757) that 'It was superfluous to compliment the author of David Simple upon her merits as a writer' (1969: p. xi). As a novelist, Sarah Fielding enjoyed high esteem during her own lifetime, and for many decades afterwards.

On December 7th, 1756, Samuel Ricahrdson wrote to Sarah Fielding to pay his own compliments, and to convey those of another great critic:

> What a knowledge of the human heart! Well might a critical judge of writing say, as he did to me, that your late brother's knowledge of it was not (fine writer as he was) comparable to yours. His was but a knowledge of the outside of a clockwork machine, while yours was that of all the finer springs and movements of the inside.

The critical judge was Samuel Johnson, and the references to the superiority of Sarah Fielding's writing – in some aspects – in comparison to that of her brother, were sufficiently frequent and sufficiently credible that if Henry had been the type disposed towards jealousy in the face of a woman's achievement, this was an instance where he had due cause.

Yet while Henry Fielding's achievement takes pride of place in the literary heritage, that of Sarah Fielding has, in Germaine Greer's words, virtually sunk without trace.

In those esoteric places where the work of Sarah Fielding is commented upon, it is generally caustic criticism which prevails. (This is not the case with women critics who continue to praise her work.) *David Simple* is pronounced to be not a real novel, with David Simple himself not a real character, and Sarah Fielding unable to tell a real story. These criticisms are reasonably accurate – if *real* is taken to mean the *reality* of today, if Sarah Fielding is assessed *only* in the light of contemporary conventions. But why should *David Simple* be judged solely on the basis of current standards and labelled as 'weak' when with a slight shift in perspective to the terms of its time, it can be seen more positively, as an achievement? No such monodimensional standard is applied to the early men novelists who are assessed both in their own context and against the current background, and who can therefore be congratulated for their contribution rather than simply condemned for their contemporary shortcomings. Few would suggest that Daniel Defoe, Henry Fielding or Samuel Richardson write real stories or present real characters when compared with novelists of today, but they are accorded an historical place in fiction and are highly praised for their introduction of realism. And if it is permissible for the fathers of the novel to be assessed in the terms of their time, it seems quite in order to extend the same indulgence to the mothers of the novel. In this context, Sarah Fielding made a remarkable contribution.

The subtitle of *David Simple* announced that the novel contains 'An account of his travels through the Cities of London and Westminster in the Search of a Real Friend', and David Simple – as the title suggests – is very simple. He is an 'innocent', devoid of duplicity, who is repeatedly disappointed by the double dealing which he meets. But because he is simple and sentimental, he serves as a vehicle for Sarah Fielding to satirise society and to make her ironical observations on the misleading appearances of life.

As David Simple is decidedly 'wet' he in turn has been satirised by critics and commentators. In a letter to Samuel Richardson, Catherine Talbot (27th June, 1744) cannot resist the temptation to mock David Simple's quest, and she wittily comments that it is not a friend to solve his problems he is in search of – but a wife. This was not a dismissal of *David Simple*: on the contrary, women writers and critics then – and since – have shown a distinct partiality for *David Simple* and its frame of reference. It served as a model for many a novel for years to come. The innocent educated by experience in the world was a favoured form right through to Fanny Burney and Jane Austen who – like Sarah Fielding – have also been seen in danger of creating 'prigs' as they have used the innocence of the heroine as a means of making their own satirical comments on the hypocrisy of society.

But I suspect that there's more than 'form' at the root of women's partiality for *David Simple*. Both women writers and women critics have pointed out that this is a novel which only a woman could have written, and while this in itself does not account for women's positive response, the change in perspective provided by Sarah Fielding helps in part to

186

explain the attraction for women.

After the novels of the men, the women come as a refreshing change, according to Clara Whitmore (1910) who notes the feminine touch in the description of surroundings. It was women writers, she states, who 'saw and recorded many interesting scenes of British life which quite escaped the quick sighted Fielding, or Sterne with the microscopic eyes' (p. 25). She gives Sarah Fielding full marks for introducing this dimension and writes of her that her 'chief charm to her woman readers is the feminine view of her times. In *David Simple* we have the pleasure of travelling through England but with a woman as guide' (p. 27). While I do not want to detract from this achievement I do not think it is Sarah Fielding's skill with scenic detail alone that marks *David Simple* as a women's novel, or which makes the literary tradition immeasurably the richer with the addition of a women's view.

Admittedly the distance between current conventions and those of the eighteenth century makes *David Simple* heavy reading on occasion – although, I hasten to add, no more so than its contemporary counterparts such as *Pamela* and other comparable male classics. But there is one scene in *David Simple* where the difficulties ordained by distance are completely overcome, and where it becomes obvious that nothing much has changed in two hundred and fifty years. It is a scene which is assuredly written from the perspective of a woman and which – to quote Virginia Woolf again – reveals an aspect of male behaviour which men do not ordinarily see in themselves. And with its measured manner and satirical insights it is an entertaining and yet serious appraisal of the relationship between the sexes, which is no less relevant or revealing now than it was when it was first written.

It concerns the heroine, Cynthia, who is travelling in a stage coach in the company of three 'gentlemen' whom the author characterises variously as 'the clergyman', 'the atheist', and 'the butterfly'. Cynthia is preoccupied with her own thoughts, is perfectly self-contained, and not only refrains from talking but is quite oblivious to what the 'gentlemen' are saying. But is she to be permitted her solitude and her independence of her male travelling companions?

Oh no. Unable to forgo an interested and flattering audience, the clergyman begins to exclaim on the Beauties of the Day, until Cynthia feels obliged to give him her attention. And while he engages her in conversation, the atheist and the butterfly yawn and groan about the tedium of it all. 'At last he who yawned' (the butterfly), writes Sarah Fielding, 'from the desire of putting an end to what he undoubtedly thought the dullest *stuff* he ever heard, turned about to Cynthia, and swearing he never studied any beauties of nature, but those possessed by the *fair sex*, offered to take her by the hand' (Book II, chapter 4: 1969: p. 176).

Move number one is repulsed by Cynthia.

The three gentlemen then proceed to converse, to argue, and to make coarse jests against women – which the author insists to be not worth repeating but which she assumes are familiar and offensive to all women. But finally the four travellers complete their journey for the day and Cynthia and the clergyman, both being tired, retire to their separate rooms at the Inn, while the atheist and the butterfly get down to some serious drinking.

Believing them to be still engrossed in their task, Cynthia, after a rest, decides to go and sit quietly in the garden. The atheist intrudes. Having got the better of his drinking companion he is himself however the worse for wear, and he pushes himself on Cynthia and tries to persuade her to his pleasure-seeking purpose. Cynthia is obliged to deal with his advances:

> She immediately rose up and would have left him; but he swore that she should hear him out, and promised her that if she would but attend with patience to what he had to say, she would be at liberty to do as she pleased. He then began to compliment her on her *understanding*, insisted that it was impossible for a *woman of her sense* to be tied down by the common *forms of custom*, which were only complied with by fools; that pleasure is pleasure, and that it is better to be pleased than displeased. (Book III, chapter 4: 1969: pp. 180-1)

Sound familiar? Not even the arguments seem to have changed much with the passing of time. Nor have women's responses. As Cynthia observes wryly to herself, the atheist assumes that his pleasure will be hers as well. But for Cynthia, the reverse is true; her own pleasure would be served by doing the very opposite of gratifying his. Yet he does not seem able to appreciate this, and in order to extricate herself from his unwelcome sexual harassment, she is obliged to resort to flattery.

Move number two is repulsed.

Next day, the coach is overturned and the atheist, 'who had stupified his senses in such a manner by the breakfast he *chose to drink*' (p. 182) is hurt and his journey is involuntarily terminated. The butterfly, having reached his destination, takes his leave. Cynthia is alone with the clergyman, who falls first into a general discourse on love, but who then makes a declaration, and a proposal.

Move number three has to be repulsed.

On a short and simple stage coach journey, Cynthia has been subjected to the unsolicited advances of all three of her travelling companions. Upon reaching London she declares she has had quite enough and her feelings would be appreciated by most women today: 'She almost made a resolution never to speak to any man again, beginning to think it impossible for a man to be civil to a woman, unless he has some designs upon her' (Book III, chapter 5: 1969: p. 184).

It is this description – and others like it – which brings together the woman writer and the woman reader. This is a woman's experience of the world, an 'everyday' experience which is not, however, found very frequently in the writing of men. In some ways it is but a subtle shift to go from the androcentric perspective of novels such as *Pamela* where the course of events is termed in blasé fashion 'procrastinated rape', to the gynocentric perspective of Cynthia which portrays such behaviour as sexual harassment: but if it is a subtle shift it marks a wealth of different meanings. And if literature is to embody the diversity of *human* experiences then *both* perspectives need to be represented within it. Whilever the literary heritage is comprised almost entirely of the views of men, it is much the poorer for the omission of women's view.

Sarah Fielding's appeal to the literary ladies of her time consisted in part of her ability to depict the world as it impinges on women. She was a well-educated woman who certainly felt much of the disapprobation that befell women who knew Latin and Greek. So when she comments – with justifiable bitterness – on the paltry provisions for girls' education, and on the jibes and jeers which were the lot of women who acquired an education despite the difficulties, she was presenting a picture that was all too familiar to the emerging blue-stockings. Which is one reason they were so favourably disposed towards her writing and why they declared that only a woman could have written it:

> I loved reading, and had a great desire of attaining knowledge [explains Cynthia], but whenever I asked questions of any kind whatsoever, I was always told, *such things were not proper for girls of my age to know*; If I was pleased with any book above the most silly story or romance, it was taken from me. For, *Miss must not enquire too far into things: it would turn her brain; she had better mend her needlework, and such things as were useful for women; reading and poring on books would never get me a husband.* (Book II, chapter 5; 1969: p. 101)

Whether or not a husband was considered an attractive item in Sarah Fielding's frame of reference it is difficult to tell (neither she nor her three sisters married). But she certainly valued education. And whether or not she resented the education of Henry it is also difficult to tell. Yet clearly she *understood* such resentment. While all the accounts of Henry's life suggest that Sarah was a devoted and uncritical sister, it is possible that had Sarah Fielding been free to provide her own version, she might have told another tale. To return to *David Simple* and Cynthia's account of her education:

And yet what aggravated my misfortunes was my having a brother who hated reading to such a degree, he had a perfect aversion to the very sight of a book; and he must be cajoled or whipped into learning, while it was denied me, who had the utmost eagerness of it. Young and unexperienced as I was in the world, I could not help observe the error of this conduct, and the impossibility of making him get any learning that could be of use to him, or of preventing my loving it. (Book II, chapter 5: 1969: p. 102)

No doubt, Cynthia spoke for many women of her time when she said:

Thus was I condemned to spend my youth, the time when our imagination is at the highest, and we are capable of most pleasure, without being indulged in any one thing I liked: and obliged to employ myself, in what was fancied by my mistaken parents to be for my improvement, although in reality it was nothing more than what any person, a degree above a natural fool, might learn as well in a very short time, as in a thousand ages. (Book II, chapter 5: 1969: pp. 101-2

Sarah Fielding felt very strongly about the denial of imaginative and moral education to girls. It was one reason she wrote *The Governess* (1749). That *The Adventures of David Simple* is supposed to 'lack unity' is not surprising, given that it was published over almost ten years and *The Governess* appeared in between. (Volume I of *David Simple* was published in 1744; the second volume, entitled *Familiar Letters between the Principal Characters in David Simple*, appeared in 1747 and *The Adventures of David Simple*, Volume the Last, in 1753).

According to some critics (Jill Grey, 1968, among them), *The Governess or The Little Female Academy* is Sarah Fielding's best work. It was in print until 1903 and as the first book written specifically for young people it provided the model for children's literature for more than a century. It is still a pleasurable (if somewhat pious) read and while the high moral tone is perpetually present, this is balanced by the lively and realistic accounts of the behaviour of the girls who are tempted to stray from the thoughtful, responsible and prudent path. To summarise the book in this way is, perhaps, to give the unfortunate impression that it is dull and dry, which is far from the case: with its wonderful fairy tales and its amusing accounts of the young scholars, it has considerable entertainment value. That it proved to be so popular and so influential for so many years (with Maria Edgeworth and her father according it a prominent place) is some indication of its enduring qualities. Again, Sarah Fielding's practice of educating the innocent through experience provides an excellent means for satirical observations on society – even in a little female academy.

The Cry: a new dramatic fable, written with Jane Collier (herself the author of *An Essay on the Art of Ingeniously Tormenting*, 1753) was published in 1754. In it a fantastical, allegorical world is created where the heroine tells her story to those who represent truth and justice, and those who stand for malice and exploitation. *The Cry* has a structure which allows for an examination of the values of life and in its subplots contains what some believe to be Sarah Fielding's best and most reasoned discourses.

The contemporary attitude towards this experimental novel is revealed in the correspondence of some of the literary ladies, particularly that of Elizabeth Carter (1717-1806, poet, essayist, translator, letter writer) and Catherine Talbot (1721-1770, poet, essayist, letter writer), and is quoted by Jill Grey:

> Miss Talbot comments 'On the whole it pleased me mightily. There is sometimes rather too strong a spirit of refining in it, which I believe is the case in all Mrs Fieldings compositions, and she often puts me in mind of Tacitus. But is she not in general a most excellent writer?' To which Mrs Carter replies that 'on the whole, Mrs Fielding is a favourite with us all, though what you say of refinements is perfectly just and what we think.' (1968: p. 24)

Samuel Richardson was full of praise for Sarah Fielding's work and was for ever offering his assistance – and his printing services. Which given the rivalry and recriminations between Samuel Richardson and Henry Fielding says something for Sarah Fielding's powers.

Samuel Richardson was the printer of Sarah Fielding's next novel, *The Lives of Cleopatra and Octavia* (1757). Another experimental and pioneering psychological novel, in which Cleopatra and Octavia return to the world and give their different versions of events. The two heroines represent different groups of women, with Cleopatra showing a distinct distaste for the intellectual woman and a predilection for feminine wiles, while Octavia displays the intellectual qualities admired by Sarah Fielding.

Henry Fielding died in 1754 and whether it was because Sarah Fielding's economic needs were greater or her brother's influence was less, Sarah Fielding produced more novels which were further removed from Henry's picaresque plots in the years after his death. In 1759 came *The History of The Countess of Dellwyn* (again, printed by Samuel Richardson) and it was another criticism of male dominance and another indictment of sexual harassment where women are seen as 'prey'.

191

But according to Malcolm Kelsall (1969), because Sarah Fielding did not give free rein to her experiments in fiction, because she struggled to make her insights fit the prevailing picaresque forms and to find favour in the eyes of the experts, including her brother, she never succeeded in her writing as she might have done. 'Partly because of the influence of Henry Fielding, which led to the peripatetic hero and episodic structure, and partly because of the unmistakable pull of romance,* Miss Fielding failed to keep control of her material' (p. xiii). Had she followed her own bent – that of allegory and an exploration of human values – the consensus seems to be that her achievement would have been greater. As *no* woman writer of her century has been granted the status of 'great achievement' this seems something of a spurious argument.

There is some speculation that Sarah Fielding was also the author of *The Histories of Some of the Penitents in the Magdalen House: As Supposed to be Related by Themselves* (1760). The Magdalen House was a home for penitent prostitutes and Sarah Fielding could well have been familiar with its practices and purposes (and have had access to the inmates) because her half-brother, John, with whom she was in close contact, was one of the founders and a governor of the home. Clearly Sarah Fielding's contemporaries believed she was the writer of this work.

Mrs Elizabeth Montagu (1720-1800, essayist, patron, letter writer and 'Queen of the Blues', and one of Sarah's friends) referred to Sarah Fielding as the author of this not-so-refined book, and Mrs Montagu's friends, Mrs Carter and Miss Talbot, were of the same mind – about the identity of the author, though, not the nature of the book. To Miss Talbot, Mrs Carter wrote on 27th November, 1759 that 'the book you inquire after is "The History of some of the Penitents in the Magdalen House". I think that is the title of the very pretty book we have been reading. I know not who writ it but it is at least a very good likeness of Mrs Fielding' (*Letters*, vol. I, p. 448).

But there was no doubt about the author of *The History of Ophelia* (1760) and no equivocation in the response of 'the blues' who found this novel of Sarah Fielding's very lively, direct and amusing. Likewise they were impressed with her last and most learned publication, the translation of Xenophon's *Memoirs of Socrates* in 1762.

All in all, Sarah Fielding's literary output was substantial and significant, and was highly acclaimed in her own time. She was widely read and widely appreciated and was ranked among the great in terms of her scholarship and her creativity. Her status is reflected in the appraisal of the critic, Clara Reeve, who in 1785, in *The Progress of Romance*, remarks on the value of *The Governess* and states that 'Miss Fielding was one of those truly estimable writers, whose fame smells sweet, and will

*(Ha!)

do so to late posterity, one who never wrote "A line that dying she would wish to blot"' (p. 143).

This is a long way from Malcolm Kelsall's summation of her achievement in 1969. In a manner which denies the substance and significance of women's intellectuality and creativity he reduces the contribution of Sarah Fielding to small proportions and justifies her consignment to obscurity with the statement, 'At her best, however, she has something of the vision of a child' (p. xvi). Children, like women, are not to be taken seriously.

Table 5: Sarah Fielding (1710-1768)

1744 *The Adventures of David Simple*
1747 *Familiar Letters between the Principal Characters in David Simple*
1749 *The Governess, or The Little Female Academy*
n.d. *Remarks on* Clarissa *addressed to the author*
1752 *Contributions to* The Covent Garden Journal, *nos 63 and 64*
1753 *The Adventures of David Simple, Volume The Last*
1754 *The Cry: a new dramatic fable* (with Jane Collier)
1757 *The Lives of Cleopatra and Octavia*
1759 *The History of the Countess of Dellwyn*
1760 *The History of Ophelia*
1762 *Xenophon's* Memoirs of Socrates (translation)

CHAPTER 11

•

Charlotte Lennox and North America

The question has recently arisen as to whether Charlotte Lennox (1727?-1804) is the first American novelist: apart from the thorny issue of whether the first novelist should have been *born* in America or *published* in America, one reason that the debate continues is because there is so little substantiated information about Charlotte Lennox's life. Was she, or was she not, American?

Another eighteenth century woman novelist about whom 'so little is known'. And another woman writer who – like Aphra Behn and Delarivière Manley – is blamed for the absence of definitive detail and is accused of deliberate deception. Instead of a closer examination of the record keeping habits of society, instead of an investigation of the sex bias which collects and preserves more, and classifies more accurately, documentation on the dominant group, there is the charge that members of the subordinate group – individual women themselves – are at fault in that they have misled biographers, commentators, critics. So the mystery which surrounds Charlotte Lennox's life can be explained by reference to her own behaviour: 'She herself can be held responsible for creating a legend around her own name' (Philippe Séjourné, 1967: p. 11).

I do not mean to suggest that women writers have not tried to present favourable but false impressions of their lives. They have. But they have had good reason. There has been great pressure on them to be acceptable women in order that they might be acceptable writers. The same is not true of men who on occasion have benefited from the reverse arrangement and have enjoyed prestige as writers partly because they have been 'unacceptable' men. (No names mentioned.) Yet this is not the end of the double standard. Some men have also been guilty of presenting a more 'glossy' or 'romantic' image of their origins than the reality has warranted, and not only has this discrepancy been more readily

3   Charlotte Lennox

recognised and rectified, but among men, departure from accuracy is judged more tolerantly. There are few diatribes in literary criticism against deceitful men who have tried to mislead the public about their lives. Nor have the discrepancies become a major issue in literary commentary. (For example, there are but 'passing comments' on some of the inaccuracies in Charles Dickens's account of his life: see Phyllis Rose, 1985.) But in the sparse criticism that does exist on women, much of it is *not* concerned with their writing, *not* with the conditions under which they wrote, but with their character, and their 'honesty', and whether they were what they claimed to be.

Charlotte Lennox is no exception. This is evidenced in Philippe Séjourné's (1967) impressively scholarly study entitled *The Mystery of Charlotte Lennox: First Novelist of Colonial America (1727?-1804)*. It is devoted entirely to an examination of her two 'American' novels (*The Life of Harriot Stuart*, 1750, and *Euphemia*, 1790) and is concerned to establish her status as the first American novelist. But there are difficulties.

These are reflected in some of the conflicting claims that are made in the information on Charlotte Lennox. For example, Duncan Isles (1970), who provides the chronological table in the Oxford University Press edition of *The Female Quixote*, has her born 'possibly in Gibraltar' about 1729-30: Alison Adburgham (1972) states that Charlotte Lennox 'was an Irish girl, born 1720, who came to England to stay with an aunt' (p. 117). And Philippe Séjourné sums up the 'received wisdom' which prevailed prior to his investigation: 'Almost everybody agrees in more or less precise words that she was born in New York – the town or the colony – in 1720; her father is said to be a field officer, generally a colonel, by the name of Ramsay, Lieutenant Governor of New York. It is then generally stated that she was sent over to England at the age of fifteen to reside with a wealthy aunt whom she found "incurably insane"; some give the date of her arrival as 1735 and many agree that this almost coincided with the death of her father who left his family "without any provision"' (p. 12). And, adds Philippe Séjourné, 'the essentials of Charlotte Lennox's story all seem to be derived from her obituary published in the *Gentleman's Magazine* of January 1804. This article was very probably based on what was known to her friends' (p. 13).

But after all the exhaustive searches that have been undertaken there are really only two details which are at the crux of the debate on Charlotte Lennox: her birth date and her father's status. It seems that there never was a Lieutenant Governor of New York by the name of Ramsay – although his 'promotion' by his daughter seeking to make a name for herself in London is understandable; and it seems that she was *younger* than she claimed to be – although this modification in her age is not accompanied by comment on women's penchant for disguising their years.

What has been substantiated is that Charlotte Lennox grew up in New York and was familiar with Albany, Schenectady, the Hudson area, and 'Mohawk' country. Her mother remained in America (and died there in 1765) and from an early age Charlotte Lennox was to be found in London, alone, poor, and trying to earn a living as an actress and a writer. The last report of her appearance on stage was 1750, the year in which her first novel, *The Life of Harriot Stuart*, was published. Not that this was her first time in print: in 1747, *Poems on Several Occasions* had appeared and it too contains evidence of her American origins.

It would have been very difficult for a young woman without 'connections' to have obtained an entrée to the literary world of London, but not only did Charlotte Lennox overcome these difficulties and find for herself some of the most prized patrons of the time, she soon became a highly acclaimed writer.

While it was a constant struggle to get some of her work published she did not lack assistance – from some of the leading literary lights of the day. Dr Johnson, Samuel Richardson and Henry Fielding all thought she merited the label 'genius', with Henry Fielding rating her *Female Quixote* as surpassing that of Cervantes's work. Dr Johnson was her devoted friend until he died and not only gave her every support, but went so far as to hold celebratory parties for her (most uncharacteristic) and to crown her with laurels. Philippe Séjourné writes that Dr Johnson 'never stopped helping her in every way; he wrote several dedications for her works; two of the essays of Father Brumoy's *Greek Theater* which she could not translate in time were done by him; he may well have suggested that she collect the sources of Shakespeare's theatre and compose her *Shakespear Illustrated* (1967: p. 21). (She may well have thought of this project herself, of course.)

Dr Johnson was always trying to help her get published because he was aware of how great her need for money was. Her entire adult life seems to have been one long battle with poverty – ending in her destitute state at her death. One reason for her lack of funds was her husband. She supported both him and her children, and numerous are the references to the shiftless Alexander Lennox who was a constant financial drain on his wife, who was 'a bad influence' on their son, and who Charlotte Lennox finally left. Running through her novels, and a particular focus of *Euphemia* – published forty years after the effervescent *Harriot Stuart* – is the theme of frustration and despair on the part of the long suffering wife who is required to be loyal and submissive to her husband for whom she has no respect. *Euphemia* 'tells us the story of Charlotte's own relations with her husband and the intimacy of her tone helps to convey a sense of authenticity; no reader could at any time doubt that she really expresses the deepest feelings of a disillusioned wife' (Philippe Séjourné, 1967: p. 150).

Because they knew of her considerable financial pressures, but more importantly because they had such high regard for her work, Dr Johnson and Samuel Richardson were most keen to see Charlotte Lennox in print. So substantial was their contribution to her literary endeavours, the Oxford University Press reprint of *The Female Quixote* (1970) contains an appendix by Duncan Isles which documents the support provided by these literary men. 'By introducing her to Richardson,' writes Duncan Isles, Dr Johnson 'provided her with a particularly valuable new ally, who helped her in at least three distinct ways; as a novelist he gave her literary advice; as a printer, he printed the first edition of *The Female Quixote*; as one of London's most prominent men of letters, he used his influence in the literary world on her behalf' (p. 418).

For Charlotte Lennox such patronage was in itself a remarkable achievement and to have enjoyed the favour of these leading literary men should surely have helped to establish her reputation as a writer of substance? But no. Again we find that it is the woman rather than the writing which comes to the fore of literary judgment, and instead of accepting the word of the great men as to her literary ability, the wiles of the woman are used to explain the 'mitaken' assessments of the men. Though Dr Johnson, Samuel Richardson and Henry Fielding could all testify to her merit, there is the (groundless) implication that they were all 'taken in' by Charlotte Lennox. In other words, that they were duped, and that this woman novelist – like all the rest – was not as good as her contemporary critics would have her be.

So frequent are the assertions that Charlotte Lennox's 'popularity' among the men was a product of her 'charm' rather than her writing, and so insidious are the implications that she was not at all popular among the women, I was sufficiently suspicious to start searching for the basis of these charges. In spite of the fact that Charlotte Lennox enjoyed the patronage of the Countess of Rockingham and of Lady Isabella Finch (to whom she dedicated *Poems*), that she was assisted by the Duchess of Newcastle (who at one time helped find employment for her husband), that she was a friend of Sarah Fielding and Jane Collier (see Margaret Dalziel, 1970) and was supported by Lady Chambers for a pension from the Literary Fund, there is the constant intimation that Charlotte Lennox was disliked by her own sex.

I do not know if this is true. I do wonder if it is relevant. And I do ask myself why this 'issue' for a woman writer would go unnoted with a man.

I can find some cryptic comments about Charlotte Lennox in Fanny Burney's *Diary* ('though her books are generally approved nobody likes her', 1778: vol. I, p. 86), and apart from the fact that it is not mandatory for a writer to be liked in order to be good, there is the issue that if we take Fanny Burney as the guide, no one would escape censure. Fanny Burney was a sharp and merciless satirist whose quick wit was used against friend and foe alike. It was because they thought that she would be misunderstood – and shunned – that her advisers, Dr Burney and Mr Crisp, were against the publication and performance of her play, *The Witlings*, which exposed the foibles of the blue-stockings – including those of her dear friend, Mrs Thrale. Yet apart from the 'evidence' supplied by Fanny Burney there is little else to support the belief that Charlotte Lennox was spurned by her own sex while she held unwarranted sway with the literary men. I can only conclude that this is yet another example of the way aspersions are cast on the character of women to deflect interest and to detract from their writing.

For I do not think that Dr Johnson, Samuel Richardson, or Henry Fielding were mistaken in their judgment. By 1755, Charlotte Lennox 'was one of the most famous and highly praised writers in London' (Kathryn Shevelow, 1984: p. 197), and to my mind her reputation was well deserved. I am impressed by her literary achievement but I am also fascinated by the way she fits into the female tradition, for in the writing of Charlotte Lennox we have one of the 'links in the chain'.

When Charlotte Lennox is placed in context – with Aphra Behn and Delarivière Manley before, and with Fanny Burney, Maria Edgeworth and Jane Austen yet to come – when she is placed alongside Eliza Haywood, we can see her writing helping to form part of that 'continuum' of women's writing to which Elaine Showalter referred. In the work of Charlotte Lennox we find some of the vigour of Aphra Behn, the barbed wit and the bathos of Delarivière Manley, and the plot pace of Penelope Aubin; we find some of the seeds that will bloom in the writing of Fanny Burney, Maria Edgeworth and Jane Austen. And we can see that *The Life of Harriot Stuart* shares much in common with *The History of Betsy Thoughtless* which was published not long afterwards.

Harriot Stuart is another lively young woman but she has the added romantic dimensions of 'New World' vivacity and 'New World' adventures. (Charlotte Lennox's account of the Indians, and the dangers, parallels those of her predecessor, Aphra Behn, in *Oroonoko*, and of course gave rise to comparable scepticism about the veracity of the writer.) Harriot is careless; in such a new country it is relatively easy to neglect some of the 'old forms' but there is a price to be paid for such negligence: Harriot's actions are often misconstrued as she flirts and fancies and flaunts some of the most cherished social practices of the day, including those of being a docile and dutiful daughter. Harriot is not quite so 'thoughtless' as Betsy, but she is definitely more determined. And although, like Evelina (who was to make her appearance almost thirty years later) (*Evelina*, Fanny Burney, 1778), Harriot too learns from experience, she has few of the sober and reflective qualities that were to stand Evelina in such good stead when that young lady made her entrance into the world.

But Harriot is a warm and likeable (as distinct from admirable) character, and as with many of the other heroines in the writing of Charlotte Lennox, there can be no doubting her authenticity. One critic, Philippe Séjourné, has been struck by this. While I am always suspicious of claims which would have a particular woman as 'the first' in any field of literary endeavour (because it is often nothing other than evidence that their predecessors have been forgotten or ignored), in terms of today's realism, there is some justification for Philippe Séjourné's stand that in Harriot Stuart we have the first real portrayal of a woman, by a woman:

> Harriot herself, like Eliza Haywood's Betsy Thoughtless the same year,* is drawn with considerable art. As readers we are carried along because of her compelling personality. Fielding's Sophia, Richardson's Pamela and Clarissa were men's creations but she is one of the first portraits by a woman, and she is so convincing, in spite of all the incredible elements in the novel, that we may go one step further and ask ourselves whether this is not one of the first, if not the first self portrait of a woman in fiction? (Philippe Séjourné, 1967: p. 148).

As Harriot Stuart did precede Betsy Thoughtless, it may well be that it is Harriot rather than Betsy who should take pride of place in the gallery of women characters who embody some of the experiences of their creators. But it is not an essential exercise – and perhaps not even a useful exercise – to attempt to establish who was 'the first'. I am cautious about accepting such assertions. Not just because I have not read *all* Eliza Haywood's earlier novels (I do not even pretend to know whether I am aware of *all* her earlier novels), or because I have not read *all* of the novels by other women who preceded her, but because to insist on Charlotte Lennox as the first woman writer to present a self-portrait, is to overlook the contribution of Delarivière Manley in *Rivella*, to put aside Cynthia and Octavia in the writing of Sarah Fielding, and to ignore the 'personal' dimensions in women's letter writing and epistolary novels from the Duchess of Newcastle to Mary Davys.

Whether Charlotte Lennox is even the first novelist of North America is in a sense a 'side-issue'. It is more generally to Susanna Rowson that the title of first woman novelist of America is accorded, and to Frances Brooke, the title of first woman novelist of Canada – although both

---

*I have the date for *The History of Betsy Thoughtless* as 1751 and that of *Harriot Stuart* as 1750.

these women were born in England. *Charlotte: A Tale of Truth*, one of Susanna Rowson's novels about America, was published in 1791 in England and when she went to America it was reprinted there in 1794 and was an astonishing success.* And because she was in Canada, and because it was about Canada, Frances Brooke's *The History of Emily Montague* (1766) is considered to be the first Canadian novel. Not wishing for one moment to deprive North America of some of its early literary contributions, it still seems an unproductive task to insist which woman was the first to do what. It is more important to establish the cross-links in women's literary tradition than to establish a series of starting posts.

And with Charlotte Lennox there are many links to be found between her work and that of other women writers. There is the link with Susanna Rowson and Frances Brooke who wrote about the New World – from firsthand experience.** There is the link with Frances Sheridan who wrote about women's disillusionment with marriage – from firsthand experience. In 1761, Frances Sheridan's *Memoirs of Miss Sidney Biddulph* appeared and in this three-volume novel we have a heroine who marries to please her mother and who lives to regret her choice of husband. Charlotte Lennox declared her indebtedness to Frances Sheridan's literary contribution, and in her own novel, *Euphemia* (1790) we are presented with a plot which has its parallels with *Miss Biddulph* for Euphemia, too, marries to please her mother rather than herself, and both heroines find themselves tested to their limits by the stupid and boorish behaviour of their husbands.

But it would be possible to make too much of this link. It could be that for very many middle class girls, the practice of pleasing a mother and of gaining a dreadful husband was a common one indeed. If both Frances Sheridan and Charlotte Lennox were concerned to portray some of the realities of women's lives, the similarities in their novels might well be no more than an understandable coincidence.

It is neither *Harriot Stuart* nor *Euphemia*, however, on which I would want to base the case for Charlotte Lennox's achievement: while both are good, they are nevertheless surpassed by *The Female Quixote* (1752). In this novel Charlotte Lennox writes a 'romance' in which she mocks romance, and not only are her characters well drawn but her style is satirically comical and her structure distinctly clever. The novel has

---

*For further details of the remarkable Susanna Rowson, see Cathy Davidson (forthcoming).

**Susanna Rowson who was born in Portsmouth in 1762 went as a child to Massachusetts, returned to England and took up a writing and acting career in 1778, and then set sail for America again in 1794.

been criticised for its unevenness – some sections are considered too long and some too short – and although there are some grounds for complaint there are also extenuating circumstances (Charlotte Lennox was very much at the mercy of her publisher and her own pressing financial needs), and overall, I do not think that the so-called unevenness detracts from her considerable achievement.

In *The Female Quixote*, the heroine is reared by her father in retirement and isolation after the death of her mother. She is given a good education and is raised in a context of the most exemplary behaviour, so that she becomes a model of learning and decorum (and she is a beauty), except for one – almost fatal – flaw. As a result of reading so many romances she is completely immersed in a romantic world.

To Arabella it is the world of romance which *is* the real world and this leads her to make many mistakes. She sees a strange man in church and is convinced that he is a prince in disguise, come to carry her off. A new boy comes to work in the garden and is another prince in disguise: when he is dismissed by the head gardener for stealing, Arabella knows that there has been a mistake and that this is all part of the romance, for she remains sure that the boy is of noble blood and that she is part of some great mystery in the making.

There is always a ravisher lying in wait for her – or so Arabella believes – and her suspicions, and her attempts to thwart the attacks of her ravishers, place her in some hilariously funny situations.

No man is worthy, and certainly not worthy of her fair hand, unless he has performed some heroic deed (as in the romanticised accounts of 'the antiquities'), as far as Arabella is concerned. Which makes life a bit awkward for her cousin, Mr Glanville, who is a very pleasing young man of whom her father wholeheartedly approves, and who falls in love with Arabella. However, he breaks the chivalric code when he dares to mention his life and, as dictated by the rules of romance, Arabella does not hesitate to banish him for his transgression. This leads to further complications.

There are some excruciatingly embarrassing yet comic scenes when Arabella banishes for life a man who pays her a compliment, when she is convinced that she is the cause of some poor man's death because she has spoken harshly to him, when she believes that the highwaymen who hold her up are noble courtiers – in disguise, of course. The reader cannot help but feel frustration with Arabella's inability to put two and two together in the 'real' world. Because she makes sense of the world in such an unconventional way she repeatedly makes herself very vulnerable as she enters upon the most 'ludicrous' mistakes – as is the case when she attends a race meeting and transforms it in her own terms into an Olympic Games of old, where the jockeys are riding for the favours of women.

But with all her faults, Arabella is more than endearing. This is partly because Charlotte Lennox is able to cultivate such empathy with her heroine that there are few problems with 'identification' and the reader becomes distressed with Arabella's continued 'perversity'. When will she discover the error of her ways and see the true worth of Mr Glanville – and live happily ever after? She pushes his patience so far, she comes so close to losing him for he is at his wit's end what to do with her when so many of his schemes for disavowing her of her romanticism fail to have the desired effect.

There are serious concerns in the novel as well. There is of course the issue of what constitutes a good education and the question of how far fiction can corrupt young minds. But more important, as far as I am concerned, is the exploration of the nature of *reality*; what is it, how is it acquired, how does it work? How can human beings construct such different views of the world from the same evidence?

Charlotte Lennox raises so many fascinating psychological issues which are the subtext throughout the novel, and which give it an added dimension. Yet surprisingly, virtually no one has commented on this aspect of *The Female Quixote*, which is for me one of its most salient and intriguing features. Even in contemporary times it still serves as a remarkable 'case study' on the vagaries of the human mind. I found the novel marvellously satisfying at a variety of levels – for its satire, its humour, its tensions, and its insights into the human condition. It is astonishing that this novel, which has no peer in the works of Daniel Defoe, Henry Fielding or Samuel Richardson, should not be part of our literary heritage, although admittedly it might benefit from some abridgment.

So when Henry Fielding, Samuel Richardson and Dr Johnson declare that Charlotte Lennox is a genius, that her work is original, provocative, and psychologically penetrating, and that she is a great writer, I have no difficulty accepting their judgment. I would rate her in much the same terms myself.

That all her work is not of the same calibre as *The Female Quixote* does not detract from its excellence, and perhaps if she had enjoyed greater financial resources and stability, Charlotte Lennox would have gone on to write more novels on a par with *The Female Quixote*. But as it was, she was always pushed for money and she pushed her pen accordingly.

It was partly financial pressure which led her to start the women's magazine, *The Lady's Museum* (1760-1761): like Eliza Haywood she turned to journalism to help augment her funds. *The Lady's Museum* – 'consisting of a Course of Female Education and a Variety of Other Particulars for the Information and Amusement of Ladies' – lived up to its promises in one respect: it was educational and extremely informative, with its articles on everything from sense to science. In the opinion of Kathryn Shevelow (1984) 'it is one of the most intelligent and valuable early women's magazines' (p. 197).

In another respect, however, it fell somewhat short of its aims: it was considerably more informative than it was amusing. This is puzzling, given the 'amusement' of *The Female Quixote*. Charlotte Lennox did not lack a sense of humour, but it seems to have found fuller expression in her earlier works (with Harriot and Arabella) than in her later ones (with Euphemia). Which is perhaps understandable. Her living conditions steadily deteriorated throughout her life and no doubt it was difficult to write amusing prose in her destitute state.

One contribution she made to women's magazines, however (and it was an amusing one), was the introduction of the serialised novel – her own ('The History of Harriot and Sophia', later published as *Sophia*, 1762). She may have done this because it was an outlet for her own writing, or because she needed to fill the pages of the magazine, or because it was a commercially successful move. As Alison Adburgham has written, Charlotte Lennox's 'novels were probably as popular as Smollett's and almost certainly they were more highly esteemed' (1972: p. 126), and it made good sense to capitalise on the interest in her work – and the suspense of the serial form – to boost the sales of *The Lady's Museum*. Even so, the magazine did not prosper.

But one reason that Charlotte Lennox was able to produce an intelligent and educative magazine (written almost entirely by herself) was because she was an intelligent and educated woman. She was an excellent novelist but she was also a scholarly woman, as can be seen in some of her translations and non-fiction works. *The Memoirs of the Duke of Sully* (1755) became accepted as a standard history and her *Shakespear Illustrated* (which was a collection of Shakespeare's Italian sources with a commentary on their uses) was taken seriously and was the subject of debate in intellectual circles.

Her literary skills were many and varied and by any standards other than those used by 'the men of letters', Charlotte Lennox would be ranked among the great and influential writers of the eighteenth century. She should be granted unchallenged status as one of the mothers of the novel. Her eclipse constitutes a significant gap, not just in the literary traditions of women, but in the cultural heritage of society. It is wearying to be obliged to record – yet again – that Charlotte Lennox's reputation owes more to the commentary on the lives of Henry Fielding, Samuel Richardson and Dr Johnson – and the way in which her boisterous and boyish American manners won them to her cause – than it does to her writing. And the literary tradition would be enriched not simply by the inclusion of Charlotte Lennox but by the exclusion of such gratuitous and irrelevant insult which all too frequently substitutes for criticism of the woman writer. Without the distraction of the consideration of her merits as a woman we would be free to concentrate on her merits as a writer – and to grant her a distinguished role in the rise of the novel.

The writer and critic Clara Reeve accorded her this place in 1785: '*The Female Quixote* was published in the year 1752 – In this ingenious work the passion for the French Romances of the last century, and the effect of them upon the manners is finely exposed and ridiculed – the author of it is since well known as one of the distinguished female writers this age has produced among us – *Mrs Lennox*' (vol. II, p. 6).

Table 6: Charlotte Lennox (1720, 1727, 1729, 1730?-1804)

1747	*Poems on Several Occasions*
1750	*The Life of Harriot Stuart* (novel)
1752	*The Female Quixote* (novel)
1752	*The Age of Lewis XIV* (translation)
1753	*Shakespear Illustrated: vols I and II* (dedication by Dr Johnson)
1754	*Shakespear Illustrated: vol. III*
1755	*Memoirs of Maximillian de Bethune, Duke of Sully* (translation: dedication by Dr Johnson)
1756	*The Memoirs of the Countess of Berci* (translation)
1757	*Philander* (a play: never staged, dedication by Dr Johnson)
1757	*Memoirs for the History of Madame de Maintenon* (translation)
1758	*Henrietta* (novel)
1760	'The History of Harriot and Sophia', serialised in *The Lady's Museum*
1760	*The Greek Theatre of Father Brumoy* (translation: two chapters by Dr Johnson)
1760-61	*The Lady's Museum* (women's magazine)
1762	*Sophia* (novel)
1766	*The History of Eliza* (attributed)
1769	*The Sisters* (play based on *Henrietta*)
1774	*Meditations and Penitential Prayers written by the celebrated Duchess de la Vallière* (translation)
1775	*Old City Manners* (play: adaptation)
1790	*Euphemia* (novel)

CHAPTER 12

•

Elizabeth Inchbald and independence

Elizabeth Inchbald (1753-1821) has numerous claims to fame, one of them being that she is accorded the honour of being the first woman drama critic.* Having established her literary credentials, she wrote for *The Artist* and *The Edinburgh Review*, and that she was considered a leading authority on the drama was made obvious when, in 1806, Mr Longman undertook his ambitious project, *British Theatre*, and invited Elizabeth Inchbald to write the prefaces for the twenty-five volumes of plays.

Her skills as a critic were developed in part through many years of close association with the theatre: she began as an actress and then turned to writing and although she wrote two novels (one of which – *A Simple Story* – is quite remarkable) it was primarily as a playwright that she was known in her own time. And it seems as if her writing was actually profitable; after years of pressing poverty and by virtue of parsimonious habits she was able to make a substantial sum from her writing and she could well have been among the privileged few women to do so.

Born in 1753 near Bury St Edmunds, one of the youngest of a large Catholic family, Elizabeth Simpson does not seem to have enjoyed any educational advantages. In her preface to *A Simple Story* (1791) she declared with not a little resentment that her learning had been within 'the narrow boundaries prescribed her sex'. She regretted her absence of a 'lettered' education and not just because she was taunted by some of the more fashionable men of letters who were galled by her literary prominence and did not take kindly to her criticism. For Elizabeth

---

*I 'repeat' this information: I do not know how many women before her tried and failed, or who succeeded – and have been forgotten.

4   Elizabeth Inchbald

Inchbald, education was a joy in itself and she was genuinely distressed by what she saw as her own 'deficiencies'.

Like many other women writers, she was 'self-taught'. Even had it been thought appropriate to provide her with any formal education as a child it would not have been financially possible, particularly after the death of her father in 1761. From that time any learning that she acquired had to be obtained free, so it was very much the result of her own reading. She was aware that better provision would have been made for her had she not been a girl, and for more than one reason, she thought this unfair: 'It is astonishing how much all girls are inclined to literature, to what boys are,' she wrote, 'My brother went to school for seven years and could never spell; I, and two of my sisters, though we were never taught, could spell from our infancy' (quoted in Anne Elwood, 1843: vol. I, p. 311).

Just as her brothers wanted to lead lives of independence, so too did Elizabeth Inchbald, but whereas attempts were made to equip them to earn their living in the wide world, no such efforts were made on her behalf. If she was going to have a 'career' rather than a conventional marriage, she had to do it all herself.

Her life during her early years in Standingfield appears to have been relatively uneventful and heightened only by occasional visits to the theatre. Which helps to explain Elizabeth Inchbald's fervent desire to leave home and to go on the stage. It was one of the very few options available to a woman who wanted to make her own way in the world. But apart from all the usual obstacles which stood in the way of stage success, Elizabeth Inchbald had one more pronounced difficulty to contend with if she was to achieve her ambition. She had a speech impediment (which Ann Elwood refers to as 'an imperfection in her organs of utterance', p. 310).

To many, a stammer would have been sufficient to discourage any thoughts of a stage career, but not to Elizabeth Inchbald who was absolutely determined to lead an independent life and who didn't have much choice about the way this could be achieved. Her speech impediment was just another problem which had to be overcome. So she disciplined herself to recite aloud and to practise on troublesome words so that the 'imperfection' was not quite so obvious. Such determination and hard work in the face of seemingly overwhelming odds were characteristic of her.

From a young age she was resolved on an independent (and exciting) life and her commitment to a career emerges in her initial response to Joseph Inchbald. She first met the actor/painter on a visit to her sister, in London, in 1771. When she returned to her home in Standingfield, he wrote to her with an offer of marriage, which she unequivocally declined, on the practical grounds that marriage (and children?) would interfere with her life: 'In spite of your eloquent pen, matrimony still appears to me with less charms than terrors,' she replied, and 'to enter into marriage with the least reluctance, as fearing you are going to sacrifice part of your time, must be greatly imprudent' (quoted in Julia Kavanagh, 1863: vol. II, p. 6).

But it was a very different matter a year later when Elizabeth Inchbald had run away from home (leaving her mother a most apologetic letter) and had gone to London to make her fortune and to lead her independent life. She was no sensitive or delicate innocent (Joseph Inchbald had two sons and no wife but this did not debar him from decency to her mind), but life in London for an unknown young woman – without property, position or protection – was fraught with dangers. Elizabeth Inchbald went looking for acting engagements and met with harassment and molestation. She was almost driven to distraction as she tried to establish a theatrical reputation without losing her reputation – or worse.

She was not oblivious to the misery and suffering of women around her who had begun with much the same aims as she had but who could support themselves now only by prostitution and who invariably met with an early death. So when Joseph Inchbald renewed his offer of marriage and accompanied it with an offer of entry to the stage, Elizabeth Inchbald accepted his 'protection' and made use of the 'promotion'.

Almost twenty years older than she, Joseph Inchbald had attained some small success as an actor, and after their two marriages (one Catholic, to comply with their own religious bleiefs, one Protestant, to comply with the laws of the land) the couple went to Bristol and Bath where Elizabeth Inchbald made her stage debut as Cordelia, playing opposite her husband's King Lear.

For the next few years, Mr and Mrs Inchbald toured round playing various parts without obtaining great rewards. Acting experience Elizabeth Inchbald certainly gained, but money she did not. Neither were ever popular actors and while it is not possible to comment on Mr Inchbald's limitations it is possible to say of Mrs Inchbald that she never completely overcame her stammer and that this in some way must account for any shortcomings in her performance.

Money was always a problem, but they appear to have had some marital difficulties as well. Mr Inchbald's grounds for jealousy are given as the great beauty of his wife which attracted a flock of admirers. Mrs Inchbald's grounds for jealousy seem to be based on more well-founded objections to her husband's behaviour.

But whether they were acting or he was trying to supplement their income by painting, life was very hard, and they were constantly on the move. In 1776 they set out for Paris in the hope of better financial rewards, but once more they were unable to support themselves. And every account of Elizabeth Inchbald's life contains the information that on their return to England the couple were forced to go into a field and dig up turnips as their only means of sustenance.

Then it was to Liverpool where Mr Inchbald had been fortunate enough to obtain an acting engagement, and if it did not lead exactly to theatrical success, this venture made life more pleasant for Elizabeth Inchbald, who became firm friends with Mrs Siddons and her brother John Kemble. Not that these two were in much better circumstanes than the Inchbalds. In order to give some idea of what life was like for actors who had not scaled the heights of popularity – and to remind readers that not even for Mrs Siddons had the path to success been smooth and easy – Julia Kavanagh points out (as a woman commentator would) that these were difficult days for Mrs Siddons: she 'was not yet the great tragic actress of later years, but a sorely tried, hard tasked woman, who acted at nights in the stately parts for which her genius and her person fitted her so well, but who washed and ironed her children's clothes in the morning' (vol. II, p. 8). Life was not all that rosy for Elizabeth Inchbald, either.

From Liverpool it was on to Birmingham where the Inchbalds, Mrs Siddons and John Kemble took lodgings together, and where a strong bond developed between Elizabeth Inchbald and John Kemble. This was the period when *A Simple Story* was in the planning stages and as Mr Inchbald became established in regular work, life began to look a little more secure. But then in 1779 Mr Inchbald died of a heart attack, and although now older, and more experienced in the ways of theatre and the world, Elizabeth Inchbald was back in the precarious position of trying to make her way once more on to the London stage. In 1780 she made her first appearance at Covent Garden as Bellario in *Philaster*.

She was, however, sufficiently realistic to recognise that it would be no glamorous and independent life she would be leading if she was to rely exclusively on acting engagements, and so she began to give time and attention to writing. Her years in the theatre, and her concentration on speech patterns and rhythms, had given her a good practical grounding in dramatic form, and she decided to turn her talents to play writing.

Initially she met with little success: she could find no one to stage or publish her first two plays – 'Polygamy' written in 1781, and 'The Ancient Law' written in 1782. But her fortunes changed with *The Mogul's Tale or the Descent of the Balloon* (a play which capitalised on the current craze of ballooning); it was staged in 1784 and for it she received the sum of £100. After that the plays flowed regularly from her pen and the money flowed regularly to her pocket. In 1785, *I'll Tell You What* met with considerable acclaim; in 1787, *Such Things Are* gained for the author the handsome payment of £900. By 1789 she had left the stage and established herself as one of the foremost playwrights of her time.

Elizabeth Inchbald was a beautiful woman (no one fails to mention her beauty and how long it lasted): she was also a single woman and a most successful dramatist, who was eagerly sought after by a number of men (including William Godwin, who proposed to her). She seems to have been disposed towards the attentions of John Kemble but he appears to have been one of the few who did not offer marriage. And what is surprising is that so many commentators should be surprised that Elizabeth Inchbald did not accept any of the proposals made to her. It is as if there is great resistance to the idea that a woman could be content – and not married.

I do not find it at all surprising that she did not remarry. She had what she had always wanted – an independent and exciting life. I assume she was perfectly content, even if other commentators on her life do not.

Her refusal to remarry, however, is not the only area where perplexity is expressed. Many are the criticisms of her anti-social behaviour. She was not always available, not part of the fashionable scene, and she had the peculiar habit of shutting herself away from the world to write. It is almost with resignation that Anne Elwood concludes, 'At all times Mrs Inchbald seems to have determined to retain perfect independence and to have chosen to have her time and her property at her own disposal' (1843: vol. I, p. 322). Which seems reasonable enough to me.

Her commitment to independence is not only evidenced in her own lifestyle, however, but is clearly stated in her writing. Her recurrent theme is that of love and marriage and its implications for women, and for females who found themselves in dreadful circumstances, Elizabeth Inchbald was not at all reluctant to countenance divorce. Not that she was of the opinion that women would necessarily be better served by replacing one man with another. She could well have been voicing her own sentiments when her heroine in *Wives as They Were and Maids as They Are* (1797) demands of her lover who wants her to end her marriage, 'And what shall I have gained by the exchange when *you* become churlish, when *you* become ungrateful?'

Elizabeth Inchbald's single and semi-solitary life requires no explanation. Perhaps her early poverty did make her a little peculiar and excessively parsimonious, although if she would not spend money on her own comfort her generosity to her sisters (one of whom *did* become a prostitute) and to her dead husband's sons, is proof that she was no miser despite the carping criticisms of her financial cautiousness. She shrewdly invested her money to provide herself with an income in her later years and this was nothing other than a sensible move; no doubt turnip digging was one performance she did not care to repeat.

Her experience of publishing practices provided plenty of evidence that the whole business was unpredictable. For example, she had completed *A Simple Story* (in one version) in 1779 but not until 1791 was she able to get it published (in revised form). For this lengthy manuscript she was paid £200 – yet it sold so well that within three months a second edition was required. Payment for her novels contrasts unfavourably with payment for her plays: for *Nature and Art* (1796), another long novel, she was paid £150 whereas for *The Widow's Vow* (1786) she received £900 and for *Everyone has his Fault* (1793), she was paid £700.

The financial rewards, however, did not correlate with the literary accolades and while there was more money to be made from successful play writing, there was more prestige to be gained from successful novel writing. Which is why the literary world took more interest in Elizabeth Inchbald's novel. *A Simple Story* was begun with the encouragement of John Kemble, and there are numerous suggestions that the author's feelings for him, and his 'unavailability', were an inspirational force for the work. *A Simple Story* was revised with the assistance of William Godwin who is not only seen as responsible for the increasingly didactic element in the final version but who seems to have played a prominent role in 'advising' some of the foremost literary ladies of the day – Mary Wollstonecraft, of course, but Mary Hays, Elizabeth Inchbald, Harriet Lee and Amelia Opie as well. *A Simple Story* was sold to Samuel Richardson who had earned himself a reputation as a patron of women of letters, and it was praised as original by *The Gentleman's Magazine* (1791, vol. I, page 61) and as dramatic by *The Monthly Review* (1791, no. 4).

But more significant than the response of the men to Elizabeth Inchbald's fiction is the reaction of the women, particularly the women writers. For it must be noted that while the literary tradition has been comprised of the commentary of men it is to the male authors of the eighteenth century that the credit has gone for the attainment of realism in the novel, whereas the female writers have been bypassed on the grounds that their reveries of romance fell far short of the desired realism. Yet this is *not* the judgment of women writers like Maria Edgeworth who saw in *A Simple Story* the apotheosis of realism. Once more we can see that the values of a woman are not those of a man for to Maria Edgeworth (writing to Elizabeth Inchbald) the realistic elements of *A Simple Story* were unsurpassed:

I have just been reading for the third, I believe for the fourth time, the 'Simple Story'. Its effect upon my feelings was as powerful as the first reading; I never read *any* novel – I except *none* – I never read any novel that affected me so strongly, or that so completely possessed me

212

with the belief in the real existence of all the persons it represents. I never once recollected the author while I was reading it; never said or thought, *that's a fine sentiment* – or, *that is well invented.* I believed all to be real and was affected as I should be by the real scenes, if they had passed before my eyes; it is truly and deeply pathetic.* (quoted in Anne Elwood, 1843: vol. I, p. 325)

Unqualified praise for the achievement of realism; if *A Simple Story* was part of the literary heritage we would have a very different appreciation of realism, a much modified respect for women writers, and a greatly altered literary tradition.

A Simple Story draws upon Elizabeth Inchbald's experience of Catholicism, it reflects her high regard for the benefits of a sound education and it reveals her concern for women's fate in love and marriage. In a pre-Freudian context it provides an illuminating account of human motivation, understanding and responsibility, and it consistently analyses the issue of choice: why do individuals behave as they do, can they behave differently, can they change? Can education provide people with a sound basis for leading a reasonable and just life?

The novel begins with Mr Dorriforth, a Catholic priest, assuming the wardship of Miss Milner, the daughter of his dead friend. He is a Catholic, Miss Milner is not; he is committed to a spiritual life, Miss Milner is not; he is a sober, pious, mature man – Miss Milner is an impressionable, fashionable young lady in search of an exciting life. From the outset this 'love affair' has more than the usual complications: the novel also has more than the usual awareness of religious, political and psychological implications.

To tell the full story would be to spoil some of the suspense, and there can be no substitute for reading the novel in full. It is one of the best – the most intriguing, the most challenging – novels I have read, and I can completely endorse Maria Edgeworth's assessment; she did not exaggerate. Part of the realism to which she refers is the realism of human nature, the complication, motivation, rationalisation of character. The 'duelling' which goes on between Mr Dorriforth and Miss Milner does not lack verisimilitude today; such testing – and consequent contrition – are by no means unknown in a contemporary context and are a testimony to the more enduring aspects of human relations.

That the novel is long, that there is a sixteen-year break in the middle, even that it has a somewhat melodramatic end, does not detract from its remarkable achievement. It should occupy a significant place within the literary tradition.

*When *pathetic* meant 'producing an effect upon the emotions, moving, stirring, affecting'. O.E.D.

Julia Kavanagh is sure that there is no precedent for Miss Milner:

> She is full of faults that scarcely admit of excuse or mitigation; she is
> vain, wilful, provoking; she cannot live without pleasure, excitement,
> and the admiration of men she despises. There is nothing great or
> heroic in her. She has not the innocence of Evelina, the dignity of
> Cecelia the sweetness and intellectual turn of Emmeline and
> Ethelinda. She is a new woman, a true one, a very faulty one,
> introduced for the first time to the world. . . . There had been no
> Miss Milner before this one, no such graceful embodiment of
> woman's failings held out, not to imitation or admiration, but to a
> surer and deeper feeling – sympathy. (1863: vol. II, p. 80)

A far cry, one might say, from the 'realism' of Pamela, or Clarissa!

But if there is commendatory comment on *A Simple Story* there is little
or nothing on *Nature and Art* (1796), not even among the women critics
who clearly knew of its existence. I have wondered about this absence of
discussion because it cannot be attributed entirely to the quality of the
novel, for *Nature and Art* has much to recommend it, even to contemporary
readers. The only conclusion that I can draw is that as Victorian
morality became more firmly entrenched, the subject matter of *Nature
and Art* became more distasteful, more offensive.

My reason for this conclusion is that a comparable fiction appeared
later in the nineteenth century – *Tess of the D'Urbervilles* – and despite
the fact that it was a more sanitised version of the story than *Nature and
Art*, it provoked widespread hostility. It is this which leads me to believe
that the more refined women critics – like Julia Kavanagh for example –
would have found it virtually impossible to discuss at length the issues of
Nature and Art.

Julia Kavanagh says of *Nature and Art* that it has no charm, which is
perfectly true, but not necessarily a fault. What it does have is an
examination of justice – from the justice of the French Revolution to the
injustice of women's treatment by men, and the distortion of justice
within a court of law. The theme is played out in the characters of
Hannah and William, with Hannah, who has been seduced by William
and abandoned when pregnant, finding herself brought before William,
the judge. And there is the cruel irony that she has no one to speak for
her, for it is the judge who is responsible for her downfall, and who
proceeds to pronounce her execution. 'Charm' is the last quality one
could expect in a realistic description of these circumstances.

It is no pretty picture of life that Elizabeth Inchbald paints in her
novels; there are no delightful young women with minor faults who learn
the errors of their ways and save themselves in time to reap romantic
rewards. Rather we have flawed characters in the tragic style, women

whose values and traits lead them (inevitably?) to tragic ends.

I do not know how much of Elizabeth Inchbald's fiction was written out of her own personal pain. I do know that such novels could not be written by someone who was not acutely aware of the human condition and deeply distressed by the circumstances of women's existence. I do know that Elizabeth Inchbald balanced the flaws within human nature against the flaws within society. And I do know that with the excision of such experience from our cultural heritage has been removed the realm of women's suffering – and insight.

More could have been learnt about the parallels between Elizabeth Inchbald's life and art, had her *Memoirs* survived. But it seems as if she destroyed them on the advice of her confessor. She first finished the manuscript in 1786 and was then offered £1,000 for the work by 'Phillips, the bookseller in St Paul's Churchyard' (Anne Elwood, 1843: vol. I, p. 321) but she was unsure of the wisdom of proceeding and declined the offer. By 1818 the *Memoirs* had increased to four volumes and with the aid of William Godwin they were offered to Constable, and this time the publisher declined. Found among her papers on her death was the following note:

Query – 'What should I wish done at the point of death?' Dr Poynter, 'Do it NOW' – four volumes destroyed.

When Mary Wollstonecraft wrote *A Vindication of the Rights of Woman* (1792), she made explicit some of the demands that had guided Elizabeth Inchbald's life and which were reflected in her writing. Elizabeth Inchbald had put her own case for women's rights – and wrongs – and was one of the woman writers who was realising in fiction some of the concepts of women's freedom. Among her friends and literary acquaintances were Mary Wollstonecraft, Amelia Opie, Maria Edgeworth, Ann Radcliffe, Anna Laetitia Barbauld – and Madame de Staël. Quite a support group. Quite an 'alternative' tradition in fiction.

I can only speculate on the shape of the literary tradition had *A Simple Story* and *Nature and Art* been among the early models of fiction to which we looked for inspiration and meaning. But I can claim with confidence that had we been allowed the existence of the mothers of the novel, had we been allowed Elizabeth Inchbald, that tradition would be different indeed. It would be fuller, it would be richer, it would be better. The absence of Elizabeth Inchbald from the literary tradition is not only a loss – it is a disgrace.

Table 7: Elizabeth Inchbald (1753-1821)

1781	'Polygamy' (not staged, not published)
1782	'The Ancient Law' (not staged, not published)
1784	*The Mogul Tale, or The Descent of the Balloon*
1785	*Appearance is Against Them*
1786	*I'll Tell You What*
1786	*The Widow's Vow*
1787	*The Midnight Hour*
1787	'All on a Summer's Day' (not published)
1787	*Emily Herbert or Perfidy Punished* (attributed)
1788	*The Child of Nature*
1788	*Such Things Are*
1789	*The Married Man*
1789	*Animal Magnetism*
1790	*Confessions* (translation of Rousseau)
1791	'Hue and Cry' (not published)
1791	*Next Door Neighbours*
1791	*A Simple Story* (novel)
1792	'Young Men and Old Women' (not published)
1793	*Everyone Has His Fault*
1794	*The Wedding Day*
1796	*Nature and Art* (novel)
1797	*Wives as They Were and Maids as They Are*
1798	*Lovers' Vows*
1799	*Wise Man of the East*
1805	*To Marry or Not to Marry*
1806-9	'Prefaces' to *British Theatre* (25 volumes)
1809	*A Collection of Farces and Other Afterpieces, selected by Elizabeth Inchbald* (7 vols)
1833	*A Case of Conscience* and *The Massacre* (not staged)
n.d.	*Deaf and Dumb*

CHAPTER 13

•

Charlotte Smith and real life

Reading about the lives of early women novelists and then reading their novels can be rather confusing: so often the dramatic detail of the biographies rivals that of the fiction. Not infrequently the lives the authors led contained more romance – and more tragedy – than the lives they wrote about, and Charlotte Smith (1749-1806) is one woman for whom the real world held more misfortunate and misery than the fictional world she created. Many of her problems stemmed from her marriage, but if being a wife caused her so much suffering, it must be acknowledged that it also caused her to turn to novel writing. While for Elizabeth Inchbald marriage may have meant a threat to independence, for Charlotte Smith marriage generated the need for independence – when she had no choice but to leave her husband and support her large family, by writing.

Charlotte Smith started relatively late in life to earn her living by her pen but she produced thirty-eight volumes in the twenty years from her first publication in 1784 (*Elegiac Sonnets and Other Essays*) until her death in 1806. While more inclined to write poetry, it was fiction that paid, so few are the volumes of poetry in her published work. Some of her novels were held in high esteem at the time (and were the source of considerable controversy), and they well deserve attention today.

But back to Charlotte Smith's harrowing life and her forced entry to the world of letters. She was married in 1765 at the age of fifteen to a foolish, pleasure-seeking, profligate man (who seems to have had no redeeming features), and by the age of seventeen she had lost her elder child who died while she was giving birth to her second. She had to face more deaths among her many children in her own lifetime. But births and deaths were not the only causes of her suffering. Her spendthrift husband was thrown into jail for debt – and for seven months she lived

5   Charlotte Smith

with him in prison. He then fled to France to avoid his creditors where his wife joined him and, under appalling conditions, gave birth. The pattern of their existence was debt and disaster and no matter how many 'fresh starts' they were given the end was always the same – and not long in coming. Finally, Charlotte Smith could take no more: although it was a daring and indecent thing to do, she left her husband.

Julia Kavanagh (1863) gives the date of their separation as 1785 but Anne Elwood (1843) puts it a couple of years later, and though there may be some disagreement about the time, both agree that it was a miserable union and better ended. Once she left her husband not only was Charlotte Smith free from his presence and constant debts, she was also free from constant pregnancies and free to devote herself to writing. Anne Elwood, the most circumspect and discreet of commentators, surmises that 'it might have been better had she taken the step at an earlier period' – almost an outrageous suggestion, but one quickly followed by the cautionary note that, of course, it wasn't all that easy, as it exposed Charlotte Smith 'to much censure for the world generally imputes blame to the wife who leaves the protection of her husband' (vol. I, p. 298). (It was some 'protection' that Mr Smith offered!)

But there had been little in the first fourteen years of Charlotte Smith's life to prepare her for her later fate. Born Charlotte Turner, her mother had died when she was three and she had been raised by an indulgent father and aunt. She had been well acquainted with the printed word. She could never remember not being able to read, was supposed to have read everything she could get her hands on (such lack of discrimination being cause for some concern among her critics), was talented at drawing, dancing and acting – and was forever 'writing verse'. Her education was not neglected. At six 'she was placed at a respectable establishment in Chichester', and at eight 'was removed from hence to a school in Kensington, at that time in high repute, and where the daughters of several persons of distinction received their education' (Anne Elwood, 1843: vol. I, p. 285). The comments of one of her Kensington school friends are revealing:

> . . . she excelled the greater part of them in writing and drawing, and being the best dancer, she was always, when there was company, brought forward for exhibition. She had a taste and ear for music, but never applied with sufficient steadiness to ensure success. She was considered romantic by her young companions; she had read more than anyone in the school, was continually composing verses, and was thought too great a genius for study. (quoted in Anne Elwood, 1843: vol. I, p. 185)

At twelve she left school and returned to her father's home where she continued her literary education and her verse writing. She was a spoilt and sensitive girl, moved by the beauty of nature, interested in the lessons of her tutors, and her life reads like something out of a pastoral romance. But how within the space of two years she came to be married, is a story which more closely approaches melodrama.

Her father decided to take a wife, and 'Charlotte's aunt,' writes Julia Kavanagh, 'alarmed at the prospect of a stepmother for her favourite, found no better remedy for the future evil than the present dangerous risk of a husband. A Mr Smith, aged twenty-one, was found and prepared to fall in love with her niece, who also received the injunction to welcome his passion; the young people proved docile, and in February 1765, Miss Turner was married' (1863: vol. I, p. 189).

Mr Smith might have looked like the 'advantageous match' that Charlotte's aunt desired – he was 'the second son of Richard Smith, Esq., an East India merchant, and also an East India director, a young man only just of age, but in easy circumstances, as he was already admitted a partner into the lucrative business of his father, who had realized a considerable fortune' (Anne Elwood, 1843: vol. I, p. 287). But it was not just the fact that Mr Smith proved to be so irresponsible which brought about Charlotte Smith's first taste of unhappiness and despair. Marriage meant living in London – in one of the narrowest and dirtiest lanes in the City – and in a house where commerce was looked upon as the real business of life, and literary pursuits were dismissed as a waste of time. When Mr Smith senior did discover that Charlotte had talent with her pen he offered her the job of being his clerk.

But it was not until 1784, after many trials and tribulations, that Charlotte Smith decided to put her pen to 'practical' use. Whenever possible she had throughout her life written verses for 'private gratification', but finding herself in financial trouble – yet again – she sought to relieve the pressure by having some of her sonnets printed. Unable to find a publisher she took the risk and had them printed at her own expense, 'and so great was their success that a second edition was rapidly called for in the same year. The profits arising from this success temporarily released the writer from her pecuniary embarrassments' (Anne Elwood, 1843: vol. I, p. 295).

This marks the beginning of Charlotte Smith's literary career, although she still had not determined on novel writing and self-support. While in Normandy (where her husband had been forced to take refuge from his creditors) she not only gave birth, she translated a French novel by Abbé Prévost (*Manon Lescaut*, 1785) and it was followed by another translation in 1786 – *The Romance of Real Life* – which was a collection of stories from *Les Causes Célèbres*. And then came the separation from her husband, and the novel writing.

The first two novels – *Emmeline or The Orphan of the Castle* (1788) and

Ethelinda or The Recluse of the Lake (1789) – were somewhat predictable love stories with a dash of mistaken identity and worthy sentiment, and while they have some of the characteristics of the despised romance, they have some monumental strengths as well and should not be dismissed out of hand. Charlotte Smith's reputation as a poet and her passion for the beauties of the English countryside are well substantiated in these two novels, and critics then (and since), have been impressed by her ability to include long – and laudable – descriptions of rural scenes in her prose. In her hands, the setting becomes an integral part of the novel in a way that it had not been before, and she is accorded the credit for introducing passages of poetry which are interwoven with the plot. But this is not all that she introduced in *Emmeline* and *Ethelinda*; she introduced new women characters as well.

As Julia Kavanagh has noted, the entry of Emmeline and Ethelinda heralds the beginning of mature women heroines in fiction. By no stretch of the imagination could these two be called 'girls'. They are not fresh young things on the brink of pleasant lives, but serious women who are fully stretched and strained by the exigencies of a harsh world. And English fiction had not seen their likes before.

In discussion of Charlotte Smith there are many comments about her inability to write 'frothy' novels, many criticisms about the weight of her work which is seen as a result of the cares of her life, and while there may be some grounds for the suggestion that her fiction is serious – even heavy at times – the other side of this coin is that she does present us with more than the flighty heroine who has a few lessons to learn in order to live a happy life. Charlotte Smith's heroines may not be tragic but they are often sadly troubled and sorely tried women and the novel is the richer for their existence.

In her commentary on Charlotte Smith, Julia Kavanagh 'digresses' to include discussion on the significance of 'women's women' in fiction, and it is fascinating to find that more than a century ago she made many of the contemporary points about the deficiencies of an all-male literary tradition. There is little difference in meaning between Tillie Olsen's quote, 'There is a wide discrepancy in American culture between the life of women as conceived by men and the life of women as lived by women' (1978: p. 179) and Julia Kavanagh's assertion that men's view of women is *limited* and that a repository of men's views alone is a limited and distorted representation of women. While ever we have only the views of men – only the females created by men – she argues, literature embodies but a half-truth. Not only are such male creations generally superficial and one-sided in her view, but they display a peculiar bias against woman and the purposes of her existence because they so frequently reduce her to nothing other than the object of passion of a man.

Today we would label Julia Kavanagh's criticism as a protest against women being seen as sex-objects, but more than one hundred years ago she phrased her objection somewhat differently. She deplored this convention among men which 'women of any refinement must by instinct have detected – the delineation of woman as mere woman – as the embodiment of beauty and the object of passion' (vol. I, p. 198).

There is much more to woman than can meet the eye of man, insists Julia Kavanagh, and it must be women themselves who articulate what woman is and can be. It is female authors – including Charlotte Smith – who have 'delighted in the internal woman, that mystery which man has rarely fathomed' (p. 202), and to have a literature of 'twofold' humanity (and any other form is a nonsense to her mind), we must have women and men characters portrayed by women and men writers. Julia Kavanagh is adamant that the literature *of* full humanity ('twofold' humanity) can only be constructed *by* full humanity, which means that the creations of women must be granted the same space and validity as those of men.

While it is a pleasure to find this clearly defined female tradition within literary criticism, the recognition is not without its frustrations. Not just because more than a century later the same point must be made yet again, but because when Julia Kavanagh made it she believed that the logic was so self-evident that the point would never need to be repeated. That all that was necessary was to expose the absurdity of an all-male literary tradition and the practice would end. That her argument was so sound and sensible it would serve to convince and would certainly ensure the demise of the foolish and false premise that men alone could represent a great literary tradition.

'For a long time men wrote alone and their minds were the minds of humanity,' she comments with a mixture of scorn and regret (p. 197). But she remains convinced that such folly will now be a feature of the past and she celebrates the advent of Charlotte Smith's mature heroines who are 'women's women' and who help to represent the full range of females in literature. She welcomes the woman novelist and announces that literature will be the richer for her inclusion.

Yet we know now that for all the consideration Charlotte Smith and her woman characters have received within the literary tradition, for all the prominence and permanence the author and her 'women's women' have been accorded, Charlotte Smith might just as well never have written. She has been lost, her heroines have been lost – and Julia Kavanagh's commentary has been lost. So today attention must again be drawn to the deficiencies of an all-male tradition: and to the sustained suppression of female writers who might offer a challenge to that male monopoly. Nothing has changed. Not with the writing of Charlotte Smith or the writing of Julia Kavanagh. Because nothing has changed there is every likelihood that the 'lock-out' and consequent limitations which have characterised the literary tradition in the past will continue in the future.

The creation of mature women characters, however, was not Charlotte Smith's sole achievement as one of the mothers of the novel. More than any other woman of her time she entered the political arena in her fiction – and caused considerable consternation among some contemporary critics. Not just because they disagreed with her but because even then there was a conviction that 'politics' should be kept out of 'art'. But her partiality for the American War of Independence and the French Revolution, and the democratic principles they represented, is embodied in her fiction and did not endear her to the establishment. As a writer she made direct comments on politics, and she also gave indirect support for more egalitarian arrangements in the world she devised. For example, many of her characters fail to make the prescribed social distinctions and see no bar to the union of the wealthy and 'well-born' with the poor and 'low-born': to Charlotte Smith the issue was not one of parental position but of individual worth and she certainly did not subscribe to the view that the worthy were to be found predominantly among the wealthy and well-born. While such a view may be acceptable today, it was one that was considered dangerous by many at the time.

Which is why there were objections to the love story of Monimia and Orlando in *The Old Manor House* (1793). There is no suggestion that the wealthy Orlando is marrying beneath himself when he weds the poor Monomia, and no suggestion, either, that Monimia should be impressed by anything other than his personal qualities. As Clara Whitmore (1910) has said of this work, 'A great change had come over the novel since Pamela was overpowered with gratitude to her profligate master, Mr B., for condescending to make her his wife' (p. 78). Social position did not count in Charlotte Smith's world and Mr B's offer of marriage would have been scorned within her novels, on the grounds that the man was unworthy. A threatening idea to those who measured their value in terms of their social position.

Charlotte Smith's explicit and implicit criticism of social organisation, of English life and law, earned her a reputation as a 'subversive' among the Tories of her time. Her novels contain some of the earliest attacks upon the legal system and although in comparison to Charles Dickens' later exposés, Charlotte Smith's attack appears somewhat timorous, what cannot be denied is that it was she who introduced such a target – who established a model for 'Jarndyce versus Jarndyce' – and that when she did it, it was considered so audacious it laid her open to the charge of being a 'menace'.

She had her own experiences of the injustices and 'circumlocutions' of the law to draw upon; her husband's financial entanglements, her father-in-law's contested will, her own horrifying months in prison. And even if some of her critics thought it inappropriate to bring such matters into the realm of fiction, she most certainly did not: 'Mrs Smith was a good hater,' writes Anne Ehrenpreis, 'her reply to her critics was blunt':

> *I* have 'fallen among thieves,' and I have occasionally made sketches of them – and I have made only sketches of them, because it is very probable that I may yet be under the necessity of giving the portraits at full length, and of writing under those portraits the names of the *weazles, wolves,* and *vultures* they are meant to describe. (from Preface to *The Banished Man*, 1794: vol. I, p. ix: quoted in Anne Ehrenpreis, 1969: p. ix)

Both the legal and political systems were the focus for Charlotte Smith's criticisms. In *Desmond* (1792), when feeling against France ran high in some circles in England, she revealed her preference for a republican government and even has the hero 'blushing for his country' for its failure to support the fight for freedom. She is adamant that people are better provided for when they have some say in the provisions being made. When placed alongside her attacks on the appalling social arrangements of England which reduce so many to desperate poverty, her political message is difficult to ignore. And again she denounced the law, the vicious legal system which is loaded against the poor, and which would put to death a person who steals the sum of forty shillings.

Understandably, her writing promoted consternation and condemnation. Charlotte Smith 'was accused by reviewers of parading her woes too openly, both in her nakedly confessional prefaces and in her characters which she all too clearly drew from life,' says Anne Ehrenpreis (1969: p. ix). She was judged to be a woman who had had a bitter life and who as a result wrote bitter novels. This is not an uncommon response by critics to a woman writer who disconcerts by leaving the 'proper feminine field' to expose some of the injustices of the wide world. Easier it is to dismiss the woman as embittered than to treat the protest as serious and valid.

Not that Charlotte Smith kept her protests out of the 'proper feminine field' either. Like many contemporary feminists she saw *politics* at work in the home as well as on the public stage, and she was equally critical of injustice in both spheres. It was no sentimental scene of domestic bliss that she presented in Mr and Mrs Stafford, in *Emmeline*, for example. The portrayal of their marriage is held to be autobiographical (see Jane Spencer, 1984b: p. 288) but it is not idiosyncratic 'personal experience' that Charlotte Smith relates; it is a stinging commentary on the relationship between the sexes:

Mr Stafford was one of those unfortunate characters, who having neither perseverance and regularity to fit them for business, or taste and genius for more refined pursuits, seek, in every casual occurrence or childish amusement, relief against the tedium of life. Tho' married very early, and tho' father of a numerous family, he had thrown away the time and money which should have provided for them, in collecting baubles which he had repeatedly possessed and discarded, 'till having exhausted every source that the species of idle folly offered, he had been driven, by the same inability to pursue proper objects, into vices yet more fatal to the repose of his wife, and schemes yet more destructive to the fortune of his family. . . .

Mrs Stafford, who had been married to him at fifteen, had long been unconscious of his weakness; and when time and her own excellent understanding pressed the fatal conviction too forcibly upon her, she still, but fruitlessly, attempted to hide from others what she saw too evidently herself. (*Emmeline*, 1788, vol. 2, p. 147)

If 'public' politics was a focus of her novel *Desmond*, so too was 'private' politics, for this is where Charlotte Smith – again drawing on her own bitter experience – poses the question of whether a woman should leave her husband. In raising this issue the author also draws on some of the ideas about women's rights which were current (among some) at the time. *Desmond* was published in 1792, the same year as *A Vindication of the Rights of Woman*, and Charlotte Smith expressed great admiration for Mary Wollstonecraft, so it is not surprising to find that she endorses the position of women's rights, and women's right to end impossible marriages. She herself wrote late in her life 'that she had been sold into marriage before she was old enough to realize its implications' (Jane Spencer, 1984b: p. 287).

Geraldine, the heroine of *Desmond*, is married to a profligate man who tries to solve his financial difficulties by selling his wife's sexual services to his friend. Geraldine leaves him and returns to her mother – who insists that a wife's duty is to stay with her husband, and sends her away. So, penniless and without protection, Geraldine is cast adrift in the cruel world until rescued by Desmond – who does not try to take advantage of her.

The dilemma of where lies a wife's duty is resolved with the death of the dreadful husband, but the moral issue remains. And it was a very serious moral issue for women. When wives could be treated so barbarously and had no access to redress, how binding were the marriage vows? That so many women novelists should have taken up the question of marriage – Eliza Haywood, Charlotte Lennox, Elizabeth Inchbald, Charlotte Smith, Mary Wollstonecraft, Amelia Opie – is not just an indication of how deeply women were concerned by this issue of paramount importance: it is also a measure of the tradition that has been lost. All the questions about the human condition – about society, the individual and the relationship between the two, about duty, loyalty, morality, freedom and responsibility – all these questions which have figured prominently in women's consciousness and have been reflected in women's fiction writing, have been eliminated from the cultural heritage when these female novelists have been cast aside.

Had the novels of eighteenth century women been retained it would have been impossible to present the image of Mary Wollstonecraft as 'alone of all her sex' or 'years before her time'. Mary Wollstonecraft might have put forward one of the best arguments for women's rights (although even this is debatable given the work of her friend, Mary Hays – *An Appeal to the Men of Great Britain on Behalf of Women*, 1798), but there were many women – Mary Wollstonecraft and Mary Hays among them – who were using fiction to present much the same case. And with the elimination of this body of fiction there has been the elimination of the tradition of women's struggle for self-realisation and independence.

Where Charlotte Smith's work is remembered, however, it is not for her contribution to women's rights that she is known. Her most noted achievement is considered to be *The Old Manor House*, which is sometimes praised for its rural setting and sometimes criticised for its weakness of plot. For Charlotte Smith – who produced ten novels in ten years to support her eight surviving and dependent children – the task of writing *The Old Manor House* afforded something of a respite for it was undertaken in the pleasant surroundings of William Hayley's villa at Eartham and in the company of the host and his friends, the poet William Cowper and the painter George Romney. Life was a little like an artists' colony with everyone working of a morning and relaxing of an afternoon. And there was no doubt that the distinguished company had a high regard for Charlotte Smith's ability when each evening she read the chapter she had written that day. William Cowper (1904) wrote, 'None writes more rapidly or more correctly – twenty pages in a morning, which I have often read, and heard reread at night, and found not a word to alter' (vol. IV, p. 271).

But if this time was a welcome interlude for Charlotte Smith it did not compensate for the demands of her life and William Cowper was not only aware of the draining effect they had on her but was moved to sympathy on this 'gifted' author's account:

> I know not a more pitiable case. Chained to her desk like a slave to
> his oar, with no other means of subsistence for herself and her
> numerous children, with a broken constitution, unequal to the severe
> labour enjoined by her necessity, she is indeed to be pitied . . . she
> will and must 'ere long die a martyr to her exigencies. I never want

riches except when I hear of such distress. (William Cowper, 1904: vol. IV, p. 367)

No man has ever had more pressing need to produce in order to be paid than had Charlotte Smith, yet the myth of the dilettante woman writer persists. We are aware of the hardships endured by lone male artists – in garrets – as they have struggled for their bread, but we are lulled by a false image of women writers whose art has been accomplishment and whose lives have been superficial.

If *The Old Manor House* is Charlotte Smith's best novel – and I am not sure that it is – then perhaps it says much about the conditions under which she wrote it: they were better conditions than she enjoyed at any other time in her writing life. But with my reservation I do not want to suggest that *The Old Manor House* is a poor novel. On the contrary, I must admit that having started it, I could not put it down. It is as much the combination as the particular parts which contributed to my delight and satisfaction in reading it.

There is the central love story of Monomia and Orlando and all the tension that accompanies their secret and innocent meetings. There is the harshness of deception and greed and the cruelty of a marriage that is not a wise match. There is the ridicule of wealth and the respect for power; the setting of the American War of Independence and the commentary on democratic ideals. There is the superb description of rural scenery and the creation of Miss Grace Ryland who must stand as one of the best and most mercilessly drawn female characters in the history of the novel. There is the 'subversive' element which some of the critics of the time did not like.

Orlando is 'held up as an example for all young gentlemen of family and fortune to marry any pretty young servant maid they chuse,' wrote the reviewer in the *Critical Review* (1793: vol. VIII, May, p. 52) with unconcealed contempt for the failure of the author to preserve the distinctions of social class. And some of the 'villains' went unpunished, hardly a fitting ending for a worthy woman writer to devise.

But if Charlotte Smith had her critics she also had her supporters, and she was a well-known and highly regarded writer in her day. There were reviewers who had praise for her novels and there were women writers who learnt from her work. Ann Radcliffe 'borrowed from her in creating her heroines' (Jane Spencer, 1984b: p. 289) and profited from her introduction of setting to provide atmosphere and enhance the action. The quiet humour and controlled satire of *The Old Manor House* are to be found later in the writing of Jane Austen – who had read and benefitted from Charlotte Smith's work.*

Charlotte Smith is an excellent writer in her own right. She is also one of the significant links between women writers and makes an important contribution to the female literary tradition. And she has disappeared.

It is tempting to suggest that one reason for her disappearance is that she challenged the status quo and was perceived as a dangerous writer. But this would mean that it was possible that if she had not been so political she might have found a permanent place in the history of letters. And, of course, there are no grounds for asserting that had she done it differently, she could well have been retained. Many other women *did* do it differently, many other women writers were apolitical, yet they have come to share the same invisible fate as Charlotte Smith. When one hundred women novelists are excised from our heritage we could find one hundred different reasons to justify their omission. But we would be overlooking the fundamental reason for their exclusion – that they were women.

So, another woman writer who contributed to her development of the novel goes the way of women writers before and since. Charlotte Smith, who has no lesser claim to inclusion than many of the men who stud our literary heritage, sinks, and is submerged from view. Only the men remain. To them go the recognition, the credit and the acknowledgment, that they were the creators of the novel.

I am a non-believer.

Table 8: Charlotte Smith (1749-1806)

1784	*Elegiac Sonnets and Other Essays*
1785	*Manon Lescaut* (translation)
1786	*The Romance of Real Life* (translation)
1788	*Emmeline, or The Orphan of the Castle*
1789	*Ethelinda, or The Recluse of the Lake*
1791	*Celestina*
1792	*Desmond*
1793	*The Old Manor House*
1794	*The Wanderings of Warwick*

*See *Northanger Abbey* and 'Catharine, or The Bower', in *Works*, edited by R.W. Chapman, 1954, p. 199. 'One critic has argued persuasively that the behaviour of Catherine Morland in *Northanger Abbey* is a deliberate inversion of Mrs Smith's Emmeline [Mary Lascelles, *Jane Austen and Her Art*, 1939: 60]' (Anne Ehrenpreis, 1969: p. vii).

1794	*The Emigrants*
1794	*The Banished Man*
1795	*Rural Walks*
1795	*Montalbert*
1796	*A Narrative for the Loss of the Catharine*
1796	*Marchmont*
1796	*Rambles Farther*
1798	*The Young Philosopher*
1798	*Minor Morals*
1799-1802	*The Solitary Wanderer* (5 vols)
1805	*Conversations*
1806	*History of England for Young People*
1807	*Natural History of Birds*
1807	*Beachey Head*

CHAPTER 14

Ann Radcliffe and the Gothic

With the 'Gothic novel' it becomes obvious that it's not possible to treat women novelists as independent entities. This is a particular genre where cross-connections and influences can be traced and where the interweavings that are the basis of a tradition require recognition. There are literary links, educational links, friendship links and amorous links among many of the women writers of the late eighteenth century. Even William Godwin provided a link as he appears once more pressing his suit, this time to Harriet Lee, who also rejected him (which suggests that Mr Godwin's public denunciation of marriage may have been more a matter of necessity than choice).

To return, however, to the Gothic novel and its most celebrated author, Ann Radcliffe (1764-1823). Yet even she is not the beginning, for although the best known she was not the first woman to use this fictional form. No discussion of women writers of Gothic novels could commence with anyone else but Clara Reeve; and no discussion of Ann Radcliffe's contribution would be complete without reference to Harriet and Sophia Lee.

Clara Reeve is the starting point. Born in 1729 in Ipswich, she had earned for herself a reputation as a 'minor' writer for her book of criticism (*The Progress of Romance*, 1785, reprinted by Garland Publishing, 1970) and for her highly acclaimed (at the time) Gothic novel, *The Old English Baron* (first published in 1777 under the title *The Champion of Virtue* and not now in print). A well-educated, even erudite woman, Clara Reeve displayed from an early age an interest in politics and a concern for the fate of women writers – which helps to explain the appearance of *The Progress of Romance*, which was not in the usual mould of ladies' publications. Among her literary heroines were Katharine Philips and Charlotte Lennox – with whom Clara Reeve felt she had much in common.

One reason for her strong identification with Katharine Philips was that Clara Reeve had also been on the receiving end of scornful barbs about learned and pretentious ladies: and one reason she felt such a strong attachment to Charlotte Lennox was that she too resented being paid so poorly for her work. It wasn't (and isn't) easy to earn a living by the pen, and Clara Reeve was not always gratified by being asked for her literary contributions: she also wanted to know how much she was going to be paid. 'She abandoned a translation of the *Letters of Aza* commissioned by the *Ladies' Magazine* on learning that she would not be paid for the work,' writes Jane Spencer (1984c), and it is possible to appreciate the dimensions of her problem when it is realised that although *The Old English Baron* went on to be a great success, Clara Reeve was paid but £10 for the copyright (p. 266).

But it was not simply her desire to explore some of the problems faced by the woman writers – and her determination to accord them their rightful place in the history of letters – which prompted her to write *The Progress of Romance*. She was also concerned to bring together the old and the new, to remind readers of the ancient romance tradition and to incorporate it into the then contemporary form. She developed her theories in *The Progress of Romance* and she put them into practice in *The Old English Baron* where in the preface to the second edition of the novel, she explicitly stated that it was her intention to write the ancient romance and the modern novel.

Influenced by Horace Walpole's *Castle of Otranto* (1765), Clara Reeve tried to bring back some of the traditions she thought that the modern novel was in danger of losing. She could see the direction in which fiction was moving, with its preoccupation with pleasantries. She wanted to reinstate some of the 'grander' themes of old, when human beings could be reduced to insignificance, and struck with awe.

As Charlotte Smith was later to see the potential of 'setting' to give added dimension to the plot, Clara Reeve could see the potential of 'atmosphere' in the shaping of a story. She wanted something more than an anonymous backdrop for social interaction, something bigger than the morals and manners of human beings, on her stage. She wanted a different context for her characters where they could be seen from a different perspective: where they were at the mercy of greater forces than their own reasoning and self-control. She wanted doubt, uncertainty – even horror – in the world she created.

While it has become commonplace to decry the excesses of the Gothic novel, it is worth noting that one thing which Clara Reeve did *not* want was supernatural terror which could be neither combated nor explained. To go too far would be to undermine the effect. In her view, Horace Walpole had gone to ridiculous extremes in *Castle of Otranto* and his readers, far from being impressed, were invariably amused. For her, it was important that the play on the imagination be real, and for this reason she kept events well within the realm of possibility. What was frightening, mysterious, unknown, could (later) be plausibly explained. A device which has since become widely used but one which Clara Reeve consciously explored and experimented with.

The Old English Baron was not her only Gothic novel, although it was her most successful. In 1793 she published *Memoirs of Sir Roger de Clarendon* but her emphasis on morality (her praise of the past with its absence of cards, dice, swearing and drunkenness) somewhat detracted from the appeal of this work – according to her many critics.* While *The Old English Baron* was included in Anna Laetitia Barbauld's *British Novelists* (in 1810, a long run), *Memoirs of Sir Roger de Clarendon* was not. Nor were any of her other works, although quite a few of them enjoyed favour at the time. They include *The Two Memoirs* (1783), *The Exiles* (1788), *The School for Widows* (1791), *Plans of Education* (1792)** and *Destination* (1799). All reveal serious concern for women's position in society and all place great faith in education as an agent for bringing about change.

In 1796 Clara Reeve published *Original Poems on Several Occasions*, and with her steady flow of publications across a range of forms she established herself as one of the leading literary ladies of her day. Historically her work has received very little attention but the fact remains that she was a thoughtful and skilful writer who not only made a contribution to the development of the novel but who is still an illuminating source on women's writing.

Clara Reeve moved in a different circle from her contemporaries, Harriet and Sophia Lee. While Clara Reeve was reading parliamentary reports and reflecting on theoretical issues, the Lee sisters were gaining a much more practical education in the theatre. The daughters of actors, Sophia was born in 1750 and on the death of her mother, reared her younger brother and four sisters – including Harriet who was born in 1757. Finances were certainly a problem in the Lee household, and writing plays was one obvious solution, and in 1780 came Sophia's first venture – *The Chapter of Accidents*.

It was a great success and the beginning of good fortune, for the money it made was used to establish a girls' school in Bath. From 1781 to 1803, Sophia and Harriet kept the school which provided them with a secure living and evidently afforded them enough time for writing, as the flow of best-selling books which emanated from Bath testifies.

*I have been unable to obtain a copy.
**My thanks to Sue Butterworth for the information that this too has been reprinted by Garland Publishing.

Perhaps their fame attracted students: perhaps the literary lives of the teachers were a model for the students: perhaps they taught their students to write novels. It seems that Ann Radcliffe was a pupil at their school.

Once the school was established, Sophia Lee settled down to writing again and produced her historical fiction, *The Recess* (1783-85). Set in the time of Queen Elizabeth, it shows signs of serious historical research and is not an altogether unlikely fiction of the period. The interest centres on two female characters – twin sisters – who are the daughters of Mary Queen of Scots, a product of her secret marriage with the Duke of Norfolk. Matilda and Ellinor, the two heroines, are buffeted about and treated harshly by a cruel world. They themselves cannot quite believe that they are able to survive such a series of calamities and disasters. But they are not without appeal and they help to illustrate the powerlessness of women, and the injustices of society.

The growing contemporary concern with women's rights was reflected in the writing of both Sophia and Harriet Lee, and their return to the past to make points about the present – a fundamental feature of their writing – represented quite a change in the direction of the novel. What Clara Reeve had started, they continued, although they appear to have been more interested in finding something that worked (and sold well) than with an analysis of form and a specified literary aim.

Warbeck (1786) was the next of Sophia Lee's novels and it was followed in 1787 by a ballad (in medieval style), *A Hermit's Tale*, and in 1796 by a play, *Almeyda, Queen of Granada* – which, despite the appearance of Sarah Siddons (Sophia's friend) as the leading lady, was no great success and did not produce anything like the profits that *The Chapter of Accidents* had so providently provided.

However, the greatest success to come out of the school at Bath was a joint production of the sisters and was entitled *The Canterbury Tales* (1797-99). For Clara Whitmore (1910), 'The *Tales* represent the beginning of the modern short story' (p. 107) and deserve more praise and greater attention. Harriet's contribution to the *Tales* has been accorded more critical acclaim than Sophia's and one story in particular has been singled out as a significant achievement. 'The German Tale: Kruitzener'* is the story of a man destroyed by his own egotism: it was one to which Lord Byron was extremely partial and he was quick to provide a commendation for the author, Harriet Lee. Later Byron dramatised the tale as *Werner, or The Inheritance* (1822), and declared that the work had 'made a deep impression on me, and may indeed be said to contain the germ of much of what I have since written' (quoted in Katharine Rogers, 1984: p. 194).

*Note: two spellings, Kruitzner, Kruitzener.

I have made only a cursory study of the literary records on the influences of Lord Byron but have failed to find any discussion of Harriet Lee. Yet clearly her work was taken seriously by some of the great men and there can be no doubt that they gained from her writing.

Harriet Lee seems to have kept her pen as busy as her sister's, although whether the writing was undertaken inside or outside the classroom is not quite clear. She writes vigorous prose and is often prompted to express outrage as she repeatedly exposes injustice particularly as it applies to women – in her novels and plays. I wonder about the significance of the title of one of her novels – *Clara Lennox* (1797) – and while I would not want to make too much out of what could be coincidence, it does seem unlikely that Harriet Lee was unaware of what she was doing when she linked the names of two of her real heroines – Clara Reeve and Charlotte Lennox – to provide the title of her novel, and to name the heroine of her fictional world.

She also wrote another novel – *The Errors of Innocence* (1786) – and a few plays. Her fiction was more successful than her drama: *The New Peerage* (1787) did not contribute to the family coffers and *The Mysterious Marriage* (1798) was never staged.

If the influence of Sophia and Harriet Lee on the world of letters has long since been forgotten, their writing was widely known, much appreciated and frequently emulated in their own day. With her explicit goal of returning to the past to bring back some of its rich traditions to the present, Clara Reeve had opened a new door in fiction and Sophia and Harriet Lee were not slow to enter and to sample some of the new delights of old ways. With Clara Reeve's evocation of 'atmosphere' (and Charlotte Smith's introduction of landscape), and with Harriet and Sophia Lee's historical fiction, we see these women setting out in a new direction in fiction. That they were soon overtaken by Ann Radcliffe does not minimise the achievement of their pioneering ways.

But before proceeding with any discussion of Ann Radcliffe it is necessary to clear up some of the confusions about the name and identities. When I first came across numerous references to Ann Radcliffe (sometimes Anne Radcliffe, or Mary Ann Radcliffe) in the late eighteenth and early nineteenth centuries, I was initially excited, and perplexed. Excited by the possibility that the many works which bore the name 'Ann Radcliffe' might all have been written by the one woman (spellings of names were often inconsistent); perplexed, because there were so many differences in the writing. And I was frustrated in some of my early efforts to confirm or refute the supposition that all the 'Ann Radcliffes' were one and the same person. However, Janet Todd's (1984) *Dictionary of British and American Women Writers 1600-1800* helps to clarify who is who and who wrote what.

Ann Radcliffe, the renowned author and writer of *The Mysteries of*

Udolpho and *The Italian* (and more), is not to be confused with that other Gothic novelist, Mary Anne Radcliffe, whose works include *The Fate of Velina de Guidova* and *Radzivil* (both published in 1790 by William Lane of the Minerva Press); who also wrote the highly popular *Manfroné* or *The One Handed Monk* (1809) and who produced *Radcliffe's New Novelist's Pocket Magazine* (1802) which was a selection of condensed Gothic fiction. Mary Anne Radcliffe was of an entirely different breed from Ann Radcliffe, and instances of mistaken identity can be attributed in part to the opportunism of a particular publisher who was quite content to have his author taken for the writer of *Udolpho* and *The Italian*.

That sales might have been boosted by a case of 'mistaken identity' also seems to be the reason behind the confusion of Ann Radcliffe with Mary Ann Radcliffe (1745-1810), who in 1799 wrote *The Female Advocate, or An Attempt to Recover the Rights of Women from Male Usurpation* (Ann Shtier, 1984). Again, though the names may be similar, the work of Ann Radcliffe and Mary Ann Radcliffe is poles apart.

Confusion is compounded by the absence of detail on the lives of all three women (not even the birth date of Mary Anne Radcliffe is known) and the ritual acknowledgment must be gone through yet again: little is known about the eminently successful and highly influential novelist, Ann Radcliffe. It would be desirable indeed to have a biography of this 'discreet but nevertheless daring eighteenth century lady' (Frederick Garber, 1981), but the prospect seems remote. Others have attempted the task and been defeated. Bonamy Dobrée (1983) has stated that Ann Radcliffe's 'life was so uneventful that one of her admirers, Christina Rossetti, who wanted to write her biography, had to abandon the idea for want of material' (p. viii).

While I would never concur with Bonamy Dobrée's assumption that because Ann Radcliffe led a very private life it was necessarily uneventful, I do appreciate the predicament that Christina Rossetti found herself in. Ann Radcliffe is a writer who invites questions about her personal life – about the nature of her imagination, the nuances of her beliefs – and these are precisely the sort of questions which must go unanswered, because of her determined reticence.

So far did she keep from public view there was considerable confusion surrounding her in her own lifetime. 'In 1809 she was reported to be dead,' writes Julia Kavanagh (1863), 'and as she did not contradict the report, her name was duly chronicled in biographical dictionaries. . . . In reality, Mrs Radcliffe did not die until 1823' (vol. I, p. 243). This is quite extraordinary. Where not reported dead she was held to be confined to a mental asylum and Julia Kavanagh concludes that 'She who could allow herself to be proclaimed dead or insane and not remonstrate, was no ordinary woman' (vol. I, p. 250). With this verdict on Ann Radcliffe I wholeheartedly agree.

Ann Radcliffe's objection to public view could have been based on an overwhelming distaste for exposure; alternatively, she could have chosen – as women writers have often done – to avoid the contradiction of being a proper woman and a published writer by removing herself from any situation in which this conflict could arise. But whatever her reasons, Ann Radcliffe, like so many women writers before her (and after her) provided little grist for the mill which manufactured maligned reputations for women. She ensured that there could be no comment on the woman no matter how widespread the criticism of the writing.

'The care with which she shunned attention has concealed even the few incidents of Mrs Radcliffe's life,' writes Julia Kavanagh, who expresses her regret. 'We know what books she wrote, what journeys she took, and there our knowledge ends. How it fared with her in that inner world which it is both the art and the charm of biography to unravel, we may vaguely surmise, but we can never know' (vol. I, p. 244).

Ann Radcliffe certainly protected herself from prying eyes: not just by refraining from any involvement in literary life or even by ensuring that no letters remained. Although she kept journals, once more her personal reticence resounds: 'Mrs Radcliffe never moved in literary society,' states Julia Kavanagh, and 'We have no letters of hers – her journals, though copious, do not deal with her life, nor even with her feelings, unless as they were manifested with regard to scenery. When she took up her pen it was not to trace any records of herself, but to note the changing aspects of nature – that great passion of her life' (vol. I, p. 249).

About any other passions, we have no clue. We would not even know if William Godwin had proposed to her. On friends, acquaintances, influences, little can be said. We know she met Mrs Thrale and Elizabeth Montagu. We suspect that she was taught by Harriet and Sophia Lee – and, if so, we can allow that she had a novel education. (Irresistible!)

Ann Ward was born in London in 1764 of middle class parents, and 'When her family moved to Bath, she probably attended a school kept by Harriet and Sophia Lee' (Katharine Rogers 1984: p. 262). Shy and reserved, at twenty-three she married William Radcliffe who later became the owner and editor of the *English Chronicle*. It seems that she took up writing in response to his encouragement – and absence – and on the many nights that he was at work, she spent her evenings in front of the fire writing her manuscripts, which she read to him on his return. She wrote rapidly, with few revisions, and if her husband's reaction was anything to go by, there was every indication that a wider audience would be drawn into her fiction – and would be well pleased.

In peaceful, private, and well-ordered surroundings, Ann Radcliffe founded an imaginative literary movement which was to inspire and influence writers of both sexes for many generations.

Her early novels are not accorded great acclaim, although they attracted sufficient interest to lead to what was, then, magnificent remuneration for her later ones. She would not have been paid £500 for *The Mysteries of Udolpho* (1794) had not *The Castles of Athlyn and Dunbane* (1789), *A Sicilian Romance* (1790) and *The Romance of the Forest* (1791) proved to be so popular and attracted such literary interest. But it is *The Mysteries of Udolpho* and *The Italian* (1797) on which much of her reputation rests.

Both novels were immensely popular – and *stayed* popular. *Udolpho*, for example, was printed twice in 1794, and again in 1795, 1800 and 1803. It was reissued in Anna Laetitia Barbauld's *British Novelists* in 1810 and in a series of British novels edited by Sir Walter Scott in 1821 (Ballantyre, 1821-4). There were two more printings in 1823, and more before the edition of 1832. The novel was still being reprinted later in the nineteenth century – in 1870, 1877, 1882, 1891, etc. It is currently in print in The World's Classics, having been issued in 1966 and 1970 by Oxford University Press and in 1980, 1981 and 1983 in The World's Classics (OUP).

Popular for many years afterwards, *The Mysteries of Udolpho* also created quite a stir at the time of publication. Commenting on its reception, Sir Walter Scott said, 'the very name was fascinating; and the public who rushed upon it with all the eagerness of curiosity, rose from it with unsated appetite. When a family was numerous the volumes always flew, and were sometimes torn from hand to hand; and the complaints of those whose studies were interrupted, were a general tribute to the genius of the author' (quoted in Anne Elwood, 1843: vol. I, p. 159).

In other words, it was a sensation. But this is not for a minute to suggest that it was 'sensational'. *The Mysteries of Udolpho* – as the reprint record reveals – was no passing craze, no excessively emotionally charged outpouring which enjoyed vulgar popularity by its play upon the feelings and its appeal to terror. It was a novel that was taken extremely seriously and which exerted a powerful influence on the world of letters.

'For some years after its publication in 1794 – one may hazard fifty years,' writes Bonamy Dobrée (1983), '*The Mysteries of Udolpho* was a "must" or in the phrase of today "required reading" for anybody who had any pretence at all to being a person of education or culture' (p. vi). One reason for this is that far from being a superficial parade of heightened sensitivities, *Udolpho* marks a change in world view and embodies significant philosophical concerns. If today Ann Radcliffe's work represents little more than an 'embarrassment' to the contemporary literary community, this contrasts with the position it attained in the nineteenth century, when it was held to be a superb achievement which opened up new areas of literary opportunity – and debate.

I was a victim of the 'received wisdom' until I began my work on Ann Radcliffe, for I had believed (on the basis of hearsay) that her novels would be examples of the worst form of early romances, that they would be so excessive as to be ludicrous and so 'escapist' as to be tedious. Nothing had prepared me for the surprise that was in store.

Yet what I have found raises once more the issue of the sexual double standard in literary judgments. For in reading her novels I was obliged to confront the fact that Ann Radcliffe was one of the founders – if not *the* founder – of the romantic movement. She was followed by many men who were influenced by her work and who acknowledged their great debt to her. But while the men who drew on her work for inspiration have been granted the prestigious status of writers of the *romantic* school, the woman who started it all is consigned to the derisory status of the writer of *romance*. There can be little clearer evidence that when women engage in the same work as men, the women's contribution is devalued by calling it by another name. It doesn't have to be a spectacularly different name. Phonetically there's not a lot of difference between *romance* and *romantic*; but there's a world of difference between a writer of 'romance' and a member of the 'romantic school'.

Ann Radcliffe helped to found the romantic movement. She was one of its first and most articulate spokeswomen. She reacted against the separation of intellect and emotion, against the glorification of reason, and she sanely suggested that life was a matter of head *and* heart. 'In an age that, publicly at least, supported the bright light of intelligible universality, she argued for the half stated, and the covert' (Frederick Garber, 1981: p. viii). *The Mysteries of Udolpho* suggested that there *were* mysteries in life.

When the Industrial Revolution was getting into its stride, when men were beginning to put their faith in science and to 'worship' machines (see Dora Russell, 1984), Ann Radcliffe focused attention back on nature, on the mystery and the beauty, and the human capacity for experiencing them.

The romantic movement is often held to be 'the only alternative to nineteenth century rationalism and science' (Kathy Overfield, 1981: p. 244): the part that Ann Radcliffe played in this movement is rarely mentioned.

Yet a steady stream of great male writers who followed her owe her much: 'Mrs Radcliffe established for herself a position which few other novelists, Gothic or otherwise, could seriously challenge until the appearance of the Waverley novels,' writes Frederick Garber (1981). 'Whether or not they acknowledged her influence all of the Romantics read her. Keats, Coleridge, and Byron, dissimilar in so many other ways, show strong touches of the Radcliffean mode. Scott and Lewis obviously knew her work well. So widespread a popularity and influence could not help but establish, in the literature that followed her, a tone and way of looking at the world which, but for her novels, might well have died out, and been mummified in large libraries' (p. vii).

Well – Ann Radcliffe has pretty much 'died out'; she has 'been mummified in old libraries' although the men who followed her have retained a prominent place in the literary tradition. Men who mentioned her in their acknowledgments but whose record of debts has been overlooked: Lord Byron who acknowledged the inspiratonal source of Ann Radcliffe in *Childe Harold's Pilgrimage* (vol. IV, p. xviii); John Keats who referred to her significantly as 'Mother Radcliffe' and of whom Bonamy Dobrée says, 'It would seem more than likely that Keats' *Eve of St Agnes* was coloured by memories of *Udolpho*' (1983: p. xiii).

'Minor' she may now be but Ann Radcliffe was one of the major literary figures of her day and for a long time after she ceased writing. 'Her contemporary reputation is beyond question,' writes Bonamy Dobrée. 'All the critics of the day praised her, including Coleridge' (p. xiii). He goes on to list the writers who were influenced by her and includes William Thackeray, Charles Dickens – and even William Faulkner.

And this is just the long line of great men. Her influence can be traced in women writers too – particularly in the work of Mary Shelley; more than one critic has suggested that *Frankenstein* is the romantic protest against 'the possible horrors of the scientific world view' (Kathy Overfield, 1981: p. 244), the reaction to the rationalist split of intellect and emotion.

Few were the women writers who followed Ann Radcliffe who were not swayed by her concerns or responsive to her synthesis of reason and feeling. The Brontës stand firmly within the tradition she helped to create, and with her emphasis on a balance of 'sense' and 'sensibility' one wonders whether Ann Radcliffe did not exert an influence on the writing of Jane Austen. *Udolpho* was admired by Jane Austen, even if she could playfully mock some of its Gothic features: that it was a reference point for *Northanger Abbey* and required no explanation although *Northanger Abbey* was not published until 1818, almost twenty-five years after *Udolpho* made its appearance, helps to reveal how central and enduring Ann Radcliffe's influence was in literary circles – and among the reading public.

No writer, however, would have enjoyed such prestige had their achievement been purely theoretical. No writer would have been so widely quoted and so well considered had they experimented – and failed. It is that Ann Radcliffe's fiction is *good* fiction that establishes her claim to fame and it is part of the achievement of good fiction that it should move in a new direction and enlarge the range of vision.

There is an underlying philosophy in her writing, a conviction that reason alone is not enough and that there must be sensibility as well, but this thesis is not presented in didactic form or as explicit authorial comment. It is a thesis which is realised in her characters and setting, and is given shape and substance throughout her novels. It is in the descriptions of her characters, their lives, their feelings, their experiences that Ann Radcliffe makes her points: it is no coincidence that her upper class villains are immune to the beauties of nature.

Her heroines – who do respond to the beauties of nature – are seen by Clara Whitmore (1910) to represent another achievement of Ann Radcliffe. Clara Whitmore makes a very similar case to that of Julia Kavanagh (see page 221) and argues that in the work of Ann Radcliffe – and Charlotte Smith – we find the first fully formed heroines of 'sensibility' whose creation has eluded men and whose appearance was a source of inspiration for women's creativity:

> . . . the heroines of Mrs Smith and Mrs Radcliffe have a quality which not even Scott has been able to give his women. It is expressed by a word often used during the reign of the Georges, but since gone out of fashion. They were women of fine sensibilities. Johnson defines this as quickness of feeling, and it has been used to mean a quickness of perception of the soul as distinguished from the intellect. The sensibilities of women may not be finer than those of men, but they respond to a greater variety of emotions. This gives to them a certain evanescent quality which we find in Elizabeth Bennet, Jane Eyre, Maggie Tulliver, Romola, the portraits of Madame Le Brun and Angelica Kauffman and the poetry of Elizabeth Barrett Browning. This quality men have almost never grasped whether working with the pen or the brush. (Clara Whitmore, 1910: p. 103)

This emotional distinction between women and men – which some would say was characteristically 'Victorian' and even 'erroneous' – is nonetheless a distinction which is made by many women writers and critics, and there does seem to be a consensus among women of letters that it is a particular dimension of 'woman' which men writers do not, or cannot, construct. Clara Whitmore is of the opinion that though men may try they are usually defeated. When Walter Scott consistently tried to do what Ann Radcliffe had done, he failed, argues Clara Whitmore. His heroines are 'immobile' in comparison (p. 103): and he fails in his attempt to infuse his settings with the qualities which impinge on women and at which Ann Radcliffe excelled.

Of Walter Scott's 'imitations' of Ann Radcliffe, Clara Whitmore writes, 'Again and again he selected the same scenes that had appealed to her, and in his earlier novels and poems he filled them in with the same details that she had chosen' (p. 104). But he did not succeed: his work 'is tediously prosaic in description, far inferior to Mrs Radcliffe, and in the description of romantic scenery he never excels her' (p. 105).

Walter Scott did believe that Ann Radcliffe had attained 'poetic' heights in her fiction that few could match, and there can be no doubt that she exerted a pervasive influence in his work as he tried to emulate in his writing the quality he found in hers. In her praise he said that she had the distinction of being

> . . . the first to introduce into her prose fictions a beautiful and fanciful tone of natural description and impressive narrative, which had hitherto been exclusively applied to poetry. Fielding, Richardson, Smollett, even Walpole, though writing upon an imaginative subject, are decidely prose authors. Mrs Radcliffe has a title to be considered as the first poetess of romantic fiction, that is, if actual rhythm shall not be deemed essential to poetry. (quoted in Anne Elwood, 1843: vol. II, p. 165)

This evaluation contrasts with that of Walter Allen (1954/1980) who gives Ann Radcliffe credit for writing 'the first successful thriller' (pp. 97-8) but who proceeds to minimise much of her achievement in *The Mysteries of Udolpho* when he says of the heroine, Emily, that 'she was a dim enough character; but she is adequate to her creator's purposes: she is incarnate sensibility, and her function in the novel is simply to feel, to feel the appropriate emotions of wonder, awe and terror. From this point of view, *The Mysteries of Udolpho* may be considered as a machine for making the reader feel similar emotions' (p. 98).

I do think this is a bit excessive.

But Walter Allen does acknowledge the extent of Ann Radcliffe's influence on writers like Walter Scott and Lord Byron ('it has been said that "the man Lord Byron tried to be was the invention of Mrs Radcliffe"', p. 99); and her influence on writers right up to the present day ('she points to Poe and all the nineteenth-century novelists and story-tellers who use, however subtly, the supernatural, the psychic, and even morbid psychological states in man, as well as to the great host of crude thriller writers of the present day', p. 99).

What is extremely interesting is Walter Allen's explanation of Ann Radcliffe's relationship to the romantic movement. He lists those who follow her but he provides no precedents for her romantic creations: he does not allow her to be a founder or originator of this movement. With Ann Radcliffe, he writes, 'we are already plumb in the middle of the romantic movement' (p. 99), so one is obliged to conclude that this is a movement which started in the middle.

Is it such a lot to ask that women should be given some credit for creation?

Walter Allen aside, the women critics have been prepared to give Ann Radcliffe her due and *The Mysteries of Udolpho* and *The Italian* (which is judged to be better but which was not so popular) are consistently praised – for the poetry, the scenery, the characters – and the plot.

To attempt to summarise *The Mysteries of Udolpho* and *The Italian* would be to do these novels a disservice: summaries would omit some of the most moving features of the writing. (They would also take up a lot of space – they are complicated plots – and besides, they would spoil some of the exquisite suspense that awaits those who have not read these works.)

But some of the characters are superbly portrayed, the men as well as the women (Father Schedoni, for example, in *The Italian* is exceptionally well realised). And the achievement which is represented in the integration of setting, action, and emotion renders the production of many modern visual horror stories amateurish in comparison. When it is recognised that so much of the spectacular scenery which Ann Radcliffe describes with such powerful effect was not directly witnessed by her (but drawn from travel and reference books), her accomplishment appears even more remarkable.

Only once, it seems, did Ann Radcliffe leave England and her experiences are outlined in *A Journey Made in the Summer of 1794 through Holland and the Western Frontier of Germany ... To Which are Added Observations During a Tour to the Lakes* (1795). Apart from this and the novels previously mentioned, she wrote only one other work, which was not intended for publication and not made available until after her death: *Gaston de Blondeville, or The Court of Henry III* (1826) reveals the author's more arduous attempt at historical accuracy and authenticity but Julia Kavanagh (1863) says of this novel that Ann Radcliffe's indulgence 'with an amount of architecture and costume ... sat awkwardly on her story and injured it' (vol. I, p. 325).

From the point of view of the reading public, Ann Radcliffe disappeared after the publication of *The Italian* in 1797 – which is probably one of the reasons for reports of her insanity or death. But *The Italian* 'was the last book that Mrs Radcliffe published,' writes Clara Whitmore (1910), without any attempt to conceal her perplexity: 'Neither the fame it brought her, nor the eight hundred pounds she received for it from her publishers, tempted its author from her life of retirement. Publicity was distasteful to her. At the age of thirty four, at an age when many novelists had written nothing, she ceased from writing, and spent the rest of her years either in travel, or in the seclusion of her own home' (p. 100).

'Mother Radcliffe' left behind an invaluable literary legacy from which many still profit: she warrants more thanks; she deserves more deference.

In her own day and for many years afterwards, Ann Radcliffe established the Gothic novel as the predominant form in fiction and she was followed by many proficient and prolific women writers who, even if they do not always match her literary achievement, do not deserve to be automatically dismissed without a fair hearing. All of the women who wrote Gothic novels have since been derided – with the term 'Gothic' being used almost synonomously with 'female' – and yet in the history of literary criticism there is virtually no evaluation of their work. The fact that they were Gothic novelists seems sufficient of itself to damn them yet in the late eighteenth and early nineteenth century the Gothic novel knew no such deadly devaluation: in the novels of Ann Radcliffe are the seeds of one of the most powerful literary movements that has ever emerged and it is more likely than not that similar strengths could be found in the Gothic novels of other women writers – if only they could be read.

For example, I would dearly like to know more about Eliza Parsons (1748?-1811) who is purported to have written sixty books, two of which are referred to (not at all flatteringly) in *Northanger Abbey*. We know that late in life, on the death of her husband, Eliza Parsons was obliged to turn to writing to support her large family (she had eight children) but economic pressure alone is not enough to explain her phenomenal success. Nor is her speed by definition a failing, for to be swift is not necessarily to be bad, despite such frequent assertions by unthinking critics.

Eliza Parsons 'borrowed' from Ann Radcliffe (Robin Riley Fast, 1984), but she introduced elements of her own into her fiction, particularly as they related to women. She argued that if women were weak then there was all the more reason to educate them, and she was consistently concerned with women's vulnerability which was a product of their economic dependence.

Regina Maria Roche (1764-1845) is another Gothic novelist who has attracted my interest but about whom little or nothing is known, except that she was 'a public celebrity' and received 'royal notice for her writing in the late 1790s' (Ann Shtier, 1984b: p. 272) – which one could be forgiven for thinking should provide some insurance against the fate of oblivion! Regina Maria Roche was also influenced by Ann Radcliffe and her most successful novel, *The Children of the Abbey* (1796), rivalled the popularity of *The Mysteries of Udolpho* having been through eleven editions by 1832.

Regina Maria Roche too rated a mention in *Northanger Abbey*

(*Clermont*, 1798), although again the reference is hardly flattering. But this author of approximately twenty novels – who enjoyed a considerable reputation and high sales in her own lifetime – cannot blithely just be passed by.

Nor should Agnes Maria Bennett (?-1808) be summarily dismissed. She too had some outstanding successes with her first novel, *Anna, or Memoirs of a Welch Heiress* (1785), which sold out on the first day, and her last novel, *Vicissitudes Abroad, or The Ghost of My Father* (1806) which sold two thousand copies on publication day. In between was the well-received *Juvenile Indiscretions* (1786) which was published 'Anonymously and was first attributed to Fanny Burney to whom Agnes Maria Bennett bears a striking resemblance' (David Temes, 1984: p. 46) as well as the highly praised and best-selling *The Beggar Girl and her Benefactors* (1797). Agnes Maria Bennett's personal fortunes fluctuated: she left her husband, endured a poverty-stricken period, became the housekeeper of Admiral Sir Thomas Pye (by whom she had several of her many children, including the famous actress Hester Esten), and she had a period as a literary success. Perhaps because she experienced some of the 'ups and downs' of life, reversals in fortune and position became a favoured theme in her fiction.

Witty, lively, satirical (and long), her novels range from the Gothic to social criticism and there can be no doubt that Agnes Maria Bennett constitutes an interesting link in women's literary traditions. But she too has been wiped from the literary record – to our loss.

So overwhelming is the evidence that there have been good women writers – and good women writers of good Gothic novels – who have been excluded from the literary tradition that I cannot suggest with any confidence that this coverage does justice to the women writers. There are bound to be more women who have not been included here, women writers of great talent who have been buried under years of studied neglect and deliberate denial. But those who have been unearthed here demonstrate beyond doubt that women were still making a creative contribution to the novel in the late eighteenth and early nineteenth centuries, a creative contribution that has been disallowed within the male literary tradition.

Table 9: Clara Reeve, Harriet Lee, Sophia Lee, Ann Radcliffe

Clara Reeve (1729-1807)

1772	*The Phoenix* (translation)
1777	*The Champion of Virtue* (*The Old English Baron*)
1783	*The Two Mentors*

1785	*The Progress of Romance* (criticism)
1788	*The Exiles*
1791	*The School for Widows*
1792	*Plans for Education*
1793	*Memoirs of Sir Roger de Clarendon*
1796	*Original Poems on Several Occasions*
1799	*Destination*

Harriet Lee (1757-1851)

1786	*The Errors of Innocence*
1787	*The New Peerage* (play)
1797	*Clara Lennox*
1798	*The Mysterious Marriage* (not staged)
1797-99, 1801, 1805	*Canterbury Tales*

Sophia Lee (1750-1824)

1780	*The Chapter of Accidents* (play)
1783-85	*The Recess*
1786	*Warbeck*
1787	*A Hermit's Tale* (ballad)
1796	*Almeyda, Queen of Granada* (play)
1804	*The Life of A Lover*
1807	'The Assignation' (play: performed, not published)

Ann Radcliffe (1764-1823)

1789	*The Castles of Athlyn and Dunbane*
1790	*The Sicilian Romance*
1791	*The Romance of the Forest*
1794	*The Mysteries of Udolpho*
1795	*A Journey Through Holland and the Western Frontiers of Germany*, etc.
1797	*The Italian*
1826	*Gaston de Blondeville*
1826	*St Albans Abbey and Other Poems*

CHAPTER 15

---•---

Mary Wollstonecraft, Mary Hays and autobiographical fiction

In front of me are the introduction and notes which serve as a guide to The World's Classics edition, (published by Oxford University Press, 1980), of Mary Wollstonecraft's novel, *Mary and The Wrongs of Woman*. Within what I have come to regard as the typical tradition of literary men, I am informed by the editors – James Kinsley and Gary Kelly – in their concluding remarks in the notes, that feminist scholars have failed to make a contribution to an understanding of Mary Wollstonecraft (1759-1797) and her work. In supercilious and sarcastic tones, the editors declare that when it comes to Mary Wollstonecraft, 'The feminist movement has devoted much attention to her life and works, but as yet has produced little comment of scholarly or critical value, and shows a recurring tendency to misspell the title of her best known book' (p. xxv).

I quote these comments because I think they are significant. They demonstrate that the dismissal and denial of feminism – the use of the snide and sneering remark as a *substitute* for an impartial evaluation of women's achievement – is a practice which persists. These petty comments are yet further support for Virginia Woolf's thesis that men critics are not simply surprised to find the view of women different from their own, but see in it a view that is sentimental, trivial, weak, 'substandard', because it is different from their own. And if Messrs Kinsley and Kelly are any guide to the value judgments that are made by literary men, then nothing has changed over the centuries. Their testimony reveals that the ways and means that have been devised to ensure that women's writing is not taken seriously – that there is not even any need to consult it as it is so inferior – continue to prevail.

(Unfortunately, I have not resisted the temptation to stoop to the sarcastic level of Messrs Kinsley and Kelly and so I should like to point out that on the first page of their edition of Mary Wollstonecraft's novels, the title of her best-known book is also misspelled.)

Spelling is not my only criticism of the editors' efforts. If 'authorities' are going to hold in contempt those views which differ from their own, then they place themselves in a vulnerable position unless they are extremely careful about the accuracy of their own assertions. To failed feminist scholars I am sure that it will come as something of a shock to learn from this edition of Mary Wollstonecraft's fiction, that *A Vindication of the Rights of Women* (sic) was written not as a repudiation of Rousseau's misogyny or even as a claim for women's autonomy, but out of 'a general change of heart engendered by the French Revolution' (p. i). So far removed is this assessment from Mary Wollstonecraft's stated motives that it can be classified as nothing other than false.

What to me remains a puzzle, however, is why two such patently anti-feminist literary men (both are professors of English and authorities on the novel) should have elected to edit the fiction of such a fervent feminist as Mary Wollstonecraft. So condescending and condemnatory is the introduction, one wonders why the publishers saw fit to include such a counter-productive prelude. It hardly qualifies as an invitation to the reader; it does little to enthuse, excite, or promote the novels. The emphasis is on failure: 'The conclusion must be that both these novels are failures. Like their author's life they are not even complete since *Mary* shrivels into a hasty and carelessly written ending and *The Wrongs of Woman* was ended arbitrarily by death' (p. xx). With their focus on the limitations and weakness of Mary Wollstonecraft's fiction, the question that arises is why these novels should have been reprinted at all.

I do not think it is making a mountain out of a molehill to draw so much attention to the negative elements of the introduction. On the contrary, I think it raises in microcosm the fundamental issue of the consequences for women's writing when only men sit in judgment. This introduction to Mary Wollstonecraft's fiction is a classic example of the way women are obliged to put aside the damning words, the devalued status, the denials and dismissals, if they are ever to get through to women's writing and to construct their own literary tradition. In this context I would suggest that the assessment of James Kinsley and Gary Kelly is *not* a good guide to Mary Wollstonecraft's novels.

For many reasons I see her fiction as significant: significant in itself, and significant too for its overtly feminist qualities and aims. But her novels are also significant for the contribution they made to the development of fiction. Mary Wollstonecraft was well aware of the tenet that the personal is political and she quite deliberately turned some of the experiences of her own life to fictional account so that she – and others – could gauge some of the personal dimensions of an oppressive social structure. Mary Wollstonecraft's novels were about herself and

6   Mary Wollstonecraft
painted by John Opie

few novelists had ventured before into such exposed territory.

I do not propose to give a detailed account of Mary Wollstonecraft's life and philosophy, for unlike James Kinsley and Gary Kelly I do recommend to readers the considerable body of feminist scholarship which exists on her.* But I want to counteract in some measure the unfavourable impression given by the introduction in the only edition of her novels in print: I also want to establish that the novels of Mary Wollstonecraft – and those of her friend Mary Hays – are very much part of women's literary tradition. For *both* women made abundant use of autobiography in their fiction. Their novels are personally political as they display some of the detail of their authors' lives in their demands for women's autonomy. While it may now be commonplace for women to write introspective novels which dwell upon their own psychological state and its relationship to social conditions – and while it may even be unremarkable for women to use their own lives as propaganda for reform and women's liberation** – it certainly was not common practice in the late eighteenth century when these women put themselves in their fiction.

There are numerous accounts of Mary Wollstonecraft's early life, but her first 'fiction' (which she distinguished from 'a novel') is, in many respects, yet another version. *Mary* is an attempt by the author to make sense of her own life, to find a meaningful framework for her own emotional experiences. At a time when she was feeling lonely, pessimistic, unhappy about her past and unsure of her future, she turned to fiction and allowed herself 'an outpouring of the trials of ... years of uncertainty' (Miriam Kramnick, 1978: p. 13).

This is not to suggest that *Mary* is sheer self-indulgence. There is a serious and defined intention behind it. Like Ann Radcliffe, Mary Wollstonecraft was interested in the relationship of sense and sensibility, in the interplay of reason and emotion, particularly as it applied to women, and to undertake a fictionalised autobiography was one way of trying to work out the relationship of these factors in one's self. But unlike Ann Radcliffe, Mary Wollstonecraft was also concerned to relate self to society, to understand the connections between the individual and the wider world. She wanted to link the personal and the political. While consistently aware that human beings were largely a product of their social conditions, Mary Wollstonecraft was also forever fascinated with the extent to which sensibility – and perception, knowledge, understanding, will – modified the influence of social conditions.

*See particularly Miriam Brody (1983), Miriam Brody Kramnick (1978), Claire Tomalin (1974), Alison Ravetz (1983).

**Since the consciousness-raising sessions of the 1970s this technique has been widely adopted in many contexts.

Mary illustrates the veracity of the old adage – how do you know what you think until you see what you write! In setting down her own experience the author was able to develop a better appreciation of the significance of events in her own life, a better understanding of the relationship between the conditions under which she was raised and the emotions she had experienced. With the result that we find in *Mary* 'the awakening consciousness of a young woman to degrading and inhibiting social forces' (Miriam Kramnick, 1978: p. 13). For Mary Wollstonecraft, the writing of her fiction was a consciousness-raising activity. As it can be for her readers.

Regrettably, we are probably now no closer than Mary Wollstonecraft was to definitively solving the riddle of the relationship between self and society. We do not know with any degree of certainty the extent to which human beings can become paralysed victims of oppressive social conditions, or the extent to which individuals can transform their circumstances. But what we have in *Mary* is an exploration of the tensions between the two and a search for a framework in which to place them.

That it was women themselves who were at fault was a possibility that Mary Wollstonecraft admitted, but one which she defiantly resisted in the face of the evidence. Her position is boldly stated in the 'advertisement' which prefaces *Mary*: she will not accept the tenet of women's weakness, even though women's strength may be a fiction. Commenting on *Mary* she says,

> In an artless tale, without episodes, the mind of a woman who has thinking powers is displayed. The female organs have been thought too weak for this arduous employment; and experience seems to justify the assertion. Without arguing physically about *possibilities* – in a fiction, such a being may be allowed to exist, whose grandeur is derived from the operation of her own faculties, not subjugated to opinion; but drawn by the individual from the original source.

If women could not be thinking and independent beings, what sense was Mary Wollstonecraft to make of her own life? What validity was there for the feelings, the aims and aspirations of the 'original source' if the fictitious Mary was but a dream?

Granted that she had a genuine need to write *Mary*, I would not want to claim, however, too grandiose a purpose for Mary Wollstonecraft's venture into fiction. Her own social circumstances should also be taken into account. She was at the time employed as a governess to the daughters of Lord and Lady Kingsborough, and was not at all happy. She deplored the idleness and frivolity of the upper class existence she was forced to witness, and became increasingly convinced that there was a strong link between character and hard work. Perhaps she wrote to exact some satisfaction from an otherwise superficial day; perhaps she took up her pen for many of the same reasons that other women have taken up their pens – for intellectual stimulation, self-realisation, enjoyment, relaxation, money.

Some of what she saw around her certainly went into the novel. Sentiments which were later to be given more powerful voice in the *Vindication of the Rights of Woman* (1792) were already evident in 1787 when Mary Wollstonecraft wrote *Mary*. In the first few pages emerges the author's unconcealed contempt for the langourous, indolent woman who skims across the surface of life, who *will not think*, and who will not take upon herself any form of responsibility. In Eliza – the heroine's mother – we have a woman who is weak in mind and body; a reclining and declining semi-invalid who keeps on her bed two beautiful dogs for whom she professes the most ardent warmth: 'This fondness for animals was not that kind which makes a person take pleasure in providing for the subsistence and comfort of a living creature; but it proceeded from vanity, it gave her an opportunity of lisping out the prettiest French expressions of ecstatic fondness, in accents that had never been attuned by tenderness' (p. 3). But even as this pitiless portrait is painted, even as Mary Wollstonecraft expresses her anger against the idea of 'woman as ornament', there is the lingering doubt as to who is to blame. Where should responsibility be fixed? Is it Eliza's fault that she affects but a mere show of life: are women weak or does the world make them that way?

Mary Wollstonecraft had much to work out. Explanations which today we take for granted were unknown to her; one of the reasons they are available today is because of the contribution she made in formulating them. Surrounded by evidence of women's 'weakness', Mary Wollstone-craft was trying to fathom the cause in order to envisage the change.

Through the fictitious family in *Mary*, Mary Wollstonecraft reworks some of her own family relationships. Eliza – as did Mary Wollstonecraft's mother – undisguisedly reveals her preference for her son over her daughter, and the daughter must come to terms with her rejection, as no doubt Mary Wollstonecraft was obliged to do. The husband, Edward, in his tyranny and irascibility, closely resembles Mary Wollstonecraft's father, and the relationship between Eliza and Edward parallels that of Mary Wollstonecraft's parents. The mother is ill and weak and unable to protect herself from the father who was 'so very easily irritated when inebriated that Mary' – the heroine like Mary the author – 'was continually in dread lest he should frighten her mother to death' (p. 5).

But this painful account of her own life is, on Mary Wollstonecraft's part, no simple plea for pity. It is the examination of a problem. In 'real life', Mary Wollstonecraft's attitude towards her mother was ambivalent;

she condemned her mother for not finding the personal strength to counteract the tyranny and temper of her father, but she was also well aware that her mother, as a wife, was denied any of the rights and resources which could give her strength. Her mother was not in a position to resist her father. The ambivalence Mary Wollstonecraft felt towards her own mother finds expression in her fiction where the harsh portrait of Eliza is ameliorated by the overall themes of *Mary* which denounced the deficiencies of education and the oppressive restrictions of marriage for women. When wives have not been educated, when they have no rights, how can they be expected to act in a strong and autonomous manner?

In worrying away at these issues Mary Wollstonecraft was shifting the ground for explanations of women's weakness. What has to be noted is that Mary Wollstonecraft found herself surrounded by 'weak women' and, according to the prevailing wisdom, women were weak because it was their nature to be so. While she could not accept this explanation she was not able to satisfactorily account for the 'weakness' she could so readily observe. In 1790, Catharine Macaulay was to assert – with brilliant insight – that women were made, not born, and Mary Wollstonecraft was immensely enthusiastic about and grateful for Catharine Macaulay's *Letters on Education* with their analysis of social conditioning (and sex-role stereotyping). But in 1787 such full understanding was yet to come although, in *Mary*, the author can be seen to be moving in the direction of an 'environment' (as distinct from 'heredity') explanation. This in itself was a remarkable achievement and was directly related to her reflections in the 'case study' of Mary.

Another area where Mary Wollstonecraft distanced herself by her own writing, and allowed herself the opportunity to clarify her own relationships, was in the friendship of the fictitious Mary for the consumptive Ann. Fanny Blood – Mary Wollstonecraft's close friend – had been dearly loved but not beyond reproach and the fictitious Mary is able to be critical of Ann in a way in which for the author Mary it would have been almost impossible to have found fault with Fanny. But by putting under the miscroscope the life of another woman as well as her own, Mary Wollstonecraft was gathering her data and sensitising her consciousness for her demand for women's rights. There are few (if any) precedents in fiction for this strategy of self-analysis – and social criticism.

Throughout *Mary*, the author keeps returning to the theme of education. For Mary Wollstonecraft, ignorance corrupted body and soul. That the upper class women she observed at close range while *Mary* was being written were so unthinking, so shallow – when a woman's 'voice was but the shadow of a sound, and she had, to complete her delicacy, so relaxed her nerves that she became a mere nothing' (p. 2) – was for

Mary Wollstonecraft the evidence of the damage done by deficient education. How can people think, exist, fulfil themselves if they are not given any intellectual life, if they are given no sound basis for making sense of the world, we hear the author demanding, again and again? And what a crime it is to deliberately deprive people of education, to specifically exclude women from educational benefits. Those who are not educated are, in Mary Wollstonecraft's terms, condemned to a half-life, to ignorance, unawareness: this makes for brutality in men and pretty lisping in women.

The story which carries the weight of these psychological, philo-sophical and political reflections is a relatively simple – if unusual – one. The heroine's brother dies and so Mary is an heiress who is suddenly shown more regard by her parents (this might have been a bit of creative wishful thinking on the part of the author). Edward, Mary's father, decides to settle a law suit with a nearby landowner by joining in marriage the two estates, and at seventeen, Mary is called from the sick bed of her consumptive friend Ann to the deathbed of her mother, and acquainted with the plan. The mother's dying wish is granted and the clergyman performs the marriage ceremony between Mary and the fifteen-year-old heir of the neighbouring estate: 'Her husband set off for the continent on the same day, with a tutor, to finish his studies at one of the foreign universities' (p. 15).

The rest of the fiction is primarily an account of Mary's resistance to cohabitation.

Mary does not like the idea of having been bartered in marriage. Nor does she like the idea of intimacy with her husband. While she conforms to some of the conventions, her rebellious spirit, nonetheless, cannot be concealed. On the death of her father, Mary 'wrote to the man she had promised to obey' (p. 19) to obtain his permission for a visit to Lisbon. She wanted to take Ann there for her health and offered her husband the explanation that her own physicians had recommended for her a change of air. 'She would have added "you would very much oblige me by consenting" but her heart revolted' (p. 20).

Permission, however, is granted, and Mary and Ann set sail for Portugal, where, sadly, despite Mary's tenderness and nursing, Ann dies. (Fanny Blood too died in Portugal with Mary Wollstonecraft as her nurse.) But in Portugal, Mary meets Henry – another consumptive who is there for his health – and she finds that she is strongly drawn to him. She returns to England, alone, however, Months pass before she sees Henry again. Too soon, he dies, but not before Mary comes to appreciate the bond that can be forged between two people of sensibility.

With the death of Henry, Mary's life is all upheaval and despair. What does it all mean? The unhappiness, the grief – the absent husband? At this stage the author seemed to see the only solutions in good works – and religious resignation.

But the day of reckoning must come. Mary has a husband who wants to be a husband and not forever can she avoid his company. She finally agrees to live with him if he allows her one more year to travel without him accompanying her. He acquiesces. But:

> The time too quickly elapsed, and she gave him her hand – the struggle was almost more than she could endure. She tried to appear calm; time mellowed her grief, and mitigated her torments; but when her husband would take her hand, or mention anything like love, she would instantly feel a sickness, a faintness at her heart, and wish involuntarily, that the earth would open up and swallow her. (p. 67)

A strong woman, a determined woman, a rebellious woman, who must finally submit. A woman of 'sensibility' who is sickened and affronted by the demands of her marriage. A woman who has no rights, who was traded by her father, who has no control over her destiny. Well might she have struggled against her fate, but to no avail. The only way out is death:

> Her delicate state of health did not promise long life. In moments of solitary sadness a gleam of joy would dart across her mind – She thought that she was hastening to that world *where there is neither marrying*, nor giving in marriage. (p. 68)

This is the 'shrivelled' ending referred to by James Kinsley and Gary Kelly. While it is far from a satisfactory ending on many levels – the only way out for women is death – it is a powerful ending, and well exemplifies Mary Wollstonecraft's values. There couldn't be a much more forceful denunciation of marriage, and in concluding her fiction, Mary Wollstonecraft has reached her own conclusions.

While ever women are *reduced* to marriage, there is no hope.

What the writing of this fiction did for the author it is difficult to determine in any definitive way. But what the novel itself does for women's literary traditions is more readily evaluated.

Had Mary Wollstonecraft not wished to make the connections between the personal and the political, no doubt she would have chosen some name other than her own for her heroine. But what she set out to do – and to my mind what she assuredly accomplished – was to link personal suffering with political, social and economic conditions. To find a framework for explaining and evaluating women's existence.

It is important to remember that *Mary* is *not* autobiography: it *is* fiction. But its authenticity is enhanced by the author's use of her own name, by the inclusion of many of her own heartfelt experiences, by her attempts to make sense of her own world, and hence to provide insights for all women. *Mary* is an example of 'speaking bitterness'* and fiction had not been used in this way before.

It seems to me – substandard feminist critic and scholar though I may be – that many contemporary feminist novels are well within the literary tradition that Mary Wollstonecraft helped to forge. Today's fiction may not be so self-consciously autobiographical, it may not be so explicitly political, but the attempt to explain one's self and one's society when one is a member of a subordinate group, the attempt to understand the links between individuals and social structures – as they impinge upon women – is now a salient characteristic of many women's novels. While such fiction may be labelled inappropriately as 'romance', female critics have acknowledged the personal/political dimension of much of women's writing, and although there is an enormous 'gap' between *Mary* (1787) and Doris Lessing's *The Golden Notebook* (1962), the distance in terms of genre does not strike me as very great.

But if it is not unusual to trace the source of contemporary feminist *ideas* to Mary Wollstonecraft, it is so unusual as to be virtually unknown to trace some of the sources of contemporary women's *fiction* to her pen. Yet the mother of feminism is equally entitled to acknowledgment as one of the mothers of the novel. Unfortunately, however, any contribution Mary Wollstonecraft has made to the development of the novel – to the women's novel – has been wantonly wiped away.

And it is not as if there were only *one* fiction on which her reputation were required to rest: *The Wrongs of Woman* was equally innovative and equally significant. However, to emphasise the incomplete nature of *The Wrongs of Woman* (as James Kinsley and Gary Kelly do) is to ignore the experimental element, to deny the intent. It is also to be crass. For in a sense it is a sad irony that this novel, which was a brutal itemisation of the burdens under which women laboured, should have been arbitrarily terminated by the author's own death in childbirth. Where James Kinsley and Gary Kelly see an unfinished novel, I see the blurring of the lines between fiction and 'real life'. In her passionate autobiographical writing, Mary Wollstonecraft did not have her view of the world out of reasonable proportions when she focused on untimely death for her heroines. For me there is added poignancy in *The Wrongs of Woman* when the fate that the author entertains as a possibility for the heroine, Maria, is the one which claims the writer herself.

While there are many similarities between *Mary* and *The Wrongs of Woman*, there are differences too. Much had happened to Mary Wollstonecraft in the intervening ten years and the changes that she had

---

*'Speaking bitterness' is the Chinese term for women's consciousness raising.

undergone manifest themselves in her intensely personal writing. No more a governess in search of the reality of women's intellectual life and independence, Mary Wollstonecraft had started to live the life she had previously doubted could exist. The author is now a woman who knows what she is talking about – not someone looking for her way.

Since her governessing days she had supported herself by her pen. She had worked for the *Analytical Review*, written much publicised books, become a member of literary, political and philosophical circles, and had abandoned her religion: she had written *A Vindication of the Rights of Woman*, formed a close friendship with Mary Hays, been to France to observe the Revolution firsthand; she had lived with Gilbert Imlay, given birth to a child, been to Scandinavia, been rejected, and attempted suicide; she had remet William Godwin and while writing her second novel had become pregnant – and married him.

This wealth of experience finds expression in *The Wrongs of Woman*: Mary Wollstonecraft had learnt a great deal in ten years: she had been educated by travel, by reading, by involvement in learned discussions and by the tutelage of scholarly men who were prepared to help the women denied access to formal instruction. She had learned by living her own life and if once there had been ambivalence about the origin of women's weakness, there was certainly none now. Her accusing finger pointed to male tyranny as the explanation – and it did not waver.

With her greater awareness of the machinations of power and her astute analysis of the significance of political circumstance, in *The Wrongs of Woman* Mary Wollstonecraft shifts her emphasis from the individual in search of self-development, to social conditions which frustrate and block self-development in women. And she calls on women to rebel. Her purpose in her novel is patently political and she acknowledges in her preface that she is more concerned to make her points than to provide a pleasing narrative.

> In many instances I could have made the incidents more dramatic, would I have sacrificed my main object, the desire of exhibiting the misery of oppression, peculiar to women, that arise out of the partial laws and customs of society. (p. 73)

It is fiction about women and for women that she writes, and the novel had not been so determinedly bent in this political direction before. The author's aim is to strip away the myths of the dominant reality which would have women suitably served by marriage, and to expose the misery which is being masked. Never does she lose sight of her awareness that what happens to the individual woman is the result of the division of power in society – that the personal is political.

It is a public institution she wants to expose – marriage; but it is the private cost she chooses to count. At the core of *The Wrongs of Woman* is the *everyday reality* of many women – and the assertion that women's feelings are valid and real – and while the author is the first to admit that such mundane matters are not ordinarily the stuff from which novels are wrought, she stands firm in her insistence that the degradation of women in marriage is tragedy on a grand scale. 'What are termed great misfortunes, may more forcibly impress the minds of common readers,' she acknowledges in deference to the more customary concepts of grand tragedy, but she will not relinquish her position that in the personal suffering of the ordinary marriage lies the potential for great art. 'It is the delineation of finer sensations, which in my opinion, constitute the merits of our best novels,' writes Mary Wollstonecraft (p. 74) as she proceeds to embark on an exposé of the barbarisms of marriage.

To omit such a novel from women's literary traditions is to exclude one of the most powerful portrayals of women – in society.

While she denounces marriage, Mary Wollstonecraft structures her attack by concentrating on the personal degradation which occurs when women are required to live with brutalising men. We are introduced to Maria, the woman of fine sensibility who is degraded by her husband, and to Jemima, who appears to lack fine sensibility but who is shown to have been degraded by her previous successive exploitations by men. And in these two women characters Mary Wollstonecraft not only resolves the dilemma of the weak and debased woman when she shows how women are demeaned by the conditions under which they are obliged to live, she also casts light on the class differences among women. Her purpose, the author declares unequivocally, is to expose the private agony which is the result of public oppression and 'to show the wrongs of different classes of women, equally oppressive, though, from the difference of education, necessarily various' (p. 74).

Pure contemporary feminism: in fiction: almost two hundred years ago. *The Wrongs of Woman* is an unapologetic attempt to present the fictionalised version – the more personalised construction – of *A Vindication of the Rights of Woman*.

In this fiercely protesting novel we find Maria, who has endured every harrowing assault on her senses that her husband could contrive and who is finally imprisoned in a mental asylum as her husband makes his last desperate bid to gain control of her fortune. Maria's keeper is Jemima, a woman who has been seduced (read 'raped') and abandoned, who has been mocked and maligned, starved and scarred, and whose behaviour, if at times coarse, must be understood in context. Brutalising circumstances can produce brutalised human beings.

In her attempt to stay sane in confinement, to explain to herself what has happened, and to provide an account for her daughter from whom she has been roughly separated, Maria writes the story of her life and marriage, and in the process compiles an impressive list of grievances against a male-dominated society.

It's all here: the double standard that shows preference for the boy and punishes the girl. 'Such indeed is the force of prejudice,' says Maria of her brother, 'that what was called wit in him was cruelly repressed as forwardness in me' (p. 126). In contrast to the rigid restrictions placed on women, there is the leeway shown to men who err: 'Master must have his little frolics – but – Lord – bless your heart! – men would be men while the world stands' (p. 172).

There is the fulmination against the absence of education for girls and the readily recognised despair of feeling dull and stupid when one is treated as dull and stupid: 'I have imagined myself the most stupid creature in the world,' confesses Maria in relation to her husband's treatment of her, 'till the abilities of some casual visitor convinced me that I had some dormant animation' (p. 145).

There is the diatribe against the sexual exploitation of women, and case after case of sexual harassment: returning from his revels, Maria's husband 'would repeat when wine had loosened his tongue, most of the common place sarcasms levelled at [women], by men who do not allow them to have minds, because minds would be an impediment to gross enjoyment' (pp. 146-7).

The novel is savage: it is effective. It is the substance of consciousness raising sessions – and of much women's fiction – almost two centuries later.

'I had been caught in a trap and caged for life,' says Maria of her marriage (p. 144). The door to freedom cannot easily be opened for the fate which awaits the separated wife is a world apart from the one which awaits the separated husband:

> The situation of a woman separated from her husband, is
> undoubtedly very different from a man who has left his wife. He, with
> lordly dignity has shaken off a clog; and the allowing her food and
> raiment, is thought sufficient to secure his reputation from taint. And
> should she have been inconsiderate, he will be celebrated for his
> generosity and forbearance. Such is the respect paid to the master key
> of property! A woman on the contrary, resigning what is termed her
> natural protector (though he never was so but in name) is despised
> and shunned, for asserting the independence of mind distinctive of a
> rational being, and spurning at slavery. (pp. 157-8)

One may debate the propriety of personal bitterness in art, the desirability of propaganda in fiction, but one cannot dispute the force of Mary Wollstonecraft's novel.

It is a harsh world for women that Mary Wollstonecraft describes. It is the private anguish, customarily 'veneered' or ignored, that she places in the cold, hard light, for inspection. Presumably much of the personal experience and many of the accusations about 'marriage' are associated with her depressingly unhappy relationship with Gilbert Imlay to whom she had felt herself honour bound* but who treated her as a toy he soon tired of: who abandoned her. That she should reach the conclusion that only a foolish woman would risk marriage is not unexpected in the circumstances. Yet at the very time of writing this diatribe against women's exploitation in marriage, Mary Wollstonecraft elected to wed William Godwin. Which for me raises the question of how she reconciled her theory and her practice. It must have been extremely difficult for her to make such a concession to the conventions she so unreservedly despised and which she knew so well could become a prison with few opportunities for release or escape. Perhaps she admitted for herself the possibility that she allowed her heroine, Maria: that of renouncing he who proved to be a rotten husband. But as she showed in *The Wrongs of Woman*, this was a perilous course of action to undertake.

What is clear is that Mary Wollstonecraft would not have been able to ignore the significance of her own 'compromise'. She did not protect herself – or others – with cushioning rationalisations. One quality which she possessed – in abundance – was the ability to 'cut through cant' and to face full square the bitter everyday realities beneath the euphemistic surfaces. This is one reason that so many of her assertions retain their cutting edge today. Her exposés are still relevant; they have a sense of immediacy.

For example, Jemima, who again and again has been exploited, who has been forced to support herself by prostitution, indicts the entire social system and the spurious justifications which support it when she says scornfully, 'How often have I heard ... that every person willing to work may find employment.' Two hundred years later the claim has its pertinent irony.

Not for one moment did Mary Wollstonecraft relax her hold on the denunciation of injustice and degradation. But if she demands nothing short of perfection from the social order, so too does she demand nothing short of perfection from women. There are to be no social conditions which weaken women but neither are women to choose to be weak. Even when the odds are against them, women must be strong. There can be no giving in, no opting out, no abdication to irresponsibility. Unrealistic it may have been but uncompromising it also was, when Mary Wollstonecraft demanded that women who did not

*For further discussion see the section on Adeline Mowbray, page 319.

want to be debased by living with base men had no choice but to rebel.

She was aware that rebellion was not easy, that the price to be paid was high, but the strain of ruthless romance is there, nonetheless, as she makes clear in her attitude to her heroine, Maria:

> I cannot suppose any situation more distressing, than for a woman of sensibility, with an improving mind, to be bound to such a man as I have described, for life; obliged to renounce all the humanizing affections, to avoid cultivating her taste, lest her perception of grace and refinement of sentiment should sharpen to agony the pangs of disappointment. . . . I should despise, or rather call her an ordinary woman, who could endure such a husband as I have sketched.
> (pp. 73-4)

The message is plain enough. Women must leave bad marriages. And not necessarily by recourse to the law.* When in her prison Maria finds a man whom she can love, who does not degrade her, the author gives her wholehearted support to Maria's renunciation of her husband and her relationship with her lover, Henry Darnford.

Society, of course, did not endorse such a subversive view. Mary Wollstonecraft knew the nature of the threat she was posing – and she knew what the response was likely to be: in *The Wrongs of Woman*, Maria's lover is tried for adultery, for appropriating another man's possession. That she was aware of the consequences of rebellion, however, did not stop her from advocating it for herself – and other women. And it was because she incited wives to disobedience that Mary Wollstonecraft was so vituperatively denounced. For almost two centuries the name of Mary Wollstonecraft has been used to symbolise the worst of womanhood; in her own time she was the 'hyena in petticoats' and the 'philosophizing serpent' who was publicly ridiculed, while more recently, with the aid of sophisticated Freudian concepts, she has been labelled 'the archetypal castrating female,' 'a man-hater whose feminist crusade was inspired by nothing more than a hopeless, incurable affliction – penis envy' (Miriam Kramnick, 1978: p. 7).

The least censorious judgment I can find of her comes from Ann Elwood (1843), writing almost fifty years after Mary Wollstonecraft's death, and who says of the author and *The Wrongs of Woman* that the 'plot was decidedly an immoral one inasmuch as her heroine, a married woman, is represented as forming an attachment to another man during her husband's life time' (vol. II, p. 151).

*It was the patriarchal law that Mary Wollstonecraft objected to because of its oppression of women; it was the law which made it virtually impossible for women to separate or divorce.

Such 'immorality' is a matter of little consternation today and cannot be proffered as a cause of her neglect. But that Mary Wollstonecraft – *novelist* – has not been reclaimed, and reinstated, as one of the primary figures in women's literary heritage is a matter of some surprise. For in form, style, content, she is one of the mothers of the novel, and she made a significant contribution to the birth of women's literary traditions.

Until Mary Wollstonecraft's fiction, the more intimate details of women's lives went, for the most part, unexpressed. There is a tradition of suggesting the suffering of women's lives but no woman novelist had stepped beyond the bounds of convention, had defiantly departed from what was 'proper', or had 'coarsely' conveyed the cruel existence to which so many women were condemned. To be sure, Charlotte Lennox, Frances Sheridan and Charlotte Smith had hinted at the frustration and the bitterness below the surface in the lives of many wives, but they *had* maintained the surface: Mary Wollstonecraft swept it all away. Sarah Fielding had discreetly commented on the undesirable treatment of women as sex-objects, and Elizabeth Inchbald had subtly suggested that happiness could even be found in an independent life: but Mary Wollstonecraft would not be constrained by convention or restricted by refinement. She broke the taboo when what had been previously shrouded in secrecy was seized upon by Mary Wollstonecraft and paraded before the public to behold.

Within a well-developed tradition of 'ladylike' novels, Mary Wollstonecraft threw down the gauntlet and made it clear that there was more to women's lives than had previously been allowed. Decorum was thrown to the winds when Mary Wollstonecraft took the 'female sensibility' which was becoming so revered and showed that while it had its advantages for women, it was not without its costs. Sensitive women could suffer even more at the hands of coarse men!

With all the developments that had taken place in the novel, with all the ventures into the territory unknown and the introduction of 'women's women' in fiction, there comes the sudden realisation, with Mary Wollstonecraft's novels, of just how much has been left out, just how great has been the omission. This recognition has its parallels in the early days of the contemporary women's movement when it was realised that despite all that was supposedly known about women, it had to be admitted that what was known was partial, biased, distorted. That the everyday reality of women's lives remained a mystery. And consciousness raising sessions helped to generate some of that personal information that was glaring in its absence from the public records. In her own time, Mary Wollstonecraft's fiction fulfilled the same function; it helped to generate the private detail that had not been admitted to the public knowledge about women.

261

Although women had been writing novels for more than one hundred years when *Mary* and *The Wrongs of Women* appeared, the omissions in women's fiction were considerable. It has always struck me as strange that at a time when for so many women childbirth was such an overwhelming issue in their lives, no mention is made of it in women's writing. I am familiar with the male hero who on the eve of battle contemplates the meaning of the universe before he risks death, but where are the accounts of women who on the eve of childbirth give voice to their fears and doubts as they risk death?

Women did write about their anxiety, their anguish – and their resentment: in their diaries (see Cynthia Huff, forthcoming): they did *not* articulate their experience in fiction. In her private correspondence Mary Brunton revealed that she was convinced that she would die with the birth of her first child, rather late in life (see page 337): but nowhere is such emotion registered in her novels. Babies are born 'off-stage' and the mental and physical pain endured by mothers does not even waft in as a whisper. Never does Charlotte Smith – despite her 'women's women' and the charge that she utilised too many of her woes and too much of her bitterness in her fiction – never does she have a character who expresses her feelings about repeated pregnancies – or about a husband she despises.

Mary Wollstonecraft does not discuss the fears and pains of childbirth in *The Wrongs of Woman* though she could not conceivably have been without concern; this is one area of her private life she does not make public, one aspect of women's experience that she does not generalise from. But in *The Wrongs of Woman* she does have Maria express her distaste, distress, and despair, when she is coerced into sexual relations with her husband, and finds herself pregnant. Writing her account of this for her daughter, Maria says:

> . . . I am ashamed to own that I was pregnant. The greatest sacrifice
> of my principles in my whole life, was allowing my husband again to
> be familiar with my person, though to this cruel act of self denial,
> when I wished the earth to open and swallow me, you owe your birth
> . . . his tainted breath, pimpled face, and blood shot eyes, were not
> more repugnant to my senses, than his gross manners and loveless
> familiarity to my taste. (pp. 153-4)

Such sentiments had not been stated before, no matter how commonly they were felt in women's everyday lives. And it is because Mary Wollstonecraft made women's lives – as they were experienced by women – the substance of her novels, it is because she authenticated the personal and placed it firmly within the realm of the political, that her fiction is central to women's literary traditions. It is no authentic female tradition if women are confined to writing within parameters decreed by men, if women are not to be permitted to write about personal intimacy because it is not decent, nor about brutalising men because it is not flattering; it is when women write about what men do not know and what men may not want to hear – and when this version of experience is validated – that there is a legitimated female tradition.

That none of these qualities of Mary Wollstonecraft's fiction is commented upon in the introduction to the contemporary reprint of her novels is one indication of how far we are from having a women's literary tradition. In the terms decreed by men it could well be that her novels failed, that they shrivelled away, that they do not conform to the standards of the early 'romantics': that they are weak, trivial, sentimental and substandard. But the point is that men do not have – or should not have – a monopoly on standards, which originate in a male view of the world.

If, however, Mary Wollstonecraft has been criticised for her failure, she is still better known and more widely read than her close friend Mary Hays, who tried to continue in the tradition that Mary Wollstonecraft had forged – who was another pioneer of women's rights and another pioneer of the autobiographical and personal novel.

Of Mary Hays (1760-1843), Gina Luria (1977) has said, 'Little is known about her earliest years. . . .' The only fragments which are known consist of evidence 'that she was born into a family of Rational Dissenters and was taken at an early age to hear great preachers teach in the environs of her parents' home in the London suburb of Southwark' (p. 524). Which can't have been a wholly satisfying or exciting life.

The adult life of Mary Hays is better documented, partly because some of her letters have survived. She wrote numerous letters, many of them 'love letters', and during the later stage of her life she actually incorporated some of her own letters in her fiction. In this respect she was very different from some of her predecessors: where Delarivière Manley and Eliza Haywood professed to have found real letters which were in reality their own fictional creations, Mary Hays employed a reverse strategy when she used her real letters to help create her fictional heroine, Emma Courtney.

The first of these love letters were to John Eccles, the man Mary Hays wanted to marry when she was eighteen. About one hundred of these letters survive,* written in 1779-80, and while there are touching professions of love to be found in them, what emerges is Mary Hays's 'fevered desire to learn whatever Eccles knew in the way of theology,

---

*They are now part of the Carl H. and Lily Pforzheimer Library's Collection of Mary Hays's Letters and Manuscripts.

philosophy, science, but most particularly Latin' (Gina Luria, 1977: p. 524). Such requests for knowledge are not surprising. How else could a woman who wanted to learn gain access to knowledge except through the 'teaching' of some man who was prepared to share the benefits that a men-only education system had conferred upon him?

But despite the love and interest that Mary Hays showed John Eccles (and which was returned) there was parental opposition, on both sides, to their marriage. John had no profession and Mary had no money; the marriage was forbidden and the lovers were disconsolate. So obvious was John's despair that Mr Eccles informed his son that he was 'sorry he should trouble so much about one woman as there were so many in the world' (A.F. Wedd, 1925: p. 2).

But Mary, who lived in Gainsford Street, Southwark, showed some of her characteristic independence and defiance of convention when she continued to meet John clandestinely (he lived nearby), and the parents finally relented and gave permission for the marriage – for fear of something worse eventuating. But before the two could be united, John became ill, and died, and Mary Hays was plunged into depression and despair. She mourned him, wrote melancholy verse, and tried to find some consolation in a life of study and learning.

Such a response may seem excessive today but at the time when women saw marriage as their only condoned vocation, the death of a prospective husband could represent more than the loss of a loved one; for Mary Hays it represented the loss of a way of life and the end of her dream of being 'taught' much of what she wanted to know. To turn to scholarly pursuits (without a tutor) was not an unusual or unreasonable response under the circumstances: she could see little apart from books, from reading and writing, as a source of sustenance in her life.

For almost a decade she led a quiet and contemplative life, engaged in solitary self-education, but by the end of the 1780s she was venturing into 'protected' religious circles and was attending lectures on religion and politics at the new Dissenting Academy at Hackney. There she could cultivate some of her more scholarly interests, have contact with some of the learned figures of the day, and she could undertake her own theoretical explorations. In 1791, under the pseudonym of 'Eusebia', she published her first pamphlet, *Cursory Remarks on an Enquiry into the Expediency and Propriety of Public or Social Worship.*

Her publication attracted considerable attention and was well received: it also brought her into contact with various prominent men – the ardent reformer William Frend of Jesus College, Cambridge, Dr Disney, Dr Robert Robinson, and Dr Priestley. George Dyer not long afterwards bought Mary Hays Mary Wollstonecraft's book, *A Vindication of the Rights of Woman.*

It changed her life. It was 'a work full of truth and genius', according to Mary Hays, who was so impressed and enthused that she wrote to the author to thank her for her 'spirited support of the just and natural rights of her sex' (A.F. Wedd, 1925: p. 5).

This ebullition led to a meeting of the two women at the house of Mary Wollstonecraft's staunch friend, Johnson, the publisher; and in the following week Mary Hays breakfasted with Mary Wollstonecraft in her own apartments in Store Street, Bedford Square. Mary Hays thus describes the occasion: 'I was extremely gratified by this interview. This lady appears to me to possess the sort of genius which Lavater calls the one to ten million. Her conversation, like her writings, is brilliant, forcible, instructive and entertaining. She is the true disciple of her own system, and commands at once fear and reverence, admiration and esteem. She was then on the point of passing over to the continent, and promised on her return to favor me with her company in Gainsford Street.' (A.F. Wedd, 1925: p. 5)

Mary Hays was deeply moved. She prevailed upon Mary Wollstonecraft to comment upon her latest literary venture – *Essays Moral and Miscellaneous* (1793). Like the *Vindication*, these essays of Mary Hays's were feminist, a protest written in women's name, and Mary Wollstonecraft was only too pleased to oblige her new admirer. She commented – and edited – and advised Mary Hays to delete the reference to women's weakness in her preface. There was by now no room for a plea for women's disability or inferiority in Mary Wollstonecraft's book, and Mary Hays readily followed the example and advice of her friend.

In the year from the time of their introduction until Mary Wollstonecraft's (delayed) departure for France, these two women met and corresponded frequently. They talked freely and at length about the rights and wrongs of women and they undoubtedly drew strength from each other's presence and support. It was partly because of the example of Mary Wollstonecraft (her own independent life! her own apartment!) and partly perhaps because Mary Hays realised that her friend would not be made particularly welcome in her mother's home, that Mary Hays decided on an independent life for herself. She too got her own apartment and supported herself by her pen.

'Her letters to family and friends during this period', comments Gina Luria (1977), 'reveal the turbulence of her new experience, particularly the intoxicating and frightening sense of working hard – reviewing, translating, ghost writing – to support "being free"' (p. 526). Mary Hays was living the life she wanted other women to be able to lead; she was living well outside the boundaries of convention and she was tasting some of the delights of 'being free'. But she was also counting some of the costs.

From her letters it is clear that Mary Hays was an emotionally vital and passionate person and yet her circumstances dictated the absence of a relationship with a man. She was a single woman – already under suspicion. Theoretical and practical considerations were an obstacle to free heterosexual relations; theoretical in that such a relationship would inevitably mean social ostracism and practical in that it could well result in pregnancy. But the fact that such a relationship did not seem possible did not prevent Mary Hays from reflecting on its desirability or from speculating on the ways and means that could remove the obstructions. Her rebellion lay in part in her insistence on women's emotional and sexual identity and in her advocacy of women's right to sexual fulfilment – outside marriage! Mary Hays broke another taboo.

In 1794 her friendship with William Godwin began. He assumed the role that John Eccles had once held in that he was a trusted tutor who could be relied upon for learning and advice. And Mary Hays felt the need for both at the time:

> Early on Hays and Godwin fashioned a mode of communication conducive to their respective needs and temperaments. In person, often cold and taciturn, Godwin was nonetheless willing to *talk* at tea with Hays; uncertain, easily cowed, Hays was happy to *write* letters that ran into volumes, for Godwin to dissect and criticize in person. (Gina Luria, 1977: pp. 526-7)

Among the many topics which came under discussion and which occupied an extensive part of the letters which Mary Hays penned, usually between eighteen and twenty-four closely written pages, were women's position inside and outside marriage, Mary Wollstonecraft's 'experiences' in France, and Mary Hays's unrequited love for William Frend. Because she was so concerned about the void in her own life, because she was concerned with her personal frustration in John Eccles and William Frend, and with the public frustration of the denial of women's sexual autonomy, William Godwin suggested that she explore this issue in fiction. Whether or not he had read *Mary* at this stage (he had met the author only once and had not liked her) or whether it is coincidence that he counselled Mary Hays to engage in the same process that Mary Wollstonecraft pursued in her first fiction, it is not possible to tell. But when Mary Hays took his advice and embarked on her fiction, *The Memoirs of Emma Courtney*, she was doing much the same thing that Mary Wollstonecraft had done almost a decade before. She was trying to make sense of her own life, in its social context, by setting it down in fictional form.

There are differences between the two authors, of course. Mary Hays does not have the proud defiance of Mary Wollstonecraft: she sets out a plea rather than asserts a demand. But there is no lack of courage in her stand. For she moves into an area where Mary Wollstonecraft did not tread. The heroine of *Mary* may have contented herself with a platonic relationship with Henry, she may have preferred celibacy to intimacy with a husband she did not love, but the heroine of *Emma Courtney* wants her desires to be known – and gratified. Such an explicit statement of women's sexual needs had not been given such unapologetic prominence in fiction before.

The plague of Emma Courtney's life is the bind of dependence and sexual needs, the constraints of inaction and the pressure of active desire. 'Interestingly, the novel is concerned far more with the question of autonomy – sexual, intellectual, vocational – than with either romance or manners,' writes Gina Luria (1977: p. 528). This is one woman's plea for a fuller and more active life for all women.

Mary Hays did not give her heroine her own name; but she did give her her own letters and some of the authentic details of the author's life. Augustus Harley is William Frend (the unresponsive lover) and Mr Francis, the philosopher, is William Godwin, and little attempt is made by the author to conceal the identity of her characters. This put Mary Hays in the unusual position of having to defend her novel as fiction when public opinion would have it as the undisguised – and disgraceful – fact. The objections to *Emma Courtney* however could just as easily have been based on the subtle arguments as on the more scandalous superficialities: 'Emma', writes Gina Luria, 'suffers because she seeks intellectual prowess, and existential freedom, thrusts inimical to the sedentary life of the eighteenth century gentlewomen and their customary marriages of convenience' (p. 528). In her own way and in the same mode, Mary Hays was no less subversive than her friend Mary Wollstonecraft; her novel, no less successful.

It was Mary Hays who reintroduced Mary Wollstonecraft to William Godwin, and she 'evidently remained for some time in ignorance of the rapidity with which the friendship begun under her auspices was progressing' (A.F. Wedd, 1925: p. 10). She was also one of the few to whom William Godwin wrote to inform her – on 10th April, 1797 – that the despised ceremony of marriage had taken place two weeks before. From the birth of Mary Godwin (Shelley) until Mary Wollstonecraft's death ten days later, Mary Hays was constantly at her friend's bedside; she was deeply grieved at her death.

Mary Hays soon had a falling out with William Godwin: some have suggested that her 'devotion to Godwin's first wife may well have caused her to resent his immediate and repeated attempts to replace her' (A.F. Wedd, 1925: p. 10). But in more ways than one, a light went out for Mary Hays when Mary Wollstonecraft died.

Increasingly 'unfashionable' though it may have been, Mary Hays continued to hold her feminist views. In 1798 she published (anonymously) *An Appeal to the Men of Great Britain in Behalf of Women*. In 1799 her second novel, *The Victim of Prejudice*, appeared and once more the conventions which constrained and victimised women were exposed. In 1802, in her attempt to show what women had done rather than what they might do, she wrote *Female Biography, or Memoirs of Illustrious and Celebrated Women of all Ages and Countries* (in six volumes). But her feminist efforts were ridiculed and without Mary Wollstonecraft, Mary Hays felt she had little support.

Like Mary Wollstonecraft had been in her own lifetime, Mary Hays was openly mocked for her vulnerability and her 'failure to get a man'. She was satirised as Bridgetina Botherim in Elizabeth Hamilton's *Memoirs of Modern Philosophers* (1800-01) and frequently sneered at in the *Anti-Jacobin Review*:

> Among those who disapproved of Mary was Coleridge, but for no better reasons than he did not admire her personal appearance, and resented scepticism in a woman. He writes to Southey: 'Of Miss Hay's intellect I do not think so highly as you or rather, to speak sincerely, I think not *contemptuously* or *despectively* thereof, yet I think you likely in this case to have judged better than I; for to hear a thing, ugly and petticoated, exsyllogize a God with cold-blooded precision, and attempt to run religion through the body with an icicle, an icicle from a Scotch hog-trough! I do not endure it. . . .' (A.F. Wedd, 1925: p. 11)

If the presence of good looks and the absence of an analytical mind were necessary requisites for entry to the male literary tradition, we would have a markedly different one from that with which we are currently presented. But there has been little room for plain sharp women in the heritage constructed by men.

Which is why the novels of Mary Wollstonecraft and Mary Hays have not found an enduring place in the cultural heritage. Yet these two women writers with their feminist autobiographical fiction conceived new possibilities for the novel and established a tradition of women's consciousness. They deserve recognition for the contribution they made to the novel – for their angry young woman protests of the eighteenth century – and for their skill in translating the personal into the political. Mary Wollstonecraft ranked among the mothers of feminism – and of the novel – and Mary Hays, her staunch supporter, was not far behind.

Table 10: Mary Wollstonecraft and Mary Hays

Mary Wollstonecraft (1759-1797)

1787	*Thoughts on the Education of Daughters*
1788	*Mary, A Fiction*
1787-90	*Original Stories from Real Life; with Conversations Calculated to Regulate the Affections and Form the Mind to Truth and Goodness*
	The Female Reader
	Of the Importance of Religious Opinions (translation)
	Elements of Morality for the Use of Children (translation)
1790	*A Vindication of the Rights of Men*
1792	*A Vindication of the Rights of Woman*
1794	*An Historical and Moral view of the Origin and Progress of the French Revolution*
1796	*Letters written During a Short Residence in Sweden, Norway and Denmark*
1798	*Memoirs and Posthumous Works* (including *Letters* to Gilbert Imlay, 'The Cave of Fancy' and *The Wrongs of Woman*)

Mary Hays (1760-1843)

1792	*Cursory Remarks on an Enquiry into the Expediency and Propriety of Public or Social Worship* ('Eusebia')
1793	*Letters and Essays, Moral and Miscellaneous*
1796	*Memoirs of Emma Courtney*
1798	*An Appeal to the Men of Great Britain in Behalf of Women*
1799	*The Victim of Prejudice*
1802	*Female Biography, or Memoirs of Illustrious and Celebrated Women of all Ages and Countries* (6 vols)
1804	*Harry Clinton, or A Tale of Youth*
1815	*The Brothers, or Consequences. A Story of What Happens Every Day*
1817	*Family Annals, or The Sisters*
1821	*Memoirs of Queens*

CHAPTER 16

Fanny Burney,
Maria Edgeworth
and the height of achievement

There are reasons for treating these two women writers together: they had much in common. Although their achievements are separated by two decades, they both enjoyed comparable eminence and acceptance, and it is interesting to note that there were no male challenges to their ascendancy, even in their own day. Of them, Marilyn Butler (1972) has said, 'For both women success in novel writing led to social success and a place in London Society. At the time the art of both was taken seriously and by good judges – for they were by a large margin, the best novelists available' (p. 1).

The success of Fanny Burney (1752-1840) and Maria Edgeworth (1768-1849) represents the full entry and recognition of women in the literary world in that they were both admired rather than maligned for their achievement. To be sure, they were not beyond suspicion and Fanny Burney was constantly plagued by doubts about the propriety of her position, but the snide insinuations that women of intellectual and literary bent were curious and unfortunate creatures, and that women who made for themselves a public name should expect to acquire automatically a 'reputation', were not the predominant considerations by which they were assessed. Partly because few wanted to contest the greatness of their achievement – for they were clearly without peers – and partly because of the exemplary womanly – and domestic – behaviour of the authors themselves, the issue of whether women *should* write was overshadowed by the issue that women *had* written, and that the work and the women were worthy of congratulation. If ever there was a period in the history of letters when women unquestionably led the way it was in the last quarter of the eighteenth and the early years of the nineteenth century when the only challenges to the pre-eminence of Fanny Burney and Maria Edgeworth came from other women – like

Elizabeth Inchbald and Ann Radcliffe.

I do not think that women writers have since enjoyed the same high status as they did then. While Jane Austen, the Brontës, George Eliot, Elizabeth Gaskell, and the poet Elizabeth Barrett Browning all gained a well-deserved place in the history of letters, it was always within the overall context of a male literary tradition. That the presence of a handful of women in a century of writing which allowed the greatness of a multitude of men led to the assertion that literature had become the business of women, attests more to the threatened pre-eminence of men than to a 'takeover' by women. When Fanny Burney and Maria Edgeworth reached the heights, women constituted *the* literary tradition – which makes it even more remarkable, and lamentable, that the work of these 'leading lights' should have been lost.

The fact that there are a few contemporary discussions on the lives and works of Fanny Burney and Maria Edgeworth has a number of advantages: it means that they have not completely disappeared from the literary heritage – although they are rarely studied – and it removes the necessity of introducing them as 'unknowns'. Many have heard of these two women writers even if they have not actually read their novels. But there are disadvantages too in that much of what has been written about them is nothing other than a charge that they have been overrated, and that their prominence (or mere presence) in the literary records is unwarranted. With a few exceptions (Marilyn Butler's 1972 literary biography of Maria Edgeworth and Joyce Hemlow's 1958 *History of Fanny Burney* among them), I would heartily discourage readers from acquainting themselves with the commentary on Fanny Burney and Maria Edgeworth. The most likely response to the received literary wisdom would be confirmation that here were yet two more women's novelists of limited vision and reforming zeal – and better ignored. Nothing could be further from the truth.

Initially, I toyed with the idea of omitting any extensive coverage of these two women writers (the line must be drawn somewhere!) on the grounds that they were already known and that their work was elsewhere evaluated. But having read some of what is purportedly known, I concluded that it would be most remiss to let it stand unchallenged and to exclude Fanny Burney and Maria Edgeworth from discussion. If they do not receive due credit and plentiful praise in other places, they will most assuredly have their excellence proclaimed here. For they are both magnificent writers and they provide the incontrovertible evidence that women had forged a full, fascinating – and fantastic – literary tradition, before Jane Austen.

But their comparable success on the literary scene was not all that Fanny Burney and Maria Edgeworth had in common: in examining some of the detail of their lives and works one is struck by the extraordinary similarity between the two. Both deeply admired their fathers and were trained as their amanuenses, writing and copying books which were published in their fathers' names. Both were prepared to use their talents in the interest of family entertainment and were 'wicked' imitators of speech patterns and peculiarities of character, with Fanny Burney more disposed towards displaying her skills in acting and Maria Edgeworth more likely to write stories to be read to the family circle. Both women valued their domestic harmony (although Fanny Burney appears to have had more trouble with her one stepmother than Maria Edgeworth had with two of hers) and both women rejected suitors whom their fathers initially encouraged them to accept, and were relieved when the pressure was removed and they were allowed to remain in their fathers' households where they felt secure.

Both women were inveterate and witty letter writers and they used the form to practise their art, to experiment with dialect, dialogue, and character sketch – and to amuse members of the family. Both were comic and satirical, and although Fanny Burney had the more cutting edge in her fiction, she had a little less assurance in her life; she worried more about what people would think of her and how her efforts might prove embarrassing for her father, while Maria Edgeworth thought more to please her father who was not overly concerned with what other people should think.

Both Fanny Burney and Maria Edgeworth were guided by their fathers who do not seem always to have given very good advice, and the responsibility for some of the 'defects' in the writing of these two women can be laid at the door of their fathers' directions.

Both were serious women who did not see fiction as frivolous diversion but who placed their writing firmly within the honourable tradition of letters. They invested their work with ethical concerns and high ideals and they were intent on providing genuine exploration and insight into the human condition. They were literally interested in a better world, where human motives were better understood and human judgment better exercised. In the days before psychology took upon itself the status of a scientific discipline – and before Sigmund Freud had espoused his fantastic theories – Fanny Burney and Maria Edgeworth played the part of psychologists as in their fiction they probed the human mind and plumbed the depths of human consciousness, will and judgment. They were analysts who were preoccupied with the age-old questions of why human beings do what they do and whether they can learn to do things differently, particularly when they can be made aware of the unfortunate consequences of their actions.

They were both proponents of a doctrine of human responsibility. Not for them the disclaimer that the insecurities and traumas of their childhood prevented them from being responsible for their own actions;

no abdication from the duty to learn, to understand, to exercise better judgment, no matter how deficient the early education or how debilitating the emotional experiences. Both had good reason to find fault with their own family backgrounds which had undermined their confidence and inflicted inner turmoil, but both stated clearly – in their lives and their work – that human beings must be reasonable, must strive to do 'the right thing', must aim for perfectability, and overcome any flaws or weaknesses of character which were impediments to fair and sound judgment and practice. It was a very dignified and autonomous view of human beings that they held, and while their novels are frequently concerned with the tension between social demand and individual conscience, and their characters who err are often treated with sympathy, their framework is always one in which it is possible for people to learn from their mistakes and to enjoy personally enriched lives, as a result.

This is their normal vision. It does not embody contemporary values but it is nonetheless the representation of a world view which has been reflected upon and which is a realistic one for its time. It is not fair to suggest that they simply countenanced 'self-sacrifice' and it is not appropriate to sneer at these two women writers as 'goody-goodies' who were no more than little didactic moralists. Given the constraints of their day, the conditions under which women were obliged to live, they advocated the greatest freedom of moral judgment that women could hope to attain, and such moral concerns are no less substantial simply because they focused predominantly on women. Since their period of ascendancy, both Fanny Burney and Maria Edgeworth have been belittled for the narrowness of their morals (more often referred to derogatively as 'manners', of course) and the paltriness of their vision, yet, in context, they were both intent on illuminating the sources of human weaknesses and strengths in order to construct a better world. Both were well able to use the sting of satire to apply 'corrective' force but this does not negate their aims or their achievements.

In their own ways, each was a ruthless judge of human foibles and one test of their skill is that some of the scenes they construct are so excruciatingly embarrassing that there is a real tendency on the part of the reader to 'look away' rather than to see someone so fearfully exposed. And it must be remembered that these were very ladylike authors – *who were doing the exposing.* They were not little-minded moralists who saw but the surfaces of life at tea parties, but unflinching, highly critical and open-eyed observers of humanity. They saw the best and the worst.

When Jane Austen's letters were first made available in 1932 they 'started a literary fracas ... they were not what ' "gentle Jane's" letters should have been like,' writes Marilyn Butler (1985). They were found to be 'punctuated by oases of clever malice' and gave rise to evaluations of her work as 'regulated hatred' (p. ix). What surprises me is that there should have been such surprise at this aspect of Jane Austen's perception. To have portrayed the characters that she did with the faults that they had – and to use the sting of irony as a corrective force – demands an understanding of 'the darker side of life'. While the novels of Jane Austen, Maria Edgeworth and Fanny Burney are all beautifully crafted to provide the civilised veneer, one of the reasons that they are so good is that these women were all well aware of what lay beneath. In their private writing – in their journals and letters – they made this clear; they did vent their anger, and reveal their rage, albeit in controlled form, and they did display their cutting edges. In Fanny Burney's diaries there are examples of 'regulated hatred' and in Maria Edgeworth's letters there are cruel comic sketches. How else could it be?

And how indicative of the dilemma that women writers find themselves in. Damned if they don't know, and damned when they do; condemned for their gentility and tragedies at the tea party in their public work and condemned, yet again, when it is learnt that harsh – and bitterly perceptive judgments – are made in their private writing.

While Jane Austen was yet to come, Fanny Burney and Maria Edgeworth were very conscious of their role as *women* novelists and they required no reminders of the restrictions under which they worked. They knew that they were 'at risk' and they knew the odds that other women writers had faced and which had often proved too great to be overcome. Both sought to establish connections with authors of their own sex, and while they taxed their minds to clarify the position of women writers, Maria Edgeworth went further than Fanny Burney (whom she followed) in claiming her place within a women's literary tradition. Not that Fanny Burney ever saw herself *outside* women's literary traditions; she was just not so assertive when it came to stating her place. Fanny Burney was ever-ready to make known her debt to her fellow women writers – particularly to Eliza Haywood and Frances Sheridan. But she always had reservations about intellectual and clever women and was frightened to be ranked among them.

This is readily seen in her attitude to the blue-stockings. On the publication of *Evelina* (1778), Fanny Burney was soon claimed by Mrs Thrale (and Dr Johnson) and she could have occupied a prominent place in the set of intellectual and literary women who comprised the blue-stockings. But she was never more than a fringe-dweller. More significantly, her play, 'The Witlings' – her next literary effort after *Evelina* – was a pointed satire on clever, intellectual, literary women, with Elizabeth Montagu, the 'Queen of the Blues', given pride of pretentious place as Lady Smatter. Because her father thought its production would *not* win friends and influence people in high places,

7   Fanny Burney

and would not contribute to the worthy image of his daughter that he wanted to cultivate, the play was suppressed. But it reveals Fanny Burney's ambivalence to the tradition of women writers. Yet Maria Edgeworth had no such doubts. She saw her own fiction writing following firmly within the tradition of women writers which Fanny Burney had helped to establish.

Perhaps Fanny Burney made it easier for Maria Edgeworth; certainly these two great women writers made it immeasurably easier for Jane Austen.

When it was realised that Fanny Burney was the author of the highly acclaimed *Evelina* (1778), astonishment was expressed at the range of lifestyles depicted in the novel; questions were asked as to how a young lady could know so much about the world. It was not just that characters from the 'highest' to the 'lowest' stations in life were portrayed authentically, but that the author had also looked on the best and the worst of the human soul, and it was the *extent* of Fanny Burney's inner and outer observations which prompted the questions. Subtitled 'The History of a young Lady's Entrance into the World', it was clear that *Evelina* had been written by one who knew quite a lot about 'the world' when she described the heroine's entrance to it, and it was the wit and wisdom of Fanny Burney's wide-ranging perceptions which were at the root of much of the respect she earned.

But all that has long since passed. For while Fanny Burney has been accorded a minor historical place in the literary tradition, it is not for her wide-ranging perceptions that she is known. On the contrary, it is the very narrowness of her view and the triviality of her concerns which has been the substance of most critical comment. And once it has been decided that she is no more than a 'miniaturist', it is but a short shift to decree that past praise of her work as 'significant' was a result of overrating her writing. Yes, she was considered good in her day – but the critics were misguided.

Now, I do not want to insist that all there is to know is contained in the world that Fanny Burney described and is embodied in a young lady's entrance into the world. But I do want to insist that when a young man makes his entrance into the world – and experiences comparable initiation difficulties – then although the world and the young man portrayed may be extraordinarily limited, *his* 'adventure' is accorded greater significance and universality than that of the young woman. He may see no more of 'life' than she, and his perceptions and understandings may be far less astute, but his experience will not be considered automatically trivial, sentimental, 'small', or substandard. Because he is male. Because it is assumed that the world of men is intrinsically of greater value than that of women.

Throughout literary judgments runs the unquestioned assumption that the views and values of men are superior to those of women, and that more can be learnt about the human condition by the carefree young man who cavorts and carouses through the countryside than by the more circumspect young woman who must always be attuned to 'which way the wind is blowing' as she moves from but one social gathering to another. This is the assumption of Walter Allen (1980), for example, when he compares the work of Fanny Burney with that of 'the great men' and contrasts the broad canvas of *Tom Jones* with the tea-party-tinyness of *Evelina*. Walter Allen's assessment of Fanny Burney is a classic example of the double standard, and of the back-handed compliment, for he reveals more explicitly than most the way a woman writer can be damned with praise for her 'feminine' achievement.

Her 'historical importance is undeniable,' he says, asserting her value, but this is quickly undermined with the statement that of course 'her actual achievement has been over-rated' (p. 93). And while he is in the process of outlining the directions in which Fanny Burney went – and where Henry Fielding had not gone – he is able to give the impression that they were not particularly profitable directions in which to go. Fanny Burney's writing 'represents the feminization of Fielding's art,' he says, and if there is any suspicion that this is not a compliment, confirmation is soon at hand when he proceeds with the pronouncement that this 'involved, of course, a tremendous diminution of Fielding's range' (p. 94). And so he undoes Fanny Burney's reputation at the same time as he extols her virtues:

> . . . the sweep of a novelist like Fielding was too great to take in small discriminations of rank and position. Small discriminations, however, are precisely the subjects that most exercise ladies at tea parties, and Fanny Burney's fiction, like the world she lived in, is full of people who, absurd as it may seem to her, do not know their place. They are Miss Burney's natural victims; she observes them with a camera-eye and picks up their speech with a microphone-ear . . . and her best comedy lies in the malicious rendering of the vulgar. (Walter Allen, 1980: p. 95)

In one short paragraph, Walter Allen is able to get it all in. Note that women are small-minded, that they are nasty and gossipy at tea parties, that they are myopically concerned with issues of rank and status: when Fanny Burney describes the tragi-comedy of human relations – pretensions – her effort is not truly creative but an extension of her malice and her technical capacity for accurate detail (her 'camera-eye' and her 'microphone-ear'). Such writing is not to be taken seriously, not to be judged 'great' by the critics whose minds are exercised by small discriminations and whose task it is to put writers in their place.

Walter Allen views the concerns of Fanny Burney as trite and banal and in so doing he misses completely the purpose and significance of her work – and of that of other women writers. With a young lady's entrance into the world, Walter Allen does *not* see a human being obliged to make one of the few and most important decisions of life – without being allowed to show or declare an interest and in the absence of any straightforward evidence. For a young lady for whom the only permissible occupation was marriage, who must find a husband without being seen to do so, who must sedulously guard her reputation in the wide world where envy, malice, greed and pretension are as abundant as in any other field of commerce, the difficulties were incalculable. And so much depended on the result. So she must observe, weigh, evaluate; she must be good at character judgment – an art at which even the greatest of men, with the best of education and the widest possible experience, have often failed.

Serious consideration might be given by a man to the choice of occupation but if his judgment were unsound, it was not necessarily a disaster. He could change his mind; try something else; find new friends; put his assets into a different venture. No such luxury was available for the young lady whose choice was for life, and which could mean death. This is no trite and banal matter for women, even if it is mocked by men. Marriage, for women, was a dangerous business.

Consider what marriage meant to a young lady in the late eighteenth century. On becoming a wife she was completely at her husband's mercy, and if she had made a mistake there was no way out. No wonder Fanny Burney and Maria Edgeworth – and Mary Wollstonecraft and Jane Austen – deplored the lack of training for young ladies in making their decisions; no wonder women writers tried to remedy in their novels some of the deficiencies of girls' education. When women writers made women's judgment – and assessment of the worth of men – a central issue in their work, they were not giving the subject undue emphasis. The quality of a man in fundamental human terms was a question of crucial importance to those who were to be wives.

Not that Fanny Burney (or Maria Edgeworth) condoned the marriage market. In their own ways each revealed their objections to the trade in women.* But both were determined to demonstrate that in making their decisions, young ladies should not be taken in by those who put on a good show, that they should not be influenced by the glamorous and gallant. Ironically, these women writers of the so-called romances,

---

*Maria Edgeworth's novels *Belinda, Patronage* and *Helen* all have lengthy discussions on the degradation of the marriage market and the desirability of a single life.

allowed 'romantic love' (as it is known today) little place in their novels: heroines were charged with the task of looking beneath the surface to take the measure of a man. If a woman was to be so dependent on the good will of a man, then it was necessary to ensure that he had good will, and that he was to be trusted. In their quests to determine the soundness and reliability of a man, young ladies were required to make some of the most astute and sensitive assessments of human nature. And to fail to see this dimension of women's novels – to dismiss as trivial, sentimental and insignificant this aspect of Fanny Burney's writing – is to miss one of the richest and most rewarding documentations of the human condition.

Which is why I lose respect for Walter Allen's judgment when he states that 'The whole world of his time was open to Tom Jones' but 'To read Miss Burney is rather like having a mouse's view of cats' (p. 94). Perhaps identification with cats – who play with mice – give Mr Allen a very different perspective from me: what he finds amusing, I find cruel.

There is no escaping his sneering tone as he compares the scope of Fanny Burney with that of Henry Fielding, and instead of commenting on the insights that the description of women's world provides, instead of examining the whys and wherefores of reducing human beings to such circumstances, he preens himself with the assurance that men do so much better. The world of Fanny Burney, he writes, was the only one

. . . accessible to a conventionally brought up upper middle class young lady constantly chaperoned, a world of routs, assemblies, balls and tea parties, dominated by the quest for marriage, or rather, dominated by the manoeuvering, innocent or otherwise, necessary to place a girl in the way of an eligible young man. In this world men are awful and incalculable when seen in the light of possible husbands or potential seducers, or ludicrous, if, as often, they think themselves possible husbands but are seen quite otherwise by the young women. (Walter Allen, 1980: p. 94)

No acknowledgment here of the far-reaching and illuminating perceptions of the author, no credit given for her penetrating gaze and her propensity for describing the highest and the lowest, the best and the worst – and the most sober and the most amusing – aspects of society. Walter Allen has assumed – with particular denseness – that because Fanny Burney's settings are often (but by no means exclusively, or even predominantly) balls, assemblies, tea parties, that her novels are about balls, assemblies and tea parties! No doubt if I were to assume that *Tom Jones* or *Joseph Andrews* were guided tours to the English countryside, he would soon point to the limitation of my view, yet how frequently are male critics challenged for their superficial – and supercilious – evaluations of women's writing? How frequently it is accepted without question that women's world and women's writing is intrinsically inferior, that in any judgment to the contrary the work must be overrated, and that it is not even necessary to examine the writing in detail to know that women's novels are in a different and markedly minor category from those of men?

That the detail of Fanny Burney's life and work is not fully known to Walter Allen is evidenced by some of his (predictable?) mistakes. Fanny Burney's heroines may have been upper middle class ladies who were closely chaperoned but she herself was not, and it seems a considerable collapse of critical judgment to confuse the author with her characters.

Charles Burney, Fanny Burney's father, was a musician who became highly respected but in his early years, and upon his marriage to 'the humble Esther Sleepe', life was a struggle for patronage and an exhausting round of lessons as a music master. Many of the pressing problems were overcome by his appointment in the winter of 1751-52 as the organist of St Margaret's Church in King's Lynn, but such an existence was a far cry from that of the upper middle classes.

So too are there inaccuracies in Walter Allen's representation of Fanny Burney as closely chaperoned. She was not. At least not until 1770 when the Burney family was united under the roof of her stepmother: 'Until the year 1770 such discipline as Fanny knew for the employment of her time was of her own devising. Up to her nineteenth year she had had unusual freedom "following my own vagaries, which my papa never controls"' (Joyce Hemlow, 1958: p. 35). But in her stepmother's home, all was to be different. That Fanny Burney had had too much freedom – that she had been at risk among some of those she knew, such as Mrs Pringle and Mr Seton – was a point made by friends, Mr Crisp among them. Old acquaintances were to be dropped: a new regimen was begun. But not before Fanny Burney had seen quite a few 'slices' of distinctly *non*-upper middle class life.

If anything, Fanny Burney's upbringing was rather 'bohemian'. Born at King's Lynn in 1752, she was back in London in 1760 where her father soon acquired 'pupils of rank, wealth and talent' and a circle of artistic friends. Among the frequent and fascinating callers to the house, in Poland Street, was the actor David Garrick, who took a keen interest in the children. 'As soon as the young Burneys were old enough to go to the theatre – and that seemed to be from the age of three or four – he frequently offered them his wife's box at Drury Lane,' writes Joyce Hemlow (1958), 'and before they could read they saw him on the stage as Lear, Hamlet, Bayes and Abel Drugger' (p. 12).

David Garrick was an excellent comic and mimic and he taught the Burney children everything he knew. Fanny – quiet, serious, slow to learn to read and write – was his best pupil. Her capacity to memorise what she heard spoken was extraordinary and her ability to mimic was considered excellent. Writing in his *Memoirs*, Charles Burney said of his daughter that she had

> . . . a great deal of invention and humour in her childish sports: and used, after having seen a play in Mrs Garrick's box, to take the actors off, and compose speeches for their characters; for she could not read them. But in company, or before strangers, she was silent, backward and timid, even to sheepishness; and from her shyness, had such profound gravity and composure of features, that those of my friends who came often to my house, and entered into the different humours of the children, never called Fanny by any other name, from the time she had reached her eleventh year, than The Old Lady. (quoted in Joyce Hemlow, 1958: pp. 13-14)

While Fanny Burney's mother lived, life was pleasant and secure, but when in 1762 Esther Burney died, Fanny was deeply distressed. Sent with her sisters to Mrs Sheeles's boarding school to be out of the way during her mother's illness, Fanny was devastated when told of her mother's death. 'Upon the arrival of the sad news the intensity of Frances's grief was so great that Mrs Sheeles afterwards declared "that of the Hundred children she had had the care of, she never saw such affliction in one before – that [Fanny] would take no comfort – and was almost killed with crying". Fanny never forgot the last melancholy week of September 1762' (Joyce Hemlow, 1958: p. 11).

Life changed drastically in the Burney household after Charles Burney lost his much loved wife. The happy home became a somewhat empty one as Charles Burney taught all day and translated Dante – often all night. There was never any question about his tenderness and concern for his children, but they didn't get much of his time. 'The Old Lady' was a neglected child.

Fanny Burney's education was very much of her own making. She had a slow start and not much encouragement on the way. Two years after her mother's death her father decided that it was important for girls to learn French and he proposed to accompany them to France for the purpose of doing so, but he could only afford such education for two. It was Fanny whom he left at home. There is even the suggestion that she was considered the least likely to benefit from the experience.

Off to France for two years went Esther and Susan Burney with their father, and the shy, reserved, and lonely Fanny was thrown back even further on her own resources. And it seems that this was when she took to literary amusements. Her reading lists of the time are long and exemplary, but her writing achievements are even more impressive. She wrote witty letters to her absent sisters, she kept a journal, and by the age of fifteen she had written a novel, 'The History of Caroline Evelyn', which concluded with the birth of Caroline's daughter, Evelina.

All the Burney children seem to have kept journals and written long and amusing letters, but even at the age of fifteen, questions about the propriety of female authorship were being raised in Fanny Burney's life. Her aunt thought it most unwise for a girl to keep a diary because you could never tell who might get hold of it – and what would happen then? When young ladies were not supposed to even think certain thoughts, it was most injudicious to keep a record of them – and to leave it lying around.

Which is why much of Fanny Burney's writing was undertaken in secret. In March 1768 she began her diary with the entry ' – to *whom* dare I reveal my private opinion of my nearest relations? My secret thoughts of my dearest friends? My own hopes, fears, reflections, and dislikes? – Nobody!' (Joyce Hemlow, 1958: p. 26). And for a few years the diary – with all its indiscreet comments – was addressed to Nobody.

But the doubts about the wisdom of women revealing their thoughts in writing had been planted. And these doubts were to grow. All the Burney children wrote injudicious letters and diaries in their teens and,

> As this practice was by no means approved by their elders it had to be pursued fugitively, and much of the early scribbling was consigned by command, or caution, to the flames. The first recorded bonfire of Burney manuscripts was that which blazed in the paved play-court of Dr Burney's house in Poland Street, London, on June 13, 1767, when on her fifteenth birthday, Fanny obediently burnt her novel 'Caroline Evelyn' along with 'Elegies, Odes, Plays, Songs, Stories, Farces, – nay, Tragedies and Epic Poems' – all the writings of her first fifteen years. (Joyce Hemlow, 1958: p. 1)

The bonfire of 1767 was not, however, the only major event of the year: in October, Charles Burney married the wealthy widow Mrs Allen, and Fanny acquired three stepsiblings. She also acquired a stepmother whom she fervently disliked and although it was another three years before the family were to unite, and before Fanny was called upon to practise great self-control, the new Mrs Burney provided Fanny with a target for satirical and stinging observations, some of which (when not later deleted) were revealed in the letters which, despite the danger, continued to be written. (The second Mrs Burney also 'appears in Fanny Burney's last novel, *The Wanderer*, as the fury Mrs Ireton, who abuses the heroine, her hired companion, with self-pitying tirades,' writes Katharine Rogers, 1984a: p. 65.)

Charles Burney appears to have been oblivious to the discord between his daughter and his wife, and while Mrs Burney was concerned about her husband's welfare, she was also convinced that the Burney children were engaged in a conspiracy against her. Her fears could have been heightened by the fact that she seems to have been excluded from much of the literary and artistic life of the family and as Dr Burney turned more and more to the publication of scholarly books on music – and as Fanny Burney spent longer and longer periods with her father copying out his work for the printer – no doubt Mrs Burney's resentment grew, and Fanny Burney's perception of her stepmother acquired sharper dimensions.

Fanny Burney was twenty-six when *Evelina* was published. The story of 'Caroline Evelyn's' daughter, the writing itself came readily enough to her; the difficulty was always trying to find the time to write – and to avoid detection. She spent an inordinate amount of time rewriting manuscripts for her father and this was the source of more than one problem. Because she was frightened of the consequences of being known as an author – frightened of what her father would think and of what people would say – she was determined to avoid recognition. This meant that she not only needed someone to represent her to the publisher (her brother and cousin being called on in this capacity), it meant that she did not want her handwriting to be recognised. So late at night, whenever opportunity permitted, Fanny Burney copied *Evelina* in a feigned hand.

She need not have worried. Once her father (and his friend Mr Crisp) knew that Fanny Burney was the author of *Evelina*, admiration and not admonition was their response. It was Charles Burney who insisted that she make public appearances as an author and who proudly paraded her at Mrs Thrale's in the presence of the great Dr Johnson. And it was Charles Burney and Mr Crisp who became her literary advisors and who helped to ensure that Fanny Burney no longer had an opportunity to write what she wanted, with only her own counsel to guide her.

There was no ill-will on their parts. They wanted only the best for Fanny Burney: but they also wanted her style to be more elevated and her subject matter to be safe and salutary. Which is why they were against 'The Witlings', and why they advised her to write more moral, more substantial, more refined works.

Once 'out' in the literary world, Fanny Burney still found it difficult to find time to write. 'The Witlings' and her next novel *Cecelia* (1782) were squeezed in between social engagements she often found harrowing, and bouts of ill health. And whether it was because she had insufficient time, whether it was the pressure of expectation that she should produce another brilliant book, or whether she heeded too closely the counsel of her cautious advisors, *Cecelia* has not the same freshness, vitality, playfulness and delight as *Evelina*: it is a much more self-conscious and weighty effort.

There is more than one version of *Evelina*, and in her *History of Fanny Burney* (1958) Joyce Hemlow places the drafts and the published version side by side to show the 'polishing' processes that the author undertook. The dialogue becomes more extended in the published version, the distinction between individuals as expressed in their language becomes more pronounced. Without becoming stilted or heavy, it is possible to see Fanny Burney adding to her drafts and developing her art. It is to be regretted that she was not permitted to continue in the way that she had begun.

Because her father wanted for her a prominent place in society, he prevailed upon her to accept the Queen's offer of a post at court – as Second Keeper of the Robes. For five years from 1786 she was at court, leading a life that was anathema to her, and in her spare moments, stealing time to write lofty and melancholy blank-verse tragedies which could not have been further removed from the witty, 'wicked', racy and seemingly spontaneous style of the epistolary *Evelina*. Finally she faced the fact that she could not continue and braced herself to request permission from the Queen – and her father – to resign.

It was after her difficult time at court that she met the impoverished French emigré Alexandre d'Arblay, and in 1793, at forty-one years of age, and against her father's wishes, she married him. Fanny Burney's literary efforts were to be their source of income:

The necessities of her new position quickened Madame d'Arblay's exertions. The tragedy begun under the Queen's roof ('Edwy and Elgiva') was completed and acted in 1795, shortly after the birth of her only child. It failed, and was withdrawn after the first night. *Camilla*, a tale, also begun whilst she was with the Queen, was finished in 1796, and published by subscription. Its success was remarkable: three months after it appeared, only five hundred copies remained of an edition of four thousand. . . . Madame D'Arblay would now have divided her life between happy domestic duties and literature had not her friends and her husband shaped her life differently.

She had always had a desire to try her fortune on the stage . . . and now her father, affectionately alive to her fame as a writer, interfered and prevented her from having a comedy entitled 'Love and Fashion' acted at Covent Garden. With great deference to his wishes, she consented to withdraw it, and thereby forfeited the £400 she was to have had for the manuscript. 'Cerulia', a tale which she had turned into a four-act comedy, had some years previously given him the same uneasiness (as had 'The Witlings') and like 'Love and Fashion' been sacrificed to his fears.

Without intending it her husband interfered even more than her father with her literary career. In 1801 . . . M. D'Arblay went to France. His wife and child soon followed him, and the war which broke out in 1803 kept them there all three for ten weary years. (Julia Kavanagh, 1863: vol. I, pp. 110-12)

Fanny Burney faced many problems in her literary career. As a result of her father's advice her plays went unperformed and unpublished (and are now mostly to be found in the Berg Collection of the New York Public Library). Because of his influence she made much less money for her work than might otherwise have been the case: he and Mr Crisp sold *Cecelia* for £250 (ridiculous!), and there is every indication that Fanny Burney managed her own financial arrangements far better than her father had ever done. It was primarily from him that she derived her fears about authorship for he was unreasonably concerned that her work should be respected and that her reputation should be for moralising rather than racy satire. He wanted his daughter placed on a literary pedestal and advised her against the use of a playful and witty style (which was one of her greatest strengths) in favour of the cultivation of a high and lofty tone. When in the later years of her life Fanny Burney edited her father's *Memoirs* (1832) she was fiercely criticised for her pomposity and pretentiousness. For a writer whose first published work had been a brilliant attack on pomposity and pretentiousness, this was not a fitting end. It was an end that was not likely to have come about without the benefit of fatherly advice.

In some respects her marriage released her from the bond of seeking her father's approval: she did after all defy him in her choice and it was perfectly proper for her to be bound by the counsel of her husband (who had a vested interest in a greater income) rather than that of her father, once she was a wife. She could have perhaps gone on – and gone back to – some of the strengths of her secret writing days, had not circumstances conspired to prevent her. She was clearly very happily married and except for the anxiety caused by her somewhat shiftless son and the occurrence of breast cancer (an horrendous account of a mastectomy is contained in her diary), she might have had the opportunity to indulge in some more witty and playful writing if there had not been the constant struggle for survival for many years in France. The only literary work she undertook during this period was *The Wanderer* (1814) and although it has some brilliant patches was not the exposé of French morals and manners that the public had been led to expect, and while she made some money from it (£2,000), the verdict was – and is – that it does not come up to her early brilliant standards.

But even if it was 'downhill all the way' after *Evelina*, Fanny Burney nonetheless scaled the heights. Her achievement should not be denied, nor diminished by her later falls from artistic grace. In *Evelina* it is possible to look back to *The History of Betsy Thoughtless* and to look forward to *Emma* and *Pride and Prejudice* and to appreciate the continuity in women's literary traditions. It is also possible to discern the dimensions of those literary traditions, with their marvellous portrayals of women's world and their insistence that it was a world to be valued and one which could afford great insight into the human condition.

What is interesting but not widely known is that Fanny Burney's half-sister, Sarah Burney (the daughter of the 'dreadful' stepmother) was also a novelist of considerable repute in her day. Sarah Burney (1770?-1844) wrote a number of novels which sold well, were published in America, and which were translated into French and German. Among them were *Clarentine* (1796), *Geraldine Fauconberg* (1808), *Traits of Nature* (1812), *Tales of Fancy* (3 vols, 1816-20) and *Romance of Private Life* (3 vols, 1839). Margaret Patterson (1984) says that 'Contemporary reviews comment on the resemblance between Sarah Burney's characters and situations and those of Fanny Burney, but they note that Sarah Burney lacks Fanny Burney's raciness of humor and power of painting the varieties of the human species' (p. 67).

Unfortunately much of what Fanny Burney did best, her father and Mr Crisp liked least, and sought to suppress. While men writers, too, have often been given poor literary advice, they have usually been in a better position to resist. That Fanny Burney was emotionally and financially dependent on her father made it extremely difficult for her to go her own way – had she desired to do so. That she did not, that she was frightened of the public world, distressed at the thought of being seen as a blue-stocking, and was prepared always to comply with the wishes of her male 'betters', is a comment not only on the position of women but an indication of the 'interference' that has characterised the lives of literary women *and* women's literary traditions. No doubt Fanny Burney would have benefited from the absence of male judgments. So too would women's literary traditions.

But despite the disadvantages, Fanny Burney remains one of the remarkable mothers of the novel; *Evelina* stands as one of the best books in the entire literary tradition. The 'feminization of Fielding's art' she may have provided, but if 'feminization' were not a derogatory term – if the female were accorded the same status as the male – then the literary critics would have noticed that Fanny Burney added a valid and valuable dimension to the novel.

Maria Edgeworth led an extraordinary domestic life and it seems to have been this facet of her existence, rather than her literary achievements, which has captured the interest of biographers and commentators. Yet she is one of the most important early novelists, one of the most significant fiction writers, and one of the most central figures in women's literary traditions. She 'was undoubtedly the most commercially successful and prestigious novelist of her heyday, 1800-1814,' writes Marilyn Butler (1984). 'No English woman had a comparable literary career before George Eliot' (p. 111), and to omit her from consideration in the rise of the novel is to distort the literary records beyond measure.

By the literary men (and women) of her time she was judged to be excellent – 'better than Fielding', as the saying seems to go. She was paid unprecedented sums for her writing and she had spectacularly successful sales. She also exerted an enormous influence over other writers for generations to come. Jane Austen admired her work, sent her a copy of *Emma*, and 'paid her respects' in *Northanger Abbey*.

> Byron thought the impression of intelligence and prudence left by her
> novels very profound. . . . Scott claimed that he owed his own
> successful career as a novelist about Scotland to her Irish example.
> Turgenev is reported to have said that his sketches of the Russian
> peasantry were inspired by hers. Ruskin declared that he had read her
> tales, and her novel *Patronage* 'Oftener than any other books in the
> world, except the Bible . . . they are it seems to me the most re-
> readable books in existence'. (Marilyn Butler, 1972: p. 2)

The sad irony is – as Marilyn Butler notes – that the comments by famous men about Maria Edgeworth's writing are better known now than the work which prompted them. Where Maria Edgeworth is praised (and where her novels have been reprinted) the honours are accorded for her authentic and innovative portrayal of Ireland, for her faithful rendition of the Irish dialect, and her introduction of the regional novel. What has steadfastly been ignored is her substantial contribution to the novel in general and to the women's novel in particular.

Maria Edgeworth was consciously a woman writer who saw herself as very much part of women's literary traditions and who was aware of her links – literary and social – with other women writers of her time. She knew all the objections to the propriety of female authorship – her own entry into print had been delayed by the arguments of her father's friend, Thomas Day, who thought public writing an inappropriate activity for a proper woman. She knew what writing women were up against and it is no coincidence that in the first tale, in her first published book (*Letters for Literary Ladies*, 1795), two gentlemen debate the issue of whether women should be authors. Given Maria Edgeworth's penchant for portraying scenes from real life, there is every likelihood that she had heard these very words – for and against – in her

287

own home, most probably between her father and Thomas Day. That she elected to write – and did not think she was compromised – is an indication of her adherence to the premise that it was perfectly proper for women to have a vigorous and independent intellectual life.

The concentration on the authentic detail of real life is a hallmark of Maria Edgeworth's writing and one of her attributes that is most highly commended, particularly in relation to her portrayal of the Irish. But if she was not satisfied with anything less than 'authentic realism' in her regional creations, nor was she satisfied with anything less in the realisation of her characters. She wrote for women and men and she presented a cross-section of women and men characters, and one of her greatest strengths is the absence of types among her heroines (and heroes). Yet to know her settings and her versatile characters, Maria Edgeworth needed access to a far wider range of places and people than were customarily available to a woman of her position, to a lady. This is one reason she was repeatedly requesting her friends and relatives to send her firsthand accounts of their experiences: it was why she was always urging her brothers, for example, to provide her with meticulous details of the nature of their professions and the scope of their views. She was conscious of the conventions that circumscribed women's lives – particularly the life of a 'lady' – but she did not allow that the woman writer should be limited to a portrayal of 'woman's world' and she made a great effort to transcend the restrictions placed on women, and women writers.

In fact, Maria Edgeworth never did subscribe to the thesis of separate virtues, values or spheres, for the sexes: if a particular quality or characteristic of human existence was considered to be good – it was good for both sexes. If strength of mind was an admirable feature, then it was to be cultivated in women as well as men – there was no recoil from the idea of the 'strong-minded woman'. (In *Helen*, 1834, the heroine is repeatedly 'lectured' for not being sufficiently strong-minded.) If independence and responsibility were the desired blend of attributes in the ideal person, they were to be desired in both sexes. So Maria Edgeworth's women talk politics (independently and responsibly) and her men raise and educate children and as both are to be taken equally seriously there is a peculiarly modern twist to much of her writing.

'Romantic love', however, as it is now more commonly understood, figured little in her 'romances' where the 'perfect' relationship between women and men was portrayed as one of true partnership.

In breaking down some of the dividing lines between women and men, Maria Edgeworth helped to establish a tradition which more often than not was cast aside during the nineteenth century (when the strong-minded woman was deplored). Her framework was drawn upon by a few women writers, Elizabeth Gaskell, 'the Victorian novelist who most closely resembles Maria Edgeworth' (Marilyn Butler, 1984: p. 112) being one woman who did follow in the form that Maria Edgeworth had helped to forge. (See particularly Elizabeth Gaskell's *Wives and Daughters* which bears a close resemblance to *Helen*.)

To draw attention to the accuracy of the reporting which Maria Edgeworth demanded of her own writing is not to suggest that she was some unthinking recorder, a passive medium through which passed the detail of real life. To portray women writers as lacking creative and intellectual resources may have been common practice, but is highly inappropriate when it comes to Maria Edgeworth. That she needed people, places, incidents to be authenticated is more a sign of her determination for perfection than an absence of creative talent, and the inclusion of reliable information (even in her 'romances') is not a fault but an added dimension which contributes to her 'consummate art' (Clara Whitmore, 1910: p. 111).

Maria Edgeworth knew there were realms of experience to which women were denied entry and when writing about these areas she was careful to ensure that her material was accurate and that her creations could be taken seriously. While seeing herself as a *woman* writer and the inheritor of a tradition that Fanny Burney had helped to create, she nonetheless extended the boundaries of the world that Fanny Burney had described. She drew on the work of other women writers and she innovatively fashioned her own new world. Never associating herself with the trenchant demands for freedom as expressed by Mary Wollstonecraft (and Mary Hays), Maria Edgeworth, however, was aware of the contribution they had made, and was not wary of utilising some of the features of their style or some of the value of their insights. Maria Edgeworth is the 'first novelist to apply an insight articulated by Mary Wollstonecraft that women have their own language,' states Marilyn Butler (1984: p. 112). She may not have presented such a forcible picture of women's previously 'private' world as Mary Wollstonecraft had done, but she certainly evoked – brilliantly at times – the authentic world of women, and the dimensions of women's emotional lives. With such a realistic range of responses – always within the context of restrictions placed upon women – Maria Edgeworth was able to make her own subtle and often highly political points about women's place in society.

Nor were they *incidental* points as some have suggested – implying that Maria Edgeworth could not have known what she was doing. No woman writer who perceived her links with Fanny Burney, Elizabeth Inchbald, and Anna Laetitia Barbauld would *unintentionally* convey feminist overtones throughout her novels. No woman writer who proposed to Anna Laetitia Barbauld – as Maria Edgeworth did – that

289

they start a politically liberal women's journal called *The Feminead* would be unaware of the messages about women's independence which run through her fiction. That one sees growing, responsible intellectual women characters in Maria Edgeworth's fiction is because that was what Maria Edgeworth intended her (positive) real women to be.

Not all her women characters are positive, of course. In *Belinda* (1801) (one of the least put-downable novels I have read), Lady Delacour, with her pursuit of pleasure, is held up as a warning not as a model for emulation. And Mrs Harriott Freke, who has to be one of the most amazing women in literature, is an example of the worst that can happen, not the best. While I am fully aware of the author's disapproval of the rude, inconsiderate, Mrs Freke, I must admit a sneaky admiration for the woman on occasion. She so blatantly defies convention. And although I'm not partial to duels, if they are to be part of the plot it makes a pleasant change to have women duellists.

I haven't read all of Maria Edgeworth's novels: I look forward – eagerly – to the pleasure of reading her last novel, *Helen* (1834),* written after her father's death and which Marilyn Butler (1984) describes as 'a sympathetic study of the conflicting loyalties of two young women caught between patriarchal authority, with its moral absolutes, and their affection for one another' (p. 111). Yet what I have read (the novels are difficult to obtain) has made a deep impression on me. I do not cease to be astonished that such a superb writer should so easily have been discarded. There has been as much joy for me in reading Maria Edgeworth as I have gained from reading Jane Austen, and I can only express my amazement and dismay that such a rich resource has so arbitrarily been removed from our cultural heritage. I only wonder that Maria Edgeworth is not extolled as one of the great writers of the English tradition and I can only presume that Ian Watt (1957) does not rank her among the originators of the novel because he has not read her work. One might debate the relative merits of her novels but one could not deny the merit of her writing – if read.

I deeply regret the omission of Maria Edgeworth in my own literary education.** I would dearly love to have a course on Maria Edgeworth's

---

*I have since read it: it is superb.

**I checked the course offerings of the English Department of Sydney University for 1985 to see if great changes have been made since my day. There is a course – number 204 – 'The rise of the novel': it lists Defoe, Richardson, Fielding, Smollett and Sterne as the authors to be read. No Eliza Haywood, no Fanny Burney, no Maria Edgeworth: in fact as far as this English Department is concerned it is as if these three authors never existed. Their names do not even appear in the extensive reading lists.

novels, but predictably most of her work is not in print. The novels that are available (*Castle Rackrent* and *The Absentee*, one volume, J.M. Dent, 1976) are the Irish stories, which, powerful though they be, do not exemplify the full range of Maria Edgeworth's talent. Perhaps it is because she has been pigeonholed as an Irish regional novelist that her work has been so peremptorily dismissed. Assuming of course that an explanation apart from that of being a *woman* writer is required.

But what has struck me in the criticism of her writing that I have encountered is the focus on her didacticism and moral tone, and the condemnation of such use. I would not want to quarrel with the idea that Maria Edgeworth does have a moral purpose in her writing. She does see character development as primary: if the character is sound the life is good; if the character is weak – and the circumstances debilitating – then the life is difficult. But I see little to object to in this approach. When William Shakespeare explored the flaws of character it was called tragedy; when Maria Edgeworth undertakes a similar exploration it is called didacticism.

Much of the critical comment associated with her overarching moral purpose is attributed to the wilful and baneful influence of Maria Edgeworth's father, who appears to have countenanced her literary leanings in so far as they helped to illustrate his own educational theses. But to understand more of the relationship between Maria Edgeworth and her father – and what she termed their 'literary partnership' – it is necessary to know something about the domestic setting in which she lived – which she prized – and which made its presence felt throughout her novels.

Richard Lovell Edgeworth was a remarkable man and not just because he had four wives and twenty-two children. He had immense vitality, great enthusiasm for practical science, an avid interest in education. As a man of means he was able to devote his life to intellectual and scientific pursuits – to improvements – agricultural improvements, mechanical improvements in his home and political improvements in his country, and of course, educational improvements in his family. It is clear that the household in Edgworthstown, County Longford, Ireland, was a hive of intellectual and practical/creative activity. And with twenty-two children, Edgeworthstown for all intents and purposes functioned as an experimental school.

The second surviving child of Richard Edgeworth's many children,* Maria Edgeworth was somewhat disturbed in her early years. Her father had no great affection for her mother and the two did not often reside under the same roof, so Richard Edgeworth was a distant and awesome figure on the death of her mother when Maria was five years of age. Having already been struck by the beauty (of mind and body) of Honora Sneyd whom he thought could share his life in a way Maria's mother

Anna Maria had been unable to do, Richard Edgeworth wasted no time in wedding the love of his life on the death of his first wife. From this new amorous relationship the children of the previous marriage felt roughly excluded and it is understandable that the young Maria, required to live with virtual strangers, should have felt rejected, and expressed her loneliness and unhappiness in a few acts of outrageous, 'undisciplined' behaviour. But for such actions she received not understanding, but further censure.

Maria's stepmother, Honora, seems to have been willing to grant acceptance – on condition of good behaviour – and so early in life, when Maria Edgeworth desperately craved entry to the magic circle of warmth and affection in her home, she learnt the necessity of winning approval from her stepmother – and her father. The pattern of her life which was firmly (obsessively?) based on seeking approval and acceptance from her father – above all else – seems to have begun with the disturbed and lonely child who had lost the security and love of her mother, who found little comfort in the replacement (who was the centre of her father's attention), and little room in the relationship between the newly and very 'happily married' parents.

When Richard Edgeworth began to train Maria as his 'helper', his 'amanuensis', she was overjoyed by such attention and the importance of her responsibility. Her father *needed* her. She accompanied him round the estate, kept the records, and of course, came into contact with sections of society she would never have encountered in the drawing room. So while on the one hand it is true that from the outset Richard Edgeworth encouraged his daughter's notetaking and writing in his own interest, it is also true that for Maria Edgeworth the experience was not without its advantages. It was in the company of her father and with his direct encouragement that she familiarised herself with the dialect, the circumstances, and the tales of the Irish workers that she later put to such good literary use.

Much of the influence/interference of Richard Edgeworth in his daughter's writing can be viewed in this double-edged manner. If he tried to direct Maria Edgeworth's literary skills to the servicing of his own practical and educational interests, it must also be acknowledged that he did encourage her education and provide her with ample opportunities for writing. That she attached such importance to being his helper and that she was so concerned to maintain their 'literary partnership' which assured her of a place in her father's life, says as much about Maria Edgeworth – and the dependent position of women – as it does about her father.

Maria Edgeworth had two basic reasons for writing – and both of them in the end were to please her father. She pleased him when she wrote something which would exemplify his educational theories, and she pleased him when she wrote something which could be read aloud to the large family of an evening. With the twenty-two children and the experimental school there was a need for educational literary materials during the day and more diverting and entertaining literary materials at night, and Maria Edgeworth wrote for both audiences, often with a particular individual in mind and always with the overriding aim of gaining approval from her father. For example, the writing of *The Modern Griselda* (1805) was undertaken in secret in order to provide her father with a surprise. Writing in 1803 to her cousin, Sophy Ruxton about it, Maria Edgeworth said:

> I shall work hard with the hopes of having something to read to my
> father – This has always been one of my greatest delights and
> strongest motives for writing – *Lazy Lawrence* – *The Bracelets* and *The
> Limerick Gloves* and *The Prussian Vase* were all written while my father
> was out somewhere or other, on purpose to be read to him on his
> return. (Quoted in Marilyn Butler, 1972: p. 288)

That part of Maria Edgeworth's purpose in writing was to please her father and to provide entertainment for the family does not seem to me to be – by definition – an impediment to her writing. The attainment of a 'trusted audience' can be a distinct advantage, desired by many writers, and is one of the reasons that women today have formed writing groups, and why manuscripts are passed round for comments from friends. That the friends were family and the critics ready-made is but a minor difference, for while the domestic circle may not have been quite so well endowed with resources and judgment as some literary circles, it was not without its talented members of discerning taste. Maria Edgeworth's father, his fourth wife Frances (who was a year younger than Maria), the 'countless' brothers and sisters who had all been reared according to the liberal 'Edgeworth education system', the aunts and cousins who were kept regularly informed, all constituted a remarkable audience, prepared to comment, criticise, correct. And if, in addition, Maria Edgeworth's writing won the approval and a place in the affection of he whom she so very much wanted to please, this hardly qualifies as a liability! When other women risked losing reputation and the rewards of affection because they would persist with their writing, Maria Edgeworth was in the more fortunate position of finding favour in the family through her literary efforts.

More difficult, distracting – and damaging on occasion – to Maria Edgeworth's writing were Richard Edgeworth's educational priorities which worked to pressurise Maria into writing material which gave her little joy and sometimes amounted to nothing short of drudgery. There can be no doubting Richard Edgeworth's genuine interest in education which was given full scope in the heady days of happy marriage with Honora. The two adults had kept detailed educational journals which charted the progress of the children and recorded how and what they learnt; the theories that were derived from these observations and experiments were contained in *Practical Education* (1798), the product of the 'literary partnership' between Maria Edgeworth and her father where the 'ideas' were held to be his and the 'secretarial' efforts held to be hers – by Maria herself.

The entire day at Edgeworthstown was directed towards the encouragement of learning in the young, and the adults (including the older children) devoted an enormous amount of time to teaching. If Edgeworth appropriated for himself the role of 'headmaster' and delegated much of the responsibility for daily instruction, he was nonetheless serious about his educational purposes and proud of his results. He wanted to make public the principles of his education system, and *Practical Education* was widely influential in educational circles, even in France.

But it was not just the principles of education that needed to be articulated to the wider world; there was also the issue of teaching materials, and it was here that Maria Edgeworth played such a significant private and public role. She wrote the stories from which children were intended to learn; from which they were supposed to learn to read and where they could learn all manner of practical skills – and moral lessons. Her *Henry and Lucy* stories (among others) are really the first planned reading programme for young children and I have no hesitation in claiming that they are infinitely superior to *Janet and John*!

While ever Maria Edgeworth employed her literary talent to expound her father's educational principles (*The Parent's Assistant*, 1796; *The Practical Education*, 1798; *Early Lessons*, 1801), while ever she wrote stories as educational aids, her father was well pleased. This was solid, worthwhile writing as far as he was concerned and he was content to maintain the 'literary partnership'. He was even prepared to sing his daughter's public praise as he did in the preface to *Tales of Fashionable Life* (1809):

It has . . . been my daughter's aim to promote, by all her writings, the progress of education, from the cradle to the grave. Miss Edgeworth's former works consist of tales for children – of stories for young men and young women – and tales suited to that great mass which does not move in the circles of fashion. The present volumes are intended to point out some of those errors to which the higher classes of society are disposed.

All the parts of this series of moral fictions . . . have . . . arisen from that view of society which we have laid before the public in more

didactic works on education. In *The Parent's Assistant,* in *Moral* and *Popular Tales,* it was my daughter's aim to exemplify the principles contained in *Practical Education.* In these volumes, and in others which are to follow, she endeavours to disseminate, in a familiar form, some of the ideas that are unfolded in *Essays on Professional Education.*
(quoted in Marilyn Butler, 1972: p. 286)

Significantly, Richard Edgeworth does not mention his daughter's novel writing – although *Belinda* had been published in 1801 and *Leonora* in 1806 to considerable acclaim. The novels do not interest him; they have no place in the 'literary partnership' of father and daughter. And because that partnership was so crucially important to Maria Edgeworth she wrote – though not exclusively – what her father valued: in a letter to her cousin Sophy Ruxton of 26th February, 1805, Maria Edgeworth makes her priorities patently clear – but one cannot ignore the ironic elements, or the 'rebellion':

I am now laying myself out for wisdom, for my father has excited my ambition to write a *useful* essay upon professional education: he has pointed out to me that to be a mere writer of pretty stories or novellettes would be unworthy of his partner, pupil and daughter and I have been so touched by his reason or his eloquence or his kindness or all together, that I have thrown aside all thoughts of pretty stories and put myself into a course of solid reading. Now Sophy, dear Sophy! mixed with all this filial piety and obedience, and goodness etc., which I see you ready primed to praise, there is one little tiny grain of folly, which is visible to no eye but that of conscience and which I might keep snug concealed from you, if I pleased, but I do not please to cheat – I have the same lurking hope which first prompted me to write Leonora – that it will be read and liked by —— vide page 63 of Monthly Magazine for February 1805.
(quoted in Marilyn Butler, 1972: pp. 209-10)

That Maria Edgeworth elected to do what her father wished does not mean that it came easily to her. As Marilyn Butler (1972) has pointed out, *Professional Education* – a study of vocational education for boys – was outside Maria Edgeworth's frame of reference, and 'It cost her two or more years hard reading, and months of drudgery in the writing' (p. 210). But that was not all. *Professional Education* was to have her father's name alone on the title page (!) and for Maria Edgeworth this was a source of great anxiety: note, it was not resentment or injustice that she felt but nervousness that she would not have done her wonderful father justice (!!).

Now this denial of authorship and dread of unworthiness must be put into perspective. The conditions under which women have written – and been acknowledged – have never been very good, and if Maria Edgeworth's working conditions were a little more peculiar than most, they were also not far from the ordinary. That women's words have been 'stolen' from them is a charge which resounds through women's literary records, and there is little qualitative difference between Maria Edgeworth labouring for love for her father, and the numerous women writers and researchers who today labour for love of their husbands. Maria Edgeworth may have severely deprecated her skills to see herself as her father's secretary with the responsibility to present his 'ideas', but such practice has not been, and is not, uncommon among women who want to make themselves indispensable in a 'partnership'. What distinguishes Maria Edgeworth from 'research wives' today who are referred to in the ritual one-line acknowledgments by the acclaimed writer, who (as Marion Glastonbury, 1978, has inferred) sometimes has done little more than append his name? The only significant difference is that it was father rather than husband who was the object of affection and on whom the writer was dependent.

As twentieth century women writers from Virginia Woolf to Tillie Olsen and Adrienne Rich have so adamantly maintained, women are rarely free to please themselves, to write what they want in a way that they want, and far from being unusual, Maria Edgeworth is part of the ordinary tradition of women writers in that her literary talents were sometimes exercised for tasks that were not of her own choosing – and she was sometimes not accorded credit for her contribution. She is but another example in the long line of women writers who have seen it as necessary (and even desirable) to please a man – or men! That it was her father, not her husband, publisher or critic, who was the significant figure, is her point of departure.

Perhaps she did lack confidence, assurance – *independence* – when she complied with her father's wishes and produced work which illustrated his theses and enhanced his reputation – but one should never underestimate the power that dependence can exercise over the mind. Perhaps she did go too far with the preservation of the 'literary partnership' but at the same time she was engaging in real work which was highly valued, and many were the women who never received such positive feedback. As Julia Kavanagh (1863) has said in relation to Maria Edgeworth, 'It is not the Greek and Latin of boys that gives them a future advantage over their more ignorant sisters. It is that they are trained to act a part in life, and a part worth acting, whilst girls are either taught to look on life, or, worse still, told how to practise its light and unworthy arts' (vol. II, p. 87). By writing for her father, Maria Edgeworth was trained to act an important part in life and far from undermining her confidence, such valued literary work could have helped to boost it.

But this is not to divert attention from the fact that she was her father's amanuensis and this often meant hard work and little joy. Perhaps her judgment is to be questioned when she revealed her anxiety about the responsibility of holding her father's reputation in her hands – yet in the late eighteenth and early nineteenth century there are 'extenuating circumstances' which help to explain such vulnerability. It is as well to remember the context in which she was working when on January 23rd, 1808, when *Professional Education* had been completed, Maria Edgeworth wrote to her cousin Sophy Ruxton expressing her pleasure and her fears:

> I am well repaid for all the labour it has cost me by seeing that my father is pleased with it and thinks it a *proof of affection* and gratitude – I cannot help however looking forward to its publication and fate with an anxiety and apprehension that I never felt before in the same degree – for consider my father's credit is entirely at stake! And do you not tremble for me, even when you read the heads of the chapters and consider of how much importance the subjects are and how totally foreign to my habits of thinking or writing. (quoted in Marilyn Butler, 1972: p. 210)

From Maria Edgeworth's point of view – given that the book was well received and her fears ill-founded – *Professional Education* was probably a success. It was taken as '*proof of affection* and gratitude' by her father and that was her motivation in writing it. One might regret the fact that in the two years of 'drudgery' that *Professional Education* took, she had little or no time for writing fiction which we might well have appreciated more – but this is a different matter.

One can also regret the fact that Charlotte Brontë spent so many years in the drudgery of looking after her father that her literary work was curtailed, and that Tillie Olsen spent so many years in domestic drudgery that we have been deprived of the books she would otherwise have written – but all this does is demonstrate how rarely women have been free to devote themselves exclusively to their writing. Think of what Jane Carlyle might have given the world had she not been obliged to spend her life ensuring that the writing of husband Thomas was not disturbed?* There have been those who have suggested that the world

*"Some people said that Jane was the cleverest woman in London. ... Her friends had the highest estimates of her talents on the basis of her conversation and her brilliant letters. Dickens thought she would have been a great novelist, and Forster agreed. ... George Eliot sent her and not Mr Carlyle copies of her first two novels' (Phyllis Rose, 1985; pp. 239-40).

would have been a better place had Thomas Carlyle done the housework, and Jane Carlyle the writing, but such things were not to be. Few are the women who had good conditions for writing – 'a room of one's own and £500 a year' as Virginia Woolf put it.

And if Maria Edgeworth did her share of the drudgery – albeit literary drudgery – she was not completely deprived of the opportunity to write her fiction. It may have been an 'extra', to be fitted in after the obligations of family living had been met, but she has left some superb novels. I do not want to dismiss (out of hand and without diligent perusal) *all* her tales and stories that were designed for educational use. Some of them can still stand in their own right as excellent examples of Maria Edgeworth's literary (as distinct from educational or moralising) skill. But I do want to commend – in the highest possible terms, Maria Edgeworth's novels. I do want to deplore (and to shout and shake my fists in frustration) the loss of such a superb body of work. I have become somewhat apprehensive about the use of the word 'tragedy' (given the sexual double standard of its literary applications) but I have no hesitations in insisting that it is nothing short of a *tragedy* that Maria Edgeworth has been denied her place as one of the mothers of the novel.

Walter Allen (1980) does accord Maria Edgeworth a place in English fiction: 'She invented . . . the regional novel' (p. 103), and many were the men who followed who were indebted to her (Walter Allen mentions Walter Scott, Gustave Flaubert, François Mauriac, Mark Twain, Ivan Turgenev, Charles Dickens). But while he extols some of her virtues he is also at pains to point out that she was not a great writer – 'with all her gifts she was less than a great novelist,' he insists (p. 107): he sees her major weakness as that of making her characters bend to suit her moral purposes:

> Miss Edgeworth's characters are free up to a point; but they are still tethered to their creator. The rope may be a long one, but they are tugged to conformity all the same. Miss Edgeworth was essentially a didactic writer for whom the virtue of the novel was that it was a particularly graphic form of tract. Fiction was an aid to education, and Miss Edgeworth's theories of human nature and right behaviour trip her up as a novelist. (Walter Allen, 1980: p. 107)

The educational element aside, the same may be said of Jane Austen and George Eliot: that they had a moral vision and aimed to show the difference between good and bad judgment and the consequences of both. To impose such *order* on their novels does not seem to me to constitute weakness in itself, and I do not find that Maria Edgeworth's fiction suffers from what is referred to as her 'didactic' practice but which could just as readily be termed her philosophical point of view, or her social criticism. As for the 'educational' component, I suspect that such an assessment is derived more from Richard Edgeworth's prefaces than his daughter's novels.

Walter Allen provides a reference to Maria Edgeworth on a page that his book does not contain (p. 364), so perhaps he has some positive statement to make which I have missed; in some of the criticism he does provide there is much with which I would not agree. This is not an issue. Part of the delight of literary criticism *could be* a debate over what is good and what is not, what works and what fails. In the end, literary criticism is a subjective activity with readers bringing their own experience and values to the writing that is being assessed, and I have no doubt that my experience and values are very different from Mr Allen's and would lead me to very different conclusions. But the activity is not *all* subjective: there are objective criteria which must also be met – among them, that the books should be available to be read. That in the absence of the ready accessibility of Maria Edgeworth's novels the debate on her work must be esoteric is one of my major objections. 'Better than Fielding', she needs to be as widely available as Fielding, and as freely discussed. But then of course we would be the inheritors of a very different literary tradition, and one in which the mothers of the novel took their rightful place.

Table 11: Frances Burney and Maria Edgeworth

Frances Burney (1752-1840)

Novels

1778	*Evelina*
1782	*Cecelia*
1796	*Camilla*
1814	*The Wanderer*
1832	*Memoirs of Dr Burney*

The Berg Collection of the New York Public Library
Diary and Letters of Madame D'Arblay (7 vols, 1842-46)
The Early Diary of Frances Burney, 1768-1778 (2 vols, 1889)

Plays (unpublished manuscripts)
   'The Witlings'
   'Edwy and Elgiva'
   'Elberta'
   'Hubert de Vere'
   'The Siege of Pevensey'

'A Busy Day'
'Love and Fashion'
'The Woman-Hater'

Maria Edgeworth (1768-1849)

1795	*Letters for Literary Ladies*
1796	*The Parent's Assistant*
1798	*Practical Education* (with Richard Lovell Edgeworth) (2 vols)
1800	*Castle Rackrent*
1801	*Early Lessons*
1801	*Belinda* (3 vols)
1802	*Irish Bulls*
1804	*Popular Tales* (3 vols)
1805	*The Modern Griselda*
1806	*Leonora* (2 vols)
1809-12	*Tales of Fashionable Life* (1809, 'Ennui and Manoeuvering'; 1812, 'Emilie de Coulanges' and 'The Absentee')
1814	*Patronage* (4 vols)
1817	*Comic Dramas*
1817	*Ormond*
1834	*Helen* (3 vols)

CHAPTER 17

·

Lady Morgan and political fiction

There are few more colourful characters among women of letters than Sydney Owenson (Lady Morgan, 1778? 1783?-1859). A prolific writer (more than seventy volumes), a passionate political writer who championed Ireland and denounced English tyranny, a marvellously rapid writer who undertook long and serious research for her 'political fictions', an outrageous woman in word and deed who fearlessly employed her satire to good effect, she seems to have been a successful author who earned herself a lot of money – and many enemies.

Writing of Lady Morgan in 1863, but a few years after her death, Julia Kavanagh is still impressed by the wit, vitality – and audacity – of this woman, and it is to be greatly regretted that her prophecy about Lady Morgan's permanent place in the literary tradition did not prove to be an accurate one.

'The mere name of Lady Morgan is not one that can or will be readily forgotten,' writes Julia Kavanagh. 'She was a brilliant woman of the world – she travelled and saw much – she wrote upwards of seventy volumes – she was original, witty and fearless – she had vehement and cruel enemies and ardent friends – she braved sarcasm and slander', and in the years to come, adds Julia Kavanagh, 'her name will hold no contemptible position in the political and literary history of her times' (vol. II, pp. 285-6).

Oh, that she should hold any position at all in the political and literary history of her times! For despite her many novels and works of non-fiction, despite the huge (if harassing) exposure her work received in the *Quarterly Review*, the furore that her fictions on Ireland fermented, her well-publicised controversies with prominent figures, despite her feminist protest in the two-volume *Woman and Her Master* (1840) and the fact that her writings were placed on the Index of forbidden books,

8   Lady Morgan, Sydney Owenson

Lady Morgan has *no* place in the political, literary, religious – or feminist – history of her time. She is a classic example of Germaine Greer's (1974) thesis of the transience of women's fame.

Famous she was. Dazzlingly famous. As writer, wit, conversationalist, society figure. Lady Morgan was no retiring person who shunned publicity but a flamboyant presence in the world. So openly did she court celebration that some there are who suggest that 'she got what she was asking for' when she was so widely and vituperatively attacked and reviewed. But if it were ever believed that one reason for women's eclipse in the historical records was a result of the retiring nature of their lives, the existence of Lady Morgan would refute such a view. She helps to make it clear that whether women withdraw from society (as did Ann Radcliffe) or whether women are publicly prominent, either way, they and their work can fade from view.

That Sydney Owenson enjoyed prominence and prestige in her own life time is incontestable: so too it is incontestable that she has almost completely disappeared. Yet it is not as if she were a passing fashion. Her writing career, which was successful from the outset, commenced with the beginning of the nineteenth century and spanned almost fifty years.

She started young, although just how young it is difficult to say for there is some confusion about her birth date – a confusion for which Sydney Owenson is herself held responsible! While Mona Wilson (1924) gives the year as 1783 it appears to me that Julia Kavanagh's date of 1778 is better substantiated. For Julia Kavanagh quotes from a variety of sources to support her assertion that Sydney Owenson was a most precocious girl.

Not only does Julia Kavanagh give Sydney Owenson's date of birth – 1778 – she also gives the place: on the Irish Sea. Such a location between England and Ireland strikes Julia Kavanagh as significant for it seemed to decree that Sydney Owenson 'should belong to neither country' (1863: vol. II, p. 286). Sydney's parents were actors, on their way to an engagement in Ireland, her father's native land. She was their eldest child and was given the name Sydney by her father 'in commemoration of Sir Henry Sydney, under whose rule the family from which he was descended had settled in Ireland' (p. 287).

Sydney had a sister, Olivia, but their mother died when both were young and the two were reared by a devoted father.

Julia Kavanagh says of the young Sydney Owenson that she did not receive much formal education but that her desire for learning, for reading and writing, was almost insatiable. 'Something she was taught, but far more did she teach herself,' comments Julia Kavanagh who goes on to describe some of Sydney Owenson's literary practices: 'She early fell into the youthful sin of poetry, and Miss Siddy was known for getting up at night, and raking up the kitchen fire, when the fit was on her. Her verses show much talent, and some poetic feeling' (vol. II, p. 289).

Writing verses, however, was not her only occupation. In 1788, in Castlebar, Sydney Owenson was introduced to the world on a public stage as 'An Infant Prodigy'. She appears to have acted regularly with her father.

But family finances were not sound and Sydney Owenson early made her attempt to contribute to the coffers by the use of her pen. While I cannot find the precise date of publication, Sydney Owenson's first foray into the world of letters was *Poems by a Young Lady Between the Age of Twelve and Fourteen*. Julia Kavanagh makes her point: Sydney Owenson was a precocious girl.

This first publication was a reasonable success and convinced Sydney Owenson that she could support herself (and her father and sister) by obtaining a position as a governess and by writing in her spare time. Such career aspirations were unusual in a young woman, but more unusual was her father's response. While he considered acting an acceptable occupation for his daughter, he didn't want her to become a governess.

Her reaction was characteristically spirited and defiant: 'What objections *can* you have to my occupying a position as teacher to the young? It is a calling which enrols the names of Madame de Maintenon, Madame de Genlis, and I believe at this moment, even of the young Duke of Orleans; . . . and I believe Dr Moore is the tutor to the Duke of Hamilton' (quoted in Mona Wilson, 1924: p. 70). It was no vulgar company that Sydney Owenson proposed to keep.

If her response to her father was unconventional so too was her entry to teaching employment. 'She arrived at her first situation in a muslin dress, pink silk shoes and stockings, and the maid's bonnet and cloak, having rushed from a dance to catch the night mail' (Mona Wilson, 1924: p. 70).

While working as a governess Sydney Owenson proceeded to publish her novels. The first, in 1802, was *St Clair, or The Heiress of Desmond* and this was followed in 1804 by *The Novice of St Dominick*. 'Both books were popular at the time, and added to the fame of their writer. But it was not till 1805, when she had reached the age of twenty seven, that Sydney Owenson published her first genuine claim on lasting popularity: *The Wild Irish Girl*' (Julia Kavanagh, 1863: vol. II, pp. 290-1).

The Wild Irish Girl was immensely popular: seven editions in two years. And the fact that Sydney Owenson reeived £300 for it – *before* publication – indicates that her previous two novels had not gone unnoted by the publishers. For the next few years the novels (and other works) continued to appear, and if Sydney Owenson did not have a great deal of time for writing, it seems that she did not need it. Commenting on her *speed*, Julia Kavanagh pays Sydney Owenson an unusual compliment by regarding it as a skill: more commonly, women writers who have been 'quick' have been condemned on the grounds that what was written in such a short time could never qualify as 'good'.

'*The Wild Irish Girl* was written in six weeks,' says Julia Kavanagh; '*The Patriotic Sketches*, which appeared in 1807, took their author but one; and *Woman, or Ida of Athens*, a tale in four volumes, begun on the 20th July, 1808, as Miss Owenson mentioned in her address to the public, and finished on the 18th of October of the same year – written, too, in the midst of society – is still more remarkable proof of her enviable facility.' Not that this was by any means all that Miss Owenson did. Musically inclined, a singer, and a good harpist, 'Miss Owenson produced an opera, *The First Attempt*, in which her father appeared in 1807, and *The Lay of an Irish Harp and Metrical Fragments*' (Julia Kavanagh, 1863: vol. II, pp. 291-2).

The time taken for the actual task of writing should not be used as an indication of the total time Sydney Owenson spent on her books, for many of them were based on a great deal of research. *The Wild Irish Girl*, for example, with its erudite heroine Glorvina (the name often after given to Sydney Owenson herself) is a serious history of Ireland. The wealth of information and the authoritative sources quoted in the extensive footnotes which feature on page after page, give a new twist to the concept of romantic fiction.

It was *The Wild Irish Girl* that launched Sydney Owenson. In the space of a few years she made the transition from governess-cum-writer to celebrity, and her achievement was considerable: 'She had combined her literary work, on which she expended no light amount of research, with a gay and independent life in Dublin. Her books had brought her a reputation for genius; like Glorvina she played the harp and sang to her own accompaniment; she was a brilliant talker and a pretty girl. Small wonder that she found patrons of fashion, and lovers galore. Supreme among the former were the Marquis and Marchioness of Abercorn, who thought that a young person of Sydney's parts would be an enlivening addition to their household' (Mona Wilson, 1924: p. 74). An invitation was offered and duly accepted, and Sydney Owenson became a semi-permanent guest at the Abercorn home, Barons Court, in Ireland, and at their English home at Stanmore Priory.

It was at Barons Court that Sydney Owenson met Charles Morgan. He was a personable man, the Marquis's private physician, a friend and follower of Jenner – and he fell in love with the petite Sydney Owenson (she was not much more than four feet tall). But she was not to be rushed into marriage: she even had reservations about marriage which could mean an end to her independent and literary life. But her serious concerns could be concealed by a facetious facade. When the Duke of Richmond enquired of her how soon he would be able to congratulate her on her marriage, Sydney Owenson gave a satirical reply:

> The rumour respecting Mr Morgan's *devoument* may or may not be true; but this I can at least, with all candour and sincerity assure your Grace, that I shall remain to the last day of my life in single blessedness unless some more tempting inducement than the mere change from Miss Owenson to Mistress Morgan be offered me.
> (quoted in Julia Kavanagh, 1863: vol. II, p. 294)

Whereby the Duke promptly knighted Charles Morgan.

But still Sydney Owenson demurred. Her friends counselled acceptance. She continued to resist. This was no decision to be taken lightly. Sydney Owenson was thirty-four years of age, she had established her own satisfactory life of letters. Why risk all? She had 'entered upon life with three purposes,' states Clara Whitmore (1910), 'to advocate the interest of Ireland by her writings; to pay her father's debts; and to provide for his old age. And these purposes she accomplished' (p. 129). So why should she marry? Marriage would mean a new way of life, which might be better, but could be worse. It clearly required a sacrifice of independence, and Sydney Owenson was not sure.

She came under pressure. According to Mona Wilson the patience of her hostess was sorely tried: Lady Abercorn did not want to lose Sydney Owenson to literary society (a distinct possibility) and she believed the best way to keep her was to have her permanently attached to the household, as she would be once married to Charles Morgan. So 'one morning Lady Abercorn suddenly opened the library door and said, "Glorvina, come upstairs directly and be married; there must be no more trifling."' Which seems to be a less than sensitive approach. But Mona Wilson adds that 'Sydney never repented seriously or for long together of her bargain' (p. 76).

In retrospect, Lady Morgan probably did believe that her marriage had been fortunate. Her literary career was not interrupted. She had no children and she enjoyed substantial encouragement and support from her husband. 'Sir Charles was in complete sympathy with his wife's political views, and he took an active part in the struggle for Catholic emancipation. He produced a considerable number of magazine articles and contributed chapters to Lady Morgan's books on Italy and France' (Mona Wilson, 1924: pp. 78-9).

In fact, so successful was Lady Morgan as a writer that it was not long before Sir Charles ceased to practise medicine in order to accompany her on her tours and to help with her research. Her work provided a more handsome living than his could have done.

While after their marriage the plan had been for the Morgans to continue to reside with the Abercorns, it was soon abandoned, partly because the couple could not abide their dependent state and because Lady Morgan took objection to the 'English conversation' to which she was regularly obliged to submit:

> I have seen the best and worst of English society; I have dined at the table of a *city trader*, taken tea with the family of a *London merchant*, and supped at Devonshire House, all in one day, and I must say, that if there is a people on earth that understand the *science* of conversation *less* than another, it is the English. . . . In England, conversation is a game of chess – the result of judgement, memory and deliberation; with us it is a game of battledore, and our ideas, like our shuttlecocks, are thrown lightly *one* to the *other*, bounding and rebounding, playing more for amusement than conquest, and leaving the players equally animated by the game, and careless of its results. . . . An Englishman will *declaim*, or he will *narrate*, or he will be silent; but it is very difficult to get him to converse, especially if he is *supreme bon ton*, or labours under the reputation of being a *rising man*; but even all this, dull as it is, is better than a man who, struck by some fatal analogy in what he is saying, immediately chimes in with the eternal 'that puts me in mind' and then gives you not an anecdote, but an absolute history of something his uncle did, or his grandfather said, and then, by some lucky association, goes on with stories which have his own obscure friends for his heroes and heroines, but have neither point, *but*, humour, nor even *moral* (usually tagged to the end of old ballads). Oh, save me from this, good heaven, and I will sustain all else beside!
> (quoted in Mona Wilson, 1924: pp. 77-8)

It is not surprising that with sentiments like this, Lady Morgan antagonised the English establishment.

In 1811 she had written *The Missionary* ('one of the worst and most imperfect books' in Julia Kavanagh's view, p. 292); in 1812 she was married; in 1813 came *O'Donnel*, a deliberately provocative championship of Ireland. In 1814 she and her husband went to France where she gathered material for her first book of that title; with its wealth of information on life in France it proved to be an authoritative source – and it made a considerable amount of money for the author.

By this time, Lady Morgan was a well-known figure in London circles: if she had her fans, she also had her foes. 'An independent, witty Irish woman of great charm, fearless in expressing her opinions, who had introduced herself into society and for whom nobody stood as sponsor,' writes Clara Whitmore (1910), Lady Morgan 'was looked upon by the old-fashioned English aristocracy as an adventuress; and later, when she came forth as the champion of Irish liberties and upbraided England for tyranny, she was maliciously denounced by the Tory party' (pp. 128-9).

To be without the protection of patronage or support in high places, to be sufficiently audacious to stand as an advocate of Ireland and critical of the English, to be sufficiently presumptuous to attempt to invade the world of letters without benefit of a 'proper' education, to be famous – and a woman – was to invoke the wrath of the English political and literary establishment. Lady Morgan was vituperatively attacked from many quarters.

'The violence with which Lady Morgan was attacked was cruel as well as unjust,' writes Julia Kavanagh (1863). 'The most insulting coarseness was levelled against her. Her age, her personal appearance, her dress, her moral, religious and political opinions were commented upon in a tone' – (oh that it were true!) – 'which has fortunately passed away from literature' (vol. II, p. 296).

There were some, of course, who thought that Lady Morgan got nothing less than she deserved. If a woman ventures on the public stage she must take what is coming to her, no matter that the most vicious attacks are reserved for women. Lady Morgan was 'uppity'; she should have expected to be put in her place. There is the suggestion that had she been a little more politely persuasive and refined she would not have 'invited' such a harsh response. But while I can find no evidence that daring women fare better if they are more diplomatic, Julia Kavanagh takes the view that Lady Morgan 'courted' some of the harassment that came her way. 'There are few of her works that are not written in a tone of defiance,' says Julia Kavanagh, expressing her regret, and 'she called in sarcasm to her aid, and sarcasm invited retaliation' (p. 296).

I think it more likely that had Lady Morgan shown herself to be cowed by the 'critics' the attacks might have ceased to be so embittered; but she gave not the slightest sign of being intimidated. On the contrary, she spiritedly – and sarcastically – hit back, and it was this defiant attitude, I suspect, that fanned the flames of character assassination.

I have no desire to take up space by quoting the contemptible castigations of Lady Morgan which regularly appeared in the *Quarterly Review*. But her response – particularly to the much reiterated and misogynistic suggestion that she should abandon writing and attempt to become the mistress of a happy family – gives some indication of the insults that were levelled at her, and some indication of the fearlessness of this amazing woman writer.

There are echoes of Aphra Behn's proud defiance of the critics in Lady Morgan's 'Preface' to *France*, published in 1815:

There is one review, at least, which must necessarily place me under the ban of its condemnation: and to which the sentiments and principles scattered through the following pages (though conceived and expressed in feelings the most remote from those of *local* or *party* policy) will afford an abundant source of accusation as being foreign to its own narrow doctrines, and opposed to its own exclusive creed. I mean *The Quarterly Review*.

In thus recurring to the severe chastisement which my early efforts received from the judgement of *The Quarterly Review*, it would be ungrateful to conceal that it placed

'My bane and antidote at once before me'

and that in accusing me of 'licentiousness, profligacy, irreverence, blasphemy, libertinism, disloyalty and atheism' it presented a *nostrum* of universal efficacy, which was to transform my *vices* into *virtues*, and to render me, in its own words, 'not indeed a good writer of novels, but a *useful friend*, a *faithful wife*, a *tender mother*, and a respectable and happy *mistress of a family*'.

To effect this purpose 'so devoutly to be wished' it prescribed a simple remedy: 'To purchase immediately a *spelling book*, to which in process of time, might be added a *pocket dictionary*, and to take a few lessons in joining-hand; which superadded to a little common sense in place of idle raptures' were finally to render me that invaluable epitome of female excellence, whose price Solomon has declared above rubies.

While I denied the crimes thus administered to, I took the advice for the sake of its results. . . . As it foretold, I am become, in spite of the 'seven deadly sins' it laid to my charge, 'not indeed a good writer of novels' but, I trust, a respectable, and I am *sure*, 'a happy mistress of a family'.

Back in print again – although not a novel this time – not one ounce deflated, and with another 'success' on her hands. Lady Morgan's productivity and rewards must have been galling to these reviewers. Publishers wooed her – even to the extent of expensive presents. And while the attacks in the *Quarterly Review* may be interpreted as 'backlash' against a prominent woman writer, its form was considered so disgraceful as to promote a 'backlash' against the *Quarterly* itself: the assaults on Lady Morgan were one of the main reasons for the establishment of an alternative publication and *The Athenaeum* came into existence. Lady Morgan was one of its regular contributors.

When she didn't 'get back' at a few of her nastiest critics in prefaces or reviews, she mercilessly satirised them in her fiction. The character of Crawley in *Florence Macarthy* is said to be based on one John Wilson

Croker who had made one of the worst and most 'unmanly' attacks upon her: and, writes Julia Kavanagh, 'it must be acknowledged that this pitiless sketch fully avenged Lady Morgan' (1863: vol. II, p. 297).

Even when she wasn't seeking retribution, however, Lady Morgan still managed to make enemies. One of the most amusing episodes I can find is that of her public altercation with Cardinal Wiseman which took place in the columns of the newspaper. Cardinal Wiseman bitterly resented Lady Morgan's statement in *Italy* (1821), 'that the Chair of St Peter had been replaced, as the original relic, uncovered by French curiosity, had been found to bear the inscription in Arabic – There is but one God, and Mahomet is his Prophet'. What must have been really maddening was that 'her story was neither a fabrication of her own nor due to a confusion with the Chair of St Peter at Venice, but that she had the authority of Denon for her assertions' (Mona Wilson, 1924: p. 117).

But it was her championship of Ireland and her unapologetic use of fiction for political ends which prompted the greatest frenzy among her many critics. She did not define 'politicians' as those who were in 'parliament' but unashamedly called herself a female politician. In 1835, *O'Donnel* was reprinted and in the preface to the new edition, Lady Morgan explicitly stated her aims:

> *O'Donnel* was the first of a series of National Tales, undertaken with a humble but zealous view to the promotion of a great national cause, the emancipation of the Catholics of Ireland. The attempt has been made the matter of grave censure, as a step beyond the position of the Author, and foreign to the scope of the genus. To this canon of criticism I cannot yet subscribe. Novels, like more solid compositions, are not exempted from the obligation to inculcate truth. They are expected, in their idlest trifling, to possess a moral scope; and politics are but morals on a grander scale. The appropriation of this form of composition to purposes beyond those of mere amusement, is not new. A novel is specially adapted to enable the advocate of any cause to steal upon the public, through the by-ways of the imagination, and to win from its sympathies what its reason so often refuses to yield to undeniable demonstration.

No separation of art and politics for Lady Morgan. And no sense of silly novels from silly lady novelists. If she has not since been taken as a serious writer it is not because she did not have a serious purpose or a considered and reasoned view of the role of 'art'. To put her in context is to realise that she made use of the limited forms that were available to women and combined them to forge a means of allowing women to become influential: at a time when women were discouraged, even precluded from political participation, she extended the boundaries as far as she could with her insistence that it was feasible to use fiction for social and political comment and criticism.

Denied a formal voice, Lady Morgan found a new one when she introduced the 'political romance'. She did not hesitate to justify fiction on the grounds that it could promote awareness, teach, and 'subvert' the conventional wisdom. Was this not what novels had been doing, but on an individual basis? When so many novels had been concerned with character flaws, with unsound judgment and unfair or immoral behaviour within individuals, why was it not proper to extend such consideration to groups of individuals?

Small shift in focus though it may have been, Lady Morgan did something new when she insisted on the validity of treating morals on a collective scale. Elizabeth Inchbald and Charlotte Smith had included some social criticism in their novels (and had been condemned for it) but Lady Morgan, like Mary Wollstonecraft, went much further when she insisted that social criticism in itself was a rationale for fiction. Like Charles Dickens – who was to follow – she was not of the opinion that the value of the novel was impaired when it was used to acquaint readers with a reality which they might not otherwise reflect upon – and which could well be horrendous.

Besides, Lady Morgan did not think it possible to write on some subjects without being political, without exposing injustice and sowing the seeds of reform. She defied anyone to write realistically about Ireland and to remain apolitical. The writer did not have to start out with explicitly political intentions to end up with an indictment of injustice: all that was necessary was a faithful representation of Irish conditions and the politics would emerge soon enough. Perhaps Lady Morgan was thinking of Maria Edgeworth when she wrote that 'whatever may have been the quality of the author's mind, every fictitious narrative that has had Ireland for its theme, has assumed a more or less decidedly political colouring. If an imitation of life be necessarily an example, Irish life, in all its combinations, can only be an example of political error' (from 1835 'Preface' to *O'Donnel*).

In her explicit advocacy of Ireland, Lady Morgan was somewhat different from Maria Edgeworth who more subtly drew her portraits of Irish life – and the inherent injustices – and invited her readers to reach their own conclusions. For Lady Morgan there was only one conclusion and her fiction was a vehicle for stating it. But her political stance was by no means confined to her fiction: it was the purpose of much of her non-fiction writing as well.

Lady Morgan's study of the history of Ireland well prepared her for reviewing the systems of France and Italy. Her books of these titles were serious attempts to describe, explain, understand – and to evaluate – the mores and manners of other countries. A sort of early anthropological

311

study – close to home. She examined the political institutions (and found herself out of favour for her preference for republicanism) and she diligently described the details of the lives of a cross-section of the community. Always concerned to expose injustice, she was equally committed to acquainting her English-speaking readers with the cultural and artistic traditions of the countries she 'explored'. Her 'Italian book is a more solid work than her volumes on France,' writes Mona Wilson (1924) 'and must have been a useful guide for contemporary travellers who shared her enthusiasm for Guido and Salvator Rosa' (p. 104).

She certainly impressed – and alarmed – Lord Byron with her descriptions of Italy: 'By the way, when you write to Lady Morgan,' he wrote to a mutual friend, Moore, on August 24th, 1821, 'will you thank her for her handsome speeches in her book about *my* books? I do not know her address. Her work is fearless and excellent on the subject of Italy – pray tell her so – and I know the country. I wish she had fallen in with *me*, I could have told her a thing or two that would have confirmed her positions.' And it was because he thought her work so good and her style so apt that Lord Byron had his own fears: he was worried that he might be accused of plagiarism. 'Much is coincidence,' he wrote; 'for instance, Lady Morgan (in a really *excellent* book, I assure you, on Italy) calls Venice an *ocean Rome*; I have the very same expression in *Foscari* and yet *you* know that the play was written months ago and sent to England; the *Italy* I only received on the 16th instant' (quoted in Mona Wilson, 1924: pp. 111-12). Clearly Lady Morgan was well esteemed among some of her literary peers.

Lady Morgan's literary life was relatively long and eventful. Until 1834 she and her husband travelled regularly through England and Europe but returned always to Dublin. Lady Morgan had endeared herself to the Irish with *The Wild Irish Girl, O'Donnel, Florence Macarthy* and her last but not least 'political romance', *The O'Briens and the O'Flahertys* (1827). 'Lady Morgan was justly popular in her own land,' writes Julia Kavanagh (1863), 'she was cheered in the theatres and publicly praised by O'Connell' (vol. II, p. 299). And she was reluctant to leave. But in 1834, not long after she had received the honour and the reward of a £300 a year literary pension for life, Sir Charles Morgan decided that he wanted to return to England and the couple settled at 11 William Street, Knightsbridge.

There is one more 'achievement' for which Lady Morgan should be given credit – that of the Albert Gate: 'Her great desire' after moving to London, writes Mona Wilson, 'was to obtain an entrance to Hyde Park at the end of William Street and after much correspondence and wire pulling, the Albert Gate was conceded in 1842': p. 113).

In London, Lady Morgan was very much part of certain political and literary circles, although she was by no means immune from jeers and snubs – one in particular from William Wordsworth (see Mona Wilson, 1924: p. 113). She retained her well-deserved reputation for repartee and was known as a brilliant conversationalist and hostess – a position not to be despised when women were excluded from political, professional and educational institutions and had need to make the world come to their door when denied entry to the world. And, of course, she continued to write.

There were her regular contributions to *The Athenaeum*; there was *Passages from My Autobiography* which she prepared with the assistance of Geraldine Jewsbury; there was her two-volume feminist protest, *Woman and Her Master* (an historical treatise that attempted to show that women had been the great spiritual force and had been conquered by man's brute strength); and there were her *Memoirs*.

Charles Morgan died in 1843 and for the next sixteen years Sydney Morgan continued to entertain – and to be entertaining. She was a celebrity until her death in 1859 and for Julia Kavanagh, writing in 1863, Sydney Morgan retains an immediacy and vibrancy that cannot be dimmed. Yet just more than one century later, she has virtually disappeared.

Why Lady Morgan should have been so decisively excluded from the literary tradition is hard to determine. It cannot be that her novels were devoid of any redeeming features, that her work was totally without merit. It cannot be because her reputation in her lifetime was at the periphery of visibility and that with her death it was but a small move to oblivion. It cannot be because she made no contribution to the development of the novel because she was a pioneer of political fiction and the innovator of 'political romance'. It cannot be that her work is without interest, relevance, wit or worth.

Not only does Lady Morgan occupy a unique place in the Irish history of letters and in the English history of letters, but she is one of the formidable links in the chain of women's literary traditions. She stands firmly between Charlotte Smith and Elizabeth Gaskell.

And yet she has disappeared. So much so that the question does not arise as to whether she warrants a place in the history of letters. One may lament the fact that the position of Fanny Burney, Ann Radcliffe or Maria Edgeworth has to be argued for in the literary tradition but at least there are those who are aware of their existence and their names are not entirely unknown in the records, even if they do figure predominantly in the footnotes. But so total has been the eclipse of Sydney Morgan, her loss does not even register. While undeniably one of the mothers of the novel, it is as if she had never existed.

Table 12: Sydney Owenson, Lady Morgan (1778-1859)

1801	*Poems by a Young Lady Between the Age of 12 and 14*
1802	*Deep in Love* (words and music arranged by Sydney Owenson)
1803	*St Clair, or The heiress of Desmond*
1804	*The Novice of St Dominick*
1805	*A Few Reflections*
1805	*The Wild Irish Girl: a national tale*
1807	*Patriotic Sketches of Ireland written in Connaught*
1807	*The First Attempt* (opera)
1807	*The Lay of an Irish Harp, or Metrical Fragments*
1809	*Woman, or Ida of Athens*
1811	*The Missionary: an Indian tale*
1814	*O'Donnel: a national tale*
1817	*France* (2 vols)
1818	*Florence Macarthy: an Irish tale* (4 vols)
1821	*Italy* (2 vols)
1821	*Letter to Reviewers of 'Italy'; including an answer to a pamphlet entitled 'Observations upon the calumnies and misrepresentations in Lady Morgan's Italy . . .'*
1822	*The Mohawks: a satirical poem with notes*
1824	*The Life and Times of Salvator Rosa*
1825	*Absenteeism*
1827	*The O'Briens and the O'Flahertys: a national tale*
1829	*The Book on the Boudoir*
1830	*France in 1829-30*
1833	*Dramatic Scenes from Real Life*
1835	*The Princess, or The Beguine*
1840	*Woman and Her Master: a history of the female sex from the earliest period* (2 vols)
1841	*Book Without a Name* (by Sir Charles and Lady Morgan)
1851	*Letter to Cardinal Wiseman in answer to his remarks on Lady Morgan's statements regarding St Peter's Chair*
1859	*Luxima: the prophetess. A tale of India* (rewrite of *The Missionary*)
1859	*An Odd Volume: extracted from an autobiography*
1862	*Lady Morgan's Memoirs: autobiography, diaries and correspondence* (2 vols)
n.d.	*Twelve original Hibernian melodies, with English words, imitated and translated from the 'Works' of the ancient Irish bards*

CHAPTER 18

·

Amelia Opie and the novel of ideas

One of the few available accounts of the life and work of Amelia Opie (1769-1853) is a *Memoir* by Cecelia Brightwell (n.d.) which was published by the Religious Tract Society, and it is far from being an extensive or illuminating account of this writer of fiction. As Cecelia Brightwell states in her opening pages, 'It is not . . . as an authoress that I wish to present Mrs Opie to my readers; my object is to trace, in the experience of her life, the goodness of God' (p. 3). But because the goodness of God was rather late in making its presence felt in Amelia Opie (for Cecelia Brightwell it is connected with Mrs Opie's conversion to Quakerism in her fifty-sixth year), not much is made of her novel writing days in the *Memoir*. 'The earlier and longer part of her history,' explains Cecelia Brightwell with little interest and no little disdain, 'was one of youthful enjoyment, successful aspiration, and worldly distinction' (p. 3). But it is not just that the period which Cecelia Brightwell passes over is one I want to explore that presents something of a difficulty: it is also that where Cecelia Brightwell does refer to Amelia Opie's novels it is in the effort to rewrite them and to remove any stains that might otherwise appear on this pure soul. There is a huge discrepancy between her reading of Amelia Opie's 'daring' novels and my own. But perhaps, if the novels were in print, this could be a matter of debate.

Amelia Alderson was born in Norwich. Her father was a medical doctor, a progressive thinker, and a supporter of some of the more radical ideas of the day. Her mother – Amelia Briggs – was 'a woman of good sense and judgement' who, according to Cecelia Brightwell, 'endeavoured early to teach her child obedience and self denial' (p. 5). Amelia was an only child and was reared as a 'rational dissenter'.

When she was fifteen, her mother died and while Amelia took over the management of her father's household it was evidently not an

9 Amelia Opie

onerous task and still allowed sufficient time for reading – and writing. In 1790, her first novel, *The Dangers of Coquetry*, was published – anonymously. Whether this warning against coquetry was the result of personal experience it is not possible to tell for scant are the details of Amelia Opie's life in Norwich, and Cecelia Brightwell certainly does not dwell on the personal involvement of the author in this particular tale. But in 1794, Amelia Opie made the first of what would be her regular visits to London, and because she wrote of her adventures to her father – who did not destroy all of her 'incriminating' letters – it is possible to glean a little more information on this stage of Amelia Opie's life.

She wanted to be an actress and, on her arrival in London, was soon friends with Mrs Siddons and Mrs Inchbald. She wanted to know more about the world – and more about the exciting ideas on democracy and freedom that were coming from France – and she was soon moving in the circles of her father's friend, William Godwin.* She wanted to know more about literature and letters and was soon on intimate terms with Mary Wollstonecraft and Helen Maria Williams (novelist, letter writer, and chronicler of the French Revolution).

Not that these details could be learnt from Cecelia Brightwell's account, where the emphasis is placed on the entry of Elizabeth Fry and religious dignitaries, and where the names of the actresses and the political philosophers are not mentioned. Obviously, however, this was an exciting time, and Amelia Opie shared in the excitement, was inspired by many of the ideas of democracy, and was aware of the claims of women's rights. She readily professed her admiration for Mary Wollstonecraft.

Perhaps the commitment to the principle of equality (a commitment which her father shared) made it easier for her to marry a man who is customarily described as 'low-born': the portrait painter, John Opie.** He was by no means 'a good match' in terms of his background or his bank account, but with Amelia Opie's interest in politics and art, her marriage to John Opie in 1798 is not only understandable, but borders on the 'romantic'.

*It is often alleged that here again William Godwin proposed – an assumption based no doubt on his predilection for making offers to young women writers. But William St Clair, 1984, states that 'The often repeated story that Godwin asked her to marry him is based on a misunderstanding of the entry in his journal for 10 July 1796 "Propose to Alderson" which refers to Godwin's successful efforts to raise money from Dr Alderson for the poet Robert Merry who was then under arrest for debt' (p. 237). It seems a strange way of making an entry. . . .

**He painted the portrait of Mary Wollstonecraft shown on page 248.

It seems as though her desire to act had met with little success, but her desire to write was still strong and unlike those women who upon marriage have put away their pens, Amelia Opie once more took hers up. For this she gives much credit to her husband: 'Knowing at the time of our marriage, that my most favourite amusement was writing, he did not check my ambition to become an author; on the contrary, he encouraged it, and our only quarrel was, not that I wrote too much, but that I did not write more and better' (quoted in Julia Kavanagh, 1863: vol. II, p. 250).

In 1801, Amelia Opie's second novel, *Father and Daughter*, was published. While it is acknowledged that Amelia Opie's later novel – *Adeline Mowbray* – is based on certain aspects of Mary Wollstonecraft's life, I have come across no suggestion that *Father and Daughter* also owes some of its detail to the experiences of Mary Wollstonecraft. Yet with a heroine who has an illegitimate child and who tries to commit suicide, the parallels between Agnes Fitzhenry and Mary Wollstonecraft cannot go completely ignored. Although if there are similarities between the facts and the fiction, there are differences as well: Mary Wollstonecraft made no attempt to hide her own animosity towards her father whereas Agnes Fitzhenry, who is seen to be responsible for her father's madness, does her utmost to make amends for her disgrace. She nurses him while he is ill and is rewarded when he recovers sufficiently to forgive her – before he dies. Agnes then falls into a 'state of stupefaction' and also dies; the reconciliatory ending takes the form of father and daughter being buried together. Such a fate would not have appealed to Mary Wollstonecraft at all.

However she would have approved, no doubt, of the fictional treatment of her life that was the substance of Amelia Opie's next book, *Adeline Mowbray* (1804). Even if Mary Wollstonecraft had not herself conveyed the details of her life to Amelia Opie, the story of her 'affair' with Gilbert Imlay (and the existence of their daughter Fanny) was widely known. And it was a story which provoked considerable interest and raised some serious questions in the free thinking and frankly speaking circles in which Amelia Opie (at least at this stage of her life) ordinarily moved. For Mary Wollstonecraft presented something of a problem to the rational intellectuals – not when she went off with Gilbert Imlay, but when she married William Godwin.

Mary Wollstonecraft had chosen to live with Gilbert Imlay in the anarchy of France at a time when, even had it been desirable, it would not have been possible for two English persons in hiding to have organised an official marriage. Nor was it such a long time since the vows of two people before God had in England constituted a binding and legal marriage. So when Mary Wollstonecraft informed her friends that she and Gilbert Imlay considered themselves husband and wife, despite the absence of a formal religious ceremony, she was not in their eyes embarking on a life of promiscuity: in the context of the rational thinkers she was leading an honourable life.

Had the relationship between Mary Wollstonecraft and Gilbert Imlay gone well, Mary Wollstonecraft could have avoided some of the slurs that were later cast on her life. But of course the romance did not go well, it did not survive. Gilbert Imlay left Mary Wollstonecraft and it was the sense of desolation and not that of disgrace which drove her to desperate lengths. It was only when she resigned herself to the fact that her life with Gilbert Imlay was over that she turned to William Godwin.

And William Godwin had publicly proclaimed his opposition to marriage.

Who changed who's mind depends very much on the sources consulted, but when Mary Wollstonecraft became pregnant, the woman who had once before been 'married' and the man who had claimed he would never marry, were married. And this is where some of the problems and the moral dilemmas start.

There is the issue of William Godwin and the abandonment of his principles: does he go up or down in public esteem for having recanted his principles and for marrying the mother of his expected child? Does Mary Wollstonecraft go up or down in public esteem for being the young woman writer who finally agreed to Godwin's offer? But more importantly, there are the issues raised by Mary Wollstonecraft's actions. Had her marriage to Gilbert Imlay not been a 'real' marriage in spite of her protestations to the contrary at the time? For Gilbert Imlay was still alive and assuredly no 'divorce' had been required in order that Mary Wollstonecraft might marry again. If she had *really* been married to Gilbert Imlay, then she couldn't *really* be married to William Godwin, so where did truth, or rationality, lie?

Should marriage be binding anyway? Why not separate, if and when love dies? But then, how just was it for one to sever the relationship, when for the other, love endured? Look at the sorrow and grief which could result if one partner was free to walk away.

These questions are not all old-fashioned. They are enduring questions about the nature and responsibility of human relationships and still constitute some of the meaningful moral issues of today. They were questions which gave rise to great interest among the rational thinkers of the late eighteenth century who were trying to work out some sort of form which was fair to women as well as to men.

They are the questions that Amelia Opie explores in *Adeline Mowbray*.

After I found and read this novel, I passed it on to some of my friends and sought their opinions. For me, it was an intensely exciting novel. Partly because I knew it was a fictional account of some of the events in

Mary Wollstonecraft's life; partly because I was intrigued with the questions it raised about relationships; and partly because it made me realise – yet again – that for women, history has not conformed to the theory of steady progress as so 'scandalous' are the issues that are explored in the novel that it could not have been published fifty years later when Victorian morality was beginning to hold sway. But I was somewhat surprised to find that my great enthusiasm for this novel was not completely shared.

With Helen Mott I engaged in a passionate argument in which I defended the 'ideas' and she decried the 'characters' (who are, at times, not all that convincing, given that they have prescribed political points to make and are not all that free to live lives of their own). Half-way through our discussion, however, we were both struck by the same thought. We were two women vigorously debating the merits of a woman novelist of the past – and of whom, *most women were unaware*! If we could not agree on the qualities of the novel we could wholeheartedly agree on the right of women to know of its existence and the desirability (necessity?) of women being able to have the discussion that we were engaged in. We were acutely aware of what women have been denied because of the lost tradition of women writers. So we concluded our 'argument' with a toast to 'Lit-crit' departments across the English-speaking world: 'May the women in them have a rigorous and riotous discussion on the strengths and weaknesses of *Adeline Mowbray*.'

Mrs Mowbray, Adeline's mother, is a widow intent on providing an erudite education for her daughter but who lacks the wherewithal to do so. There are some satirically amusing scenes in which Mrs Mowbray's limitations are revealed; on one occasion when she is perusing a philosophical text on the opportune time and means for teaching her daughter arithmetic, Adeline is to be found in the corner completing the household accounts, an arithmetical task quite beneath the contempt of her mother. The reader is left in no doubt that Mrs Mowbray's grandiose ideas on education and her inability to demonstrate any sound common sense are at the root of some of Adeline's later misfortunes.

For her mother introduces her to the thrilling thesis of one Glenmurray, who scorns marriage as a barbarous and cruel state, and the impressionable Adeline is readily convinced of the beauty of true union and the baseness of weddings. So when this pure and innocent young woman meets Glenmurray – who proves to be a handsome, sensitive and virtuous young man – she not only falls in love with him but wants to live with him without the shackles of marriage.

Which is a bit of a problem for Glenmurray. He recognises that it is one thing to publish purple prose which pronounces against wedlock, but quite another to subject the sweet Adeline – whom he loves – to the taunts and torments of a hypocritical world which will judge her harshly for her failure to comply with convention. But he is at a loss to know what to do for he realises that to propose to Adeline, to insist upon marriage, is to risk being damned in her eyes. She admires him for his lofty principles and would be deeply distressed if he were to dispense with them.*

Glenmurray's hand, however, is forced. Mrs Mowbray marries a blackguard whom Amelia Opie describes as one who 'in his dealings with men was a man of honour' but who was 'in his dealings with women, completely the reverse; he considered them as a race of subordinate beings formed for the service and amusement of men; and that if, like horses they were well lodged, fed, and kept clean, they had no right to complain.' And when the stepfather, Sir Patrick O'Carrol, not only makes advances to Adeline but reveals that he is prepared to use force, Adeline has no real alternative but to leave. With Glenmurray.

They go abroad and we are witnesses to harrowing scenes where people who are at first charmed by Adeline's beauty and refinement soon become hurtful and hostile when she scorns any pretence of marriage and makes known her single (and pregnant) state. Even those who are sensible and sensitive feel that they cannot condone her behaviour by continuing to see her; and those who have less sense and more spite show their outright contempt for her and treat her as a source of contamination. A multitude of questions are thrown up as we encounter vicious women who are perfectly acceptable to society because they are wives, while Adeline who is pure of thought and compassionate of deed is condemned, because she is not a wife.

But she and Glenmurray are happy in each other. Their joy is marred only by the jibes and barbs of a censorious world, and the declining state of Glenmurray's health.

They return to England. The end draws near for Glenmurray who is driven almost to distraction about the fate of his love when he is no longer there to protect her. He (rightly) predicts offers from 'men of the world' who would only be too pleased to take advantage of her poverty and vulnerability and to make her their mistress. That he commends his cousin to Adeline as a husband on his deathbed, then, can probably be explained in terms of his desperation because such 'bartering' in women stands in sharp contradiction to his earlier objections to marriage. He dies.

Adeline does not love the cousin. She does not feel for him the pure and noble emotion that she felt for Glenmurray so she rejects the 'offer' of marriage and elects to support herself. She sets up a school and there

---

*I suspect that here, Amelia Opie is having a go at William Godwin who so readily renounced his resistance to marriage when he found someone who accepted him.

is nothing but praise for her as a teacher – until her past catches up with her. She is forced to abandon the school. Her circumstances become intolerable. She consents to marry the cousin – and is miserably unhappy.

So we have the bliss of life with Glenmurray – outside marriage; and the misery of life with the cousin – inside marriage. Which could well be where the fiction departs from the facts of Mary Wollstonecraft's life, for there is no evidence that she was ecstatically happy with Gilbert Imlay and desperately unhappy with William Godwin.

But the happy illicit liaison and the unhappy marriage were sufficiently plausible to challenge the accepted customs of Amelia Opie's day – and sufficiently scandalous for those who later wished to defend the author to want to deny any charge of immorality in her writing. It has been suggested that the novel was not designed to encourage wantonness or promiscuity but was intended to serve as a warning to any who might be tempted to stray. Not only does this interpretation 'contradict' much of what I find in the book, however, it also suggests that Amelia Opie was condemning Mary Wollstonecraft and her life. There is *no* evidence that Amelia Opie had anything other than admiration for Mary Wollstonecraft – at least when she was writing *Adeline Mowbray*: how she felt in her fifty-sixth year and after her conversion to Quakerism is another matter entirely. But I do think it is regrettable that in one of the few instances where a woman novelist writes a fictional account of the life of a feminist she admires, the achievement can be brushed aside with the assertion that the novel is something other than it was meant to be. It seems to me perfectly clear that *Adeline Mowbray* exposes many of the hypocrisies associated with marriage and that it explicitly states the arguments for and against this holy estate – even at the expense of character on occasion. The implication that Amelia Opie was writing to illustrate the value of marriage is, I suspect, a respectable rationale constructed long after the event, the product not merely of Victorian influence, but of the author's own later entry to the Society of Friends.

For me, *Adeline Mowbray* stands as a novel of ideas based on Amelia Opie's admiration for Mary Wollstonecraft, and her very genuine questions about marriage for women – and whether it was, or was not, a good thing.

But *Adeline Mowbray* was by no means the end of Amelia Opie's writing career, although it was the end of a particular phase. In 1806, John Opie died and while *Simple Tales* was published that year, Amelia Opie's writing thereafter took on a distinctly more serious and religious tone. On the death of her husband she gave up her life in the artistic circles of London society and returned to her father's home in Norwich where 'father and daughter' each became more interested in the Society of Friends. In 1809 her *Memoir* of John Opie was included in the posthumous publication of his *Letters on Painting*. In 1812, *Temper* was published and revealed the author in the role of a severe moralist. This was followed by *Tales of Real Life* in 1813, and then in 1816 came *Valentine's Eve*, which shows 'The state of her religious feelings at the time it was written. The lesson it inculcates is, the superiority of the religious principle as a rule of action, and as a support under affliction and unmerited calumny' (Cecelia Brightwell, n.d.: p. 22).

Her writing showed an increasing moral bent and moved further away from fiction with *Illustrations of Lying* published in 1825, *Detraction Displayed* in 1828, and her final publication, a volume of poems, *Lays for the Dead* in 1834.

But if the later writings of Amelia Opie have little of appeal or merit, this does not diminish her earlier achievement nor detract from the interest of *Adeline Mowbray*. I would not want to claim for this novel the unqualified status of 'great' but neither would I want to be without the opportunity to read it. It may be one of the small links in the chain which forms the continuum of women's writing and it may be that it enriches women's tradition more by way of its association with Mary Wollstonecraft than by virtue of its own achievement. But the fact remains that in this rendition of Mary Wollstonecraft's life, and in its questioning of love and marriage, *Adeline Mowbray* makes a contribution to women's heritage.

Whether it is a major or minor contribution is a matter of debate. Perhaps discussions in 'Lit-crit' on the relative merits of Tobias Smollett and Lawrence Sterne and their contribution to the realistic novel could make way for a consideration of the strengths and weaknesses of Amelia Opie and her contribution to the early novel of ideas.

Table 13: Amelia Opie (1769-1853)

1790 *The Dangers of Coquetry*
1801 *Father and Daughter*
1802 *Poems*
1804 *Adeline Mowbray*
1806 *Simple Tales*
1809 *Memoir of John Opie*
1812 *Temper*
1813 *Tales of Real Life*
1816 *Valentine's Eve*
1822 *Madeline*
1825 *Illustrations of Lying*

1828 *Detraction Displayed*
1834 *Lays for the Dead*
n.d. *Tales of the Heart*

CHAPTER 19

Mary Brunton: premature death and a rich bequest

Jane Austen had both precedent and peer in Mary Brunton (1778-1818). In a pattern that I have now come to accept almost as the 'norm', I must admit that until a year ago, the name Mary Brunton was not one to which I attached any significance: I was vaguely aware of having come across it in the course of my research but it was not a name that had aroused my curiosity, let alone one that had impinged on my consciousness. So when I encountered those intriguing titles of her novels – *Self Control* and *Discipline* – I went back to some of my notes and sources and found, sure enough, that Mary Brunton was there, even though I had passed her by. She was there in Ellen Moers's *Literary Women* (1977) and one of her letters is quoted in Elaine Showalter's *A Literature of Their Own* (1977), but while these references were reasonably interesting they had not been sufficiently inspirational to send me off on an enthusiastic search for this first-rate and forgotten woman writer. And yet not to have read *Self Control* and *Discipline* was assuredly my loss.

However, before I begin my glowing account of the work of Mary Brunton, I should like to make a disclaimer; I have a real problem with her overt use of Christian dogma as the explanation and justification of moral development. The discomfort which I feel with her explicit religious sentiments could be the result of their 'inappropriateness' in a contemporary (and post-Freudian) context: more likely however is that it is the result of my personal prejudice. I find the passages of pious prose intrusive, even jarring, yet I would not want to give the impression that this marred my enjoyment of the novels. It did not; partly because these doctrinaire pronouncements do not interlace the text but are discreetly contained in particular sections, and so I was able to employ the tried and true literary strategy of 'skipping' the pages on which they occurred.

10   Mary Brunton

With this 'impediment' dealt with, I can now proceed with my almost unqualified praise for the writing of Mary Brunton.

She was born Mary Balfour on the island of Burra, Orkney, and while her mother (Frances Ligonier) was not noted for her domestic accomplishments, she was skilled in intellectual pursuits and was responsible for interesting Mary in Italian, French, and music. Apart from a short period in an Edinburgh school (her husband, who provides this information in his *Memoir* of her, does not say which school it was), Mary Brunton was primarily self-taught. She was an avid reader (particularly of fiction), with an abiding interest in the complexities of the human mind and character development, and she went on to become an excellent Italian and French scholar, an able musician – and of course a Christian.

But it is important to avoid the portrayal of Mary Brunton as simply a straight and sober soul who wrote fictional moral tracts. Such a representation is far from an accurate portrayal of her character or of her writing. She was lively, witty, sportively satirical; she was refreshingly free from pomposity and entertainingly perceptive when it came to an analysis of morals and manners. She was wary of being 'taken in', of being impressed when there was not due cause, and it is something of a contradiction that a woman who could be so 'religious' could be simultaneously so 'irreverent' and could mock so many authoritative institutions. Because I think some of these perspicacious attributes of hers are revealed in her attitude to mathematics (an area in which she did not excel) I quote her husband's appraisal of her opinion on this subject:

> She repeatedly began, but as often relinquished, the study of mathematics. Where the address to the intellect was direct and pure, she was interested and successful. But a single demonstration by the *reductio ad absurdum* or by applying one figure to another in order to show their identity, never failed to estrange her for a long time from the subject. She could never divest herself of an idea that the first had more of the trick of argument than was worthy of pure science; and the second was despised as a mere mechanical operation. (Alexander Brunton, 1842: p. 5)

Mary Brunton was not at all impressed by mathematics: when it wasn't a clever trick it required no true thought!

She spent most of her early years – on her own admission – reading poetry and fiction, and doing translations, but the leisure to pursue these interests was cut short on the death of her mother, when she took over the management of her father's household. This, however, was only for a few years: at the age of twenty she married the Reverend Alexander

Brunton and they moved to Bolton.

Her education continued under the influence of her more formally educated husband (he later became the Professor of Oriental Languages at Edinburgh University), but because he believed that she would profit from more than his intellectual companionship, he was pleased when in 1803 they moved to Edinburgh. In Bolton they had been isolated; he had been her only stimulus: 'It was otherwise in Edinburgh,' he writes, 'Our circle widened. She mingled more with those whose talents and acquirements she had respected at a distance.' But the Reverend Brunton doesn't want to give anyone the idea that his wife was a passive presence at these intellectual gatherings: 'She found herself able to take her share in their conversation and, though nothing could be farther from the tone of her mind than either pedantry or dogmatism, she came by degrees, instead of receiving opinions implicitly, to examine those of others and to defend her own.' This trait of defending her own stance was to serve her well when she took to novel writing – as was her sense of humour. 'There was a freshness and originality in her way of managing these little friendly controversies,' writes her husband, 'a playfulness in her wit – a richness in her illustrations – and an acuteness in her arguments, which made her conversation attractive to the ablest' (1842: p. 8).

If her writing is any guide to her conversation, this assessment of her skills by her husband need not be attributed to spousal bias; her novels contain comparable characteristics – and more – which make them 'attractive to the ablest' as well.

Mary Brunton took up novel writing as a 'pastime'; no doubt her motivation and confidence was assisted by her contact with the literary circle in Edinburgh and certainly she was encouraged in her venture by her friend, Mrs Izett. Whether she had ever experimented with writing – whether she had ever harboured a desire to write – is not completely clear, but once embarked on her novel writing it seems to have been typical of her that she did not treat it as a means of idling away the time or as a pleasant diversion. The titles of her novels tell something about the values of the author – *Self Control* and *Discipline* – and her attitude towards her writing was that if it were not done 'properly' there was no point in doing it at all.

When she started on her first novel, *Self Control*, she had no thought of publication. But as the manuscript grew and she came to trust her own efforts, her desire to see it in print took hold and grew. Much of the first volume was completed before her husband was even aware of its existence and once he was let into the secret the work of writing assumed yet more serious dimensions. Every morning, time was set aside for writing; every evening she read what she had written, to her husband. (And it is interesting to note that even at this early stage she almost never took his advice but remained firm and believed in her own work.) Mary Brunton was convinced that there was virtue in habit, in regularity and rules, and she tried not to depart from this daily discipline. As one of the themes that was to emerge in her writing was the dignity and necessity of labour, it is not surprising that she should have set for herself the same standards that she demanded of her heroines. Yet there is some evidence that what began as satisfying and enjoyable self-realisation soon became a bounden duty once Mary Brunton decided she would like to see her novel in print. By the time she came to write *Discipline*, she professed that she saw writing as her required work, a a contribution she could make to society, and while none of the 'playfulness' and seeming spontaneity is absent from the novel, Mary Brunton suggests that it was – at least on occasion – absent from the work. It is not surprising that she felt this way: though it would be surprising if she felt this way *all* the time. Few writers would deny that while the overall effort might bring pleasure there are periods when the predominant feeling is one of pain. And damned hard work.* And there is also an enormous difference between writing for self and for a public audience. When writing *Evelina* in secret and with no thought of publication, Fanny Burney found the process one of fun: when later expected to 'produce' and in a style that she found onerous, most of the fun went out of the work. She admitted that writing was grinding hard work. Perhaps a similar thing happened to Mary Brunton – although it was never the case that she bowed to the criticism of her work. Not only her husband, but the highly esteemed Joanna Baillie (poet and dramatist, 'the female Shakespeare', 1762-1851), to whom Mary Brunton dedicated *Self Control*, found that her recommendations for improvement were politely rejected. Which might be why Mary Brunton retained more of her playfulness and irreverence than Fanny Burney did.

Or it could be that Mary Brunton's insistence that her novel writing was hard work and not an immensely enjoyable pastime was a pretence designed to protect her husband. It might not have been terribly 'fitting' for the Reverend Brunton's wife to confess that she was carried away by her novel writing and was thrilled with the exhilarating task of creation. She could well have been ambivalent about the joy and the work. In some of her correspondence with Mrs Izett – which is in itself immensely entertaining – she gives every indication that she is completely engrossed in the characters that she has created, and that she finds the experience deliciously enjoyable.

Laura is the heroine of *Self Control*. To attempt to give any summary of the 'plot' would be to write a mini-novel so suffice it to say that the

*Says she drawing to a close!

story begins with a handsome seducer and ends with Laura's marriage to the truly worthy Montague de Courcy – and in between there is much action – in a variety of places.

Initially, Laura is favourably impressed with the handsome 'rake' who pretends concern with her welfare. But his base motives are soon revealed and the scene in which the unsuspecting Laura understands his real intentions is one of the most powerful that I have read. In spite of my hardened exterior as a seasoned feminist I was so 'involved' that I would not be surprised to know that I blushed for Laura and the assault on her integrity and sensitivity.

It is no melodrama that Mary Brunton writes. Confronted with attempted seduction, Laura experiences a range of feelings and doubts that are not unknown today. Should she tell her father who would be shocked by such behaviour in his 'friend'? Would she be believed? Perhaps it was all her fault anyway?

The novel continues in this authentic vein. Once rejected, the handsome suitor discovers that he really does want Laura and is prepared to marry her, and we have hundreds of pages of convincing sexual harassment. We come to understand that the 'love' he feels is the pride of possession, and is not a commitment to Laura's well-being. There are the most moving accounts where Laura is just worn down – made a victim – as we find that there is no limit to the tricks and deceptions and force that this man is prepared to use to gain possession. Mary Brunton knew what contemporary feminists have tried to signify in the slogan '*No means no!*'; again and again she satirically, and bitterly, exposes the way that Laura's unequivocal refusals and rejections are taken as encouragement for greater feats of mastery and capture.

And all the while, the worthy Montague de Courcy is in the background: the 'misapprehensions' are legion.

While revelling in her creations, Mary Brunton nonetheless had some difficulties with her heroine. As Catherine Stimpson once remarked, 'It's so hard getting a character from one room to another.' Obviously Mary Brunton felt some of the same pressures, as she confided to Mrs Izett:

April 10, 1810

Your friend Laura proceeds with a slow but regular pace; a short step every day – no more! She has advanced sixty paces, alias pages, since you left her. She is at present very comfortably situate, if the foolish thing had the sense to think so; she is on a visit to Norwood, where she is to remain for a few days; and a very snug old-fashioned place it is! Though it should never be laid open to the public at large, you shall see the interior of it one day or other. . . .

If ever I undertake another lady, I will manage her in a very different manner. Laura is so decently kerchiefed, like our grandmothers, that to dress her is a work of time and pains. Her young sister, if she ever have one, shall wear loose, floating, easy robes that will slip on in a minute. (Alexander Brunton, 1842: p. 16)

Mary Brunton may have had 'problems' with her heroine, but she overcame them. While I have some criticisms of the plot (as she herself did on reflection after publication) I have few criticisms of the character delineation, and I am awed by the style. I have always been impressed by the elegant balance of Jane Austen's sentences; I have often wondered how a writer achieves such a finely tuned tone, how the internal contrasts, the 'ups' and 'downs' are created with such apparent effortlessness? How the foil, which can be the basis of irony with the first part of the sentence rising to an unthinking peak and the second part descending to the satirical exposure, can be constructed without a hint of clumsiness? What I can attest to is that this achievement of Jane Austen's is the achievement of Mary Brunton as well, and I can understand why Jane Austen so intently studied the style of *Self Control*, and why she was concerned that she would not attain the same level of excellence.

Daniel Defoe, Henry Fielding, and Samuel Richardson are held in high esteem for their invaluable introduction of *realism* to the English novel. Perhaps I do them a disservice when I confess that for me, their accounts – particularly of women – are far from being 'realistic' and at times come so close to being absurd that I find what they meant to be serious, amusing in its incongruity. I lose patience with Pamela and Clarissa and am always full of advice as to what they can do to get out of their ridiculous predicaments; I am astonished by Moll Flanders. Yet there are no such 'distances' between me and the women whom Mary Brunton describes. With Mary Brunton (and Jane Austen) the detail and the nuances of women's existence are so finely portrayed that not one shadow of a doubt is cast on their authenticity; and this is not something which shines in irregular patches but is the fabric of their fiction.

Perhaps one reason for this ring of authenticity in the writing of Mary Brunton is that there was little separation between the reality of her heroines and that of her own life. She was actually writing in the context of what she sought to convey in her writing – as her letters to Mrs Izett reveal:

St Leonard's
August 30, 1810

I have not answered your two letters, blame not me, who had all the will in the world to do so, nor Mr B., who has teased me every day to write to you. Blame your dear friend and favourite, Montague de Courcy, of Norwood, Esq., for he has been wholly and solely in fault. He has been making love so energetically, that I have not the heart to leave him in the middle of his flames, more especially, as he has been interrupted by a score of troublesome visiters breaking in upon his privacy. To say the truth, I have been far more compassionate towards him than she who ought to have been the most deeply interested. She has not only given him his congé, but has barbarously left him, in a cold October evening, standing under a tree in his own avenue. There he has stood since last night; there he must stand all today, for today I write to you; all tomorrow, for tomorrow I go to town; and all Thursday, for I do not return till then. The thirteenth chapter is closed, and I mean that six more should bring all things to their proper issue. If I write *every* day, and *all* day, that may be done in fifty days. But I find that in one way and another, half my time is abstracted from my business, as I now begin to consider this affair, at first begun for pastime! Besides, I must take more exercise if I would not be sick, and must sew more if I would not be ragged. . . .

My hopes of popular favour are low – very low indeed. Of a work like mine the wise and the good will not be at the trouble to judge. Its faults are not such as will recommend it to the vulgar. It *may* become popular, for that is a mere lottery . . . I judge by myself; for while I have little pleasure in praise, I am on many subjects keenly alive to censure. Many a person less generally vain than I, has felt all the touchy vanity of authorship.

But I am positive that no part – no, not the smallest part – of my happiness can ever arise from the popularity of my book, further than as I think it may be useful. I would rather, as you well know, glide through the world unknown, than have (I will not call it *enjoy*) fame, however brilliant. To be pointed at – to be noticed and commented upon – to be suspected of literary airs – to be shunned as literary women are, by the more unpretending of my own sex; and abhorred as literary women are; by the pretending of the other! – My dear, I would sooner exhibit as a rope dancer – I would a great deal rather take up my abode by that lone loch on the hill, to which Mr I. carried my husband on the day when the mosquitoes were so victorious against him.

All these things considered, pray transfer your sympathy to some other circumstance of my lot. – Rejoice with me that I have the finest pease and cauliflower in Scotland; and moreover, the most beautiful appletree that can be seen. (Alexander Brunton, 1842: p. 17-19)

Her letters are a good gauge of her writing style; the blend of the serious and mockingly satirical, the contrast of mundane existence with that of lofty ideals. And while Mary Brunton gives the outward impression that she was confident in her ability as a writer, her letters help to reveal her inner apprehensions about the critics, about her fears as to how she would be judged both as woman and as writer.

In September 1810, the first part of *Self Control* went to press. Not only was the rest unfinished, it was not even definitively planned. It is a measure of Mary Brunton's faith in her own powers that she was not nervous about the first part going into print while the second part remained to be written; according to her husband, far from being alarmed she was animated at the prospect of meeting a deadline. She wrote rapidly and easily until the entire novel was with the printer (p. 15).

To my mind, the novel would have benefited from a little more planning. I can recall my own response when, about fifty pages from the end, when I believed there was every chance of Laura and Montague overcoming the fates that conspired against them, I anticipated a denouement of wedding bells and married bliss. But I was in for a surprise. Laura is abducted; the action is transferred to America; Indians appear on the scene; death looms and it seems there is no way out; I was almost in despair that the happy ending which I had expected was not going to take place and it was only by exercising the greatest 'self-control' that I was able to resist the temptation of turning to the last page to reduce the tension.

I can remember thinking – wryly – that perhaps the author might have practised a little more self-control!

But the novel was published and it was a great success. Speculation began to mount as to the identity of the author, with fingers being pointed in the direction of the Brunton household. As Mary Brunton so appositely informs her correspondent, Mrs Izett, 'It has come out, the evil spirit knows how, that I am the author of Self Control. . . . *Of course all the excellences of the book are attributed to Mr B., while I am left to answer for all its defects*' (Alexander Brunton, 1842: p. 23: my italics).

Criticisms can be made of *Self Control*, particularly with regard to its structure. But Mary Brunton makes these criticisms far more eloquently than I could do. It is unusual to find a writer with such unclouded critical judgment of her own work but the clear-sightedness, so typical of Mary Brunton, is not confined to an analysis of her fellow human beings: she casts the same illuminating light on herself. To Mrs Izett, she wrote:

April 19, 1811

Now that you have told me what you think defective in Self Control, I shall, without reservation, acquaint you with all the faults (so far as I recollect them) with which it has been charged by others; and shall even candidly confess those which – strike myself. To begin with the latter, which of course appear to me to have most foundation, I think the story of Self Control is defective – it is disjointed – it wants unity. The incidents, particularly in the second volume, have little mutual connections. This appears to me the capital defect of the book. It is patchwork; the shreds are pretty and sometimes rich, but the joining is clumsily visible. You, who know how the thing was put together, will easily account for this blemish; but I fear neither you nor I can now excuse or mend it. The American expedition, too, though, in the author's opinion, the best written part of the book, is more conspicuously a *patch* than anything else which it contains. Though I do not see the outrageous improbability with which it has been charged, I confess that it does not harmonise with the sober colouring of the rest. We have all heard of a 'peacock with a fiery tale'; but my American jaunt is the same monstrous appendage tacked to a poor little grey linnet.

In the middle of the second volume the story lags. An author of more experience would have brought out the characters without such an awful pause in incident. An author of more invention would have contrived incidents to serve that very purpose, as well as to fill up agreeably the necessary time between the close of the first love, and the triumph of the second.

I confess to you, that these are the only great faults in Self Control to which my conscience pleads guilty; but they are far from being the only ones of which I am accused. It is alleged that no virtuous woman would continue to love a man who makes such a debut as Hargrave. All I say is, that I wish all the affections of virtuous persons were so *very* obedient to reason. . . .

Nevertheless the book is both read and bought. In spite of all these faults and a hundred more (many of them contradictory), there is not a copy to be had in either Edinburgh or London.

I finished the corrections for the second edition last night; and now what shall I do next? You know I have no great enjoyment in idleness.

Meanwhile, the hurrying of that vile book into the world has put all my necessary and appropriate employments far behind. I have letters to write – books to read – presses to put in order – wine to bottle – gowns to make – and all manner of household linen and wearing apparel to mend. Today I have eleven people to dine with me, for which important event I must go and prepare. So it is lucky that my paper is full. (Alexander Brunton, 1842: pp. 25-6)

After a short rest – and determined to learn from some of her mistakes – Mary Brunton commenced work on her second novel. There are two areas where it stands in sharp contrast to her earlier work; it is much more tightly constructed, and the heroine is presented very differently. We had been introduced to Laura as a young woman with whom we were expected to sympathise; in *Discipline*, we meet Ellen, of whom we are meant to disapprove.

Reading the first few pages of *Discipline* was for me a strange experience; it seemed familiar. I had the feeling that I had covered this ground before. I was aware that the author was creating a heroine whom 'no one but herself would much like'.

Discipline was published in 1814; *Emma* was published in 1816. There can be no doubt that Jane Austen was working within a tradition of women writers and drawing upon some of their resources. The similarities in the work of Mary Brunton and Jane Austen are striking.

Within the first few pages of *Discipline* the plan for the whole novel is laid. We have the impetuous and indulged Ellen (whose adored mother dies while Ellen is still a child), and whose education, moral and intellectual, is left in the hands of a weak and unthinking father. We have the young heroine who makes painful mistakes about the world and her prominent place within it and who, during the course of the novel, undergoes a range of harsh learning experiences to emerge at the end as a responsible human being.

Whereas Emma had Miss Taylor (Mrs Weston) as a guide whose value had to be learnt, Ellen has Miss Mortimer (her dead mother's closest friend) as a mentor whom she initially mocks and whose true worth is only later perceived. In *Discipline*, the points of departure from *Emma* consist of Miss Mortimer's Christian teachings and Ellen Percy's context, for it is not the sheltered society of Hartford that sets the scenes for Ellen's sins but the shallow world of fashionable London.

Neither Mr Woodhouse nor Mr Percy provide much guidance for their daughters, but whereas Mr Woodhouse's 'selfishness' takes the form of 'withdrawal' from the world, Mr Percy's weakness is that he is too much part of the world. Like *Emma*, the plot of *Discipline* is so intricately interwoven that developments in the novel can be traced back to earlier sources, and the intimations that Mr Percy is not a refined gentleman, and that he attaches too much importance to money, is confirmed when he later loses his fortune, reduces Ellen to penury – and commits suicide.

All the seeds of significance are sown in the opening pages of the novel. We are acquainted with the deficiencies of Ellen's education and on the fourth page, Ellen herself recounts the unhealthy attention that was accorded her precocious performances:

To own the truth, my mother lay under strong temptation to report my sallies, for my father always listened to them with symptoms of pleasure. They sometimes caused his countenance to relax into a smile; and sometimes, either when they were more particularly brilliant, or his spirits in a more harmonious tone, he would say, 'Come Fanny, get me something nice for supper, and keep Ellen in good humour, and I won't go to the club tonight.' He generally, however, had reason to repent of this resolution; for though my mother performed her part to perfection, I not unfrequently experienced, in my father's presence, that restraint which has fettered elder wits under a consciousness of being expected to entertain. Or, if my efforts were more successful, he commonly closed his declining eulogiums by saying, 'It is a confounded pity she is a girl. If she had been of the right sort, she might have got into Parliament, and made a figure with the best of them. But now what use is her sense of?' – 'I hope it will contribute to her happiness,' said my mother, sighing as if she had thought the fulfilment of her hope a little doubtful. 'Poh!' quoth my father, 'no fear of her happiness. Won't she have two hundred thousand pounds, and never know the trouble of earning it, nor need to do one thing from morning to night but amuse herself?' My mother made no answer: – so by this and similar conversations, a most just and desirable connection was formed in my mind between the ideas of amusement and happiness, of labour and misery.

Ellen must endure trials and tribulations before she becomes a suitable wife for the hero, Mr Maitland – who, like Mr Knightley, is older and wiser, who has watched her growth and development, who has protected her and proffered his good advice – and who has waited for her to 'see the light' and appreciate his worth. But Mary Brunton, who has a much broader canvas than Jane Austen (and who admitted to the influence of Maria Edgeworth with her treatment of Irish life), not only transfers the action to Scotland and provides a detailed picture of Highland life – with social commentary – she goes without trepidation into areas where Jane Austen did not tread. There is more 'guts', more overt harshness, spite, and sheer viciousness in *Discipline*, not the least of which is a scene in a mental asylum where, with the most perspicacious skill, Mary Brunton depicts the futility of Ellen trying to persuade the director that she is sane and that her committal – while ill with fever – has all been a dreadful mistake. The more Ellen protests that she is sane, the more evidence she provides for the director that she is not. R.D. Laing could do no better than Mary Brunton, who, more than one hundred and seventy years ago, wrote this realistic and moving account.

Such 'lessons' were very much Mary Brunton's forte. She wanted her novels to be entertaining but she also wanted them to develop and

sharpen the intellectual and critical judgment of her readers. She
certainly did not see these aims as incompatible. With her usual
challenge to established form she demanded to know why *novels* were
held to be inferior to epics and tragedies; as was her custom, she put her
case to Mrs Izett:

August 15, 1814

Ellen is at an end. She was finished at three o'clock one morning; and
I waked Mr B. out of his first sleep to hear of her wedding. . . .

Why should an epic or a tragedy be supposed to hold such an
exalted place in composition, while a novel is almost a nickname for a
book? Does not a novel admit of as noble sentiments – as lively
description – as natural character – as perfect unity of action – and a
moral as irresistible as either of them? I protest, I think a fiction
containing a just representation of human beings and of their actions
– a connected, interesting, and probable story, conducting to a useful
and impressive moral lesson – might be one of the greatest efforts of
human genius. Let the admirable construction of fable in Tom Jones
be employed to unfold characters like Miss Edgeworth's – let it lead
to a moral like Richardson's – let it be told with the eloquence of
Rousseau and with the simplicity of Goldsmith – let it be all this, and
Milton need not have been ashamed of the work! But novels have got
an ill name; therefore 'give novels to the dogs'. I have done with
them; for, if even the best possible would be comparatively despised,
what is to become of mine? Well, what shall I do next? Give me your
advice; and if I like it I will take it. (Alexander Brunton, 1842:
pp. 37–8)

Discipline too was a great success. But Mary Brunton wrote no more
novels: her literary efforts consisted of one more short story, *Emmeline*,
which was published after her death. In 1818, at forty years of age, she
became pregnant. She believed that she would die in childbirth. On
December 7th she gave birth to a still-born son; she became feverish
and on December 19th, 1818, she died. Her life and writing career
ended as Mary Wollstonecraft's had ended; as Charlotte Brontë's was to
end.

There are many respects in which Mary Brunton represents the
traditions of women writers before Jane Austen. She is a fitting subject
for the conclusion of this book. That her superb novels should have
endured transient fame and then vanished almost without trace is not
only characteristic of women's treatment, but makes me acutely
conscious of what we have lost: it makes me more determined to
challenge the precepts and practices of those who have constructed the

literary tradition. That such writing as Mary Brunton's – so close to Jane Austen's in time, style and achievement – should have moved so far from view, and left Jane Austen to stand alone, is sufficient to convince me that there are no limits to the lengths to which the tradition makers will go to present a literary heritage which is predominantly male.

Mary Brunton was one of the mothers of the novel; she was one of the hundred good women writers before Jane Austen. Her disappearance is an indictment of the practice of literary criticism; her reclamation serves as an inspirational impetus to ensure that such travesties of justice do not occur again. Mary Brunton would have been the first to endorse the injunction to the still male-dominated circles of the literary establishment that they should 'do unto women what they have done unto themselves'. Then we would have a literary heritage in which men were equally represented – with women.

Table 14: Mary Brunton (1778-1818)

1810-11	*Self Control*
1814	*Discipline*
1818	*Emmeline*

Bibliography

ABEL, Elizabeth (ed. (1982), *Writing and Sexual Difference*, Harvester Press, Brighton.

ADBURGHAM, Alison (1972), *Women in Print: Writing Women and Women's Magazines from the Restoration to the Accession of Victoria*, Allen & Unwin, London.

ALLEN, Mary (1976), *The Necessary Blankness: Women in Major American Fiction of the Sixties*, University of Illinois Press, Urbana and Chicago.

ALLEN, Walter (1954/1980), *The English Novel*, Penguin, Harmondsworth.

ANONYMOUS (1823), *The Novels of Stern, Goldsmith, Dr Johnson, Mackenzie, Horace Walpole and Clara Reeve*, Horst Robinson, London.

BAKER, Ernest A. (1938), *The History of the English Novel*, Witherby, London.

BALLANTYNE, John (1821-4), *Ballantyne's Novelist's Library*, edited with prefatory memoirs of the authors by Sir Walter Scott, 10 vols, Hurst, Robinson & Co., London.

BALLARD, George (1752), *Memoirs of Several Ladies of Great Britain who have been celebrated for their writings or skill in the learned languages, arts and sciences*, W. Jackson, Oxford.

BARBAULD, Anna Laetitia (ed.) (1810), *The British Novelists* (50 vols), F.C. and J. Rivington, London.

BEAUMAN, Nicola (1983), *A Very Great Profession: The Woman's Novel, 1914-39*, Virago, London.

BEHN, Aphra (1984), *The Lucky Chance*, Methuen, London. (Play first performed 1686.)

BERNBAUM, Ernest (1913), 'Mrs Behn's Biography: A Fiction', *PMLA*, vol. 28, pp. 432-53.

BERNIKOW, Louise (1980), *Among Woman*, Harmony, New York.

BIOGRAPHIA DRAMATICA (1812), ed. David Erskine BAKER (3 vols), Longmans, London: reprinted 1966, AMS, New York.

BLACK, Frank Gees (1940), *The Epistolary Novel in the Late Eighteenth Century*, University of Oregon Press, Eugene.

BLAKEY, Dorothy (1939), *The Minerva Press 1790-1820*, printed for the Bibliographical Society, Oxford University Press, Oxford.

BRIGHTWELL, Cecelia Lucy (n.d.), *Memoir of Amelia Opie*, The Religious Tract Society.

BRODY, Miriam (1983), 'Mary Wollstonecraft: Sexuality and Women's Rights', in Dale Spender (ed.), *Feminist Theorists*, The Women's Press, London; Pantheon, New York, pp. 40-59.

BROWNSTEIN, Rachel M. (1982), *Becoming a Heroine: Reading About Women in Novels*, Viking Press, New York.

BRUNTON, Alexander (1842), 'A Memoir of Mary Brunton', in Mary Brunton, *Discipline*, Richard Bentley, London, pp. 2-56.

BURNEY, Fanny (1778), 'The Early Diary of Frances Burney, 1768-1778' (2 vols), Berg Collection, New York Public Library.

BUTLER, Marilyn (1972), *Maria Edgeworth: A Literary Biography*, Clarendon Press, Oxford.

BUTLER, Marilyn (1984), 'Maria Edgeworth', in Janet Todd (ed.), *A Dictionary of British and American Women Writers 1600-1800*, Methuen, London, pp. 110-12.

BUTLER, Marilyn (1985), 'Introduction', in R.W. Chapman (ed.), *Jane Austen: Selected Letters*, Oxford University Press, Oxford, pp. ix-xxvii.

CARTER, Elizabeth (1808), *A Series of Letters between Mrs Elizabeth Carter and Miss Catherine Talbot from the year 1741 to 1770. To which are added letters from Mrs Elizabeth Carter to Mrs Vesey between the years 1763 and 1787* (2 vols), published from the original manuscripts in the possession of the Rev. Montagu Pennington, F.C. and J. Rivington, London.

CAVENDISH, Margaret (1656), *The True Relation of My Birth, Breeding and Life*, Everyman edition, J.M. Dent, London, 1973.

CAWELTI, John (1976), *Adventure, Mystery and Romance*, University of Chicago Press, Chicago.

COLBY, Vineta (1974), *Yesterday's Women: Domestic Realism in the English Novel*, Princeton University Press, Princeton, New Jersey.

CORNILLON, Susan Koppelman (ed.) (1972), *Images of Women in Fiction: Feminist Perspectives*, Bowling Green University Popular Press, Bowling Green, Ohio.

COWPER, William (1904), *The Correspondence of William Cowper* (4 vols), ed. Thomas Wright, Hodder & Stoughton, London.

DALZIEL, Margaret (1970), 'Introduction', in Charlotte Lennox, *The Female Quixote*, Oxford University Press, Oxford, pp. xiii-xix.

DAVIDSON, Cathy N. (1982), 'Flirting with Destiny: Ambivalence and Form in the Early American Sentimental Novel', *Studies in American Fiction*, no. 10, Spring, pp. 17-39.

DAVIDSON, Cathy N. (forthcoming), *The Origins of American Fiction*.

DAVIDSON, Cathy N. and Broner, E.M. (eds) (1980), *The Lost Tradition: Mothers and Daughters in Literature*, Frederick Ungar, New York.

DELANY, Sheila (1983), *Writing Woman: Women Writers and Women in Literature, Medieval to Modern*, Schocken Books, New York.

DOBRÉE, Bonamy (1983), 'Introduction', in Ann Radcliffe, *The Mysteries of Udolpho*, Oxford University Press, Oxford, pp. v-xiv.

DRABBLE, Margaret (1985), *Oxford Companion to English Literature*, Oxford University Press, Oxford.

EHRENPREIS, Anne Henry (1969), 'Introduction', in Charlotte Smith, *The Old Manor House*, Oxford University Press, Oxford.

EHRENPREIS, Anne Henry (1971), 'Introduction', in Charlotte Smith, *Emmeline: The Orphan of the Castle*, Oxford University Press, Oxford.

ELWOOD, Anne (1843), *Memoirs of the Literary Ladies of England* (2 vols), Henry Colburn, London.

EVELYN, John (1850), *Diary and Correspondence* (4 vols), ed. William Bray, Henry Colburn, London.

FANSHAWE, Lady Anne (1830), *Memoirs of Lady Fanshawe*, ed. Sir N.H. Nicholas, Henry Colburn & Richard Bentley, London (first published 1829).

FANSHAWE, Lady Anne and HALKETT, Lady Anne (1979), *Memoirs*, ed. John Loftis, Clarendon Press, Oxford.

FAST, Robin Riley (1984), 'Eliza Parsons', in Janet Todd (ed.), *Dictionary, op. cit.*, pp. 241-2.

FIGES, Eva (1982), *Sex and Subterfuge: Women Novelists to 1850*, Macmillan, London.

FRASER, Antonia (1984), *The Weaker Vessel: Women's Lot in Seventeenth Century England*, Weidenfeld & Nicolson, London.

GAGE, Matilda (1873/1980), *Woman, Church and State: The original exposé of male collaboration against the female sex*, Charles Kerr, Chicago, reprinted 1980 by Persephone Press, Watertown, Massachusetts.

GARBER, Frederick (1981), 'Introduction', in Ann Radcliffe, *The Italian*, Oxford University Press, Oxford, pp. vii-xv.

GILBERT, Sandra M. and GUBAR, Susan (1979/1980), *The Madwoman in the Attic: The Woman Writer and the Nineteenth Century Literary Imagination*, Yale University Press, New Haven, Conn.

GLASTONBURY, Marion (1978), 'Holding the Pens', in Sarah Elbert and Marion Glastonbury, *Inspiration and Drudgery: Notes on Literature and Domestic Labour in the Nineteenth Century*, WRRC Publications, London, pp. 27-47.

GOLDBERG, Philip (1974), 'Are women prejudiced against women?', in Judith Stacey *et al.* (eds), *And Jill Came Tumbling After*, Dell Publishing, New York, pp. 37-42.

GOREAU, Angeline (1980), *Reconstructing Aphra: A Social Biography of Aphra Behn*, Dial Press, New York.

GOULIANOS, Joan (ed.) (1974), *By A Woman Writt*, New English Library, London.

GREER, Germaine (1974), 'Flying Pigs and Double Standards', *Times Literary Supplement*, July 26th, p. 784.

GREY, Jill, E. (1968), 'Introduction', in Sarah Fielding, *The Governess*, Oxford University Press, Oxford, pp. 1-82.

HAMILTON, Catherine, J. (1892), *Women Writers: Their Works and Ways*, Lock Bowden, London.

HELSINGER, Elizabeth K., SHEETS, Robin Lauterbach and VEEDER, William (1983), *The Woman Question: Literary Issues, 1837-1883*: vol. III of *The Woman Question, Society and Literature in Britain and America, 1837-1883*, Garland Publishing, New York.

HEMLOW, Joyce (1958), *The History of Fanny Burney*, Clarendon Press, Oxford.

HILL, Christopher (1985), *Collected Essays: Writing and Revolution in Seventeenth Century England: Vol. I*, Harvester Press, Brighton.

HORNER, Joyce M. (1929/30), *The English Women Novelists and Their Connection with the Feminist Movement, 1699-1797*, vol. X, nos. 1, 2, 3 of Smith College Studies in Modern Languages, Collegiate Press, Northampton, Massachusetts.

HUFF, Cynthia (forthcoming), 'Chronicles of Confinement: Reactions to Childbirth in British Women's Diaries', in *Women's Studies International Forum*.

HUNTER, Jim (ed.) (1966), *The Modern Novel in English*, Faber & Faber, London.

ISLES, Duncan (1970), 'Chronology and Appendix', in Charlotte Lennox, *The Female Quixote*, Oxford University Press, Oxford.

JENSEN, Margaret Ann (1984), *Love's Sweet Return: The Harlequin Story*, The Women's Press, Toronto.

JERROLD, Walter and Clare (1929), *Five Queer Women*, Brentanos, London.

KAVANAGH, Julia (1863), *English Women of Letters: Biographical Sketches* (2 vols), Hurst & Blackett, London.

KELSALL, Malcolm (1969), 'Introduction', in Sarah Fielding, *The Adventures of David Simple*, Oxford University Press, Oxford, pp. ix-xvii.

KILPATRICK, Sara (1980), *Fanny Burney*, David & Charles, Newton Abbot.

KINSLEY, James and KELLY, Gary (1980), 'Introduction', in Mary Wollstonecraft, *Mary and The Wrongs of Woman*, Oxford University Press, Oxford, pp. vii-xxi.

KOSTER, Patricia (1971), 'Introduction', in *The Novels of Mary Delarivière Manley*, Scholars Facsimiles and Reprints, Gainsville, Florida, pp. v-xxvii.

KRAMNICK, Miriam Brody (ed.) (1978), *Mary Wollstonecraft: Vindication of the Rights of Woman*, Penguin, Harmondsworth.

LASCELLES, Mary (1939), *Jane Austen and her Art*, Clarendon Press, Oxford.

LEE, S.E. (ed.), *Dictionary of National Biography*. See under Stephen.

LESSING, Doris (1962), *The Golden Notebook*, Michael Joseph, London.

LOFTIS, John (ed.) (1979), *The Memoirs of Anne Lady Halkett and Anne Lady*

342

Fanshawe, Clarendon Press, Oxford.

LONGE, Julia (ed.) (1911), 'Letter to Dorothy Osborne', in *Martha, Lady Giffard: her life and correspondence, 1664-1772*, George Allen, London, pp. 38-42.

LUDLOW, J.M. (1853), 'Ruth', in *North British Review*, no. 19, pp. 169-71.

LURIA, Gina M. (1977), 'Mary Hays's Letters and Manuscripts', in *Signs*, vol. III, no. 2, pp. 524-30.

MacCARTHY, Brigid M. (1944), *Women Writers: Their Contribution to the English Novel 1621-1744*, Cork University Press, Cork.

MacCAULAY, Catharine (1790), *Letters on Education*, Reprinted 1974 by Garland Publishing, New York.

MAEROFF, Gene (1979), 'Journals' Problem: What to Publish', *New York Times*, 14th August, pp. C1 and C4.

MAHL, Mary R. and KOON, Helene (eds) (1977), *The Female Spectator: English Women Writers Before 1800*, Indiana University Press, Bloomington and The Feminist Press, Old Westbury, New York.

MANLEY, Mary de la Rivière (1714), *The Adventures of Rivella, or, The History of the Atlantis. With secret memoirs and characters of several persons her cotemporaries* [sic]. *Deliver'd in conversation to the young chevalier D'Aumont in Somerset-House Garden, by Sir Charles Lovemore*, n.p., London.

MANSFIELD, Katherine, (1977/1981), *Letters and Journals*, ed. C.K. Stead, Penguin, Harmondsworth.

MARTINEAU, Harriet (1877), *Autobiography: With Memorials by Maria Weston Chapman* (3 vols), Smith, Elder, London.

MASEFIELD, Muriel (1927), *The Story of Fanny Burney: Being an Introduction to the Diary and Letters of Madame d'Arblay*, Cambridge University Press, Cambridge.

MASEFIELD, Muriel (1934), *Women Novelists from Fanny Burney to George Eliot*, Nicholson & Watson, London.

MAYO, Robert (1962), *The English Novel in the Magazines 1740-1815*, Northwestern University Press, Evanston, Illinois.

MILFORD, Nancy (1975), *Zelda Fitzgerald*, Penguin, Harmondsworth.

MILLETT, Kate (1970), *Sexual Politics*, Doubleday, New York; 1972, Abacus, London.

MISH, Charles C. (1967), *English Prose Fiction 1600-1800: A chronological Checklist*, Bibliographical Society of the University of Virginia, Charlottesville, Virginia.

MOERS, Ellen (1977), *Literary Women: The Great Writers*, Anchor Books, Doubleday, New York.

MORGAN, Fidelis (ed.) (1981), *The Female Wits: Women Playwrights of the Restoration*, Virago, London.

MORGAN, Lady (1835), 'Preface' to *O'Donnel*, Henry Colburn, London.

NEEDHAM, Gwendolyn B. (1938), 'Mrs Manley: An Eighteenth Century Wife of Bath', *Huntingdon Library Quarterly*, no. 3, April.

OLSEN, Tillie (1978), *Silences*, Delacorte Press/Seymour Lawrence, New York.

OSBORNE, Dorothy (n.d.), *Letters from Dorothy Osborne to William Temple 1652-54*, ed. Edward Abbot Parry, J.M. Dent, London.

OVERFIELD, Kathy (1981), 'Dirty Fingers, Grime and Slag Heaps', in Dale Spender (ed.), *Men's Studies Modified: the impact of feminism on the academic disciplines*, Athene series, Pergamon Press, Oxford, pp. 237-48.

PAPASHVILY, Helen Waite (1972), *All The Happy Endings*, Kennikat Press, New York (first published 1956).

PATTERSON, Margeret (1984), 'Sarah Burney', in Janet Todd (ed.), *Dictionary, op. cit.*, p. 67.

PEPYS, Samuel (1928), *The Diary of Samuel Pepys* (10 vols), ed. Henry B. Wheatley, G. Bell, London.

PERRY, Ruth (1980), *Women, Letters and the Novel*, AMS Press, London.

PHILIPS, Katherine (1705), Letters from Orinda [Katherine Philips] to Poliarchus [Sir Charles Cotterell], n.p., London.

PRIESTLEY, J.B. (1929), 'Introduction', in Mary Priestley (ed.), *The Female Spectator: Being Selections from Mrs Eliza Heywood's* [sic] *Periodical (1744-1746)*, John Lane, The Bodley Head, London.

RAVETZ, Alison (1983), 'The trivialisation of Mary Wollstonecraft: a personal and professional career revindicated', in *Women's Studies International Forum*, vol. 6, no. 5, pp. 491-500.

REEVE, Clara (1785/1970), *The Progress of Romance through times, countries and manners; with remarks on the good and bad effects of it, on them respectively, in the course of evening conversations* (2 vols), W. Keymer, Colchester, 1785; reprinted 1970 by Garland Publishing, New York.

RICH, Adrienne (1980), *On Lies, Secrets and Silence*, Virago, London.

RICHETTI, John J. (1969), *Popular Fiction Before Richardson: Narrative Patterns 1700-1739*, Clarendon Press, Oxford.

ROBINS, Elizabeth (1924), *Ancilla's Share: An Indictment of Sex Antagonism*, Hutchinson, London.

ROGERS, Katharine (1982), *Feminism in Eighteenth Century England*, University of Illinois Press, Urbana.

ROGERS, Katharine (1984a), 'Fanny Burney', in Janet Todd (ed.), *Dictionary, op. cit.*, pp. 64-7.

ROGERS, Katharine (1984b), 'Harriet Lee' and 'Sophia Lee', in Janet Todd (ed.), *Dictionary, op. cit.*, pp. 193-5.

ROGERS, Katharine (1984c), 'Ann Radcliffe', in Janet Todd (ed.), *Dictionary, op. cit.*, pp. 262-4.

ROSE, Phyllis (1985), *Parallel Lives: Five Victorian Marriages*, Penguin, Harmondsworth.

RUSS, Joanna (1984), *How to Suppress Women's Writing*, The Women's Press, London.

RUSSELL, Dora (1984), *The Religion of the Machine Age*, Routledge & Kegan

Paul, London.

SACKVILLE-WEST, Vita (ed.) (1923), *The Diary of Lady Anne Clifford*, Heinemann, London.

SACKVILLE-WEST, Vita (1927), *Aphra Behn*, Gerald Howe, London.

SADLEIR, Michael (1927), 'The Northanger Novels', *Edinburgh Review*, no. 246, July, pp. 91-106.

ST CLAIR, William (1984), 'Amelia Opie', in Janet Todd (ed.), *Dictionary, op. cit.*, pp. 236-7.

SEELEY, L.B. (1890), *Fanny Burney and Her Friends*, Seeley, London.

SÉJOURNÉ, Philippe (1967), *The Mystery of Charlotte Lennox: First Novelist of Colonial America (1727?-1804)*, Publications des Annales de la Faculté des Lettres, Aix-en-Provence.

SHEVELOW, Kathryn (1984), 'Charlotte Lennox', in Janet Todd (ed.), *Dictionary, op. cit.*, pp. 196-8.

SHOWALTER, Elaine (1977), *A Literature of Their Own: British Women Novelists from Brontë to Lessing*, Princeton University Press, Princeton, New Jersey.

SHOWALTER, Elaine (1984), 'Women Who Write are Women', *The New York Times Book Review*, December 16th, pp. 1, 31, 33.

SHTIER, Ann B. (1984a), 'Mary Ann Radcliffe' and 'Mary Anne Radcliffe', in Janet Todd (ed.), *Dictionary, op. cit.*, pp. 264-5.

SHTIER, Ann B. (1984b), 'Regina Maria Roche', in Janet Todd (ed.), *Dictionary, op. cit.*, pp. 272-3.

SIMPSON, Hilary (1979), 'A literary trespasser: D.H. Lawrence's use of women's writing', in *Women's Studies International Quarterly*, vol. II, no. 2, pp. 155-70.

SINGER, Godfrey Frank (1963), *The Epistolary Novel*, Russell & Russell, New York.

SMITH, Margarette (1984), 'Elizabeth Inchbald', in Janet Todd (ed.), *Dictionary, op. cit.*, pp. 173-6.

SMITH, Margarette (1984;, 'Delarivière Manley', in Janet Todd (ed.), *Dictionary, op. cit.*, pp. 209-10.

SPENCER, Jane (1984a), 'Eliza Haywood', in Janet Todd (ed.), *Dictionary, op. cit.*, pp. 157-60.

SPENCER, Jane (1984b), 'Charlotte Smith', in Janet Todd (ed.), *Dictionary, op. cit.*, pp. 287-9.

SPENCER, Jane (1984c), 'Clara Reeve', in Janet Todd (ed.), *Dictionary, op. cit.*, pp. 266-7.

SPENDER, Dale (1982a), *Women of Ideas – And What Men Have Done to Them: From Aphra Behn to Adrienne Rich*, Routledge & Kegan Paul, London.

SPENDER, Dale (ed.) (in press), 'Women's Autobiographical Writing', Special Issue, *Women's Studies International Forum*.

SPENDER, Dale (forthcoming), *The Writing or the Sex? The Judgement of Literary Men*, Athene Series, Pergamon Press, Oxford.

SPENDER, Lynne (1983), *Intruders on the Rights of Men: Women's Unpublished Heritage*, Pandora Press, London.

STEAD, C.K. (ed.) (1981), *Katherine Mansfield: Letters and Journals*, Penguin, Harmondsworth.

STEPHEN, Sir Leslie (ed.) (1885), *Dictionary of National Biography*, vols 1-21; vols. 22-26 ed. Leslie Stephen and Sidney Lee; vols. 27-63 ed. Sidney Lee, Smith, Elder, London.

SUMMERS, Rev. Montague (1917), 'A Great Mistress of Romance: Ann Radcliffe 1764-1823', in *Transactions of the Royal Society of Literature of the United Kingdom*, vol. XXXV, 24th January, pp. 39-77.

TEMES, David (1984), 'Agnes Maria Bennett', in Janet Todd (ed.), *Dictionary*, *op. cit.*, pp. 45-6.

TILLOTSON, J. (n.d.) *Women of England*, Thomas Holmes, London. (Joanna Baillie, Frances Burney, Hannah More, Lady Morgan, Mrs Piozzi, Charlotte Smith).

TODD, Janet (ed.) (1984a), *A Dictionary of British and American Women Writers, 1600-1800*, Methuen, London.

TODD, Janet (1984b), 'Introduction', in Janet Todd (ed.), *Dictionary*, *op. cit.*, pp. 1-26.

TODD, Janet (1984c), 'Mary Hays', in Janet Todd (ed.), *Dictionary*, *op. cit.*, pp. 156-7.

TOMALIN, Claire (1974), *Mary Wollstonecraft*, Weidenfeld & Nicolson, London.

TOMPKINS, J.M.S. (1932), *The Popular Novel in England 1770-1880*, Methuen, London.

TOMPKINS J.M.S. (1980), *Ann Radcliffe and Her Influence on Later Writers*, Arno Press, New York.

WALTERS, Anna (1977), 'The value of the work of Elizabeth Gaskell', unpublished MA thesis, University of London.

WATT, Ian (1957), *The Rise of the Novel: Studies in Defoe, Richardson and Fielding*, Chatto & Windus, London.

WEDD, A.F. (ed.) (1925), *The Love Letters of Mary Hays (edited by her great/great niece)*, Methuen, London.

WHICHER, George Frisbie (1915), *The Life and Romances of Eliza Haywood*, Columbia University Press, New York.

WHITMORE, Clara H. (1910), *Woman's Work in English Fiction: From the Restoration to the Mid Victorian Period*, G.P. Putnam's Sons, Knickerbocker Press, New York.

WILLIAMS, Raymond (1975), *The Long Revolution*, Penguin, Harmondsworth.

WILSON, Mona (1924), *These Were Muses*, Sidgwick & Jackson, London

WOLLSTONECRAFT, Mary (1792/1978), *Vindication of the Rights of Woman*, Penguin, Harmondsworth.

WOOLF, Virginia (1928/1974), *A Room of One's Own*, Penguin, Harmondsworth.

WOOLF, Virginia (1938/1970), *Three Guineas*, Hogarth Press, London.

WOOLF, Virginia (1972), *Collected Essays: Vol. II*, ed. Leonard Woolf, Chatto & Windus, London.

WOOLF, Virginia (1984), *The Common Reader, 1*, Hogarth Press, London.

WÜRZBACH, Natascha (ed.) (1969), *The Novel in Letters: Epistolary Fiction in the Early English Novel*, University of Miami Press, Miami.

Index

acting, 85, 98-9, 101, 208-10; *see also* drama; theatre
Adburgham, Alison, 104, 106, 196, 204
Addison, Joseph, 104, 107
Adelaide, Debra, 115
'agony columns', 104-5; *see also* women's magazines
allegory, 191-2
Allen, Walter, 44, 45, 60-1, 74, 94, 99, 141, 241-2, 277-80, 298-9
Analytical Review, The, 256
anonymity, 13, 24-5, 83, 84, 95, 117, 244, 317; *see also* pseudonyms
Anti-Jacobin Review, 268
Arblay, Alexandre d', 284
Arblay, Madame d', *see* Burney, Fanny
Artist, The, 206
Astell, Mary, 28-9
Athenaeum, The, 164, 309, 313
Aubin, Penelope, 119-20, 199
Austen, Jane, 1, 2, 6, 106, 115, 116-17, 145, 148-50, 152, 161, 163, 175, 178, 179, 186, 199, 227-8, 239, 271, 273-4, 276, 278, 287, 290, 325, 331, 335, 337-8; *Emma*, 106, 286, 287, 335; *Northanger Abbey*, 149-50, 228n, 239, 243, 287; *Pride and Prejudice*, 167, 286; *Sense and Sensibility*, 1
autobiography, 29, 30-5, 41, 43, 67, 78, 84, 246-69

Bage, Robert, 6n
Baillie, Joanna, 329

Baldwin, James, 146n
Barbauld, Anna Laetitia, 215, 232, 237, 289-90; *British Novelists*, 232, 237
Barker, Jane, 120
Beckett, Samual, 146n
Behn, Aphra, 4, 11, 47-66, 72-3, 79, 83, 84, 85, 89, 91, 93, 117, 139-40, 141, 156, 175, 178, 183, 194, 199, 308; *The Fair Jilt of Tarquin and Miranda*, 58; *The Lucky Chance*, 53; *The Nun or The Fair Vow-Breaker*, 58, 59-60; *The Nun or the Perjured Beauty*, 58; *Oroonoko*, 50, 60-1, 62-3, 199
Bennett, Agnes Maria, 4, 120, 149, 160, 244; *Anna or Memoirs of a Welch Heiress*, 244; *The Beggar Girl and Her Benefactors*, 149, 160, 244; *Juvenile Indiscretions*, 244; *Vicissitudes Abroad*, 244
Bernbaum, Ernest, 50
Bible, The, 16
biography, 6, 14, 29, 30, 32-3, 41-2, 45, 66-7, 78, 84
Blakey, Dorothy, 160-1
Blood, Fanny, 252
blue-stockings, 274-5
Bodichon, Barbara Leigh Smith, 31
Bonhote, Elizabeth, 120, 160
Boyd, Elizabeth, 120
Brightwell, Cecelia, 315, 317
Briscoe, Sophie, 120
Brody, Miriam, 249n
Bromley, Eliza, 120

Index

</>
Index

Norman, Elizabeth, 131
novel: epistolary, 6, 77, 79, 81, 95-7, 100, 158; gothic, 150, 230-45; historical, 234; of ideas, 315-24; of manners, 158-9, 162; rise of, 1-2, 4-5, 6, 11, 19-20, 34-5, 42, 44-5, 81, 83, 91-5, 107, 115-19, 173-7, 228, 286-7, 290, 331-2; science fiction, 42-3; sentimental, 5, 8; serialised, 204; utopian, 42; 'women's', 5, 57-8, 152-4, 157, 161-2, 166, 243-4; *see also* children's literature, political fiction, popular fiction, psychological fiction, realism, romance, pastoral, romantic fiction

O'Brien, Edna, 140
Olsen, Tillie, 5, 23, 85, 175n, 221, 296, 297
Opie, Amelia, 131, 139, 150, 175, 179, 212, 215, 225, 315-24; *Adeline Mowbray*, 318-23; *The Dangers of Coquetry*, 317; *Detraction Displayed*, 323; *Father and Daughter*, 318; *Illustrations of Lying*, 323; *Lays for the Dead*, 323; *Memoir of John Opie*, 323; *Simple Tales*, 322; *Tales of Real Life*, 323; *Temper*, 323; *Valentine's Eve*, 323
Opie, John, 317, 322
Osborne, Dorothy, 27, 36-7
Owenson, Olivia, 303
Owenson, Sydney (Lady Morgan), 130-1, 158-9, 174, 175, 179, 301-14; *Florence Macarthy*, 309-10, 312; *France*, 308-9; *Italy*, 310; *Memoirs*, 313; *The Missionary*, 307; *The Novice of St Dominick*, 304; *The O'Briens and the O'Flahertys*, 312; *O'Donnel*, 307, 310, 312; *Passages from My Autobiography*, 313; *St Clair*, 304; *The Wild Irish Girl*, 304-5, 312; *Woman and Her Master*, 301, 312

Palmer, Charlotte, 131
Parker, Mary Elizabeth, 131

parody, 100-1, 201-3
Parry, Catherine, 131
Parsons, Elizabeth, Phelp, 131-2, 150, 160, 243
Patterson, Margaret, 286
Pearson, Susanna, 132
Peddle, M., 132
Pepys, Samuel, 34, 35
Perry, Ruth, 13n, 77, 95
personal as political, 247-69, 317-23
Philips, Katherine, 24-9, 36, 45, 230-1
Pilkington, Letitia, 97
Pilkington, Mary, 132
Pix, Mary, 79, 132
plagiarism, 18, 72, 83; *see also* literary theft
Plantin, Arabella, 132
Plunkett, Elizabeth, 132-3
poetry, 17, 35, 217, 232
political fiction, 223-5, 301-14
Pope, Alexander, 68, 71, 76-7, 84, 87, 90, 100, 101, 154-5; *The Dunciad*, 84, 161
popular fiction, 76, 95
Priestley, J.B., 94-5
printing: invention of, 17; 'pirate', 26-7
print runs, 6-7n, 25
private circulation, 25, 33
propaganda, 54, 249
prostitution, 14, 192, 209
pseudonyms, 4, 13, 24, 67-81, 78, 90, 162, 164-6; *see also* anonymity
psychological fiction, 96, 249
publicity and promotion, 71, 78, 79
Publisher's Weekly, 153n
Pye, Sir Thomas, 244

Quarterly Review, 301, 308, 309

Radcliffe, Ann, 61, 133, 150, 175, 178-9, 215, 227, 230-45, 249, 271, 303, 313; *The Castles of Athlyn and Dunbane*, 237; *Gaston de Blondeville*, 242; *The Italian*, 150, 235, 237, 242; *A Journey Made in the Summer of 1794*, 242; *The Mysteries of*

354

Woodfin, Mrs A., 136
Woolf, Virginia, 35, 37, 39, 45, 50, 51,
    52, 55, 85, 86, 93, 116, 143-4, 145,
    163, 187, 246, 296, 298; *A Room of
    One's Own*, 143; *Three Guineas*, 143
Wordsworth, William, 142
Wroath, Lady Mary, 11-22, 23, 31n,
    45, 58, 72; *Urania*, 11, 18-21
Wroath, Robert, 12
writing: as defiance, 3, 13, 35-40, 58;
    for financial gain, 4-5, 11-14,
    18-19, 50-2, 55, 69-72, 75-7, 89,
    97, 158, 174-5, 183-4, 197-8,
    203-4, 210-12, 217-20, 226-7, 231,
    243, 284-5; for male approval,
    55-6, 76, 78, 86; with a moral
    purpose, 30, 44, 81, 92, 103-5, 158
Wollstonecraft, Mary, 136, 139, 151,
    174, 178, 212, 215, 225, 226,
    246-63, 264-5, 266-7, 268-9, 278,
    289, 311, 318, 322, 337; *Mary*, 246,
    249, 250-5, 262, 266-7; *A Vindic-*

ation of the Rights of Woman, 155,
    215, 225, 247, 251, 256, 257,
    264-5; *The Wrongs of Woman*, 246,
    255-62
women critics, 86, 73-9, 186-93, 198,
    205, 206, 211, 212-14, 221-2,
    230-6, 240-1, 246-7, 255, 260-1
women readers, 5, 16, 81, 86, 89-90,
    92-3, 96, 102, 104-5, 187-9
women's magazines, 102-5, 153-4,
    203-4; *see also* 'agony columns',
    journalism
'women's' novels, 5, 57-8, 152-4, 157,
    161-2, 166, 243-4; *see also* male
    romance, romantic fiction,
    sentimental novels
women's rights, 51-2, 225, 233,
    249-69, 317-20

Yearsley, Ann, 4, 137
Young, Mary Julia, 137